M000207005

BEYOND NORMA RAE

Gender and American Culture

Martha Jones and Mary Kelley, editors

Editorial Advisory Board

Cathleen Cahill

Rosalyn LaPier

Jen Manion

Tamika Nunley

Annelise Orleck

Janice A. Radway

Robert Reid-Pharr

Noliwe Rooks

Nick Syrett

Lisa Tetrault

Ji-Yeon Yuh

Series Editors Emerita

Thadious M. Davis

Linda K. Kerber

Annette Kolodny

Nell Irvin Painter

The Gender and American Culture series, guided by feminist perspectives, examines the social construction and influence of gender and sexuality within the full range of American cultures. Books in the series explore the intersection of gender (both female and male) with such markers of difference as race, class, and region. The series presents outstanding scholarship from all areas of American studies—including history, literature, religion, folklore, ethnography, and the visual arts—that investigates in a thoroughly contextualized and lively fashion the ways in which gender works with and against these markers. In so doing, the series seeks to reveal how these complex interactions have shaped American life.

A complete list of books published in Gender and American Culture is available at https://uncpress.org/series/gender-and-american-culture.

BEYOND NORMA RAE

How Puerto Rican and Southern White Women Fought for a Place in the American Working Class

Aimee Loiselle

THE UNIVERSITY OF NORTH CAROLINA PRESS

CHAPEL HILL

© 2023 Aimee Loiselle
All rights reserved

Set in Arnhem by Copperline Book Services, Inc.

Manufactured in the United States of America

Cover photograph by Jack Delano,
courtesy of the Prints and Photographs Division,
Library of Congress.

Complete Library of Congress Cataloging-in-Publication Data
is available at https://lccn.loc.gov/2023034422.
ISBN 978-1-4696-7612-8 (cloth: alk. paper)
ISBN 978-1-4696-7613-5 (paper: alk. paper)
ISBN 978-1-4696-7614-2 (ebook)

CONTENTS

ILLUSTRATIONS

Figures

Tables

ABBREVIATIONS

ACTWU	Amalgamated Clothing and Textile Workers Union
ACWA	Amalgamated Clothing Workers of America
AFL	American Federation of Labor
ALU	Amazon Labor Union
BIP	Border Industrialization Program
CBI	Caribbean Basin Initiative
CIO	Congress of Industrial Organizations
CUNY	City University of New York
E&O	errors and omissions insurance
EEOC	Equal Employment Opportunity Commission
EPZ	export processing zone
FLSA	Fair Labor Standards Act
FLT	Federación Libre de Trabajadores
GE	General Electric
HERE	Hotel Employees and Restaurant Employees union
ILGWU	International Ladies' and Garment Workers' Union
INS	Immigration and Naturalization Service
LBO	leveraged buyout
NAACP	National Association for the Advancement of Colored People
NLRB	National Labor Relations Board
NRA	National Recovery Administration
PPD	Partido Popular Democrático
PRIDC	Puerto Rico Industrial Development Company

PRNA	Puerto Rico Needlework Association
PRRA	Puerto Rico Reconstruction Administration
SAG	Screen Actors Guild
SCAP	Supreme Commander of Allied Powers
SEC	Securities and Exchange Commission
SEIU	Service Employees International Union
SEZ	special economic zone
TWUA	Textile Workers Union of America
UNITE	Union of Needletrades, Industrial, and Textile Employees
WEPZA	World Export Processing Zone Association

BEYOND
NORMA RAE

INTRODUCTION

Who Makes the American Working Class

Women Workers and Culture

They say the third generation, like my grandchildren, don't
know what the struggle was. But through your effort, they will
get to know. You'll get this thing out, you'll publish it, and I hope
you get enough publicity so people will really know about it.

—Gloria Maldonado

The thing is, I wanted it to be a movie that was right—about the
union, about what we went through. In the movie they make like
it's only me that's important, and there were so many others.

—Crystal Lee Sutton

Gloria Maldonado and Crystal Lee Jordan detested their work conditions and wanted to do something meaningful with their time and energy in addition to raising children. In the early 1970s, the labor movement offered them opportunities to try, and each woman decided to become active in an industrial union. After several years with the International Ladies' Garment Workers' Union (ILGWU), Maldonado became the education director for Local 66 in New York City. Crystal Lee, on the other hand, joined a union for the first time, signing a membership card with the Textile Workers Union of America (TWUA) in Roanoke Rapids, North Carolina.[1] Although the women did not work in the same factories or attend the same rallies, their jobs and unions were interconnected parts of a textile and garment industry that served as an engine for US global ambitions during the twentieth century.[2]

On a chilly day in March 1971, Maldonado walked into the High School of Fashion Industries through one of its four metal doors, each capped with an art deco mural. She was at the respected public school in midtown Manhattan to teach an ILGWU industrial sewing class. Founded in 1926 with classes for dressmaking and garment cutting, it was the Central Needle Trades High School until the 1956 New York City Board of Education changed the name to reflect the school's expanded curriculum related to design and the fashion

Gloria Maldonado (*standing on left*) teaches a 1971 sewing class at the High School of Fashion Industries. | ILGWU Justice Photographs Collection, Kheel Center, Cornell University, Ithaca, NY

industry. As a union educator, Maldonado was carrying on a tradition of Puerto Rican women helping other women workers improve their skills and demand better pay.

Maldonado had caught the attention of several New York labor leaders because she was a vocal member determined to question both company management and men in union leadership. In 1970, these labor leaders offered Maldonado a full-time job as an organizer for Local 66, and she added the title of education director a year later.[3] At the High School of Fashion Industries, the Local 66 manager and a photographer from the ILGWU newspaper *Justice* joined her to get photos to promote the union's educational programs. She walked the close rows of sewing machines to assist the women of color most likely attending for bilingual instruction.

Two years later, in May 1973, Crystal Lee caught the attention of southern labor leaders with her determination and willingness to be vocal. When the regional TWUA organizer wanted to file a National Labor Relations Board (NLRB) grievance about a letter the J.P. Stevens Company had posted on its mills' bulletin boards, several white members, including Crystal Lee, tried to hand copy it for him. The letter offered a "special word to our black employees" and said the TWUA was making false promises that "by going into the

"I knew this union was the only way we could have our own voice, make ourselves a better way of life."

Crystal Lee

A 1979 postcard celebrating the TWUA and Crystal Lee. The ACTWU provided the background photos, and Crystal Lee provided her image and quotation, which highlights her decision-making about how to represent herself as part of an interracial working class. Printed by Helaine Victoria Press for its Bread & Roses series. | Crystal Lee Sutton Collection, Alamance Community College, Graham, NC

union in mass, you can dominate it and control it." Union members knew that less than 20 percent of J.P. Stevens workers were Black because pressure from civil rights labor activism, particularly its successes with Title VII of the 1964 Civil Rights Act, had only recently punctured the rigid segregation of mills.[4] They also knew the company wanted to trigger the bigotry and racial fears of uninformed white millhands, who would imagine the union "supported black power." If that happened, the TWUA would not get enough votes in an NLRB certification election to represent the workers.[5]

Black union members could not copy the letter because bossmen had been following them for months and had already fired one man.[6] A white worker tried but gave up after a bossman told her to stop. When Crystal Lee called the organizer, he said he needed the exact wording of the letter. She decided to get it done, writing fast and flipping through the posted pages, but a bossman walked up and told her she could not copy it. Crystal Lee kept writing. Another bossman told her to stop and go see the supervisor. Crystal Lee replied she would go after the break. Although nervous, she went to supper, where coworkers asked what had happened and said she had "guts." Crystal

Lee mentioned that the bossmen said they were going to fire her, so "y'all can expect anything." It was a collective event, which millhands discussed throughout the shift.

Crystal Lee returned to her towel-folding station, where the assistant overseer ordered her to go to the supervisor. She saw a few bossmen and her forelady waiting. The supervisor asked why she was using the pay phone on company time, and nobody spoke up for her as he listed her supposed infractions. Making such false accusations was a common means of harassing union members because supervisors could not legally reprimand them for union activity. Crystal Lee resisted, asking the men for their names and titles. They looked confused, and the supervisor shouted that she should call her husband. "Tell him to pick you up. I want you out," he yelled. Perhaps if Crystal Lee had conformed to the mill town's patriarchal gender norms and called her husband so he could take responsibility for her, the situation would have ended with a simple termination. Instead she was noncompliant.[7]

Crystal Lee said she had to get her pocketbook and walked back to the folding station. She noticed coworkers staring, and Mary Mosley, an African American woman in her section, asked what happened. "He fired me," Crystal Lee replied as a Pinkerton guard and a policeman arrived. She asked Mosley for a marker, wrote UNION on a piece of cardboard, stood on her table, and held it overhead.[8] Her fellow union members, peers, and neighbors stopped work, many raising a hand in V for victory. They could not imagine that this action, which emerged from decades of labor activism and years of interracial union organizing, would become the key dramatic scene in a Hollywood movie. They could not imagine it would generate an icon that would appear for decades as a representation of individualist defiance.

The different length and detail of these stories about Maldonado and Crystal Lee do not reflect the intensity of their work or labor activism; Maldonado had more years as a union member and more positions in the labor movement. Neither do they reflect a disparity in the women's interest in culture. Both Maldonado and Crystal Lee recognized the importance of media for how people understand the working class and unionizing. The differences between the stories reflect the quantity, depth, and type of archival sources available for each woman. And the scope of these archives derives from each woman's position in the arena of cultural politics and her relationship to the means of major media production, which are all run through with intersections of gender, race, class, status, and citizenship.[9]

Although both women participated in media projects with the intention of influencing public conversation about work and unions, only Crystal Lee,

Crystal Lee Sutton speaking at a 1988 event in Saint Paul, Minnesota. | Crystal Lee Sutton Collection, Alamance Community College, Graham, NC

an attractive, white, southern millhand, became the focus of big commercial producers. Her association with them in the 1970s led to a 1979 Hollywood movie, *Norma Rae*, which had a much wider reach than the public history project Maldonado contributed to from 1984 to 1985. The popularity of *Norma Rae*, and the effusive praise for Sally Field as the lead, forced Crystal Lee into visibility in a way she did not choose and without remuneration—yet granted her a platform for public speaking, an avenue to prominent labor events, and a basis for demanding payment.

Crystal Lee decided to step into that spotlight and make the most of mainstream media interest to critique the movie and reassert her own point of view as a labor activist. Following the March 1979 release of *Norma Rae*, she did an interview with *People* magazine and said she had not received payment for the movie or for the *New York Times* article and Macmillan biography on which it was based. While Crystal Lee mentioned the possibility of a lawsuit, her immediate concern was the ideology of *Norma Rae*. "The thing is, I wanted it to be a movie that was right—about the union, about what we went through," she said. "In the movie they make like it's only me that's important, and there were so many others."[10]

Crystal Lee's words became a central theme for this book. There were so many others—women of many races, ethnicities, geographies, migrations, and citizenships—working and organizing in the low-wage textile and garment industry. Government offices, corporate executives, factory managers, and even some workers used these categories to differentiate cost arrangements and access to pay and benefits.[11] In this catalog of labor, southern millhands and Puerto Rican needleworkers were not supposed to know each other, and Puerto Rican women were not supposed to be imagined as the American working class. Based on their own needs and priorities, however, women navigated and challenged these labor markets, which were intertwined, if not interchangeable.

Although popularly understood as solitary mills or sweatshops, manufacturers were bound parts of a global operation. National and international laws and agreements continuously reconfigured the related regional, colonial, and transnational currents of materials, products, workers, and capital.[12] The colonial quantities were often smaller than those for major industrial centers, but these connective tissues attached and lubricated the amplifying components of the US economy, transmitting and fueling its global reach. Decades of women working in this industry along the US Atlantic—the Northeast, South, and Puerto Rico—and the dynamics of global disaggregation precipitated the conditions that motivated Maldonado and Crystal Lee to become active union members. This larger history made *Norma Rae* and its story of a singular white woman possible, and returning to this history challenges the movie's cultural work and the gendered, racialized, and nationalized meanings it perpetuates.

Maldonado also entered the arena of cultural politics in the 1980s, just as *Norma Rae* was becoming a standard of American film. She joined a dozen needleworkers who spoke with three Puerto Rican scholars for an oral history project titled "Nosotras Trabajamos en la Costura."[13] Maldonado expressed her ambitions for the project to an interviewer: "You'll get this thing out, you'll publish it, and I hope you get enough publicity so people will really know about it."[14] She knew cultural contests were crucial to public understanding and wanted to contribute to an effort that articulated her version of the American working class and its struggles.

The "Nosotras Trabajamos" project produced oral history transcripts that became source material for photography exhibits, bilingual panels, and an award-winning radio documentary. These media still do cultural work from the archive, serving the creation of alternative narratives of the American working class. Without these public history productions, there would be fewer challenges to the dominant narrative of isolated scrappy white workers and the many ways it operates to impact labor policy, employment, worker resistance, and other political-economic practices.

As this book braids an examination of women in the textile and garment industry with their experiences in the arena of cultural politics, it argues that the social categorizations and identities that segmented workers also influenced mainstream representations of work and meanings for the American working class. They did this in two ways. Categorizations and identities constrained who had access to and influence over mass media resources, which impacted how, when, and where certain workers appeared in popular culture. Second, they shaped the decisions of creative professionals—their imaginative choices about topics, story lines, characters, and dialogue and their business tactics regarding viability, sales, performers, and investors. While I argue that capitalist mechanisms have tremendous power in who constructs visibility and meanings for "worker" and "working class," they are not uncontested.[15] As a result, movies cannot be observed as static reflections of a time period, because they are products made in contentious fields of cultural production within an aggressive capitalist system, and they do ongoing cultural work as they circulate through popular media.

The Movie at the Middle of It All

Norma Rae became the starting point for this book because of its high profile. The film continues to appear on cable networks and great-movie lists, and the popular-culture icon it generated has retained its relevance as an adaptable symbol of individualist defiance for television shows and websites. Labor organizations still use both to try to motivate their members. *Norma Rae* and its icon have serious cultural power to still hold people's attention over forty years later, which made me curious about the movie's creation, the reasons for its durability, and the way it has shaped how people think of American workers.

Norma Rae tells the story of a white millhand, mother, and wife in the South as she becomes active in a union in the 1970s.[16] During the opening credits, a poignant theme song with a woman's sweet voice plays, and audiences see Sally Field as Norma in sepia-toned photographs.[17] The song and images cut to the pounding of looms in an old textile mill, and in the introductory scenes, Norma shows her feisty stubborn behavior both on the job and at home with her parents, who also work in the mill. She and her two children live with her parents, and her father has a loving but overbearing involvement in Norma's life. When Reuben, a leftist, Jewish intellectual union organizer, arrives in town, Norma's father tells him to leave, but she becomes intrigued.

Reuben represents the start of the union drive and becomes Norma's mentor, directing her passions into purposeful labor activism. Other millhands eventually sign membership cards and join the organizing drive. This activism causes tensions between Norma and her new husband, Sonny, whom she married because they each promised to be caring parents for her two children and his daughter. Despite pressure and harassment by management, including Norma's termination and expulsion, the majority of workers vote to certify the TWUA. In the final scene, Reuben drives away as Norma watches, a solitary figure on an empty side street.

The movie also generated what I call the Norma Rae icon, which has two components, visual and linguistic. In the visual component, Field as Norma Rae holds the UNION sign overhead with the camera only on her. Fellow union members, allies, coworkers, and neighbors have been cropped out, and since the movie does not contain any reference to the sixteen-year campaign against J.P. Stevens or the longer history of southern labor activism, neither does the icon. Norma Rae stands alone in her rebellion. The linguistic component appears as the phrases "having a Norma Rae moment" or "going Norma Rae," which express the icon's essence: a transitory individualist defiance. The repeated visual and linguistic representation of rebellion without ideology, movement, or even context allows the icon to work on behalf of different types of defiance, for different desires and purposes.[18]

Because movies do not serve as direct reflections of society, a dominant representation such as *Norma Rae* raises questions not only about why this movie was made in this way but also about what it pushed to the side or eclipsed. When I discussed this project with a friend, she said her mother had moved from Puerto Rico to New York and then Massachusetts for factory jobs in the 1970s, which prompted immediate inquiries: Where and when did Puerto Rican women work in textiles and apparel, and were there popular representations of them as manufacturing workers? Why had I never learned this history? I found scattered archival material and three journal articles that challenged the mainstream narrative of deindustrialization, with its concentration on white workers at specific sites in the metropole.[19] When Puerto Rico is studied with US labor history—not because it is rightfully part of the United States but because of colonial realities—that focus cannot withstand scrutiny.

The questions also led me to the 1961 movie *West Side Story*, and I realized the two lead female characters, Maria and Anita, sew in a New York garment business idealized as a romantic bridal shop. Almost twenty years before a white woman millhand is the central character in a Hollywood movie, Puerto Rican needleworkers migrating from the archipelago to the Northeast appeared on the big screen.[20] The embedded cultural narrative of *West*

Side Story, however, articulated the young women as poor exotic beauties and troubled urban teens rather than as workers—and definitely not as the American working class.[21]

Braiding Labor and Cultural History

This book provides a counternarrative to the erasures of *Norma Rae*. Both labor and cultural history, interlaced with history of capitalism and its attention to finance in political economy, informed my approach.[22] Braiding these methods illuminates how labor market structures and mainstream cultural structures impede our ability to see these women as interrelated workers in US industry. All of these, both types of structures and the impeded perception, contribute to a racialized, nationalized notion of the American working class.

The cultural history at the center of the book uses theoretical tools to analyze popular media as capitalist productions at junctures of finance and property as well as creativity and narrative. This approach, which traces from Antonio Gramsci to Stuart Hall, relies on Pierre Bourdieu's model of fields of cultural production and Raymond Williams's propositions regarding cultural formations and structures of feeling.[23] These concepts undergird the overall argument that popular culture is a highly contested arena that impacts not only society's *perception* of economic relations but also *the unfolding* of economic relations. It is interactive, not merely descriptive or reflective.

Bourdieu emphasized forms of capital and the role of status in fields of cultural production. In each field, participants with unequal economic, social, and cultural capital struggle over their ability to gain access to the process, shape the product, and accrue rewards from it. The value of different economic, social, and cultural capital derives from their operative interrelationships in each setting, not from a stable intrinsic worth.[24] Crystal Lee and Maldonado, from different positions, fought to influence media productions because of their capacity to make narratives and meanings that modify or fortify ingrained mainstream dispositions.[25] The women's actions and assertions show that the exercise and reproduction of power through culture is not unilateral or unequivocal, even when a poor working woman goes up against a major Hollywood studio. The field of cultural production is fraught, like any other.

My analysis of the icon's narrative and affective reverberations uses Williams's theorizing about cultural formations and structures of feeling to elucidate the significance of popular culture for the political economy. His framework delineates an unstable but instrumental channel between agency and structures—between people's sentiments, perceptions, and values; their ideologies and behaviors; and the larger social, political, and economic systems.

According to Williams, texts are neither inert nor freestanding but rather active parts of pervasive cultural formations in which people, groups, and institutions make, view, and rehash texts and their ideas and evocations. Rich texts, including popular media and formal documents such as legislation, interact inadvertently and purposely through emotional, imaginative, social, and material processes that constitute formations. Cultural formations that become entrenched generate meanings, notions, customs, and sensations that converge over time to "legitimate a given distribution of power."[26]

Williams argues that structures of feeling are crucial to these cultural formations. They are more than a zeitgeist; they are active and facilitate a cultural formation's reproduction of power. Structures of feeling flourish through interactions with texts and their related activities and audiences when people experience reiterations of affective response mingled with ideas and concepts. Affective associations can arise with varying levels of intention, from premeditated mixes of ideology and feeling to unpredictable subconscious amalgams of narrative and emotion, yet serve the same structure of feeling. Such repeated emotional dynamics can align mental and social habits with a certain political and economic composition. Through these "regularized patterns of emotion and sentiment," the structure of feeling translates principles that support certain arrangements of power into naturalized personal sentience.[27]

Even texts that appear to express very divergent overt dogma can conduct similar embedded narrative and affect, functioning to normalize the same arrangement of power.[28] In this case, *Norma Rae* tells the story of a poor woman deciding to join a labor union, and the icon's visual component shows a woman holding a sign that says UNION. But the icon's linguistic component indicates the deeper narrative and affect: "having a Norma Rae moment," a passing act of individual defiance. *Norma Rae* and the icon transmit this antagonistic, yet aspirational, sensation tied to a narrative of the unapologetic aggrieved individual who triumphs in taking a stand. It aligned with a structure of feeling that saturated and reinforced the burgeoning cultural formation of neoliberal individualism.[29] This mainstream formation helped make certain political-economic policies and practices captivating, appealing, and normalized.

I also use two precision tools for my analysis of *Norma Rae* and its icon. The history of creative disagreements and business decisions regarding the "Crystal Lee" script employs a theory from film scholar Robert B. Ray. He argues that the postwar Hollywood consensus dictated the "conversion of all political, sociological, and economic dilemmas into personal melodramas" focused on the individual via the emotional redemption of a reluctant hero.[30] This "Hollywood tendency" minimized the collaborative, long-term efforts required for substantive political and economic change and reinforced the notion that an individualist actor serves as the bedrock of power and responsibility. Although it is not part of a methodical right-wing conspiracy and movies are not perfectly coherent ideological texts, there was a potent convergence of this tendency and the amplifying neoliberal projects of the 1980s.

My comparison of Crystal Lee's 1973 action at her folding station to the 1979 movie depiction of Norma's stand on a table uses James J. Kimble and Lester C. Olson's theory of visual rhetoric. They argue that workers in a shared space, such as a factory, experience posters or actions as affiliated group members. Kimble and Olson call these performances "backstage gestures," displays in a limited area where public viewing is not available. Backstage gestures rely on a "reciprocal familiarity" and operate as a means of "communal identification." When a wider unexpected audience watches such a gesture as if it is a front-stage performance, viewers can mistake it as the act of one self-possessed person. This imaginative process transforms the gesture from a unifying vernacular signal to an individualistic iconic performance.[31]

Organization of the Book

This book consists of six chapters; the first begins with a wide lens to capture women workers along the US Atlantic from Puerto Rico to the Northeast, and the sixth ends with a close-up lens on the solitary individual of the Norma Rae icon. As the lens narrows from chapters 2 through 5, it follows the process of extracting and refining raw material into a polished commercial movie and condensed, sharp icon. In this capacity, *Norma Rae* serves as an entry point into the past rather than as a reflection of the time period. It pulls readers into the historical context behind the movie, including the interconnected labor and migrations of southern and Puerto Rican women. The result sets the United States in a transnational framework while crossing common conceptual and historiographical divisions between southern, Caribbean, labor, economic, and media histories.[32]

Maldonado and Crystal Lee, studied together in the larger industrial context, anchor this history of the intertwined, but not equivalent, conditions of Puerto Rican needleworkers and southern millhands. Give-and-take between the labor markets, not simply localized circumstances, led to the volatile conditions that the women worked in, complained about, and organized against. Connecting this history to each woman's encounters in the arena of cultural politics highlights how categorizations and identities shaped their access to major media and their opportunities to participate in constructing a narrative of the American working class. Cultural theory deepens this study of power reproduced via capitalist formations in each field of cultural production, where these working women fought to gain some control over the representations of class struggle.[33] The resulting history argues that even Hollywood directors like Martin Ritt who envisioned themselves as liberal, humanistic, creative professionals made movies that converged with the neo-liberal turn.

Although it would have been simpler to remain within the conventional bounds of southern labor history, geographic constructs can camouflage the diversity of women workers, the long history of US colonial industrialization, and their impacts on the metropole as well as global sites. The familiar terms "southern millhand" and "Puerto Rican needleworker" have proven especially effective for managers and ambiguous for labor analysis. "Southern millhand" covers women who reeled and wound yarn or thread, operated weaving looms, loaded cloth, sheared, hemmed and finished edges, trimmed loose fabric off finished items, and folded items for retail packaging. In addition, many southern women, including Crystal Lee, trained as sewing machine operators and worked in apparel and home goods factories, not just textile mills.[34] And "Puerto Rican needleworker" comprises a range of labor, including working as a floor girl, reeling and winding yarn or thread, weaving, loading cloth, cutting patterns, operating sewing machines for all types of apparel and home goods, hemming and finishing edges, doing basic and fine embroidery, and packing.[35] The women and duties were not equivalents, but they had similarities, links, and overlaps that the terms work to hide rather than illuminate.

It is important to traverse academic conventions to reevaluate Puerto Rican needleworkers and southern millhands in US labor history and to reveal the workings of capitalism in both manufacturing and cultural production. The history highlights how popular culture obscures its own business maneuvers as well as historic complexities, while recirculating gendered, racialized, classed, and nationalized meanings for work and workers. Capital plays a vital role in that arena of cultural politics, especially in filmmaking, where studios administer tremendous resources on behalf of very expensive products. *Norma Rae* elided this rich historical context, and the icon entirely eliminated it. Both also performed a certain type of cultural work, participating in the construction of meanings for the proper American working class, whiteness, and individualist rights and responsibilities. They exemplify the magnitude of the fights over cultural mass production.

PART I

CHAPTER ONE

Women Workers in the US Atlantic

Seeing the Raw Material before
Cultural Production

I don't give a darn if he does it to her, then he'll do it
to me, do it to my sister, do it to the one. . . . And I will
not stand for that you know, because after all,
we're human beings, and we're all ladies.

—Louise Delgado

At the turn of the twentieth century, a Puerto Rican woman in a long white dress set her sewing machine in front of her row house on a cobblestoned street in San Juan. Her mother had taught her fine hand sewing and embroidery to make elegant curtains and table-cloths long before she could afford a machine. The woman was proud of both her needlework skills and her black hand-operated machine. She had made the white dress with the ruffle collar and puff sleeves, but now she was completing edging on handkerchiefs for an agent. He had been coming around with orders for about six or seven years, and ever since the United States had arrived, there were more orders for handkerchiefs and night-gowns. The agent had even brought gringos in suits to watch the neighbor-hood women sew. Although the woman now made one or two cents more per dozen, the pay had not increased as she had hoped with the arrival of the Estados Unidos.

She sewed almost every day while the oldest of her six children kept an eye on the little ones. It was a nice clear day when the fancy white woman with the big camera asked to take a photograph. The young seamstress said yes, because it was an opportunity to show off her work and to show the neighbors that what she did was important. Los niños hurried to the door to peek out, and neighbors came out from their row houses; even the women working inside stopped what they were doing to find out qué está pasando. Every-one had seen her sew many times, but they could not take their eyes off the

A woman shows her sewing skills on a street in San Juan in 1902. | Helen Gardener Collection, INV.04331302, National Anthropological Archives, Smithsonian Institution, Washington, DC

camera. The event became a topic of conversation for days, a morning they all experienced and remembered together.

This woman was an early needleworker who helped build the modern US textile and garment industry. Even though she carried on both a feminine tradition and a piecework contract practice from Spanish colonialism, the work changed as department stores and manufacturers in the US metropole learned about the needleworkers and insular agents. By the time of this 1902 photograph, orders had been increasing for four years as businesses sought cheap skilled labor from thousands of Puerto Rican women. The Charleston Inter-State and West Indian Exposition exemplifies this imbalanced enmeshing of Puerto Rico into manufacturing along the US Atlantic.

In 1899, a group of South Carolina businessmen set out to coordinate an exposition. Their objective was not a world's fair. They wanted to foster economic ties between the South, Northeast, and Caribbean for textiles, apparel, and home goods. The Charleston City Council approved the plan to expand commerce with the "open, growing, and profitable" Caribbean islands, allowing organizers to found a company in 1900.[1] These men understood that the cotton regime, from commodity to retail sales, served as an engine for

A 1901–2 Charleston Exposition pamphlet illustrates the commercial vision of linking the US Atlantic from the South to the Northeast and to Puerto Rico. | Rare and Manuscript Collections, Kroch Library, Cornell University, Ithaca, NY, from Osborne Library, American Textile and History Museum, Lowell, MA

US global ambitions and that establishing more labor, manufacturing, and investment options for this massive operation would mean greater flexibility for the pursuit of revenues in a world of escalating change and proliferating variables. Having multiple labor markets, segmented by gender, race, ethnicity, citizenship, and geography, to play off one another enhanced the power of political authority and capital. The Charleston Exposition highlights how Puerto Rican needleworkers were labor for this US industry yet were not perceived as the American working class.

An Extended US Atlantic

When Gloria Maldonado began sewing in New York City factories in the 1960s, she joined a long history of needleworkers navigating, pushing, and resisting the colonial labor market, and her ILGWU organizing had roots in the first years of US occupation in Puerto Rico. By the 1890s, the US cotton regime had reclaimed a strong global position, and the federal government had consolidated continental western territories through tactics that killed, restricted, or marginalized indigenous tribes, Mexican subjects, French descendants, and métis people.[2] Business executives, investors, government administrators, and military leaders turned to the erosion of the Spanish Empire and debated how to approach the Caribbean. Despite concerns about race mixing, they pushed for interventions, especially in Puerto Rico.[3] When war with Spain escalated in 1898, Theodore Roosevelt urged senators to make "Porto Rico ours."[4]

Decades of pulling needleworkers into the US textile and garment industry as demarcated, undervalued labor began with the Treaty of Paris that concluded the Spanish-American War. Unlike previous treaties of acquisition, it disregarded incorporation and citizenship for Puerto Rico. Instead of promising independence or statehood, vague classifications provided opportunities for ongoing experiments with imperialism and capitalism, including extreme tax and banking exemptions, offshore diffusion of industry and capital, wage exclusions, and labor migrations—beyond what was possible in the South, the West, and Hawai'i.[5]

Commerce was a top priority, and realignment of Puerto Rico's economy with the US Atlantic began immediately.[6] The War Department established the Division of Customs and Insular Affairs for ports and duty collections in Puerto Rico and Cuba. Staff noticed local women participated in a tradition of Spanish needlework: embroidery, drawnwork, needlepoint, and fine sewing. Affluent women continued the tradition as an expression of gentility, while poor girls and women completed "exquisite table linens, lingerie, dresses, blouses, handkerchiefs, and dress accessories" as piecework for contracting agents. By the end of 1898, US importers and department stores were enlisting insular contractors for these items.[7] This early attention to Puerto Rican embroidery and fine sewing framed the women as "needleworkers" even though they increasingly labored in industrial manufacturing in a mix of homes and sweatshops.

The Division of Customs and Insular Affairs initiated colonial policies and practices that fostered more needlework contracting and the industrialization of the women's labor. In its first year, the division increased tariffs on tobacco and coffee entering Cuba from Puerto Rico, two top products the archipelago had exported. But Congress did not open North American markets. The loss of trade drove Puerto Rican landowners from coffee to sugar and women in the coffee regions to more needlework.[8] By 1901, US manufacturing companies were sending prescribed orders to agents for finishing and embroidery on their own product lines, and the number of women dressmakers doubled between 1899 and 1910, from 5,785 to 11,200.[9]

Development of this commercial infrastructure was not a neutral result of impartial market mechanisms. US offices defined Puerto Rico and its working people in relation to metropolitan economic objectives in ways run through with gender, race, ethnicity, and citizenship. When implementing rules and legislation conceived as necessary for colonial measurement, taxation, and investment, they relied on and reconstituted racialized class formations at the intersection of Spanish Caribbean and US conceptions of race and gender. Social categories were reconstructed in and through this modern capitalist imperialism. Press releases, government memos, magazine photos, and world's fairs fostered a cultural narrative of colonial benevolence that represented Puerto Rico as backward and primitive—dependent, impoverished, uneducated—but not aggressive.[10] This narrative limited the perception of needleworkers in the US economy and contributed to their invisibility in the American working class. US political and economic authority relied on and enacted this narrative of Puerto Rican people as a passive "dark Other," even as government and business leaders employed the skilled women workers and collaborated with insular elites who had highly concentrated wealth, advanced education, and cosmopolitan networks.

Criollo hacendados, the landed elite, had complicated relationships with metropolitan officials, manufacturers, and banks.[11] Many initially welcomed occupation because they wanted release from Spain's antiquated oversight and access to the US sugar market. They realized equitable economic integration and independent political governance were not part of the deal after four generals served as appointed governors from 1898 to 1900.[12] As with many colonial occupations, however, many insular elites negotiated with US officials, politicians, banks, and investors as they sought ways to benefit and profit from contradictory combinations of cooperation and obstruction. Criollo hacendados soon realized that the expanding needlework industry, though bound to the metropole, offered lucrative opportunities.

At the same time, working men and women launched their own organizations and alliances to take advantage of occupation. Many low-income and rural workers welcomed the United States as well because they feared immediate self-rule would solidify criollo hacendado exploitation of poor workers. In 1901, the Federación Libre de Trabajadores (FLT; Free Federation of Workers) formed an affiliation with the American Federation of Labor (AFL).[13] Despite tensions within the Puerto Rican labor movement and between insular and metropolitan unions, these relationships continued into the 1960s and impacted textile and garment manufacturing, especially during the Great Depression.[14]

US occupation also required extensive political governance, and the provisions constituted Puerto Rico as a site of potential and persistent exclusions, with special attention to needlework.[15] The resulting alterations in concepts of sovereignty and citizenship; real estate and tax manipulations; and managed labor migrations exceeded practices in the South. The offshore experiments also facilitated US globalization via colonial industrialization, a source of procedural and policy scaffolding for late twentieth-century export processing zones (EPZs). This scaffolding consisted of bureaucrats and experts, legislative clauses, legal definitions, economic data and rationales, and finance mechanisms as well as geographic sites, facilities, and labor practices.[16] Such pragmatic contributions to neoliberal political economy were as important as the intellectual propositions of economists such as Ludwig von Mises, Friedrich von Hayek, and members of the Mont Pèlerin Society, who are often at the center of the neoliberal histories.[17]

Two provisions from early US governance illustrate the significance of foundational colonial practices for steering Puerto Rican women into a dual labor market as lowest-wage insular and lower-wage migrating workers. The provisions did not set unchanging codifications but rather initiated a routine of exempting Puerto Rico from constitutional or legislative frameworks as deemed necessary, often, but not always, in contentious collaboration with insular elites. The Foraker Act (1900) and *Downes v. Bidwell* (1901) implemented colonial practices later entrenched by the New Deal and repackaged by Operación Manos a la Obra (Operation Bootstrap) in the 1940s. Although often unexamined in US labor history, the provisions entwined Puerto Rico with US industry and finance while differentiating its workers.

The Foraker Act was a formative piece of legislation that drew Puerto Rican women into the United States and global capitalism as nonincorporated insular residents and lowest-wage workers to which the state and employers had malleable obligations.[18] It enacted a distinct political-economic status by creating a civilian government, yet implementing a tariff on goods coming from the archipelago despite the Constitution's "uniformity clause." This clause and related Supreme Court cases had prohibited tariffs between parts of the United States. With the Foraker Act, Congress claimed the federal government's ability to disregard the Constitution and legal precedents in one place, even as it maintains them elsewhere.[19]

Some scholars emphasize the eventual lifting of this tariff and argue that its removal initiated "free trade" with Puerto Rico, indicating things to come. This perspective aligns with a narrative of globalization as a relentless expansion of "free flows," rather than as a contested and constrained process of coalescing power and capital.[20] A lack of tariffs with open trade had been common practice with previous territories, however, so the later removal was less significant for colonial policy and future arrangements than the initial imposition. That hindrance to trade helped inaugurate the legal and bureaucratic scaffolding for colonial industrialization.

The Supreme Court decision *Downes v. Bidwell* upheld the Foraker Act, confirming the US government could redefine sovereignty via its overseas territories. It is one of the most significant Insular Cases—a series of decisions from 1901 to 1922, most of which involved tariffs, taxes, and businesses—and legitimated commerce as a core mechanism and consequence of modern imperialism. In this case, Samuel Downes sued the US customs inspector for the Port of New York after his company paid a duty on oranges from Puerto Rico, but the Supreme Court upheld the import duty.[21]

Justice Edward Douglass White wrote a concurring decision that distinguished between incorporated and nonincorporated territories, which he said were not foreign in the international sense, because they were under US sovereignty, but were foreign in a domestic sense. Justice John Marshall Harlan's dissent argued Congress was bound by the Constitution for all parts of the United States, and prominent critics said *Downes* was a rationalization for imperialism. They did little to undermine the appeal of its justification for holding land sovereign while deeming it outside the constitutional and legal framework of the nation—a template for future EPZs.[22]

At the same time as these colonial provisions, the 1901–2 Charleston Exposition opened, calling more attention to Puerto Rico. The event exemplifies how "diverse actors on the metropolitan homefront" entangled their interests with Puerto Rico and helped precipitate a transition to colonial industrialization.[23] A publicity booklet, written by and for industrial, financial, and political leaders, stated the exposition would afford "a splendid opportunity for the extension of industrial and commercial enterprise. . . . There is a fine field in Porto Rico for American occupation—not occupation by arms, or as the result of military conquest, but occupation by the merchants and manufacturers of the United States."[24] As a public expression of emerging colonial relations, it framed the archipelago as a commercial resource that would provide consumers and manufacturing for the US Atlantic.

The promotional magazine invited politicians and textile, garment, and hosiery companies from the US Atlantic to the exposition and noted that Puerto Rican needlework would be shown. The exposition's West Indian Commissioner traveled to Puerto Rico to visit Ponce, Yauco, and San Juan, where he met with the chamber of commerce.[25] An article celebrated Señorita Herminia Davila, who said the embroidery was unlike any in the United States because it had been "cultivated among the young society girls." She knew to praise the distinctive artistic embroidery rather than the piecework contract system. The narrative of feminine tradition naturalized the poor women's low-wage labor for textiles, apparel, and home goods while camouflaging the harsh conditions and exploitation.[26]

The Charleston Exposition offered the usual attractions, but the Cotton

UNCLE SAM TO THE CHILDREN OF THE SEA.
COPYRIGHT 1901. THE SOUTH CAROLINA INTER-STATE AND WEST INDIAN EXPOSITION COMPANY.

This Uncle Sam pamphlet, with a masculine tone that is both paternalist and sexualized, exemplifies the imperial perspective of the businessmen and politicians coordinating the Charleston Exposition. | Rare andManuscript Collections, Kroch Library, Cornell University, Ithaca, NY, from Osborne Library, American Textile and History Museum, Lowell, MA

Palace was most prominent.[27] Exhibits were a tangible manifestation of the US Atlantic bound by technology, financial partnerships, and racial hierarchies. Organizers highlighted the South's ability to compete with states like Massachusetts and displayed "the resources and industries of our new possessions in the West Indies."[28] The E. Jenckes Manufacturing Company of Rhode Island brought four machines from its hosiery mill. These ran near a section dedicated to Olympia Cotton Mills, one of the largest manufacturers in South Carolina.[29]

Planners expressed their ambition for this economic colonialism within a global frame. "[Our] object," they stated, "is to secure to our American Cotton

Manufacturers a greater share of the lucrative trade in cotton fabrics in South America and the West Indies. These countries import fifty million dollars of cotton goods annually, three million dollars more than the Chinese Empire with its four hundred million people. Of this vast traffic, England controls twenty million, Germany ten million, France three million, other European nations sixteen million and the United States, the most energetic people of the globe, one million or only two per cent."[30] For businessmen, the mills, factories, and investments were not isolated or local.

In this competition, each region of the US Atlantic served a related function. The Northeast had established mills, machine manufacturers, industry experts, and major banks, and the South offered cheaper real estate and labor as yeoman farmers lost their property.[31] Puerto Rico provided the cheapest offshore land and labor as colonized rural families lost their property or needed wages due to dramatic changes in commodities trade and insular taxes.

The increasing quantification and monitoring of trade, investment, production, land values, and consumption in Puerto Rico were crucial colonial mechanisms—as important as military occupation and political authority. In 1902, the Division of Customs and Insular Affairs was renamed the Bureau of Insular Affairs and expanded to oversee customs, trade, sugar, and industry. For this purpose, it gathered statistics, descriptions, and photos, accumulating quantitative and qualitative data that made Puerto Rico accessible to investors and manufacturers.[32] Depictions of needleworkers, as well as measurements of their labor and poverty, were integral to this bureaucratic work, and government-industry programs defined apparel and home goods production as a colonial priority. In 1909, the Departamento de Instrucción Pública (Public Instruction Department), a US agency, offered classes in crochet, embroidery, and sewing and encouraged piecework.[33] The government funded a department partnership with manufacturers, retailers, and the Philadelphia Textile School to implement the needlework curriculum, which reached over 26,000 women by 1926.[34]

While ties with Puerto Rico increased, companies also built southern mills and updated northeastern factories. In the New South, similar but not equivalent combinations of racialization, rural poverty, migration, and government-industry collaboration structured textile and apparel manufacturing. Like colonial representations of Puerto Rico's backwardness and imperial commerce and governance, Jim Crow narratives of Black inferiority and legal segregation helped constitute notions of whiteness and the American working class. The segregation that restricted African Americans' access to the mills was so rigid, managers did not even hire Black workers during a major strike, except on the few occasions when they thought white workers' anger about Black men in the mills would fracture the union.[35]

Owners and managers did not want to do anything that might encourage the slightest interracial worker solidarity. Mill town segregation bolstered the patriarchal race and class hierarchy of white supremacy on which their status and wealth depended. This hierarchy gave upper-class whites tremendous political and economic power; granted millhands a potent white superiority with circumscribed but unequivocal privileges; and excluded Blacks from political power and sharply limited their economic options, with violence if deemed necessary. Even as the mill town manifestation of racial capitalism grew from and perpetuated the oppression of Blacks and exploitation of poor whites, most millhands came to believe they were entitled to the jobs over any Black worker. As detestable as the jobs were, they had slightly better pay and more regular schedules than the harder jobs relegated to Black workers, and mills often provided basic housing. When segregation contorted in the 1910s because increased production pushed managers to open positions to African American men, they were limited to the dirtiest jobs, like unloading cotton bales. The racialized labor system was also gendered and served notions of femininity and family. White men took the exclusive machinist jobs, white women and children worked for lower wages in production, Black men had the heaviest dangerous jobs, and a small number of Black women cleaned restrooms.[36]

Within the seemingly unbending hierarchy, and in contradiction to New South boosters' promotion of worker passivity, many millhands resisted exploitative practices. They questioned, quit, or went on strike over convoluted labor contracts, unfair pay forfeitures, bullying bossmen, abusive treatment of women, rules about starting and stopping machines, fines for fabric assessment, various forms of the stretch-out, and low wages.[37] Walkouts, wildcat strikes, and union pickets often occurred because of unfair dismissals, such as a 1900 strike at the Haw River mill in North Carolina and a 1913 walkout at the Fulton Mill in Atlanta that coincided with a United Textile Workers (UTW) campaign. Although it ended without major wage or hour concessions, the UTW received company recognition.[38]

Advantages for companies and managers in the South had less to do with worker acquiescence than with the availability of cheaper land, child labor, landless poor, lower wages, municipal and state strikebreaking, and a prevailing anti-union outlook.[39] Even with managers, owners, politicians, and police cooperating to suppress organizing, millhands built communication networks, shared tactics, and allied with union representatives. Sharing and debating memories around a kitchen table (often overheard by children), swapping anecdotes at work, and cutting newspaper clippings or arranging photos in scrapbooks fashioned an informal archive for southern workers.[40]

Early resistance and union organizing were a foundation on which to coordinate the larger campaigns that Crystal Lee would join in the future.

Strengthening Links between Puerto Rico, the New South, and the Northeast

Starting in 1914, World War I triggered a decline in European imports and immigration, which directed more attention to domestic options, including Puerto Rico.[41] Government and business experts from the metropole and main island promoted Puerto Rico as an alternative to Europe's lace, embroidery, and female workers, and New York manufacturers increased shipments of precut fabric bundles for assembly and finishing. Two modes of labor grew simultaneously: the homeworker system multiplied with more agents, and new urban factories appeared.[42] The city of Mayagüez adopted a needlework curriculum for its public schools in 1918 and opened four apparel and home goods manufacturers with 1,000 workers. Ponce had two plants that employed 1,400 women.[43]

The war also expedited migration to the metropole for better wages. The 1917 Jones Act conferred US citizenship on residents of Puerto Rico, allowing for a military draft and easier movement, if not elected federal representation. It constructed a distinct form of citizenship that made demands on residents without increasing their ability to make demands on the government. This arrangement rearticulated the archipelago's relationship to the metropole: Puerto Rico subsumed in US sovereignty yet without full access to the nation-state or citizenship and the benefits these conferred.[44] The results boosted colony-metropole mobility, encouraged relocation of residents as a formal policy for poor or inadequate conditions, and complicated any path to independence.

Wartime production increased jobs in the South as well, and millhands observed wartime celebrations of their patriotic contributions and calls for democratic economic security. But when the war ended, so did federal interest in maintaining production by supporting labor. The downturn hit mills hard, bringing wage cuts and layoffs. In reaction to the gap between wartime propaganda and the recession, a series of strikes spread in 1919. Many owners locked out workers to sell surplus. Organized strikes continued anyway, and workers gained several contract provisions, including a fifty-five-hour week and more favorable wage calculations.[45]

The Northeast remained a prominent manufacturing hub into the 1920s. Both the Northeast and the South increased their consumption of bales of cotton during the 1910s, and all three regions increased machine activity.[46]

Although 1920 marked a turning point, when the number of northeastern bales and spindles leveled off, this change did not indicate the region's irrelevance or a predetermined "end." As an early site of dense manufacturing and finance, the initial stages of disaggregation impacted the Northeast in conspicuous ways that camouflaged how it remained a crucial source of investment, machines, and managers and served as a reserve of specialty and affordable older factories.[47]

Economic Crisis and More Worker Differentiation with More Labor Connections

The economic collapse from the 1920s into the 1930s triggered crises for businesses and workers and unexpected, but rapid, structural formalization in the industry. As a result, Puerto Rico, the South, and the Northeast became more tightly linked via manufacturing, investment, and labor migrations, even as industrial sites diversified and spread. This paradox of robust interconnection—stimulated yet disguised by gender, racial, and citizenship categorizations—within a disaggregation of manufacturing would define the industry for the next seventy years. Rather than undergoing a linear relocation of factories southward, northeast manufacturing thinned and reordered as production steps, labor, and investment adjusted into new arrangements spread along the US Atlantic. But attention to the biggest factories and quantities has created a focus on the metropole, and the cultural erasure of needleworkers has contributed to the misconception of a straightforward relocation of factories from the North to the South to the Global South.

In the Northeast, restrictions on European immigration prompted a search for other sources of cheap skilled labor.[48] More manufacturers and department stores sought alternatives in Puerto Rico, increasing their use of needleworkers on the main island. Because of their concerns that not enough women could be trained to produce at the speed and cost they wanted, manufacturers and department stores developed more precut designs to ship to the archipelago. The practice further aligned women's labor toward mass production and marked Puerto Rico as a lowest-wage labor market with "'off-shore' production" for the metropole.[49]

A 1923 newspaper article would sound familiar to anyone who followed "free trade" debates in the 1990s. The article opened in Ponce, a city four centuries old, at a concrete building with power-driven sewing machines. The reporter argued that "US reforms" had not brought modern business practices but rather promoted the old exploitative sweatshop as such. "[The sweatshop] seemed young and hopeful to Porto Rico, and now it goes by the name of industrial progress," he explained. "In the United States, the sweatshop is recognized as a menace . . . [but] in Porto Rico it is thought of as the bearer of a kind of industrial salvation."[50] He understood regional links, noting that companies preferred Puerto Rican sweatshops to southern mills because they provided skilled women at a lower cost. Although sweatshops had multiplied, piecework contracts remained for "New York concerns." The reporter believed any legislation to help needleworkers or limit Puerto Rico's "advantages" would be interpreted as "discouraging new industries."[51] That year, the US Supreme Court declared minimum wages for women unconstitutional, including Puerto Rico's rarely enforced 1919 wage law.[52]

In 1929, a few years before partnering with US economists, Luis Muñoz Marín also criticized sweatshops. He argued the island had become "a factory worked by peons, fought over by lawyers, bossed by absent industrialists, and clerked by politicians. It is now Uncle Sam's second largest sweat-shop." Muñoz Marín outlined the manipulative process by which US companies pushed external investment into Puerto Rico, extracted profit and dividends in the form of exports from very cheap labor, and then declared "a favorable trade balance."[53]

In addition to this work in Puerto Rico, more women migrated to the Northeast for higher wages, and manufacturers recruited more needleworkers. Even though the number of active machines in the Northeast declined in the late 1920s as corporations disaggregated into more sites throughout the South, Puerto Rico, and Colombia, the remaining shops and plants needed cheap labor.[54] They turned to Puerto Rican women seeking better pay and conditions, needleworkers already familiar with US specifications and business representatives.[55] Citizenship had opened these pathways for versatile migrations and labor recruitment, and women's job arbitrage ran as a corollary to the manufacturers' labor and regulation arbitrage.[56]

Starting in the 1920s, Doña Eulalia, Minerva Torres Ríos, Lucila Padrón, Luisa López, Louise Delgado, and Eva Monje worked in New York factories. Padrón and her sisters had helped their mother with piecework on the island, where they had received precut fabric to sew and finish. In 1927, Padrón walked the New York streets to find a job and noticed dresses and robes she had made in Puerto Rico for three dollars apiece selling for $100. López took turns with her mother, sister, and brother sewing coffee bags, so the machine ran nonstop in the apartment. Delgado arrived in 1923 and saw that her mother and sister ran their machine all day, but she got a job in a dress factory. Monje moved to New York in 1919 and was working in a garment factory in 1927.[57]

Extreme colonial differentials fostered the migration, but US and insular offices supported labor mobility.[58] The Bureau of Employment and Identification opened in New York in 1930 as an agency of the Puerto Rico Department of Commerce and Industry. Its Identification and Documentation Program produced thousands of English-language cards to confirm US citizenship because most employers were ignorant of Puerto Ricans' status.[59] It gave women easier access to the employment they were seeking but in a way that enabled racialized colonial labor markets for manufacturers and added to a larger destabilization of work conditions.

US manufacturing relied on this incipient pattern of mobile colonial women available for both lowest-wage insular and lower-wage metropolitan production and appreciated the malleable obligations to employees. Companies with enough logistics staff and resources could regularly move manufacturing and hiring in these "related but nonsequential currents." Women navigated and shaped the currents as well, seeking the best situation they could find depending on wages, conditions, or a desire for financial autonomy. Conceptualizing capital and labor in such related but nonsequential currents foregrounds the movement of manufacturing, workers, and investment in multiple directions and avoids misleading notions of economic advancement.

In the face of imbalanced political and economic power, women along the US Atlantic resisted the exploitation and demanded better conditions. Puerto Rican women in Brooklyn and East Harlem, where the majority of the early diaspora settled, joined groups such as Liga Puertorriqueña e Hispana and Alianza Obrera.[60] Monje and Delgado became ILGWU members and shop stewards.[61] Perhaps some women knew about the radical activist Luisa Capetillo, who organized for the FLT, traveled to New York to speak on labor and women's issues, and published a text on women's rights.[62]

As the economic crises worsened in the mid-1920s, some New York companies looked to New England for lower costs. The Princeton Thread Mill, for example, moved to Watertown, Connecticut.[63] Circumstances prompted northeastern companies to research the South as well. They compared land and construction costs, utilities, and tax and wage rates. Big companies with resources and credit formed conglomerates and bought older family mills. The Simmons Mattress Company, which J.P. Stevens would absorb in the 1950s, bought all six Patterson mills in Roanoke Rapids, North Carolina, in the 1920s, and a conglomerate that would become Cone Mills purchased the Haw River mill outside Burlington, North Carolina, from the Holt family; two of these mills would become Crystal Lee's places of work.[64]

In the South, the economic collapse hit farmers hard, and thousands of white yeoman families lost their land. The surplus of poor whites gave textile and garment businesses a tremendous advantage. Managers could fire workers and require higher productivity from the remaining millhands without worrying about strikes, because destitute rural outsiders crossed pickets and took lower wages.[65] Stretch-outs spread, with some jobs reassigned to multiple beams or looms, millhands forced to work faster for the same pay, and roles reclassified as piecework. As more white families became dependent on wages and the time clock, Jim Crow was vital to constituting a new class identity with status even more reliant on white superiority. The domestic labor of Black women supported this racial capitalism, because they cleaned homes and did laundry for extremely low wages as more white women had to work in mills for wages.[66]

This exploitation led to an explosive 1929, and one of the most famous strikes in US history occurred in Gastonia, North Carolina, at the massive Loray Mill owned by the E. Jenckes Company of Rhode Island.[67] The company, which had exhibited at the 1901–2 Charleston Exposition, purchased the mill in 1919 to become one of the first conglomerates.[68] The National Textile Workers Union (NTWU) sent representatives to organize the millhands' walkout into an official strike. Although it gained few concessions, the action increased solidarity and networks of communication.[69]

Workers' Rights and Worker Differentiation in the New Deal

In the depths of the Great Depression, from 1933 to 1934, demonstrations erupted along the US Atlantic. Scholars have often discussed the strikes from a southern perspective because of their pronounced militancy. But strikes were national-colonial, with related, if not fully coordinated, actions from Maine to Alabama and Puerto Rico.[70] The chief concern for workers in Puerto Rico was the pay structure, which had always benefited metropolitan firms and insular agents. When the economic collapse swelled the surplus of poor white women in the South, and managers there lowered wages and increased stretch-outs, Puerto Rican needleworkers had to bear large cuts to piece rates. US manufacturers could get their work done cheaply in the South, without freight charges or agent commissions, so insular agents cut their rates.[71]

Although Congress supported the short-lived Puerto Rican Emergency Relief Administration with the 1933 Federal Emergency Relief Act, the effort came too late for needleworkers. Women from homework and sweatshops in Lares, San Germán, and Mayagüez went on strike. In Mayagüez, more than 2,000 workers from almost seventy shops were involved, and groups stoned factories, including one owned by María Luisa Arcelay, the first woman elected to the House of Representatives of Puerto Rico. As in the South, owners and managers like Arcelay called the police to protect their property, and officers wounded several women and killed Luz María Santiago. Arcelay exemplifies how Spanish colonial hierarchy had adapted with US colonialism. She was from a criollo family, attended college, and became a teacher but left that career in 1917 to open a needlework shop. It was profitable, so she and a partner moved to a bigger site. She also represented insular business at the 1934 National Recovery Administration (NRA) code hearings in Washington, DC, and fought against any minimum wage for needleworkers.[72]

The workers' unrest and New Deal legislation created an opening for union organizing. Teresa Angleró of the FLT led an effort to use the NRA codes to bring in more factory workers. In 1934, she worked closely with Rose Pesotta, an ILGWU organizer sent from New York, to merge Puerto Rican locals into the Needle Workers' Union Local 300. The women wanted to support worker actions, recruit members, and improve lobbying. More than three-fourths of factory workers organized, and the union mediated for a pay increase of 15–25 percent. Needleworkers in remote areas, who defended their right to do homework for fair pay, did not gain as much because agents neglected to tell rural women and pocketed the increase.[73] Despite some misdirected criticism of homeworkers for undercutting pay rates, Local 300 pushed to enforce the raise, and Angleró organized with the ILGWU for several years.[74]

In 1934, southern millhands also went on strike over stretch-outs that included replacing people with machines, speeding up machines, increasing the number of looms per operator, hiring more job watchers, and installing clocks on machines.[75] Several strikes led to lockouts, when owners closed mills to purge troublesome workers and surplus stock, leaving families destitute.[76] Although the most remote millhands did not usually know about strikes, these actions promoted labor networks across towns.[77] They ended in October, when the UTW accepted recommendations from a mediation committee President Franklin D. Roosevelt convened to end the strikes and reduce hardships on indigent workers.[78]

The heightened activism and management-police repression along the US Atlantic led to ongoing federal involvement. The New Deal response was complicated and incongruous. It helped solidify rationales for exemptions in Puerto Rico, differentials in the South, and gender and race employment discrimination but also legitimized basic work standards and union representation. After decades of organizing, labor leaders encountered receptive national offices, and many industrial wageworkers benefited from new protections and oversight. But within this expanding scope of public-private collaboration, the New Deal developed government-industry projects in ways not fully counterbalanced by government-labor partnerships.[79] Companies and investors maintained their advantaged position vis-à-vis the state.

The results were obvious in Puerto Rico, which attracted New Deal leaders like Eleanor Roosevelt and Rexford Tugwell. Eleanor Roosevelt joined liberal reformers who had intertwined concerns with the South and the Caribbean, and needleworkers were a priority when she visited the main island in 1934.[80]

First Lady Eleanor Roosevelt on her 1934 trip through Puerto Rico with Lorena Hickok. | Associated Press photograph

She stopped at a women's prison, where inmates made fine lace for 50 percent of the proceeds, and saw women on remote coastal roads carrying bundles of material. One rural seamstress said she earned sixty cents a dozen for nightgowns but could make only one a day because of the intensive appliqués. Another woman earned ten cents a dozen for handkerchiefs that sold for fifty cents apiece in the metropole. Roosevelt's visit culminated in Mayagüez, the center of industrial needlework, where she toured an "advanced" factory with 200 workers. Upon returning to Washington, DC, she promoted manufacturing collectives and encouraged friends and allies to learn more and invest.[81]

Tugwell, a prominent economist and renowned member of President Roosevelt's Brain Trust, led an intensive assessment and recommended the formation of the Puerto Rico Reconstruction Administration (PRRA) with rigorous economic planning. Despite Tugwell's preliminary attempts to "decolonize" landownership by breaking up the sugar industry and fostering worker collectives, PRRA policies facilitated colonial governance with extreme exemptions.[82] Tugwell, like other officials, business leaders, and investors, maintained the rationale that Puerto Rico needed lowest-cost industrial employment to encourage social progress. The New Deal sought a better and more humane colonialism rather than its end and continued to cultivate imperialism through external investment and colonial industrialization.

While technocratic terms gave it a gloss of modernity, the planning built on and adapted colonial notions. A 1934 PRRA report stated that due to higher costs of credit and logistics, "the only industries which have important possibilities for development are those which can progressively profit by the utilization of a large supply of labor that is 'cheap.'" The report supported Public Act 40, pushed by the appointed governor and passed by the insular legislature in 1930 to exempt new manufacturing facilities from taxes for ten years.[83]

This rationale distressed labor activists, who understood labor markets affected one another. The Council for Pan American Democracy argued that sweatshop conditions in New York were "in part due to the working conditions in Puerto Rico. One part of trade cannot be controlled without controlling the other."[84] Despite such criticisms, New Deal justifications that perpetuated earlier US colonial practices became core presumptions of economic development.

The New Deal extended the bureaucracy that worked to make Puerto Rico more legible as an option for trade, production, and recruitment. FDR created the Division of Territories and Island Possessions in the Department of the Interior as part of a 1934 executive branch reorganization.[85] Offices provided information that lobbyists, investors, and managers could use to support established businesses and attract new enterprises. An exhaustive 1935 report called *Planning Problems and Activities in Puerto Rico* included statistics for dividend payments, interest payments, real estate rentals, freight charges, and bonded indebtedness.[86]

Such New Deal projects proved particularly mixed for Puerto Rican women, for whom attention often meant not leverage but surveillance.[87] The *Planning Problems* report listed eighteen areas for research and action, including farm debt, tariffs, and shipping—but also public "beneficencia," house-to-house slum surveys, tuberculosis, nutrition, and the activities of schoolchildren. The latter topics involved poor mothers, making them subject to public policy debates and initiatives. Questions of poverty increasingly focused on motherhood and population rather than on systemic economic reform.[88]

The New Deal also solidified labor market differentiations that obscured women's interconnected work across a globalizing national industry. Its reports continued to use "needlework" for the quantification of insular textile and garment workers, sustaining their separation from New England mill workers, New York garment workers, and southern millhands while sentimentalizing the labor and homogenizing the variety of jobs.

Debates about the 1938 Fair Labor Standards Act (FLSA) were a decisive forum for the entrenchment of Puerto Rico as an industrial site subsumed

Left: A needleworker near Ponce completes piecework for an insular contract agent, 1938. *Below:* Women sew in a San Juan factory, 1942. | Photographs by Edwin Rosskam and Jack Delano, courtesy of Library of Congress, Prints and Photographs Division, Farm Security Administration/Office of War Information Black-and-White Negatives, Washington, DC

in US sovereignty but not of the nation.[89] During the Great Depression, enacting a national minimum wage became a top concern. From 1938 to 1940, Puerto Rico officially shared the FLSA universal minimum wage intended to eliminate southern differentials. But business groups, particularly the Puerto Rico Needlework Association (PRNA), immediately advocated an exemption for the archipelago, and most managers refused to pay the legal wage. In 1939, over 8,000 needleworkers struck in Mayagüez to call for compliance with the FLSA.[90]

The PRNA wrote editorials, policy papers, and letters demanding tariff protections or wage and hour exemptions. A 1938 letter from the association secretary said the FLSA represented the "highest human achievement" but could not be enforced in Puerto Rico because a clause stated it would only be enacted if it did not curtail employment or earning power. He argued "the law means the total collapse of every needlework shop" in an industry that ranked second in importance for the island. Another dramatic letter, from former PRNA president Victor Domenech, insisted the FLSA minimum wage would cause the collapse of the industry and inhibition of development.[91] Rather than pushing for a reduced or weaker nation-state, the PRNA advocated a strong interventionist state capable of demarcating and enforcing exceptions to its laws or regulatory standards as a means to orchestrate market mechanisms.

Metropolitan industry leaders with interests in Puerto Rico agreed. Edward Leon, a New York attorney for companies that contracted with insular agents, sent a letter to the Division of Territories and Island Possessions saying people blamed the FLSA minimum wage for a needlework decline.[92] A dozen articles about needlework appeared in the *New York Times* from August to November 1938, and one declared a "Pay Plea for Puerto Rico." Another argued the FLSA had caused unemployment in needlework "despite its good intentions."[93]

Insular labor activists took different positions, aggravating rifts within the movement. Prudencio Rivera Martínez, an FLT leader who had become labor commissioner, advocated compliance with any FLSA wage amendment as long as there were "adequate remedies . . . to be applied to local conditions by the insular legislative assembly."[94] He supported an insular bureau of minimum wage and industrial homework, but the PRNA fought it. Many labor activists criticized Martínez's compromises and left the FLT to form other unions, and the ILGWU submitted a statement arguing needlework was profitable enough to pay higher wages.[95]

After two years of letters, lobbying, and negotiating, Congress passed a wage amendment that allowed a lower minimum for nonincorporated territories, and "Needlework in establishments" was top on the list of applicable jobs.[96] The New Deal strengthened the nation-state through the management of such official exceptions from national standards and legislation, not only through massive economic programs and public works. The wage amendment exacerbated exploitation and arbitrage along the US Atlantic and laid the foundation for Operation Bootstrap by supporting the notion that offshore contracting served industrial progress. Federal attention to handkerchiefs typifies the relevance of contracting for US global plans. A 1939 PRRA handkerchief report outlined industry conditions: "Puerto Rico has no part in the ownership of material, the planning of products nor the marketing of the manufactured goods. . . . Puerto Rico's concern is only with labor and this is contracted." Yet a radiogram mentioned the need to preserve the handkerchief industry through lower wages and a reciprocity agreement with Switzerland and other ruinous competitors like China.[97]

The New Deal had contradictory effects in the South as well. Even when programs targeted the region's textile and garment industry, FDR deferred to southern elites on implementation because he depended on Dixie Democrats for his legislative agenda and reelection. This meant industry and white supremacy, not the demands of white or Black workers, received top priority, and most southern offices aligned incoming federal funds with companies' interests.[98] Town officials in Ellisville, Mississippi, for example, misused a Works Progress Administration (WPA) allocation to construct a "vocational school." The Vertex Hosiery Company operated this "school" with "students" in a forty-hour week when it relocated from Pennsylvania.[99] The New Deal strengthened such government-industry relationships even as southern elites demanded "less government" regarding worker issues like wages and unionizing.

As in Puerto Rico, industry leaders in the South drafted their own NRA codes and formed the Cotton Textile Industry Committee. Although managers did not abide by their own codes, the Cotton Textile Industry Committee demanded full compliance with wage differentials, which lowered wages below northern rates and then lowered wages further for Black workers. This wage regime performed multiple functions: holding wealth at the top; reinforcing elitist white supremacy by marginalizing white workers; bolstering white superiority through the oppression of Black workers; and instigating union fragmentation, which also thwarted labor's overall political power.[100]

The New Deal was imperfect and did not transform wages or conditions to the extent workers wanted or foster the union membership labor leaders expected, yet it represents the most comprehensive progressive economic program in US history. The 1935 Wagner Act recognized unions and created the NLRB and a grievance procedure that legitimated unionizing and institutionalized a foundation, limited as it was, for organizing. The FLSA was profoundly problematic because it excluded agriculture, with its predominantly

Black and immigrant workforce, and allowed an amendment to lower wages in Puerto Rico, which hurt thousands of needleworkers. But it formalized a wage standard and validated grievances based on pay, which became a tool for worker activism. The ILGWU and TWUA demanded and used these federal laws and regulations to expand contact with Puerto Rican needleworkers and southern millhands who had never seen organizers.[101] These tools were also the primary means for building the postwar labor movement that Maldonado and Crystal Lee would join in the 1960s and '70s.

In addition to tackling colonial and domestic economic conditions, FDR's administration aimed to stabilize the global economy. A key piece of legislation, the 1934 Reciprocal Trade Agreements Act, transferred trade deals from Congress to the White House and had far-reaching repercussions for manufacturing jobs. Based on the idea that executive trade offices were more nimble, the act gave FDR the power to negotiate bilateral tariff reductions to stimulate world trade.[102] This arrangement changed the place of tariffs in US politics: by removing Congress, it limited the sway of constituents, prioritized trade relations over domestic producers and workers, and strengthened bonds between global capital and foreign economic policy.

Japan also became a point of concern. While the Great Depression hammered the United States and Europe, Japan expanded production. In 1933, its cotton textile exports surpassed those of England, France, and Germany. By the late 1930s, Japan ranked third, behind England and the United States, for global trade. Japanese production relied on low-wage labor from migrating rural women as well. Girls and young women from poor households who needed money for a dowry or the family farm moved to factory towns. They lived in dorms under paternalist supervision that lowered costs below even those of British colonial mills in India.[103] This situation laid the foundation for a postwar foreign economic policy focused on Japan's textile industry that would further destabilize employment in the US Atlantic.

Bracing the Ties That Bind Maldonado and Crystal Lee

World War II intensified the pace of change, multiplied the lines and hubs of the sprawling global industry, and increased the number of Puerto Rican women working in both the archipelago and the Northeast. Starting in 1938, Muñoz Marín and the Partido Popular Democrático (PPD; Popular Democratic Party) decided to address poverty rather than emphasizing independence, and leaders proposed collaborative, if tense, policymaking with federal offices. In 1941, FDR appointed the esteemed but controversial Tugwell as governor, allowing him to coordinate economic planning as long as it did not interfere with war strategy. Although Tugwell implemented limited state ownership and collectives, he and Muñoz Marín pushed for legislation in 1942 to create the Compañía de Fomento Industrial (Puerto Rico Industrial Development Company; PRIDC) and hired Arthur D. Little, a consulting firm in Boston.[104] Without using the word "colonial," the firm's August 1942 report endorsed sovereignty, tax, and labor exemptions and said it was already pursuing a northeastern corporation for a venture.[105]

Based on the report, Tugwell, the PPD, and the PRIDC cooperated with officials and enterprises from the metropole and main island to implement more subsidies and real estate, construction, taxation, and labor exclusions—formative steps for Operation Bootstrap. Their proposals were presented as modern scientific business solutions, even though their pastiche of initiatives adapted earlier colonial industrialization. In 1945, PPD leaders worked with the PRIDC to pass a resolution authorizing it to construct buildings for private firms, sold or leased at below-market rates. Later that year, the PRIDC went further with Aid to Industrial Development, which provided direct subsidies to external investors according to their own building specifications.[106]

Booming wartime and postwar production granted many metropolitan white workers union leverage, a sense of employment stability, and faith in the United States' unprecedented economic and geopolitical power. Even though US dominance of trade and financial institutions like the World Bank and the International Monetary Fund (IMF) was not absolute, US agencies, trade representatives, and industrial corporations directed most international agreements and projects. At the same time, they confronted global opposition in multiple ways—from military intervention and covert operations to market share and credit.

Southern millhands did not attain substantial benefits from this boom because worker organizing was hampered by white supremacy, segregation, and anti-union attitudes. Political and business elites converted New Deal planning boards into state development agencies that emphasized industrial growth and production over economic planning and work conditions, and they continued to funnel federal subsidies and state tax funds to investors, owners, and managers. Although they could not execute the extreme exemptions granted in Puerto Rico, elites developed special arrangements at the local and county levels with municipal bonds, tax waivers (abatements and temporary exemptions from property, excise, and income taxes), fee reductions, reimbursements of moving costs, and concessions for pollution or water usage and contamination.[107]

Efforts to dismantle or repurpose New Deal programs occurred in Puerto Rico as well. In 1946, Tugwell backed the first Puerto Rican governor, Jesús T. Piñero, a cofounder of the PPD. He and his administration, together with the PRIDC, developed an economic plan for managing the related but nonsequential currents of capital, manufacturing, and poor workers. Their policies often appeased conservative business interests, which had rejected even limited state ownership. They fostered public-private partnerships with firms and investors over workers, and their plan phased out import substitution for increased external direct investment in cheap exports.[108] Piñero and Muñoz Marín broadcast Operation Bootstrap with the 1947 Industrial Incentives Act, which extended the 1917 income tax exemptions and ended all import duties to the metropole, making the archipelago a bounded duty-free zone. The act also waived qualifying firms from property taxes, excise taxes on machinery and raw materials, municipal taxes, and industrial license fees.[109] Later that year, Arthur D. Little helped Textron build a mill in Puerto Rico, and its executives acknowledged the appeal of the amended lower wage, fifteen years without taxes, and elimination of duties. They announced plans for five more mills, to include rayon fabric and sewing production.[110]

When Muñoz Marín became the first elected governor of Puerto Rico in 1948, his administration continued Operation Bootstrap. A 1949 *New York Times* article declared, "Puerto Rico Urged on US Business," and said a hypothetical textile company could retain almost twice the profit due to tax exemptions and lower wages. An Office of Puerto Rico pamphlet encouraged executives to relocate manufacturing for orderly workers, who appreciated jobs due to unemployment and underemployment, and promised needleworkers with great dexterity. By 1950, homework and factories had increased, and women held 60 percent of all new jobs.[111] Despite difficult conditions, poor women such as Esmeralda Santiago's mother expressed pride at having their own income from the city factories, and the money created new, if constrained, opportunities for autonomy.[112] The increase also drew attention from ILGWU leadership as Puerto Rican women contradicted the booster "orderliness" narrative by unionizing. Even within a gendered, racialized, colonial labor hierarchy, women made increasing connections, building a union network from the archipelago to the Northeast.[113]

Operation Bootstrap encouraged poor women to migrate to the metropole for better wages or as cheaper labor, depending on the audience. During the 1940s and '50s, the needs of Puerto Rico's poor households continued to surpass industrial employment and its low piece rates and minimum wage. Efforts to alleviate the poverty focused on women rather than on employers: the PPD established a Women's Bureau (1945–52) to encourage modernization, with factory jobs and family planning.[114] The wage amendment that made Puerto Rico appealing to businesses made the Northeast appealing to needleworkers, and these dual currents constituted a labor market manipulation that undercut wages overall.[115]

In 1956, women in Puerto Rico form ILGWU Local 600 for over 3,000 corset and brassiere workers, and members stand with union managers and directors to celebrate. | ILGWU Photographs 1885–1985, Kheel Center, Cornell University, Ithaca, NY

The increased migration prompted insular and US officials to expand services in the metropole, particularly with the Puerto Rico Department of Labor. Its offices expanded for the recruitment, transportation, and hiring of workers, and insular leaders encouraged permanent migration.[116] In 1948, operations of the Bureau of Employment and Migration transferred to the new Migration Division (1948–89), which served as an employment agency in New York, Rochester, Boston, Hartford, Philadelphia, Cleveland, and Miami. Much Migration Division scholarship has centered men, especially farmworkers, but the offices were integral to the movement of needleworkers as well. Staff guided their relocation and took an active role in acquiring housing, attaining education and training, and providing descriptions of Puerto Rican culture to local organizations.[117]

The New York office held regular meetings about job applicants, employer services, counseling, and training with Puerto Rican staff and presenters focused on improving conditions. Dozens of factories sent Puerto Rican Labor

A 1955 Puerto Rico Department of Labor order form requesting women needleworkers for Fairway Skirts on Houston Street in New York City. | Puerto Rican Employment Program, Offices of the Government of Puerto Rico in the United States Collection, Centro Library and Archives , Center for Puerto Rican Studies, Hunter College–CUNY, New York, NY

Department forms to the Employment Program, requesting sewing machine operators, cutters, finishers, floor girls, and packers. In 1951, Howard Clothes in Brooklyn submitted multiple orders, including a request for three hand sewers and seven trimmers for men's coats. Fairway Skirt on Houston Street had two openings for sewing machine operators in April 1952, and the Employment Program sent Sixta and Laura Rivera.[118]

Informal networks also supported the migrations of Puerto Rican women. Women in rural training programs grew frustrated with piece rates and moved, and instructors spoke about earning more money on the mainland. Most needleworkers knew family or friends who had relocated to island cities or the Northeast.[119] Their letters and remittances carried the network to the next generations, to women like Maldonado, and helped them get hired after they arrived in New York, Philadelphia, and Chicago.[120] A 1953 survey of San Juan needlework operators indicated migration to the Northeast was the primary reason women quit.[121]

A full-page 1955 article in *Justice*, the ILGWU newspaper, reports that Puerto Rican women in New York City want women on the main island to get the same minimum wage. | *Justice*, July 1955, DigitalCollections@ILR, Kheel Center, Cornell University, Ithaca, NY

Despite a history of insular labor activism, Puerto Rican women in New York often worked in nonunion shops because of a lack of outreach from ILGWU and Amalgamated Clothing Workers of America (ACWA) locals. Discrimination marginalized women who were perceived as inferior or outsiders, and many ILGWU locals had strong ethnic identities. Some Italian and Jewish women used negative stereotypes about "newcomers" and "laziness" to block Puerto Rican women from membership.[122]

Many Puerto Rican women, however, knew their abuelas', mothers', aunties', and sisters' union stories and found ways to sign membership cards, file grievances, and initiate walkouts. By the 1950s, some were shop stewards and chairladies, and they bolstered the national-colonial network of labor organizing.[123] In July 1955, ILGWU needleworkers rallied in New York to demand that women in Puerto Rico receive the same minimum wage. Louise Delgado, as an active shop steward, exemplifies this attitude. When an owner yelled and threw a dress in a woman's face, Delgado confronted him. He did not relent, so Delgado announced a shutdown and called her ILGWU chairman. She said, "I don't give a darn if he does it to her, then he'll do it to me, do it to my sister, do it to the one. . . . And I will not stand for that you know, because after all, we're human beings, and we're all ladies."[124] Like many working women, Delgado fought derogatory treatment by claiming the status of "lady," a term reserved for upper-class women in Caribbean, Black, and white communities. Rather than a statement of social mobility, it was a classed and gendered demand for respect as an industrial wageworker.

Puerto Rican women also used membership to get the best possible job situation. In an underwear factory, María R. requested better pay because she was the only operator who could use the zigzag machine. The boss fired her, so she contacted the ILGWU. The agent required the boss to rehire María R. and compensate her accordingly. Although she received better pay, María R. did not forget the humiliation and found another job at a swimwear factory with even higher pay. The original boss offered her a raise to keep her, but she left anyway.[125]

In addition to migrations, new postwar technologies impacted workers in both Puerto Rico and the South. Military research spurred production of synthetic fabrics made with petrochemicals—cotton was no longer absolute king. Several states along the Gulf of Mexico had a petrochemical sector, and the PRIDC campaigned to develop one. By 1956, Caribe Nitrogen, Gulf Caribbean, and Commonwealth Oil Refining Company had facilities in Puerto Rico, and the PRIDC endorsed a large complex to include the manufacture of synthetic fibers.[126] A 1957 study of the synthetic fiber industry noted Puerto Rico was "a low labor-cost area and thereby furnishes an alternative." It predicted that by 1975, 80 percent of US synthetic textile production would be in the South and Puerto Rico. In the case of Puerto Rico, the author argued that the added costs of fuel and transportation would need to be offset with lower wages.[127]

Textile and Apparel Workers as Cold War Policy

Changes along the US Atlantic continued to interact with global reconfigurations and foreign economic policy. The textile and apparel industry already served US global ambitions, but Cold War diplomats, military commanders, and trade representatives adapted it for a strategy that maintained its overall importance, while downgrading the position of domestic manufacturing and workers. Rebuilding occupied Japan as an ally was a top priority, but the Supreme Commander for the Allied Powers (SCAP) and the State Department did not want any military industry. They decided on cotton textiles. In 1947, SCAP outlined production targets with allocations of capital, materials, coal, and extra food rations for textile workers. SCAP and the State Department also renewed cotton and textile trade between Japan and its former Asian colonies and even acquired cotton from India and Egypt. In 1948, George Kennan appointed the banker William H. Draper to organize a Textile Mission to Japan with businessmen and financiers.[128]

In the 1950s, the Bureau of the Budget agreed that foreign economic policy should focus on political-security issues as much as financial concerns, and the National Security Council urged Japanese imports to curtail possible economic deterioration that could lead to communist subversion.[129] The International Cooperative Association spent millions of dollars on the construction of textile and garment factories throughout East Asia, and President Dwight Eisenhower lobbied for Japan's 1955 admission to the General Agreement on Trade and Tariffs (GATT). US conglomerates looked to Japan and Taiwan as they had looked to Puerto Rico at the turn of the twentieth century: a new option in the catalog of manufacturing and labor.[130]

Puerto Rico played a crucial role in this Cold War industry realignment. In 1948, President Harry Truman established the Point IV Program, which encouraged export manufacturing in poor regions to counter communist appeals. Point IV offered technical and financial assistance to "third world" countries and promoted Puerto Rico's colonial industrialization as a model. The State Department invited students, experts, and politicians from Africa, Asia, and South America to travel to Puerto Rico and see its results. In some cases, the State Department even funded the research trips.[131]

Puerto Rico also served as a model for economic development of the Mexico-US border region. The two governments had been discussing how to manage seasonal migrant workers and, after years of debate, settled on export processing. In the late 1950s, the Mexican secretary of industry and commerce led a delegation on a tour of apparel and electronics manufacturing factories in Japan and Taiwan.[132] The governments also hired Arthur D. Little, and a consultant from Puerto Rico, Richard Bolin, moved to Mexico to coordinate research and development. In 1961, the firm produced a report recommending an export processing zone like Operation Bootstrap. As in Puerto Rico and Japan, most initial funding for the Mexican zone came from US government agencies. In 1963, the US government added Item 807 to the Tariff Code, allowing customs to assess duties only on the value added to materials sent abroad for processing. President Gustavo Díaz Ordaz took office in 1964 and supported the zone, which formally opened in 1965 as the Border Industrialization Program (BIP) but became known as "the maquiladoras."[133]

These new global supply chains led some economists to consider how they might cultivate an American middle-class lifestyle through lower consumer prices rather than through cost-of-living wages and other distributions of income and wealth. The full consequences of all these postwar policies would hit most working Americans in the 1970s, when Maldonado and Crystal Lee were active with their unions.

1958 Turning Point

The year 1958 was notable for Puerto Rican needleworkers in New York and for southern millhands in North Carolina. As the cotton regime lost its outright authority in the global economy, southern industrialists sought to maintain their elite status by investing in synthetics. Karl Robbins, a retired North Carolina textile magnate, provided 4,000 acres for a research park to attract sophisticated industries to the Raleigh-Durham-Chapel Hill region, and Governor Luther H. Hodges, a former Fieldcrest Mills executive, coordinated the planning committee. Construction on Research Triangle Park began in late 1958, and Chemstrand, a synthetic textile company from Georgia, and the American Association of Textile Chemists and Colorists were two of the first leases.[134] Like the 1901–2 Charleston Exposition, this collaboration of businessmen, politicians, and investors was intended to make the state a hub for longer lines of trade and capital.

Just forty miles northeast of "the Triangle," the TWUA organized a strike in Henderson, at an old factory where the conglomerate Cone Mills had made limited updates. The proximity of these two ventures demonstrates industrial capitalism's opportunistic tendency to use any available means to generate revenues. The TWUA local accused Cone Mills of bad-faith negotiations to wear down workers and push them to decertify the union in frustration. When a strike seemed imminent, the new generation of young white elites taking over management positions tried to avert it. Unlike many returning African American veterans, who became involved in civil rights activism, most middle-class and affluent white veterans hoped for calm to appeal to new industries and investors. But for older elites, the existence of a local in Henderson gave it a reputation as a "union town," which infuriated them. These senior members of established families still served as regional executives and board directors and intended to provoke a strike to break the TWUA.[135]

A couple months into the strike, violence erupted when outside white workers arrived. Hodges provided National Guard troops to protect the mills, but he wanted to end the crisis. He ordered an investigation and the NLRB began looking into unfair labor practices, which pushed mill negotiators to make a weak contract offer. But factories continued operating with strikebreakers. Without the ability to stop poor transient whites and without support from any regional elites, the TWUA lost the strike by attrition.[136] In Burlington, forty miles west of the Triangle, Crystal Lee had started working at another old mill and heard about the strike, beatings, sabotage, and patrols. Her father viewed it as another indicator of the futility of unions and the problems they caused, just as managers hoped.[137]

In 1958, Puerto Rican women also walked out in the Northeast with the ILGWU. Maldonado most likely knew about it because thousands of women filled Seventh Avenue and marched to Madison Square Garden for a union rally. Over several years, ILGWU organizers had increased their outreach in contracting shops, which relied heavily on Puerto Rican needleworkers. The effort paid off, prompting workers from fifty nonunion shops to join striking ILGWU members. Regional leaders also planned for simultaneous walkouts across seven states, because owners and managers were moving production to older factories in Massachusetts, Connecticut, and New Jersey. The strike lasted five days and won a wage increase and severance plan when Maldonado was probably a young woman in the city.[138]

For many decades, tens of thousands of women living, working, and moving along the US Atlantic produced cloth, fabrics, sheets, handkerchiefs, bras, pants, dresses, and coats in an interconnected array of enterprises. When Maldonado and Crystal Lee became assertive union organizers in the 1970s, they were responding to situations that had emerged from this larger context— a context that included historical laws, investments, trade deals, migrations, and labor actions, all embroiled in ongoing fights over the conditions of manufacturing. In different regions and unions, but within one US industry, Puerto Rican needleworkers and southern millhands negotiated, assailed, and changed these conditions. They sought better wages and circumstances and found ways to resist exploitation or demand better treatment. Realignments during World War I, the Great Depression and New Deal, and the postwar years both intensified and dispersed these links. Workers' simultaneous actions in 1934 and 1958 expressed overlapping demands, as changes continuously rippled through the industry. Despite all the women involved and the complexity of issues and events, only the southern millhands received mainstream media coverage and popular representation as real "American workers."

CHAPTER TWO

Gloria Maldonado and
Puerto Rican Needleworkers
Moving in Colonial Currents

An organizer is a person who tries to bring in a shop that is
non-union. They talk to the people and tell them about the
benefits of having a union and try to convince them
to join the union and to sign a card.

—**Gloria Maldonado**

My sister-in-law brought me here. She took me to
American Thread. I applied and in less than a week I got
a job as a machine operator. . . . It was easy to find
jobs when I came here in 1969.

—**Patria**

Two dozen Puerto Rican women left a third-story sweatshop and filed down the stairs onto the sidewalk. They encouraged each other, exclaiming and smiling as they merged with the crowds moving along Seventh Avenue toward Madison Square Garden. Some women hooked arms as they walked, and others looked for mamis, sisters, aunties, and cousins in the swirl of faces. It was March 1958, and the ILGWU had coordinated one of the largest regional strikes in US history. After sixty years of colonial status, thousands of Puerto Rican women were union members, shop stewards, and business agents who had spread word of the walkout. Organizers had spoken in Spanish about how the ILGWU could improve conditions when workers stood in solidarity, and they called needleworkers into the street from union and nonunion shops.[1]

Although no available record exists of Gloria Maldonado's participation, she most likely started embroidering and sewing at a young age and already had a job. The archives do show that Eva Monje, a shop steward, shut down her housecoat factory to support the dressmakers' strike. And Saby Nehama, a Jewish man who headed the Education Department for Local 22 Dressmakers and worked closely with Puerto Rican members, expressed his solidarity by giving a rousing speech in Spanish.[2] If Maldonado did not join the women marching to Madison Square Garden, she knew about them. Newspapers and radio covered the event, and workers talked about it for weeks.

At the same time as this strike, the book for *West Side Story* was published following a successful opening on Broadway. The celebrated musical, in which the two female leads are needleworkers in a romanticized New York City dress shop, dominated Broadway and sparked talk of a movie. Unlike needleworkers in city factories and contracting shops who walked out with the ILGWU, however, Maria and Anita in *West Side Story* do not discuss work conditions, wage rates, or unions. They are the exotic dark Other in colorful dresses, and their background sewing serves the play's fairy-tale quality. The writers and choreographers did not depict Puerto Rico's colonial status or the recruitment of needleworkers for textiles and apparel. When Anita sang that she preferred the consumer goods in America over the poverty in Puerto Rico, it was the only explanation for the women's presence in the city.

During the 1960s and '70s, Maldonado was one of thousands of Puerto Rican women navigating and shaping pronounced changes in the northeastern industry. Transnational corporations and investors capitalized on the favorable policies from federal trade and diplomatic offices, and then lobbied for more. They intensified the global currents, which accelerated the disaggregation of manufacturing, workers, and capital from previously dense hubs like the Garment District in Manhattan or the mill cities of Massachusetts and multiplied the lines of investment, manufacturing, labor, and trade running through the South, Puerto Rico, East Asia, and Mexico. Although diminished and realigned, northeastern production did not end. Many mills and plants remained as a reserve of older low-outlay, low-cost properties and specialty machines, and managers recruited Puerto Rican women to New England from the main island and New York until a spate of closures in the 1980s.

Puerto Rican needleworkers pursuing industrial work along the US Atlantic into the 1970s illustrate the complications of this history. They were not the largest group of textile and apparel workers, but they performed crucial functions as a particular type of mobile labor and as connective tissue for the sprawling industry and US economy. Like capital, they inhabited a large geographic terrain, even if the two functioned with unequal assets, information, risks, and rewards. The asymmetrical power impacts the agility and pace of workers' mobility, not the reach.

Examining needleworkers' history together with postwar colonial and foreign economic policy illuminates the economic, political, and social structures not usually included in the dominant narrative of "capital flight." Women moved in search of better wages and conditions, interacting with the currents of capital and manufacturing. In addition, regional companies and local businesses were unable to adapt like large corporations. When federal trade agreements implemented options like complex quota systems and contracting in East Asia or the BIP, large corporations had the logistics staff, legal teams, credit, and capital liquidity to take advantage. Regional companies and local businesses adjusted by recruiting cheaper workers to their sites, becoming contractors for global brands, or selling their plants to transnational corporations.[3]

The 1958 strike that launched the ILGWU into the 1960s was a concerted effort to address not just low wages but also specific conditions causing increased precarity. ILGWU president David Dubinsky argued textile and apparel employment had become more insecure because of three business practices: increasing section work (workers doing one action all day) to deskill jobs and drive down wages; selling businesses to move capital from manufacturing to financial investments; and relocating factories and shops out of Manhattan to Brooklyn and surrounding states such as Connecticut, Massachusetts, and New Jersey.[4]

In January and February, union negotiators met with New York employers' associations but could not agree on a renewal of the dressmakers' collective agreement. Organizers and shop stewards in the ILGWU New York City, Eastern, Out-of-Town, and Northeast Departments began setting up strike machinery with their Picket, Hall, and Settlement Committees. On March 3, New York City mayor Robert F. Wagner intervened in an attempt to avoid a major strike.[5] Union negotiators dropped the requested wage increase from 22 to 15 percent, but the employers' associations offered 5 percent. Dubinsky countered that workers had gone without a raise for five years despite hikes in the cost of living.[6]

In addition, the union wanted a severance plan to address the precarity. Dubinsky suggested the idea at the 1950 ILGWU convention because he had seen many employers make their fortunes in manufacturing, then close their city shops. He criticized them for taking the capital they had accumulated from workers and investing it in Wall Street, commercial real estate, or cheaper outlying shops. Between 1953 and 1961, the proportion of dressmakers in the Garment District near Seventh and Eighth Avenues decreased, but it increased in Harlem, Brooklyn, and the Bronx. Real estate and wages were lower in the outer boroughs, and some companies relocated even farther out. Workers who had labored twenty or thirty years were left without jobs amid shrinking opportunities.[7]

The strike started on March 5, with thousands of union and nonunion

Puerto Rican women. New York Local 22 Dressmakers and Local 23 Skirtmakers had many Puerto Rican members, and they joined the march to Madison Square Garden for a massive rally.[8] In addition, the ILGWU had increased outreach and grievance actions in contract shops to show managers they could not evade union wages by contracting and subcontracting.[9] Maldonado's name does not appear in records related to this strike, but she made the decision to become active in the ILGWU in the late 1960s, so she most likely had ties and even membership in the union by 1958. Monje called the workers in her housecoat factory to join the walkout, and Nehama spoke in Spanish to the audience of workers from a variety of backgrounds and ethnicities. It was a declaration of solidarity with Puerto Rican women.[10]

Puerto Rican women's participation in the strike built on their years of experience with the industry and ILGWU. In addition to the ongoing colonial wage reduction, Migration Division recruitment, and informal networks of family and friends, the cost of airfare from Puerto Rico to New York had dropped from $180 to $75 and increased the movement between the archipelago and the Northeast. Direct flights to New Jersey and New England were also more available.[11] The number of women living in the Northeast increased, and they sewed, embroidered, and packed in all types of textile, apparel, home goods, and accessories production in an expanding geographic terrain.

In response, the metropolitan-area Labor Advisory Committee on Puerto Rican Affairs had run a program from 1952 to 1957 to support workers who wanted to join a union and assist them with discrimination in their local or job.[12] When the time came for the 1958 dressmakers' contract negotiations, there were 8,000 Puerto Rican women working in skirt and sportswear across 322 union shops. Another 1,000 women worked in coats and suits.[13]

As strike committees prepared, they asked organizers to reach out to all workers in the seven-state area. To cover scattered factories, shop chairladies were responsible for coordinating strike times, signs, and picket numbers at each location. For example, committees formed in Bridgeport, Stamford, Hartford, New Haven, and Waterbury, Connecticut, to make sure there were strikers at strategic sites throughout each day, and Puerto Rican needleworkers participated in these cities.[14]

The work stoppage in the New York metro area, Connecticut, Massachusetts, Rhode Island, New Jersey, Pennsylvania, and Delaware was a short general strike. But it was one of the largest in geographic area covered as a single walkout. The action achieved three major objectives: it won an 8 percent wage increase, regulations for contracting and subcontracting, and a severance plan. This plan required owners and companies to contribute to a severance fund, announce closures ahead of time so workers could look for their next job, make relocations public, and pay out to laid-off employees. A similar severance plan was included in the collective agreement for skirts and sportswear signed a few months later.[15] Severance could not stop the interconnected regional, colonial, and global disaggregation, but this demand disputed and rearranged the terms of capital migration. By compelling owners and companies to pay out for the years of labor that had produced their wealth, the severance plan tempered the financial impact on women workers.

Puerto Rican women's widespread participation in the strike demonstrates the force of their identities as industrial workers with goals for their jobs. Even with recent changes, they did not see a dying industry but rather shifting pathways to jobs from the archipelago to New York and New England. They continued to use various tactics to deal with the variable work conditions, from transience and circumvention to union membership and confrontation.[16] Their actions also contradict the popular-culture representation of West Side Story, where Maria and Anita appear as poor exotic beauties who discuss love and dancing but not wages and walkouts.

Puerto Rican Workers in West Side Story and the American Thread Company

In West Side Story, audiences meet the two young Puerto Rican women in a shop with sewing machines, but the dialogue and set emphasize a fantasy of party dresses and the romantic promise of wedding gowns. Anita, who has lived in New York for years, makes a white dress for Maria to wear to her first dance since arriving from Puerto Rico. The shop is a feminine consumer space rather than an industrial one. Like chores for a poor girl in a fairy tale, sewing is associated with drudgery, not manufacturing. The girls complain about the shop owner, an older woman with a minimal presence, as an obstacle to their socializing. Rather than viewing her as a savvy industrial worker using her skills for a side business or as an oppressive manager controlling their time and pay, the young women talk about the owner like a rotten stepmother. They have a desire to get out to their men, not a drive to act in solidarity as workers. Maria and Anita talk and sing as troubled youth from a distant tropic, expressing no identification as the American working class.[17]

Articles about and reviews of West Side Story further aligned the musical with cultural narratives of dark outsiders and rough teenagers rather than with narratives of workers and labor. Before the musical opened, a reporter joked that police on Fifty-Second Avenue were having a difficult time discerning "juvenile delinquents" from the singers and dancers on their way into rehearsals for West Side Story, a musical with "tough youths," where performers have sideburns and wear "tight blue jeans." Another article noted that for a few weeks people called the area "Gangway" instead of Broadway. When reviews mentioned the Puerto Rican characters, they did not discuss working women but rather "New York's teen-age gang fights" and "the tragic hatred of immigrating [sic] Puerto Ricans."[18]

Puerto Rican needleworkers were the raw material that the creator, director, and choreographer, Jerome Robbins, and the writers, Arthur Laurents (book), Stephen Sondheim (lyrics), and Leonard Bernstein (music), had refined. They extracted the women from a complex colonial industrial reality and processed them through a Shakespearean tale of gang rivalry and young love. The resulting West Side Story musical did not erase Puerto Rican needleworkers but minimized their identity and labor, reducing the work to peripheral feminized consumerism while ignoring unions and colonial labor market manipulations.

In the northeastern political economy, long after the play closed in June 1959, Puerto Rican needleworkers continued to pursue jobs and ILGWU activism. Their interactions with the American Thread Company demonstrate how women navigated shifting and diffusing arrays of investment, manufacturing, and trade into the 1970s. The migration of Puerto Rican women to an outlying site in Willimantic, Connecticut, belies the notion that only capital has a wide range. And the company's mix of new plants, closures, labor recruitment, equipment updates, and administrative relocations expose the complicated arbitrage that cannot be seen when tracking one factory in a global company.[19]

In 1898, the year the United States occupied Puerto Rico and mainland businesses began contracting with insular agents, two companies in Scotland formed a holding company. It then created the American Thread Company and bought several mills in New England, including the Willimantic Linen Company in rural eastern Connecticut, becoming one of the first international conglomerates. By the 1920s, it was expanding in the South with a new factory in Dalton, Georgia.[20] Responding to the midcentury changes described in chapter 1, American Thread increased product lines while consolidating manufacturing. This consolidation was not a full closure in New England with direct relocation to the South, but rather a mix of closures and updates in various regions. For example, in the 1950s, it closed plants in both Fall River, Massachusetts, and Bristol, Tennessee.[21]

In the 1960s, company reports declared cheap imports were the top problem—not wages or unions. The cheaper products came primarily from Japan and Hong Kong, where SCAP and the State Department had helped build postwar textile and garment industries. Seeking to outmaneuver these global competitors, American Thread launched another reconfiguration in 1963. It opened sales offices and distribution points in Indiana and California; closed older plants in Troutman, North Carolina, and Newman, Georgia; and opened new factories in Marble and Transylvania, North Carolina. The company also fully updated the Willimantic mill with new technology from Germany rather than from the New England machine manufacturers it had used in the past. Much of the specialized equipment was for new synthetic materials, and managers set out to recruit more Puerto Rican women. Even with declining consumer retail, 1972 saw the highest sales and earnings in the company's history, with strong reliance on industrial products, such as Normex for NASA and the Apollo missions.[22]

American Thread engaged in financial arbitrage as well. In 1961, the company moved its controller and related departments from Manhattan to Willimantic. Eight years later, the full headquarters relocated to an industrial park in Stamford, Connecticut, to save on real estate and tax costs.[23] American Thread also incorporated a cotton-dealing subsidiary in Delaware, a state known for lenient credit and financial reporting laws, which allowed the company to avoid taxes and duties on raw materials. To methodically monitor allocation of company resources, executives bought cutting-edge data-processing computers for the new Technology Center installed in a large warehouse in Willimantic near the updated mill in 1968.[24]

Like Textron, American Thread saw Puerto Rico as a site of lowest-wage labor exempted from investment costs such as taxes, fees, and land regulation. During the 1960s, it opened sales offices and distribution points on the main island to serve colonial manufacturers that US foreign economic policymakers were still using as exemplars of export processing.[25] In 1961, after Fidel Castro consolidated power in Cuba, President John F. Kennedy appointed the head of the PRIDC and Operation Bootstrap, Teodoro Moscoso, to coordinate the Alliance for Progress. It was intended to foster economic cooperation between the United States and Latin America following the Puerto Rico model.[26] In 1963, an insular petrochemical complex gained momentum when Presidential Proclamation 3663 raised the limit on oil imports to Puerto Rico. The archipelago processed more petroleum for export to the metropole, and the refineries were a step toward synthetic fabric production.[27]

Despite upbeat publicity, millions of dollars in tax exemptions, and millions of dollars funneled through the PRIDC, the 1960s were years of shrinking insular employment and stagnating wages. The number of textile and garment factory workers increased from 55,000 to 81,000, but home needleworkers declined from 51,000 to 10,000. In 1962, despite his earlier support of a lower minimum wage for Puerto Rico, Dubinsky met with Governor Luis

Muñoz Marín to discuss ways to improve the living conditions and factory employment of needleworkers.[28]

Since the turn of the twentieth century, however, Puerto Rican women viewed manufacturing jobs as mobile rather than stable and rooted, and their continued migration to the Northeast resulted from and masked the employment contractions.[29] They continued to track extending pathways through an industry with lengthening supply chains and lines of trade. Women like Esmeralda Santiago's mother found their first wage job on the island in the 1950s and flew to New York in the 1960s. Santiago's mother, who also wanted better medical care for her son, had to restart as a thread cutter despite having skills as a sewing machine operator.[30] By 1970, the number of Puerto Rican residents on the continent corresponded to the number in the archipelago. Within this demographic change, insular women faced limited sweatshop options and a loss of homework, while those in New York were incorporated into low-wage manufacturing undergoing deskilling and regional disaggregation to places like American Thread.

Many Puerto Rican women followed the job opportunities to New England. They heard about shops such as Elco Dress Company, which bought the old Arrow Dress factory in Holyoke, Massachusetts, in 1962. Lesnow Manufacturing and Totsy Manufacturing opened garment assembly shops in 1968 in old factories near downtown Holyoke, where silk and rayon mills remained open. Personal listings in the city directory included employers, and dozens of entries with Latino names noted jobs in textiles, dress companies, and apparel factories—such as Maria Garcia at Bay State Mills.[31] Puerto Ricans moving for jobs in Holyoke and Springfield, Massachusetts, and Bridgeport, Hartford, and Willimantic, Connecticut, helped establish substantial demographic percentages.[32]

Hartford's office of the Migration Division became very active in the 1960s, and the Greater Hartford Chamber of Commerce invited Oscar Nieves, regional director of the Puerto Rico Department of Labor, to enroll.[33] The office provided a script for staff approaching potential employers and emphasized that "citizens from Puerto Rico" worked to "better themselves economically and socially." The Hartford field representative, Gilberto Camacho, encouraged staff to explain that Puerto Ricans are skilled, satisfied, and "good workers" with "great speed in all work requiring the use of their hands." Although his 1964 memo did not mention textiles and garments, hand speed was a common endorsement of needleworkers.[34] Sewing factories along Franklin Avenue hired Puerto Rican women to operate machines, cut threads, and sew labels into dresses.[35] The ILGWU stayed active too, pressing for an agreement with the Southern New England District, particularly for the contracting shops that made garments for jobbers registered with the New York Dress Joint Board.[36]

More Puerto Rican women moved to American Thread, with the majority arriving between 1965 and 1969. Some were recruited, some joined family members, and some heard about jobs through informal networks.[37] A young needleworker named Patria said, "Well, my sister-in-law brought me here. She took me to American Thread. I applied and in less than a week I got a job as a machine operator. Then I wrote my cousins to come here to work. . . . It was easy to find jobs when I came here in 1969." Another needleworker, Daria, came to Willimantic from Puerto Rico in 1970 because her uncle had written to her parents saying young women could get good jobs.[38]

Many women felt pride in their work, especially if they met quotas. Lupe easily learned and went beyond the quota in a few weeks. Gabriela liked her time at American Thread, saying, "I enjoyed looking at my machines filling with thread. Everything looked so beautiful. I did a good job because I was careful. My bosses praised me for my work." Others, including Renata, worried about the expectations. "I learned to operate the machines in two weeks," she said. "The difficult part was to achieve dexterity to produce the quota. That took me about three months." Tatiana had a similar experience. "I was almost always nervous because of the constant pressure to make quota," she said. "I got nervous every time the bosses came to check my work. I felt I had to hurry up." All the women recalled a particular supervisor who regularly called out, "Menea esas manos," which translates to "Keep those hands busy."

The conventional system of quotas, with bonuses for extra pieces, functioned as a veiled stretch-out requiring more and faster work to increase pay. Most needleworkers had a particular read of the exploitation, viewing the quota as making basic money for the company and the piecework, or pizual, as earning money for themselves. Proficient women expressed confident identities as industrial workers with a sense of accomplishment. In Holyoke, Maria Berríos told her two daughters that supervisors at the dress factories could put her wherever they needed, because she was good and fast on all the machines and always made extra money. She became angry if they tried to underpay her after she went over quota.[39] At American Thread, Dolores worked as a machine operator from her arrival in Willimantic in the 1960s until the factory closed in 1985 and enjoyed the job. "I like sewing," she said on her last day. "I never had any accidents. The work there is divided into piecework and the task. The task is what you are supposed to produce in order to earn your salary. Piecework is what you produce . . . so that we can earn extra money."

Maldonado and Union Power in New York City

Maldonado and Puerto Rican women who stayed in New York continued to have a severance option if they were laid off because of relocations to the surrounding states. The 1961 renewal of the dressmakers' collective agreement had a 5½ percent raise, higher minimum wages, a standard piece-rate schedule, and quotas for imports.[40] The ILGWU launched a national severance plan in March 1961 with a special ceremony for the cloak, dressmaker, and undergarment locals. Latina workers including Acela Contreras and Mary Lopez posed for photos when receiving their checks from the Supplementary Unemployment-Severance Benefits Fund.[41]

At the same time, the Migration Division of New York remained a recruitment and employment agency. Job orders for hand sewers, sewing machine operators, section workers, hand label sewers, appliqué workers, line workers, cutters, assorters, binders, floor girls, and packers passed through the office in the 1960s. Companies and shops that produced fabrics, dresses, suits, children's clothes, skirts and blouses, undergarments, hats, belts, handbags, handkerchiefs, and towels submitted requests. For example, Jorge Ortiz handled a November 1963 job order from Uptown Handkerchief for a hemstitching operator.[42]

During these years, Maldonado became involved in ILGWU Local 66, known as the Bonnaz, Embroideries, Tucking, Pleating and Allied Crafts Union. "I didn't see myself doing much, and it was a struggle. What am I doing here?" Maldonado said. "'I know English, I know Spanish. I gotta better myself.' So I started being active in the union." She began attending meetings and reporting concerns to shop stewards.[43]

Maldonado was a vocal participant willing to question both shop management and men in union leadership. In 1970, some of these leaders offered her an organizer job because, in her own words, she had been "opening my big mouth, you know, being critical." She was making $180 a week for thirty-five hours of garment work, and the ILGWU job paid only $110. Maldonado did not take it, because "that was a big hunk, $70 dollars a week less." Union representatives called her two weeks later and said they would start her at $110, then meet in six weeks to discuss a raise. She called it a gimmick but decided, "Well, this is my only chance, so I'll sacrifice myself." As an organizer, her goal was to convince workers to sign membership cards by talking about the benefits of having a union, and she was especially interested in talking to women at nonunion shops. Maldonado got the raise six weeks later.[44]

The early 1970s were years of wide-ranging experiences for Maldonado. She had opportunities for a union career and labor activities beyond what

Crystal Lee had in North Carolina. The metro area included the ILGWU, ACWA, formidable labor councils, and vibrant labor studies programs that brought together workers and students at institutions like the City University of New York (CUNY). Maldonado became involved with the Hispanic Labor Committee, which was affiliated with the Central Labor Council that coordinated actions across locals from many sectors and partnered with city and regional community groups. Maldonado met Puerto Rican and Latino/a workers from different unions, including Health Care Workers' Union 1199 and New York State United Teachers (NYSUT) with the United Federation of Teachers.[45]

She expressed a candid awareness of negative reactions to her assertiveness. "I'm known for my straightforwardness," she said. "A few people don't like to hear the truth, you know, sometimes I have to, you know, just knock them down. Really, some people don't like me because of that."[46] Maldonado, like many women organizers including Crystal Lee, had contradictory experiences with men in labor leadership. Some men did not want Maldonado stepping beyond her prescribed feminine position. But she leapt anyway, and several men supported her ambitious activism. Prominent members of the Hispanic Labor Committee backed her bid to become secretary because they admired her organizing. She also considered Murray Gross, manager of Local 66, a close mentor. Gross went on to become Dress Joint Council general manager and an ILGWU vice president.[47]

Using determination, savvy, and connections, Maldonado pursued multiple opportunities. At the Central Labor Council office, she picked up a pamphlet about the Cornell University extension program in labor studies. She asked her ILGWU supervisor if he would pay for her to attend, but he said, "No, I could teach you what you need to know." So Maldonado applied for a scholarship from a Puerto Rican leadership group and attended the Cornell program without his support. He was not happy but could not stop her.[48]

Harry Van Arsdale, financial secretary for the International Brotherhood of Electrical Workers (IBEW) Local 3 and Central Labor Council president, invited Maldonado to join his local's trip to Switzerland for a tour of the International Labour Organization (ILO), a UN agency that negotiates and helps implement labor standards.[49] When Gross found out Maldonado's supervisor did not grant her permission to go, he went to Van Arsdale and asked him to speak to her boss. She did not receive approval until a couple days before the flight but had planned as if she were going. "When [my boss] found out that I had everything," Maldonado said with a laugh, "he was very angry. When I came back from that [trip], which was something that I'll never forget, you know, he was very different with me. And my coworkers, it's hard to say,

Gloria Maldonado (*standing on left*) teaches a 1973 industrial sewing class at Local 66 headquarters. | ILGWU Justice Photographs Collection, Kheel Center, Cornell University, Ithaca, NY

were . . . started giving me, you know, like ostracizing me." Unions were sites of such contest as well as collaboration.

Although some peers resented Maldonado's elevation, she carried on. She earned quick promotion and accepted simultaneous positions as head organizer and education director for Local 66. Her education work garnered the attention of *Justice*, the ILGWU newspaper from 1919 to 1995—attention usually reserved for the white male leaders. Editors sent a photographer to her 1971 industrial sewing class at the High School of Fashion Industries, a 9–12 public school in Manhattan. The new manager for Local 66, William Schwartz, attended to help promote the educational programs.[50] *Justice* decided to photograph another of her classes in 1973, this time at Local 66 headquarters. Wearing a hip striped dress, she stands next to a woman at an industrial sewing machine, who is attending the class to improve her manufacturing skills. The women are all industrial workers but wear simple dresses or skirts and blouses, not dingy coveralls.[51] Their identities as industrial workers did not manifest in a stereotypical blue-collar appearance.

Contesting the Terms of Globalization

Maldonado's years as a Puerto Rican needleworker, ILGWU organizer, and vocational instructor in New York positioned her to take a wide view of the industry. During the 1970s, she came to a keen understanding of unions as a way to engage in struggles over the terms of global trade and capital, as well as a means to demand better immediate work conditions. She was concerned about three major issues in the contests over globalization: the quota system and imports, the conditions of low-wage workers in other nations, and the resurging exploitation of immigrant workers in New York.

Maldonado's perspective regarding imports and quotas built on decades of ILGWU efforts to control, or at least mitigate, the multiplying lines of global trade. Such actions have been lumped into a limited, generic conceptualization of "protectionism," but many union ideas were not crude provincial or isolationist reactions. In challenging foreign economic policy, they often developed forward-looking proposals with dual objectives: to maintain fair domestic employment and prevent global exploitation. The 1934 Reciprocal Trade Agreements Act, however, had transferred trade negotiation to executive offices, away from members of Congress who could be pressured by constituents like union locals and regional owners. By 1945, the United States had already entered thirty-two bilateral agreements with twenty-seven countries based on the theory that tariff reductions would increase peace through increased trade.[52] Although the consequences were not yet obvious to most rank-and-file workers, union leaders and regional companies were aware.

In the late 1950s—long before the 1994 North American Free Trade Agreement (NAFTA)—the ILGWU, TWUA, and ACWA asked members of Congress and state governors to back their demand that trade offices consider domestic employment when managing tariffs and quotas. In 1958, the New England Governors' Textile Committee complained about the increase in imports from "underdeveloped countries [that take] strong protectionist measures" to impede US exports. ACWA president Jacob S. Potofsky warned in 1961 that imports threatened to eliminate the domestic industry and called for quota enforcement.[53] The ILGWU and TWUA even formed partial alliances with regional companies that wanted to sustain the same production stake.[54] They cooperated in lobbying for import limits and testified alongside executives, although they fought over unionizing.[55] Even when successful in achieving some demands, the unions' concentration on imports and quotas, without enough effort to limit financialization and outward capital migration, could not counteract the trade and investment arbitrage.[56]

Maldonado agreed on the need to reduce imports, especially from Japan, China, and India. She understood nations gamed the quota system, with

China buying Panama's unused quota numbers so its larger manufacturers could import more to the United States.[57] But trade offices, under Democrat and Republican presidents, continued to construct rationales and procedures for cheap imports and capital export. In 1971, President Richard Nixon convened the Commission on International Trade and Investment Policy, chaired by an IBM executive. It called for monetary policy, not manufacturing and employment policy, to address trade deficits. Its main suggestion was to "eliminate all barriers to international trade and capital movements within twenty-five years." Such scaffolding would eventually provide the basis for the "free trade" proposals and comprehensive multilateral treaties of the 1990s and 2000s.[58]

Maldonado worried when unions struggled to fight this foreign economic policy. "We are being attacked by imports, attacked by sweatshops, by homework coming back," she said.[59] She and other organizers supported the 1971–74 ILGWU campaign with the TWUA to pass the Foreign Trade and Investment Act (Burke-Hartke Trade Bill). The bill had three goals: maintain production of goods "historically produced" in the United States, encourage the return of production that had been "transferred abroad," and support new production.[60] It even proposed an amendment to the 1954 Internal Revenue Code that would curb the outflow of capital, technology, and jobs by ending tax breaks for transnational corporations and giving federal offices the option to restrict capital export if they believed too many jobs were at stake.[61] TWUA leaders encouraged the rank and file to understand the bill by distributing "Technical Explanation" cards and asked workers to contact their congressional representatives.[62]

Trade groups and lobbyists such as Henry Ford II and the New York Chamber of Commerce coordinated multiple attacks.[63] Although industrial nations like Japan, France, and Germany and the European Economic Community had tariffs and quotas to safeguard domestic manufacturing, US critics attacked Burke-Hartke as "dangerous protectionism."[64] Congressman H. John Heinz III (R-PA) declared the bill would "damage" the US economy by imposing more quotas, eliminating tax provisions favorable to overseas investment, and regulating international capital transactions. He argued the bill would burden American consumers with high prices and destroy jobs. Opponents proposed "adjustment assistance" for displaced workers, a policy that promised to use unemployment statistics to direct federal funds to new job training, but the ILGWU, TWUA, and ACWA did not endorse adjustment assistance. They said past trade bills had promised funding and facilities, but these were inadequate or did not materialize.[65]

Large corporations also blocked Burke-Hartke. They had the logistics staff, technologies, capital liquidity, and credit to take advantage of global manufacturing and lowest-price consumption. In response to tariffs and quotas by other nations, these corporations became multinationals, building facilities to produce and sell within the trade barriers. They also reconfigured supply chains to utilize, instead of compete with, cheaper imports. Caterpillar Tractor, for example, was buying foreign parts for its domestically assembled products by 1971.[66]

These opponents of Burke-Hartke emphasized rates of return for investors and consumer prices, which was a change from the 1950s, when economists, lobbyists, and politicians defended open US markets based on Cold War strategy and derailing communist subversion. The new framing was successful even though 1973 saw two negative indicators: US wages stagnated for the first time in decades, and the country experienced its first merchandise trade deficit since 1893.[67]

Burke-Hartke did not pass, and unions had little choice but to tolerate adjustment assistance in future trade bills. Like severance plans, adjustment assistance could not stop disaggregation, but it provided a short-term tactic for contesting how it unfolded. Throughout the 1970s, trade offices facilitated disaggregation in more sectors, particularly electronics and automobiles. They permitted more cheap imports from foreign-based factories, reduced barriers to US corporations that invested in other countries, and cut costs for importing pieces for domestic assembly. As a result, US corporate investment in foreign countries increased at a rate 50 percent faster than in the fifty states.[68]

Maldonado also supported the ILGWU message regarding workers in the exporting countries. Although directors still pursued anticommunist business unionism, they also grappled with global exploitation. From the 1950s to the 1970s, the union researched wage rates in places such as Japan and Hong Kong and critiqued trade agreements from the perspective of workers in East Asia as well as Mexico and the United States. Leaders responded with national lobbying and international outreach. *Justice* was particularly vocal, with columns that expressed solidarity with women workers around the world and announcements of foreign unionizing.[69]

Maldonado worried about work conditions in the multiplying global sweatshops. Rather than blaming poor workers trying to survive, she recognized that large corporations were collaborating with elites to seek options in more and more countries. Maldonado knew who was really benefiting and said, "The people in the higher echelons [of these underdeveloped countries] are the ones that are getting the benefits from it, not the poor people."[70] Global elites were increasing their revenues from manufacturing contracts and from the commercial real estate and financing for these enterprises.[71]

Despite these circumstances, Maldonado and other organizers were having greater difficulty recruiting immigrants as new members. They believed it was an unintended consequence of the 1965 Immigration and Nationality Act (Hart-Celler Act), which ended the national origins formula that had been used since 1924 to determine immigration quotas. The act led to an increase in documented immigrants arriving from Caribbean nations including the Dominican Republic, Jamaica, and Haiti. Maldonado thought the act had impacted textile and garment employment and unionization because of the subsequent increase in undocumented immigrants following friends, family, and comparatively higher wages into the metro area.[72]

The increased immigration and challenges to organizing in New York prompted changes to ILGWU membership drives, new language programs, and social activities to welcome and support workers from the Caribbean and China. Maldonado and other organizers planned beach trips, visits to the UN, and parade floats with invitations and maps in multiple languages. Articles in *Justice* celebrated unity, shared information in Spanish and Mandarin, and included photos of workers of many ethnicities.[73] As with many organizations, official efforts often contradicted ground-level politics within locals, where discriminatory practices could marginalize migrant and immigrant women.[74] Despite those tense situations, regional representatives and education departments extended services to encourage all workers to build solidarity.[75]

Although Maldonado grew frustrated by the multiplying sweatshops and homework, she refused to blame the poor workers. She argued New York employers and managers were preying on immigrant fears to exploit and intimidate them. "There's a lot of undocumented workers that are scared to join the union because, you know, it's an 'institution thing,'" she said.[76] Many Caribbean and Chinese immigrants who tried to organize were fired, and managers went so far as to trigger Immigration and Naturalization Service (INS) raids on their own shops to block unionization.[77] This manipulation of newly documented and undocumented women workers allowed businesses to avoid unions, minimum wages, overtime pay, and tax reporting.[78]

Maldonado Flourishes with Labor Studies

Throughout these fights over the terms of globalization, Maldonado organized workers and designed labor education. In 1974, she received an Outstanding Leader Award from the Central Labor Council because she was a strong secretary for the Hispanic Labor Committee and a creative education director. She knew she worked hard but worried about resentment. "I didn't think that I deserved [the award] because I didn't have that many years," she said. "I hadn't paid my dues for that long. . . . It brought me problems because my [ILGWU] boss did not like that I got it, that award. And he was very, he said it was to-kenism and that I shouldn't have gotten it because they didn't talk to him."[79] Maldonado understood the realities of the labor movement, the hierarchy and seniority, the opportunities for substantive change and personal growth, and the bigotry and sexism—and she believed in the union with all that.

The years 1973 to 1976 were a peak in her career. Following the ILGWU and Hispanic Labor Committee successes, Maldonado applied for a job at the Rutgers University Labor Center. When Eddie González, a colleague from the labor councils, learned Rutgers wanted to hire a Hispanic woman to design programs for working women, he contacted Maldonado and backed her appli-cation.[80] In the summer of 1974, she left for New Brunswick to coordinate labor extension activities and planned to involve more women workers, raise aware-ness of the history of labor struggles, and expand metro-area organizing.[81]

Maldonado's job covered not only trainings for shop stewards and orga-nizers but also public events and specialty classes such as Working Women in American Society. In September, she walked into a classroom with forty students who had signed up for the class. "I was scared," Maldonado said. "It was scary. But I said, 'Well, you gotta do it.' And I introduced myself and told them, I says, 'This is my first job [controlled laugh] as a teacher, you know, my first teaching job." She invited Puerto Rican women, African American women, women union organizers and business agents, and a woman politi-cian to share their experiences.[82]

As part of her vision, Maldonado wanted to reach more Hispanic workers by listening to them discuss their priorities. She organized a November Labor Center seminar for Latino/a workers to discuss the effects of inflation and the recession, which attracted media interest. The *Central New Jersey Home News* reported, "Miss Gloria Maldonado, an associate extension specialist at the center, is serving as program coordinator," and noted that forty-five Latino/a workers attended the lively event.

A year later, Maldonado helped coordinate a visiting exhibit, *Working Amer-icans*, funded by the Smithsonian and the AFL-CIO. The tour was building momentum toward the 1976 Festival of American Folklife on that theme. The Department of Labor and AFL-CIO were supporting the future festival and its celebration of "work-related traditions, looking at Americans not as people from a certain area of the country or from a particular culture, but in terms of how they made their living." When a reporter from *Central New Jersey* asked Maldonado about the visiting exhibit, she commented on the special segment "Workers and Allies: Female Participation in the American Trade Union Movement, 1824–1976." She said, "[It] has been assembled by the Smithsonian Institution as a salute to American women workers, during the nation's Bicentennial celebration and in observance of International Women's Year."[83] Maldonado embraced her role as a spokesperson for Latinos/as and women in the labor movement.

Maldonado's dedicated labor activism had earned her city leadership positions, metro-area recognition, and creative partnerships with eminent national institutions. A year after Maldonado started at Rutgers, however, the administration cut funding across several programs, and she received a pink slip. Over the next several months, Maldonado experienced disappointments but did not allow these to deter her. She returned to New York and became education director for the Joint Board but was unable to develop her curriculum. The board was "not too gung ho on education and I had a lot of ideas in my head but they didn't come through," Maldonado said. "Nobody helped me." When her friend Louise Delgado retired a few years later, she suggested Maldonado replace her as a business agent handling forty-eight shops. Business agents monitor contract enforcement, encourage worker involvement, and serve as the liaison between members and management during grievances over wages, seniority, and terminations.[84]

Puerto Rican Women and the 1970s Crises

Maldonado and other Puerto Rican needleworkers achieved this greater prominence just as the effects of decades of disaggregation were overwhelming domestic manufacturing. Beginning with the 1973–74 petroleum embargo and hitting a frenzy with the 1975–76 recession, a web of economic crises exposed the inability of conventional centrist-left liberalism to address the domestic consequences of US foreign economic policy. A reliance on familiar Keynesian principles proved inadequate for the intense currency fluctuations, inflation, and rising unemployment. This "stagflation" further undermined industrial employment and union leverage, eroding the basis of job and economic stability for Puerto Rican needleworkers.

Several years of economic disruption and lack of effective response opened political opportunities for neoliberal economic policy to gain more traction. The ideology behind these legislative and regulatory proposals, which pushed to further open US consumer markets and eliminate all barriers to capital movement, argued the promotion of capital would eventually benefit labor. It displaced the belief of postwar centrist-left liberalism that capital and labor should prosper together through policies supporting both.[85]

The neoliberal economic policies also advanced financialization, which further diminished the domestic manufacturing Puerto Rican needleworkers depended on. As financial markets and institutions gained more influence over policies and practices, they elevated the financial sector and transferred resources and capital from others, such as manufacturing, into their drive for short-term gains.[86] The 1978 Revenue Act was a triumph for finance over manufacturing. For the first time, it implemented tax reductions for rich individuals to spur their finance investments, which Wall Street firms preferred. These replaced the established practice of corporate investment tax credits, which had supported the development of physical assets such as machines and factories that came with jobs.[87]

In northeastern cities with substantial Puerto Rican populations, financialization had tangible costs for wageworkers. The Hartford Chamber of Commerce and insurance executives prioritized finance over manufacturing and pushed "downtown development." This strategy favored real-estate speculation, office construction, and upscale retail and restaurants rather than manufacturing and fair housing, which had benefited Puerto Rican working-class households.[88] In New York, Wall Street firms and investment bankers stepped into the city's calamitous 1970s fiscal crisis with a specific solution. In return for backing municipal bonds, they demanded corporate tax cuts, investment tax waivers, and subsidies for commercial real estate.[89]

Maldonado expressed dismay at the city policies and at Ed Koch, the Democratic mayor from 1978 to 1989, who described himself as "a liberal with sanity." Maldonado did not agree and said, "Mr. Koch, you know, [he allows] real estate developers to take all of Manhattan and triple the rent, the people are just not making it, there's more shops that are closing up." She recognized the impact on needleworkers. "[Landlords] tripled the rent in the garment area," she said. "You see shops closing because of that rent. It affects our people, our generation of Puerto Rican women who have been there [for years] . . . and all of a sudden the man [who owns the shop] has to close."[90] Puerto Ricans, including union leaders, resisted this financialization. The Young Lords, a group of liberation activists, demanded public health clinics, day care, and trash pickup, and the majority–Puerto Rican students at Hostos Community College in the Bronx coordinated walkouts and petitions when the city announced it would end subsidized tuition.[91]

Like all organizers in the 1970s, Maldonado had to deal with more sophisticated anti-union tactics that further undermined union leverage in both local organizing and the national negotiations that shaped globalization.[92] As corporate executives and managers confronted the disruptive economic crises, they decided unionizing and labor were the cost factors most within their control. They worked to deter and block NLRB certification elections and collective bargaining agreements, hiring new consulting firms, such as Modern Management Methods, that specialized in legalistic strategy. In 1977, AFL-CIO president George Meany declared that union busting was experiencing a resurgence but the new "labor relations consultants" carried briefcases instead of clubs.[93] In the arena of national politics, corporate advocacy groups, from the established National Association of Manufacturers and US Chamber of Commerce to the new Business Roundtable and American Enterprise Institute, were determined to dismantle labor's formal political power, accumulated over five decades. They honed anti-union lobbying and cultural narratives that blamed union pay for stagflation.[94]

The 1970s crises crushed Puerto Rico's economy with greater ferocity than the metropole's and attracted more predatory investors. Between 1969 and 1975, only 28.7 percent of the jobs promised by PRIDC-promoted firms materialized, and the rate was even lower in petrochemical industries. Although Wal-Mart buyers noted in 1971 that much of its children's apparel came from Puerto Rico as well as Japan, the situation changed during the mid-1970s, leading to closures and the decimation of women's industrial jobs.[95] By the time of the deep 1975 recession, external investors owned 70 percent of all productive wealth in Puerto Rico.[96]

US and insular officials responded with a policy that would become a decisive instigator of the archipelago's 2014–16 fiscal crisis. In 1975, Governor Rafael Hernández Colón of the PPD lobbied Congress to revise Internal Revenue Code Section 931. It allowed metropolitan corporations manufacturing in the archipelago to place their profits in banks in any US possession and, upon liquidation of the Puerto Rican enterprises, transfer all accumulated profits to the metropole without federal taxes. Corporations often held their revenues in Guam and speculated in global currency until they closed their Puerto Rican businesses. PPD and business lobbyists convinced Congress to allow US corporations to transfer their profits to the metropole without taxes at any time. They argued it would boost Puerto Rico's industrial development and allow the US banking system to recuperate millions of dollars. In 1976, Congress passed Section 936, extending these tax exemptions to foreign corporations.[97]

From 1976 to its peak in 1993, the section spurred many "936 corporations." Capital-intensive enterprises, including pharmaceuticals and precision manufacturing, increased while labor-intensive plants for textile and garments declined. The new facilities employed fewer workers per unit and functioned even more often as subsidiaries of US corporations.[98] In the core industries producing 57 percent of manufactured goods, external ownership averaged 98.3 percent.[99]

Definitive Political Fights over Domestic Textiles and Apparel

In these relentless contests over colonial and global industrialization, Maldonado and thousands of labor activists continued to fight cheap imports. The

ILGWU coordinated demonstrations throughout the Northeast and South from 1976 to 1977 and included small New England cities with substantial percentages of Puerto Rican workers, such as Springfield, Massachussetts, and Pawtucket, Rhode Island.[100] The Amalgamated Clothing and Textile Workers Union (ACTWU) took ILGWU flyers that asked consumers to insist on the union label and stapled them to its boycott pamphlets asking buyers, retailers, hotels, and restaurants not to buy J.P. Stevens.[101] The importance of Asian textiles and garments to US relations with the surging East Asian economies impeded union success. By 1980, textiles comprised one-third of South Korea's exports, and China was the sixth largest exporter of textiles to the United States.[102]

Despite import concerns, Puerto Rican women sought jobs in textiles and apparel. The New York Migration Division still received orders from companies such as Fremitex, West Side Textiles, Zevon Textiles, Latch-On, D.C. Dress, Uilin Fashion, Pioneer Embroidery, and Kingley Trimming.[103] Irma Medina's mother, Aracelis Martínez, learned industrial sewing at the Ana Roqué High School in Humacao in 1962. She moved from Puerto Rico to New York in 1964 for better wages, returned to the island and worked in another factory for a few years, and went to New York again in 1970 for a job as a sewing machine operator in an undergarment factory.[104] Maria Salgado-Cartagena's paternal grandmother was recruited from the island to work in a New York factory in the early 1970s and stayed there as a senior seamstress for ten years.[105]

Opportunities for Puerto Rican needleworkers continued outside New York as well. Martínez eventually paid for Medina's flight from the island, and they moved to Springfield in the mid-1970s. Martínez worked at Gemini Mill, a former Carter's factory that was owned and managed by an eastern Massachusetts executive fulfilling contracts for OshKosh B'Gosh and Izod. He often struggled to find workers with the interest and sewing skills, but Puerto Rican women had the experience.[106] In the early 1970s, Salgado-Cartagena's mother, Maria Berríos, completed piecework in Swedesboro, New Jersey. She made octagonal needlework, sewed the pieces together in a pattern, and packed them in boxes shipped to New York. She then received a paycheck and another box of materials. As a girl, Salgado-Cartagena helped her mother with packing and labeling. Berríos also made embroidered doilies for their apartment, carrying on the original cultural tradition as a craft. In the late 1970s, they moved to Holyoke, where Berríos worked for Elco Dress Company until it closed in the mid-1980s.[107] American Thread still hired Puerto Rican women in Willimantic through the 1970s, sometimes paying them to fly to the main island and recruit workers.[108]

When the recession deepened, however, the effects were immediate. At

American Thread, reports showed high revenues and expanding sales in 1972 and a stable year in 1973, but the tone and content changed dramatically the next year. The 1974 report said the company had experienced a "sharp dip" and argued the United States was in its worst business condition since 1937–38 because of unemployment, underutilized capacity, lower retail sales, and reduced production in manufacturing for apparel and automotive. In 1975, American Thread lost orders and revenues and declared the nation was "at the bottom of a severe recession" with slow demand improvement. Even as executives reduced hiring, however, they planned for new packaging capability in Willimantic. In 1977, they installed an energy conservation system and computerized order processing.[109]

The effects of disaggregation and Section 936 meant US offices no longer promoted Puerto Rico as a textile and apparel export processing model. Colonial industrialization with lowest-cost exports, in an enclave of fluctuating but perpetual extreme exemptions, was adapted to new goods. Heavily automated pharmaceutical plants on the main island increased from forty-seven to eighty-four companies.[110] In 1974, the UN Industrial Development Organization (UNIDO) convened a working group to create an agency of export-processing experts. Richard Bolin, the Arthur D. Little consultant who had helped develop Puerto Rico's Operation Bootstrap in the 1940s and '50s and Mexico's BIP in the 1960s, received a UNIDO contract to establish the World Export Processing Zone Association (WEPZA). In 1976, Bolin also founded the Flagstaff Institute to promote EPZs, and WEPZA officially launched in 1978 as a council of government representatives and regulatory authorities. Throughout it all, Bolin celebrated Puerto Rico, saying it was pivotal to his conceptualization of EPZs. He and WEPZA joined government offices, corporations, and investors to develop EPZs in South Korea, Taiwan, Iraq, Egypt, and China, which replaced the archipelago as acclaimed examples.[111]

The fight for domestic textiles and apparel pushed against these federal and international agencies planning for more disaggregation.[112] Rather than a futile lost cause, these efforts manifest the unceasing political-economic contests over lines of global trade. Unions continued to ally themselves with local business groups and regional companies from New York, Massachusetts, Illinois, Virginia, Tennessee, and the Carolinas. In 1978, the American Textile Manufacturers Institute and the chairman of Burlington Industries joined union leaders to denounce the devastation of imports.[113] Unfortunately, the same business groups and companies that allied with unions over imports continued to block unionizing. This contradiction inhibited the ability of unions to fight imports and shape the terms of globalization.[114]

The federal government was not monolithic—unions also sought support from agencies including the Council on International Economic Policy,

Government Accountability Office (GAO), and Treasury Department, which questioned unfettered access to US consumer markets. The Council on International Economic Policy advised President Richard Nixon in 1971 to prioritize domestic economic conditions over diplomacy and to enforce quotas and antidumping laws.[115] The GAO criticized weak federal efforts to control dumping from other nations, with particular concern about East Asia.[116] In 1979, unions called on members to contact congressional representatives to support two Treasury initiatives. First, the Treasury proposed increased oversight of antidumping duties and a conference on countervailing regulations. Second, it outlined changes to US International Trade Commission procedures for injury investigations into the "conduct of sales at less than fair value." The ACTWU participated in numerous congressional hearings, such as the House Ways and Means Committee's 1977 discussion of consumer prices and imports. Union leaders sent reports and testified to the International Trade Commission regarding multiple products, including a targeted effort to reduce cheap gloves from China.[117]

Staff in the State Department and Trade Representative Office, however, advocated holding markets open and facilitating US foreign investment and mobile capital currents. During President Jimmy Carter's administration, US banks and corporations almost tripled their foreign investments to $530 billion. In 1978, the Carter administration pressured regional executives and trade associations to break their alliance with unions and back off opposition to tariff reductions. White House offices collaborated with members of Congress to urge a "select group of industry and union leaders to meet as soon as possible with Special Trade Representative Robert Strauss." An observer commented that the "tight coalition of apparel, textile, fiber, and union groups might be in danger of crumbling."[118]

From the 1960s to the 1970s, Maldonado and thousands of Puerto Rican women continued to maneuver through and challenge colonial and global lines of trade. At the end of the 1970s, Maldonado had an established reputation as a labor activist and advocate for women workers, and needleworkers remained crucial to northeastern factories tied to transnational corporations. Even though the urban density of shops and mills thinned as manufacturers rearranged operations, Puerto Rican women moved with them as they had for decades. They had careers and households built on the wages and benefits they had accrued from decades in the US Atlantic industry, but these were not as stable as they hoped.

PART II

CHAPTER THREE

Crystal Lee and Southern Millhands

Extracting a "Life Story"

I did do right. I know I did. I'd go down for this,
if I had to, for my black brothers and sisters.
—Lucy Sledge

I started in the canteens, on the break time.
I would talk union to my friends, and I started
getting a lot of membership cards signed.
—Crystal Lee Jordan

ozens of white women of all ages and sizes walked toward the workers' entrance for the old Haw River factory outside Burlington, North Carolina. Most had wrapped their hair in light scarves, and a few smoked cigarettes while crossing the parking lot. Many waved to friends as they went to clock in for the second shift. It was 1958, and Crystal Lee Pulley had rushed home from high school to change clothes and get supper for her first night. She was seventeen when her parents said the family needed the money, so like her grandparents, parents, and older sister had before her, Crystal Lee understood it was time to go into the mills. Her mama worked third shift and helped her get hired, but as a young worker without experience, she went where the bossmen told her. They said a woman had given notice and Crystal Lee would work with her for the next week to learn and take over.[1]

The archival record for Crystal Lee is extensive: newspapers and magazines, a television show and biography, documents in collections at diverse institutions, and her personal papers at Alamance Community College. Several sources go into detail about her early work, including training with this older woman, who had a son at the high school. The woman asked Crystal Lee not to tell anyone she worked in the mill so her son would not be labeled, and Crystal Lee bristled but understood the fear of prejudice. "She had the audacity to say that to me, and here I was a teenager working in the mill, taking over her job," she stated. "But I never said anything to her about it and I never mentioned it at school." Nor did Crystal Lee complain about the danger of filling batteries with yarn while looms were running, but she disliked the oily slippery floor and the cotton bits that coated her hair.[2]

At the same time as Crystal Lee's job training in 1958, theaters were showing the Hollywood movie *God's Little Acre*, an adaptation of the 1933 Erskine Caldwell novel. It had remained a best-selling book because it tells the story of a salacious Georgia family and contains explicit sex scenes and implications of incest. Widower Ty Ty Walden lives on a farm beyond the mill towns, where his son Jim Leslie is a rich cotton broker and his son-in-law Will Thompson works as a virile millhand who has sex with both his sisters-in-law. In the culminating dramatic scene, Will attempts to break a lockout, but security guards kill him. His martyr death prompts workers to get involved. The movie did not update the Depression-era novel, instead depicting a timeless sweaty and rumpled South with poor whites assisted by poorer Blacks. White men in gritty clothes are industrial workers, and white women are homemakers and objects of sexual desire.[3] Neither Caldwell nor the filmmakers represented women as hardworking millhands or union members; women existed only in relation to patriarchal fights for money and sex.[4]

In the 1960s and '70s, Crystal Lee was one of thousands of millhands who navigated and shaped the industry in the South. Like Gloria Maldonado, she sought her best job opportunities in a gendered and racialized labor system under increasing pressure and eventually joined a union. She started at a time when intense changes were making southern factories even more different from the popular notion of them in *God's Little Acre*. Decades of foreign economic policy had spread and solidified lines of manufacturing and trade with Asia and Mexico. Southern investors were moving capital into new technologies like automation and synthetics, disrupting the cotton regime, if not the overall social hierarchy, and the civil rights labor movement demanded Title VII and formation of the Equal Employment Opportunity Commission (EEOC) with the 1964 Civil Rights Act.

Southern women, poor white and African American millhands, pursued industrial work into the 1980s. They encountered and influenced robust intersections of gender, race, class, and geography that interacted with larger labor and capital currents. Millhands were physically and socially isolated by owner families and the conglomerates that bought them out—elites who used their positions to restrict homeownership and medical care, limit free press, constrict the local tax base, and withhold funds from public resources such as roads, schools, libraries, and sewer lines. But the jobs and factories were fully entwined in the US Atlantic, which was bound with global trade. Executives and managers understood this duality, relying on it to increase their control. They held down southern wages via class and racial divisions buffered by the social isolation while using offshore manufacturing for even lower wages and fewer regulations, which further destabilized the southern situation. Young white millhands from multigenerational families, like Crystal Lee, and incoming African American women entered the plants just as this duality became more volatile.

Examining their history in relation to postwar foreign economic policy and civil rights labor activism illuminates the correlations between gendered and racialized domestic jobs and global structures. In 1963, building on decades of union fights and civil rights lawsuits, the TWUA launched a southern membership drive to organize J.P. Stevens, and it grew into an interracial campaign to unionize the South. Black women and men fueled the early years, signing membership cards and bringing momentum from hard-fought successes in education and transportation. When Crystal Lee signed her first union card in 1973, she joined an established southern drive and prominent national campaign made possible by the intertwining of class and race in labor demands for economic justice. By this time, however, colonial industrialization, the SCAP in East Asia, the BIP in Mexico, and increasing EPZs around the world had reduced the leverage of southern millhands.

Examining this labor history together with popular media coverage of Crystal Lee illustrates how forms of capital drove the extraction of her "life story" from this larger context. It shows how even left-leaning creative professionals overlooked colonial industrialization and women of color and obscured interracial union organizing. The expansive archival sources for Crystal Lee do not exist solely because she was a vocal labor activist who gained media attention. Many documents and photos come from her labor organizing, and there would be no life story without Crystal Lee's union activism, but Maldonado was a vocal labor activist at the same time. Neither do the sources exist simply because Crystal Lee was white. There were many millhands with union stories who fit the dominant narrative of the white American working class. Crystal Lee's activism was necessary and her whiteness was mandatory, but they were not sufficient to spark the early media attention in the 1970s or to propel the resulting archive.

The earliest sources exist because three conditions made commercial media coverage of Crystal Lee viable. First, there was a general fascination with poor white southerners as seen in movies such as *God's Little Acre* and television shows such as *The Beverly Hillbillies* (1962–71). Second, the surging women's liberation movement reshaped media in two ways: women creative professionals attained more decision-making clout, and mainstream producers looking to modernize their formulas appropriated select aspects of diverse feminist activisms and helped compose a popular "women's lib" that was white and heterosexual. Lastly, Crystal Lee was an excellent candidate because of a combination of traits: her pretty appearance as a familiar white millhand, her situation as a married mother of three that could be spun for respectability, and her idiosyncratic transgression of gender, class, and race norms that many audiences would consider tolerable yet feminist audiences could applaud as women's liberation.

The ultimate sizable archive, however, with sources that continued to appear after her death, exists because Crystal Lee fought for influence in the arena of cultural politics, particularly with Hollywood moviemakers. She refused to accept her low-capital, low-status position in the movie development and her elimination from the film's production and distribution. From her first contact with a freelance journalist through her collaborations with *Ms.* magazine and Macmillan Publishing, Crystal Lee stepped into and thrived in the popular-culture arena. Throughout these productions, she also repeatedly asserted the collective ideology of her unionizing and the labor movement.

None of this argument detracts from the significance of Crystal Lee's vibrant labor activism and assertive voice. It celebrates her lifelong dedication to union action within a rich historical context, while striving to understand why, out of tens of thousands of needleworkers and millhands, her experiences had such a widespread cultural impact and archival presence. As Crystal Lee said, there were so many others—she saw herself helping to advance a labor movement, not taking a solitary stand. And she reiterated this ideology, recognizing the union movement's strengths and flaws, until her death.

Crystal Lee's South

Crystal Lee's first shift in 1958 did not come as a surprise. She grew up in southern mill town society in the 1940s and '50s and watched her family and neighbors go to and from factories, stress about bills, complain about tired bodies, and debate the efforts, successes, and losses of unions. She spent her childhood in Roanoke Rapids, North Carolina, where her parents worked first shift until 1955. That year, when she was fourteen years old, her father moved the family 135 miles west to Burlington in search of some elusive better job. At seventeen, Crystal Lee found a part-time job at a florist that she really liked, but it paid only fifty cents an hour, and she could earn a dollar working at the Haw River mill.

Regional circumstances did not predetermine Crystal Lee's experiences and identity, but they influenced her ideas, forming meanings and shaping parameters for her choices. The intentional physical and social isolation constricted millhands' understanding of the larger industry and fostered connections between poor white workers. Shared histories and families permeated the neighborhoods; relationships were close, if fraught with the tensions of gender, class, and status that ran through small towns. The stories of workers and unions, as well as contemporary circumstances, provided Crystal Lee with understanding and inspiration.

Her resentment of class discrimination and the low status of millhands simmered long before her concerns about work conditions. "I always got the feeling when I was in school that textile work was something to be looked down on," she said. "I wasn't ashamed of what [my parents] did but I would rather not been asked because there were doctors' children in the room." She had noticed that "the smarter students came from the families with a little bit more money." When Crystal Lee struggled to get homework done on breaks at the mill, however, she realized "the higher class kids" were not more intelligent; they had more time and help from parents. "They definitely dominated the school. I resented that very much," she said. "I felt like we needed more attention."[5] Students from families with more money could also act in plays and become cheerleaders—a teenage desire that would resurface in her TWUA organizing.

Crystal Lee's parents did not join the TWUA at the Haw River mill, because her father thought unions caused trouble that got workers fired. But at this first job, Crystal Lee saw a woman shop steward walking into the supervisor's office with her head up and even a smile. Crystal Lee noticed this woman had a respected position in the union and the mill, and such intersections of class and gender would be central to her later decisions.[6]

Each mill town had peculiarities, but they all operated as entrenched systems of Jim Crow with potent intersections of race, class, and gender that framed and mediated the political, economic, and social terrain. The intersections relied on and perpetuated white superiority, with strict, often brutal, divisions between white and Black. They also worked to sustain the elitist mode of white supremacy in which classed and gendered, as well as racialized, notions of fitness, intelligence, hygiene, and respectability entitled specific people to high status, with its access to landownership, private clubs, higher education, government offices, and tax revenues.

Although these vectors of race, gender, class, and status hindered working people from building political-economic leverage, most white millhands valued their share of political legitimacy, social capital, and financial benefits derived from white superiority. They also resented the elitist white supremacy, with its derogatory view of poor whites, especially "lintheads," but racial superiority mitigated the class discrimination and labor exploitation, leading most white workers to embrace Jim Crow without question.[7] Other white workers collaborated with elitist white supremacy and its enactments because the practices and institutions had marginalized alternatives.[8] They could not imagine feasible options.

Crystal Lee's family lived in the millhand part of town, distinct from the affluent white neighborhoods and the fringe areas where Black residents lived without public services or paved roads. African American residents did the dirtiest and toughest jobs: digging ditches, cleaning privies, laundering, cooking. Although no available records describe Crystal Lee's childhood ideas about race, as an adult she said she grew up hearing from her father, preachers, bossmen, and politicians that "whatever else a millhand is, he is at least above a n——."[9]

Legal ordinances about race mixing had mutable exceptions if a white employer needed labor. The few African American women in mills prior to the Civil Rights Act worked as scrubwomen, because the labor regime forced them to seek wages in cleaning, laundry, or the tobacco industry.[10] Black men had more options but within strict race and gender occupational segregation. In the 1940s and '50s, when white workers stopped taking certain mill jobs and the number of white transients dipped, jobs opened for Black men inside dusty picker rooms, where raw cotton was prepared for carding.[11]

Despite the pervasiveness of white superiority, many radical organizers understood the need to address race and class as mutually reinforcing oppression. Some union leaders even thought interracial organizing in the textile industry might be less controversial because membership would be white majority, with a small number of Blacks as a tentative step. However, when unions attempted interracial, or even parallel, organizing, business, civic, and police leaders spread fear that a "dictatorship of the pro-lat-erate" would "lead to social equality" of the races.[12] In general, cumulative union tactics were contradictory, occasionally pushing for parallel drives and frequently appealing to white superiority. Organizers who held racist ideas or wanted to increase membership at any cost stoked white working men's anxiety, encouraging them to join for solidarity defined by whiteness, brawny masculinity, patriarchal prerogative, and industrial class.[13] The manipulation of race and gender anxieties and red-baiting reinforced each other, serving the combined purposes of driving wedges between working people and undermining organized leftist challenges to capitalism.

While labor organizing remained mired in segregationist politics, civil rights labor activism, with groups including the NAACP, National Council of Negro Women, and Congress of Industrial Organizations (CIO), moved ahead. The world wars helped, forcing dramatic changes as wartime production released money, expanded industrial needs, and opened opportunities for Black workers. More African Americans moved from the deep rural South to southern, midwestern, and northern cities, which often improved conditions for Black households. Black soldiers and pilots returned with expectations regarding veteran benefits and basic rights.[14]

Wartime production and military research and development triggered changes in the southern textile and apparel industry and increased its dependence on federal defense contracts. This restructuring tempered the position of cotton and strengthened ascendant petrochemical ventures. The changes did not target segregation but drained the sense of permanence from mill towns. They also allowed the federal government to make indispensable contributions via executive orders from FDR, Truman, and Eisenhower that prohibited discrimination in defense contracts.[15] Of course, managers did not immediately comply, but the orders gave the NAACP and unions a lever for lawsuits and grievances. The cumulative impact made it easier for African Americans to demand jobs and the benefits of union membership.

In the towns, postwar changes did not appear to change the fact that mills dominated families like Crystal Lee's. School curricula were blatantly tracked, with vocational programs funneling certain students into factories. Unlike officials, executives, managers, and national union leaders, most North Carolina millhands did not have extensive knowledge of the US Atlantic. They did, however, have an awareness of elite white supremacy, ongoing exploitation, stretch-outs, and efforts by workers to improve their working and living conditions.

Gender and Race in Crystal Lee's Understanding of Class

During her adolescence, Crystal Lee's resentment of the prejudice toward millhands grew into an analysis of class. After she got married at eighteen, her interrogations expanded to question gender discrimination as well. Crystal Lee wrangled with mill town conventions and her ambition for respect, autonomy, and a sense of purpose in society for the next thirteen years. These intersecting catalysts drove her pursuit for better options, even within the restrictive mill community, and led to her interest in and dedication to the TWUA.

Unlike her siblings, Crystal Lee pushed through to earn her diploma. "The only reason I finished school was because of Daddy," she said. "I hated it because of the way the teachers treated the working-class kids." When she and other summer school seniors went to the pool after class, she met Omar Carlos Wood Jr.—who went by "Junior"—a blond young man home from the Marines who hoped for a University of North Carolina football scholarship. He did not get one, so they got married.[16]

In August 1959, when Crystal Lee was eighteen years old, they moved into an apartment and took jobs at Glen Raven Mills.[17] Her class consciousness deepened while working as a stop-checker, timing weavers to track their speed unstopping a spindle or completing a run of towels. She knew bossmen used stop-checkers to implement stretch-outs, because at her parents' mill they had reduced weavers from twenty to four per section after timing them. She was uncomfortable, but she and Junior needed money and went to work together.[18]

Crystal Lee also grew frustrated with southern white working-class femininity and its contradictory classed gender expectations. Women could work but not hold on to their own money or go out late. Yet they were excluded from the respect owed to affluent women, who were considered "ladies." After Crystal Lee gave birth to a boy in 1960, she could not socialize, but Junior still went out.[19] "Course the wives, they couldn't go, which was always disturbing to me," she said. "And of course it was one or two in the morning when Junior did come in, and I was mad as hell." Despite arguments, they were trying to stay together when Junior died in a drag racing accident in early 1961.[20] He left Crystal Lee a small insurance inheritance, but her father had to serve as the guardian. "That was so damn strange, here I was married, widowed, and a mother, and I couldn't even write my own checks. I thought that was stupid," she declared.[21]

The first indication of her willingness to transgress racial norms occurred during a second pregnancy, after she dated a former boyfriend home from the University of North Carolina for the summer. He offered to marry her, but Crystal Lee did not think he was mature enough to be a father and worried he would blame her for leaving college.[22] Crystal Lee was then fired from Glen Raven when she refused to run after a weaver bolting from loom to loom. She was single, hiding a pregnancy, out of work, and living with her parents. Despite the Jim Crow narrative that welfare was for Black women, Crystal Lee went to the Alamance County office.[23] Poor mill families were only supposed to go if they needed household help, because social workers told Black women receiving welfare they had to do assigned domestic jobs or lose their income.[24] Crystal Lee applied for welfare anyway—not an act of radical antiracism, but a telling contravention.

She increasingly transgressed intersections of class, gender, and race to seek better conditions. In 1962, she gave birth to a second baby boy and did not like that her father still provided for her. "I felt like he was glad because, well, there he had me again to where I'd have to stay at home and depend on him," she said. Crystal Lee got an attorney to demand child support and accepted a $4,000 settlement.[25] She refused to rely on her father's paternalism as the only viable resource or to tolerate gender and class privileges that allowed the college boy to evade responsibility.

Civil Rights Labor Activism and the TWUA Drive

Throughout the 1960s, Crystal Lee was focused on her sons as civil rights labor activism intensified and the TWUA launched its J.P. Stevens drive. Although she was not yet in the labor movement, these actions created the conditions for her involvement, a fact she would later recognize. In 1963, when the TWUA decided to reinvigorate efforts in the South, leaders chose J.P. Stevens because it was well known and employed 36,000 people in North Carolina. J.P. Stevens began as a nineteenth-century woolen mill but had become one of the largest "textile" corporations, with facilities that made cloth, sheets and towels, industrial filters, fiberglass fabrics, and carpets.[26] Strategists assumed a breakthrough in this conglomerate would dissolve the myth that the South could not organize.

In 1964, Title VII of the Civil Rights Act had a tangible impact on the union because it prohibited employment discrimination. The NAACP joined several groups to start a community-organizing project headquartered in South Carolina called Textiles: Employment and Advancement for Minorities (TEAM). The project paid fieldworkers to help local people apply for jobs and persuade managers to hire Black millhands. The TWUA welcomed these Black workers to its drive, because they were increasing in number yet remained locked out of higher-paying jobs and were willing to demand access.[27]

The NAACP also offered legal aid, and J.P. Stevens, Cone Mills, and Burlington Industries were sued many times. The Department of Defense delayed several 1969 contracts to the three largest companies, J.P. Stevens, Burlington Industries, and Dan River Mills, because they had not done enough to hire and promote Black workers.[28] The legal cases that helped fuel the 1960s and '70s southern drive grew from this combination of Black millhand resistance, civil rights action, and labor organizing.[29]

By the late 1960s, mill managers realized Black workers supported unions more actively than white employees and sought ways to get them out. In July 1968, a J.P. Stevens plant in Roanoke Rapids laid off two terry inspectors, an African American woman, Lucy Sledge, and a white woman. Sledge's supervisor completed a termination form that rated her a worker of good quality and quantity and recommended reemployment. Her extended family labored in cotton picking and mills, and a few months later she found out the plant had filled positions with less-experienced white women. After five applications, Sledge waited with others outside the personnel office, but managers called only white people. In the fall of 1969, she learned supervisors had hired four white women as terry inspectors.[30]

Sledge's husband had recently been fired from another J.P. Stevens plant when supervisors discovered he was active in the union at his second job at an A&P grocery. Sledge called her cousin, who put her in touch with the EEOC. In 1970, EEOC staff came from Atlanta and gathered documents for Sledge to become the lead complainant in a class-action suit on behalf of Black employees at eight J.P. Stevens plants. The TWUA and AFL-CIO supported the suit as intervenor-appellees. Three years later, Sledge worried about testifying at the Raleigh district court, saying, "I was afraid something was going to happen to me." In October 1978, after years of litigation, the US Court of Appeals for the Fourth Circuit upheld a previous finding of discrimination by legal class and reversed an earlier decision that had not supported Sledge's individual claim. "I did do right," she said after the decision. "I know I did. I'd go down for this, if I had to, for my black brothers and sisters."[31]

Efforts such as *Sledge v. J.P. Stevens* helped increase Black workers in the mills from less than 5 percent to almost 25 percent, but they still earned the lowest wages.[32] The TWUA drive consistently signed more Black than white millhands and held meetings at Black churches.[33] The determination of Black workers made the drive viable and allowed the TWUA to capitalize on mainstream coverage of NAACP lawsuits.[34] Their emphasis on J.P. Stevens's intransigence drew increasing attention at a time when newspapers and nightly broadcasts still covered a labor beat.

The TWUA, however, faced a serious challenge. J.P. Stevens had a history of breaking unions or shutting down mills. Executives encouraged managers to harass organizers, remove them from the edge of mill property, throw out or cover union bulletins, and threaten or fire workers. Corporate lawyers filed countermotions and dragged out NLRB hearings.[35] These obstructionist practices constrained the TWUA's ability to recruit the majority-white millhands, who feared losing their jobs. Many knew about the limited successes of past organizing drives in the face of elites willing to break unions by any means. The lack of signed cards from white workers hindered certification elections and caused leaders to debate their ability to target J.P. Stevens.[36]

Seeking Income, Seeking Autonomy

During these years, Crystal Lee's quest for decent work and autonomy as a poor white woman took her back to Roanoke Rapids, where Sledge was on the same mission as a poor Black woman. Crystal Lee's older sister, Syretha, had stayed there and suggested Crystal Lee return for a fresh start. Syretha also mentioned a man named Larry Jordan Jr.—who went by "Cookie"—who worked with her husband at a unionized paper mill. Crystal Lee wanted her own house and out of Burlington because she did not appreciate the looks from people who knew she had an "illegitimate child." She packed her things in June 1962.[37]

For the move to Roanoke Rapids, she relied on money from two government provisions: regular checks from Social Security child-survivor benefits and the settlement derived from state laws for child support. Crystal Lee and Cookie decided to get to know each other, but her father was anxious about white working-class femininity and gossip in mill towns.[38] Relenting to her father's pressure, she and Cookie married, and she was disappointed when the romance evaporated and Cookie insisted she stay home around the clock.

In 1965, Crystal Lee had a baby girl and wondered what she had been like before children. This growing dissatisfaction with the limits of white working-class femininity and marriage stoked Crystal Lee's interest in union activism as much as her resentment of prejudice against millhands, class analysis, and concerns about work conditions. Her labor activism occurred at this fiery intersection of class, gender, and the means of production.[39]

Cookie did not offer any nights out as relief from household monotony, and the discontent led her to a brief 1968 affair with the town "ladies' man."[40] Crystal Lee continued to search for something more than staying home that was not in a cotton mill. When a vocational school opened on the outskirts of Roanoke Rapids in 1969, Cookie let her take two courses and even hoped for a part-time job. Syretha was a head waitress at a motel restaurant, so Crystal Lee took a waitressing course. In case Syretha could not help her get a job, she also took a power-sewing course, figuring apparel was better than textiles.[41] Like Puerto Rican needleworkers, she was savvy about exploring and creating employment options across the industry.

Crystal Lee found a job in a tourist restaurant but quit after the manager said she could make more money if he arranged "dates" for her with male customers. She got a job as a power sewer at an apparel plant thirty miles away, then at one twenty miles away, where she made a lot of money—more than at the mill or restaurant.[42] But during an exhausted drive home, she saw an accident and decided it was not worth that risk. She returned to waitressing but put her name in at J.P. Stevens. In February 1972, when Sledge was participating in the lawsuit, J.P. Stevens hired Crystal Lee at $2.25 an hour in the put-up department as a gift-set operator, arranging fancy towels in boxes. She stayed until August, when a previous boss offered her a hostessing job at his new nightclub, which sounded much more exciting.[43]

As Crystal Lee questioned the limits of white working-class femininity and followed her ambitions, Cookie settled into the norms of mill town society. When he heard about a freedom march for Roanoke Rapids, he did not want to let people "tear up what little mess I got." He and his friends had heard about uprisings in Harlem, Detroit, and Newark and viewed them as "those riots [where] Black people were just stealing everything that wasn't tied down." With guidance from a state senator, they formed a political Young Men's Club to plan for a possible race war, but Cookie did not tell Crystal Lee. He knew she thought differently about race and her mind-set was not "a put-on feeling." She did not encourage racial prejudice or divisiveness.[44]

Cookie tolerated her views on race because they did not challenge his patriarchal standing as a husband, but he did not like her hostessing. The nightclub catered to men, and hostesses were there to socialize. Cookie knew the men were drinking and people saw Crystal Lee in town late at night. He insisted she quit.[45] But she stayed because she enjoyed wearing nice clothes, using makeup, and keeping her hair long. Instead of standing at the kitchen counter or towel-folding table, she chatted with nightclub members and arranged tables. Unfortunately, her arguments with Cookie increased in frequency and volume, and the children were old enough to hear and understand. Crystal Lee conceded after two months and returned to J.P. Stevens Delta #4 in October 1972. She hated walking into the mill, so when she injured her foot in December, she happily took a medical leave until April 1973.[46]

While Crystal Lee pursued these personal escapes from the constraints of white working-class femininity and the drudgery of millwork, the TWUA campaign intensified. It included plans for a boycott, and between 1970 and 1973, J.P. Stevens faced two major class-action suits in the Carolinas in addition to the Sledge case.[47] In 1973, the TWUA hired Eli Zivkovich for the southern drive, even though he was a coal miner with a wife, Pearl, at home in West Virginia. In early 1973, he had lost his job with the United Mine Workers (UMW) because of volatile internal politics.[48] While in the steelworkers' union office with a friend, he took a job with the TWUA because he did not want to leave the labor movement.[49] The union sent him to North Carolina, which had shown some results over the ten-year campaign, and he mailed out leaflets with response postcards. When 350 came back from Roanoke Rapids, the chief of southern organizing, Harold McIver, supported Zivkovich's plan to go there. At the same time, Robert Freeman, another TWUA organizer, launched a drive at the Cannon Mills plants in Kannapolis, southwest of Roanoke Rapids.[50]

When Zivkovich arrived in spring 1973, he was not the first organizer millhands had supported. Roanoke Rapids had a history of union certification votes—in 1946, 1949, 1958, and 1964—and Virginia Keyser had coordinated a town membership drive from 1963 to 1969.[51] Zivkovich moved into a room at the Motel Dixie that doubled as his office, and Margaret Banks, a millhand from upstate New York, joined him as a full-time organizer. At their first meeting, all the workers except one were Black. Although two white men were the first to show up with signed membership cards, a Black man named Joseph Williams came with his father and brother to submit fifty cards. Supervisors and bossmen quickly targeted the Black men, demanding they confine leaflets to the canteens and firing Williams.

Crystal Lee was on medical leave and did not witness these events, but they pushed Zivkovich to make dramatic displays. He wanted everyone to know that whatever had happened during past drives, this one was different and would endure.[52] Zivkovich noticed a clause in a recent federal court order regarding back pay that said the union had the right to inspect bulletin boards once a week. No organizer had been inside the fence of a J.P. Stevens mill in more than a decade, so Zivkovich made a show at each one. The bossmen helped with their attempts at intimidation—following him through the buildings and causing a commotion. At one mill, boxes and bolts of cloth blocked a board in the loading area. The bossmen refused to move them and circled Zivkovich, but five Black men stepped forward. Nobody spoke until the bossmen ordered the African American men to move the items.

When Crystal Lee returned to work in April 1973, she noticed a poster announcing a TWUA meeting at a Black church. It reminded her of a letter she had received from J.P. Stevens while she was on medical leave. It apologized for firing workers, promised not to discourage membership, and vowed not to threaten employees. In 1972, after six years of litigation, J.P. Stevens had been held in contempt of two court orders: one required the company to provide back pay to ten people fired for joining the union, and the other demanded an apology letter mailed to all employees and read aloud by an NLRB agent to each shift. There had never been a decision like it.[53]

Crystal Lee was intrigued by the coincidence of the letter and poster. Her father and Syretha warned against getting into trouble, but Crystal Lee wanted to go to the meeting. After years of Cookie talking about acting as shop steward, she thought, "If he could be in a union, I didn't see why textile workers couldn't have a union." Cookie earned more money, had his birthday off, and got decent insurance. She knew his father had been active in the 1940s CIO Southern Organizing Campaign and remembered the woman steward at her first mill job.[54]

In considering the TWUA, Crystal Lee reflected on three issues: the prejudice against millhands, her children's future, and her parents' lives. "Cotton-mill workers are known as trash by some," she said, "and I knew this union was the only way we could have our own voice, make ourselves better." She also worried her three children would follow her into the mills and get swallowed up. "They been raised just like I was, same story over and over," she explained. "All their life, all the children ever hear is JP." The complaining was even a type of programming, preparing children for the grind. "[The mills] have, JP has, in a way, brainwashed the parents: they wore out. . . . JP [just] wants to get the family into the mill." And her parents still worked, struggling to pay their bills through pain and illness into old age.[55]

Crystal Lee asked her friend Liz to join her for the meeting at the Black church. As expected, Cookie told them he did not like the idea of white women going there, but he knew Crystal Lee did not have any hesitation. When the women arrived, Black mill workers filled the parking lot and pews. Crystal Lee and Liz did not see any white people except for a man and woman at the pulpit.[56] Zivkovich knew the drive depended on Black workers but needed to bring in the white majority—J.P. Stevens had 3,700 workers in Roanoke Rapids, and only 700 were Black. He immediately noticed the two white women willing to cross the race and gender lines of Jim Crow and white working-class femininity, and he thought Crystal Lee might have the energy to bring in white millhands.[57] He and Banks found her and Liz after the meeting, and within a few days, Crystal Lee had signed a membership card, grabbed a TWUA button, and taken an organizer's card. In the mill's canteen, she talked union and recruited white members. She also took bigger risks, such as smuggling out an "opinion survey" because it asked about the union and required a signature. The NLRB prohibited such surveillance.[58]

Within three weeks, Crystal Lee was going to the TWUA office almost every day, joining millhands who had been active for months. Zivkovich advised everyone to carry a notebook and write down anything management said, because several Black workers had already been fired and reinstated. By the end of May, Crystal Lee was a recognized TWUA advocate, and bossmen began reprimanding her for supposed infractions such as talking, using the bathroom, and spending time in canteens, which she recorded in her notebook.[59]

Then Zivkovich heard about a four-page company letter that Black millhands said included an inflammatory insinuation that the union would put Black workers above whites. Historic white superiority and racial segregation, red-baiting, and manipulation of patriarchal masculinity came together in this memo. Zivkovich wanted to know the exact words from the letter so he could initiate legal action. When bossmen scared off other workers, Crystal Lee said she would find a way. She seemed fearless and knew everyone at the mill. On May 30, Crystal Lee and a friend took turns attempting to memorize lines to write them down in the bathroom. When that did not succeed, she called Zivkovich, and he expressed in clear terms that he needed the exact words.

Crystal Lee was nervous but got a clipboard from her sister, waited for a quiet time, and took it to the bulletin board. She flipped through the pages, writing in her notebook. A bossman told her she could not copy it. She kept going. It appeared to be the usual threat that the union would cause people to lose their jobs—but then she reached the paragraph with a "special word to our black employees." It advised them "against the promise [that] by going into the union in mass, you can dominate it and control it in this plant, and in these Roanoke Rapids plants, as you may see fit." Crystal Lee grew angry, because she knew J.P. Stevens wanted to aggravate white workers' racism and anxiety about racial conflict. She knew less than 20 percent of workers were Black, so they could not be a union majority, but if bigoted or uninformed white millhands read the letter, they would think the union "supported black power" and it would not win an election.[60]

Bossmen came and went, asking her to go to the supervisor. She told them she would go after the break. Although apprehensive, she went outside to the "safety supper" the plant had provided to celebrate time without accidents. The letter was a hot topic because union members knew others had tried copying it, and coworkers had seen Crystal Lee at the bulletin board. When people asked her about it, a few said she had "guts." Crystal Lee told them bossmen had said the supervisor was going to fire her, so "y'all can expect anything." Copying the letter was a collective event, discussed by many people over a couple of days.[61]

When Crystal Lee finished eating, she returned to her folding station, where the assistant overseer told her to go to the supervisor's office. She saw several bossmen and her forelady, who all knew her from years in town. At the restaurant and nightclub, she had served them food and danced with a couple of the men. Nobody spoke up for her as the supervisor listed her supposed infractions, like using the pay phone on company time. Crystal Lee resisted, asking the men for their names and titles instead of pleading for pity. They looked confused, and the supervisor stood and shouted that she should call her husband. "Tell him to pick you up. I want you out," he yelled.[62] Perhaps if Crystal Lee had complied with the patriarchal gender norms and called her husband so he could take responsibility for her, the situation would have ended with the termination.

Crystal Lee said the supervisor would have to get the police. Then, questioning this idea, she changed her mind and said she had to get her pocketbook. She walked back to the folding station and noticed her coworkers staring at her. Mary Mosley, a Black woman in her section, asked what happened. "He fired me," Crystal Lee replied. A Pinkerton guard arrived and then a policeman. Crystal Lee asked Mosley for a marker, wrote UNION on a piece of packaging, stood on her table, and held it up.[63] Crystal Lee later said she had made the sign because she was angry and wanted to make a push for the union within the mill since it was probably her last opportunity.[64] At a 1994 AFL-CIO tribute to McIver, she reiterated the point: "I held that sign up for the workers in that plant to see and little did I realize it was going to get the attention that it has."[65]

She intended the UNION sign to be a backstage gesture, a display staged in a limited area without public viewing. Backstage gestures rely on "reciprocal familiarity" and function as a means of communal identification. Crystal Lee understood her sign as a message for her coworkers, a vernacular unifying signal, not an individualistic performance.[66] The group shared both an awareness of regional union history and knowledge of the current drive, whatever their opinions. The folding stations in that room, the familiar bossmen, the recognized magnitude of opposition to supervisors or police, and the writing on a gift-set insert all had idiomatic meanings. As Crystal Lee stood, some coworkers gave her the V for Victory sign, and others held fists in the air. Her forelady, the bossmen, and Syretha pleaded with Crystal Lee to get down from the table, but she stayed, turning to share the sign with everyone.[67]

She eventually sat on a stool and laid her head on the folding station until the police chief arrived. Chief Drewery Beale was her cousin's husband and knew details about her life.[68] He stood next to her and said, "Lee, this doesn't have anything to do with the union." Crystal Lee told him she wanted a taxi and for the door to be opened for her. "I am a lady," she said, claiming the status that women in industrial jobs, including Louise Delgado in 1950s New York City, demanded as an act of resistance, rather than of respectability politics. They were not petitioning for social mobility or an entrée into gentility but asserting their right to respect and decency.

At the fence, she saw a police car, and two officers grabbed her. She reached for the gate and pushed against them, but they took Crystal Lee to the town jail and charged her with disorderly conduct. She requested her phone call, and Zivkovich bailed her out, as organizers regularly do. The next day, he and another organizer met with the town manager and police chief. Zivkovich said that his union would not tolerate such treatment, and the police were liable to be sued for conspiracy with the company. After that, the police left Crystal Lee alone and stopped openly spying on the Motel Dixie.[69]

The hours spent in jail prompted Crystal Lee to think about her three children, mill town society, and how J.P. Stevens might use her personal life. She feared supervisors and anti-union millhands would tell her children about their different fathers to try to stop her unionizing through humiliation. When she got home, Crystal Lee retrieved a box of photos and documents from the boys' fathers. She explained how they had different dads and talked to them about meeting Cookie, marrying him, and having their sister, Elizabeth. She gained strength from realizing the children saw her in a new way. "My children know what I am, but they also know that I am an honest woman, and I believe in standing up for my rights," she said. "That really set me free, because then I had nothing to hide. . . . After that I got even more

Eli Zivkovich and Crystal Lee at the 1974 AFL-CIO Convention. | Crystal Lee Sutton Collection, Alamance Community College, Graham, NC

deeper involved with the union campaign." Crystal Lee had survived her defiance of the bossmen and police and spoken the truth, further loosening herself from the expectations of mill town femininity and class hierarchy.[70]

She told Zivkovich she wanted to stay with the TWUA, and he asked McIver to put her on the payroll, which he reluctantly agreed to do. McIver's hesitation derived from regional union officials, who called her "that stripper" who got up on a table and "hootchy-kootchied." Because Crystal Lee was a poor woman, they labeled her insubordinate and unpredictable. Zivkovich relied on her more than on Banks because Crystal Lee understood the towns, but he had to convince them to move ahead with her NLRB case. He wondered how many good grievances and organizers had been ignored or lost thanks to southern patriarchal attitudes about women obeying men.[71]

When McIver submitted the June 1973 Charge against Employer to the NLRB, it covered the situations of three employees: the harassment of Ricky Martin, with write-ups for inferior work and talking; the harassment of McArthur Winborne, with write-ups for tardiness and smoking; and the termination of Crystal Lee for improper use of the phone and canteen.[72] Crystal Lee's handwritten affidavit filled seven pages and listed concerns regarding frequent office meetings, locked gates, and harassment, as well as the events of her termination.[73] She recognized the NLRB charge as an opportunity to raise collective demands about work conditions and treatment of union members. These three cases moved through the NLRB process for five years, with J.P. Stevens using every tactic to delay reinstatement or remuneration until 1978, the same year as the US Court of Appeals' decision in *Sledge*.[74]

Zivkovich appreciated Crystal Lee's commitment and granted her a prominent role in the union because he traveled frequently and she had the time and local knowledge. She got signed cards and statements Zivkovich and Banks were unable to elicit. She was willing to transgress Jim Crow divisions, so he also asked her to coordinate a workers committee of people still inside the mills. When she welcomed white and Black workers to her house, managers could not stoke racial fears by charging that outsiders were changing their ways. Crystal Lee learned more about anti-union race manipulation and red-baiting from discarded copies of *Militant Truth*, a newspaper that accused unions of race-mixing and communism and used biblical passages to call people to repent. The editors had relationships with corporations and groups such as the Southern States Industrial Council, which promoted free enterprise and individualism as antidotes to Soviet authoritarianism.[75]

Crystal Lee's class consciousness, critique of white working-class femininity, and ambitions for seeking greater purpose and meaning for her life had brought her into an interracial union drive, which sparked an enduring dedication to the labor movement and deepened her understanding of racial politics. The activism also led to opportunities with popular-culture producers that further expanded her analysis of class, gender, and race and connected her to women's liberation. She did not have the economic or social capital to impose significant control on the media productions, but Crystal Lee fought for influence and took advantage of each one's success to fight in the arena of cultural politics and express support for the working poor and unions.

Commercial Media Wants a Story to Sell

In June 1973, a few days after Crystal Lee's conspicuous termination, Henry P. Leifermann called the TWUA headquarters at Motel Dixie to ask about the drive. He was a thirty-one-year-old freelance journalist in Atlanta with an interest in the industry because, while he had grown up in an affluent town in South Carolina, he knew people in the mills from teaching Red Cross swimming.[76] He was also looking for an article that would sell, and the union drive aligned with and fueled three media trends.

First, J.P. Stevens appeared regularly in the business pages as an important national conglomerate analyzed for its revenues and share values.[77] Second, manufacturing had become a troubling news topic as the reconfigurations that started in the early twentieth century accelerated. Business sections reported import fluctuations and losses in US productivity, and newspapers still had a labor beat, in which journalists described declining opportunities for working-class Americans, presented primarily as white men in heavy industries.[78]

Third, coverage of the conflicts between J.P. Stevens and the TWUA often relied on, participated in, and adapted a popular fascination with "the South" as a region of peculiar concerns. In novels, magazines, advertisements, movies, and television shows, the fascination manifested in two broad categories: spectacles of the plantation realm or portrayals of the personal lives of poor whites as dignified, if parochial, working people; troubled exploited laborers; or ignorant "crackers."[79]

During the 1960s, video portrayals of poor whites proliferated.[80] The television shows *The Real McCoys* (1957–62), *The Andy Griffith Show* (1960–68), *The Beverly Hillbillies* (1963–71), and *The Waltons* (1972–81) presented warm depictions of good parochial white southerners with quirky habits. Hollywood movies tended toward a voyeuristic scrutiny of the South and its problems, including degenerate bigoted whites, in films such as *Cool Hand Luke* (1967), *Bonnie and Clyde* (1967), *Easy Rider* (1969), and *Deliverance* (1972).[81] These productions participated in a construction of white poverty and racism as problems of a difficult, aberrant South.

This fascination also manifested in newspapers and news segments that emphasized isolated poor whites with reports on brown lung and Volunteers in Service to America (VISTA) programs in Appalachia.[82] President Lyndon Johnson and others promoted such stories to show that the War on Poverty did not serve only urban Black people.[83] This coverage circulated photos and videos of mill towns showing hardworking poor whites, especially women. The affecting representations infused the setting and workers with poignant significance and virtue as "good southerners."[84]

When Leifermann initiated his research on the TWUA drive, he joined and advanced these national conversations. His pursuit of a marketable article also aligned with Zivkovich's need to recruit white millhands and obtain positive publicity. And these circumstances converged with Crystal Lee's situation as a working-class white woman discovering the labor movement's possibilities for millhands' living conditions, workers' political-economic power, and her sense of purpose in society.

Zivkovich answered questions and directed Leifermann to five workers, including Crystal Lee, a sympathetic and attractive example for other white workers. She agreed to an interview because Zivkovich said it would help. "He explained to me about how important it was for union people to learn about unions, doing education work and everything," she said.[85] Although Crystal Lee had been active in the union for only two months, Leifermann picked her as the central figure. She was a "real good talker" and gave Leifermann material for a personal strand to carry readers through an article covering abstract topics like industrial economics and poverty. This strand appealed to the fascination with poor white southerners, because Crystal Lee lived, labored, and organized in this geographic and imagined space.[86] Crystal Lee also served as a gendered twist on the embattled working class, which suited the growing mainstream interest in women's liberation. She transgressed gender norms in ways associated with a fourth media trend, amplification of a popular "women's lib."

The women's liberation movement demanded and initiated new ways to talk about and represent women. Women of many backgrounds and feminist ideologies organized political groups, published manifestos, and formed collectives.[87] The National Organization for Women (NOW) and *Ms.* magazine were prominent liberal examples in a movement that included radical organizations such as the Combahee River Collective, Chicago Women's Liberation Union, Redstockings, W.I.T.C.H., Lesbian Feminist Liberation, and Hijas de Cuauhtémoc.

As the movement became more ubiquitous, mainstream media produced articles and television segments with attention to liberal feminism and individual white activists. At a time when talk shows including *The Merv Griffin Show* (1962–86), *The Phil Donahue Show* (1967–96), *The Dick Cavett Show* (1968–74), *Dinah's Place* (1970–74), and *Dinah!* (1974–80) welcomed public intellectuals, feminist leaders appeared on daytime television. In movies such as *Up the Sandbox* (1972), *The Stepford Wives* (1975), *An Unmarried Woman* (1978), and *9 to 5* (1980), Hollywood studios adapted the rhetoric of women's liberation to a familiar genre, the Modern Woman film with its feisty heterosexual white heroine. *Alice Doesn't Live Here Anymore* (1974), about a divorced mother working as a waitress, triggered a flurry of commentary as well as the television series *Alice* (1976–85). Mainstream journalists, reviewers, and hosts often labeled these activists, shows, and movies as "women's lib," and Crystal Lee gave Leifermann an opportunity to take advantage of the trend.[88]

His piece ran as a three-and-a-half-page article in the *New York Times Magazine* in August 1973 and initiated the extraction of Crystal Lee's "life story" from the larger context. The story's prominence in an esteemed national newspaper was not inevitable. Leifermann had effectively maximized the four media trends—J.P. Stevens, the unsettled working class, poor white southerners, and "women's lib"—to write a highly marketable article. It did not guarantee that the movie *Norma Rae* would happen, but it laid a defined foundation for all future productions.

In the article, titled "The Unions Are Coming: Trouble in the South's First Industry," he created a strand with enthralling moments from Crystal Lee's experiences that held together his general history of the cotton industry. The article begins with Crystal Lee describing her arrest and telling her children about their fathers, which Leifermann sets up as a personal, rather than strategic, move. The editorial layout centers a close-up of Crystal Lee with a reflective expression on her face, and at the bottom of the first column, Leifermann notes that she joined the TWUA because she wanted better for her children, accentuating the maternal.[89] So although the article discusses the textile industry, the first page draws emotional attention to Crystal Lee as a poor mother.

Anecdotes from her life, without experiences from other millhands, punctuate the article, driving the piece, individualizing the conditions, and initiating the construction of her life story. The next section includes an explanation of jobs such as hopper feeder, carder, spinner, doffer, side hemmer, and terry loader, followed by a description of Crystal Lee's family and first job. It says her mother cried with relief when Crystal Lee got it because the household so desperately needed the money. Leifermann then covers Crystal Lee's early marriage and the birth of her two sons.

His discussion of the industry deploys the narrative of the peculiar South and its troubled white workers. To advocate for labor, he argues the mills are crucial yet rarely mentioned in accolades for the New South because their unhealthy, dead-end jobs lead to poverty and its problems. "Millhands are the bedrock of the Deep South's economy, religion, politics, industry," he states. "They are also the lowest paid industrial workers in the South and the nation. . . . Their wholly non-average life is plagued by alcohol, sex, violence, and an image of themselves as deserving no better than what they get."[90] The white millhand appears as an anomalous worker rather than a contingent but indicative part of a global catalog of exploited labor.

Leifermann also argues that well-intentioned critiques of poverty that focus on workers' troubled behaviors have allowed companies to perform as defenders of the South by expressing their unequivocal admiration of millhands' dignity and endurance, and evading responsibility for the exploitation causing the problems. As an example, he summarizes a 1973 article in a South Carolina newspaper that quoted two social workers who said the mills limit education and encourage parents to bring their children to work, keeping families trapped in "a society in which sex and alcohol were the only outlets." Leifermann notes that fourteen mill companies placed a full-page ad in this same newspaper declaring workers were a positive force for good and "the backbone and strength of our community." As a result, he says, millhands see the companies as their champions against judgmental do-gooders.[91]

The last page presents the TWUA drive with some analysis. Leifermann emphasizes that J.P. Stevens is an industry leader with success blocking unionization and hiring law firms that specialize in anti-union tactics, which means the TWUA measures progress in signed cards, not plants organized. Rather than highlighting civil rights labor activism or the interracial membership drive, however, he says federal contracts and a dwindling pool of poor whites have led to an increasing number of Black workers, with the percentage at J.P. Stevens jumping from 12 to 20 percent in four years. This statistic is a prelude to his description of anti-union manipulation through racism and racial anxieties, which sets the stage for Crystal Lee's riveting termination.

The article ends with her attempt to copy the "antiunion letter," her stand on the folding table with the UNION sign, and the arrival of Chief Beale. The final paragraph does not highlight the interracial drive or systematic obstruction of worker organizing. It does not emphasize Crystal Lee's view of class prejudice or the union's importance. Instead, it constructs an affecting moment of personal defiance. The last line quotes her response to the police: "I said to Drewery Beale, 'I'll tell you one thing: you're going to open that door for me to go out of here.' I said, 'I am a lady.' Because see," Crystal Lee says, "Drewery knows things. He knows me."[92] The article depicts her as a poor woman aspiring to respectability in southern society rather than as a labor activist demanding decency and respect as an industrial worker in a union movement.

Leifermann made no effort to analyze links between the South and global industry. This choice reflects not their absence or inconspicuousness but rather his reliance on the popular fascination with the South. He could have included information about J.P. Stevens's subsidiaries and affiliates in Japan, Mexico, France, and New Zealand.[93] He could have explained how GATT, the Point IV Program, and bilateral trade agreements fostered "third world" development via textile and garment exports to the United States. Congress had passed the Trade Expansion Act (1962) and revised the quota regime with Item 807 (1963) under the Tariff Schedule that each further disaggregated supply chains. He could have mentioned the BIP (1965) that the TWUA and ILGWU had opposed.[94]

Instead, the 1973 *New York Times Magazine* article skipped any mention of TWUA's lobbying regarding trade policy, which it was doing with the southern drive. Leifermann could have said the TWUA had advocated strict import quotas as early as 1945, and the AFL-CIO criticized foreign economic policy, sent memos to Congress, testified at hearings, met with pro-labor politicians, and encouraged people to buy American-made.[95] Leifermann most likely knew that from 1971 to 1973, the TWUA and ACWA lobbied hard for the Foreign Trade and Investment Act (Burke-Hartke Trade Bill), which addressed trade, capital migration, and currency in an effort to support domestic manufacturing.

He pitched to newspapers that covered trade tensions regarding Japan, Mexico, and China as well as US negotiations with smaller players including Taiwan and Hong Kong. Business and labor reporters had acknowledged the rise of imports and impact on domestic textiles and the entangled relationships between the United States, Asia, and Latin America.[96] Compared to the dominant narrative of industry relocating in a direct path from the North to peculiar South, however, the percolating narrative of "globalization" did not yet have widespread cultural recognition.

Leifermann tuned all that out and, rather than making a serious structural argument about the political economy, used personal and maternal aspects of Crystal Lee's experiences as a cohesive strand. This creative decision initiated the extraction of her life story from national and global currents as well from decades of southern activism. The embedded cultural narrative of a struggling mother wanting better for her children had an affective appeal that was advantageous and served Leifermann well. It also had repercussions that would ripple out for years.

Crystal Lee, like Maldonado, faced immediate reaction from her peers. Some said Crystal Lee received too much attention, considering other workers had also suffered harassment and termination. Arguments erupted at the motel room union office, especially when Zivkovich was out of town and asked Crystal Lee to keep the headquarters open. A malicious rumor circulated that she had done a pornographic stag film, and since it lingered, Zivkovich asked three people implicated in the rumor whether any tape had ever existed, and they all gave him a firm no.[97] As both he and Crystal Lee knew, rumors and slander about a working woman's sexuality were often used to intimidate and restrain her and send a message to other women.

Despite arguments and gossip, Zivkovich kept Crystal Lee on the payroll. She was the most committed, standing at the factory gates every day and traveling every night to talk to workers at home. As she said, "The company did me a favor [firing me] because that just gave me more time to work for the union."[98] She also helped with a tactic that flipped her gendered encounter with class discrimination. In high school, Crystal Lee had wanted to be a cheerleader, but the children of millhands were not welcome. Either with Zivkovich's permission or at his request (the record is contradictory), she organized a TWUA cheerleading squad to raise awareness of the union and get mothers involved. She recruited twenty girls and coordinated times for them to make red-and-white uniforms. "I never will forget all those patterns we cut out," Crystal Lee said.[99] In December 1973, she and a few members decided to get a float into the Christmas parade, from which millhands had also been excluded. They spoke to the town committee, rented a flatbed, printed a banner with "Good Tidings and Merry Christmas from the Textile Workers Union of America," and planned for the cheerleaders to ride on the float.[100]

These successes led to more friction. A disagreement erupted over whether Cookie should pull the float, and Zivkovich's reliance on Crystal Lee exacerbated antagonism between her and Banks, who left. Cookie started arguments by asking whether she was in love with Zivkovich or complaining about housework, and she told him, "Hell, let the housework go. I'll do it some time. I can do it, I don't need sleep. I can sleep when I'm dead." He thought he was losing her to the TWUA and did not understand her commitment to a union that seemed to offer her little.

Crystal Lee clearly had a stake beyond her goals of improving the lives of working people and supporting the labor movement. She was pushing both herself and the gender and class boundaries that had limited her as a poor white woman. "That was an exciting part of my life because I was doing something I didn't even think I could do," she said.[101] The union gave her an opening to act and lead in ways she had not been permitted to in other parts of mill town society such as school and marriage. Crystal Lee also believed that Zivkovich's strategy, the workers committee, her dedication, and TWUA resources would sway enough millhands to vote union. By early 1974, 2,000 people had signed cards—more in six months than in the previous six years.[102]

As the drive inflamed strains within the union and Crystal Lee's marriage, a crew from the television show *Woman Alive!* arrived. Leifermann's piece had caught the attention of staff at *Ms.* magazine, which had started in 1971 as an insert in *New York* magazine and began publication on its own in 1972. By early 1973, Patricia Carbine, Letty Cottin Pogrebin, Gloria Steinem, and Marlo Thomas had established the Ms. Foundation for Women to share women's voices for change.[103] When the Corporation for Public Broadcasting called for proposals for a "women's show," Steinem and the *Ms.* staff were ready to expand their media reach. They partnered with KERA, the Dallas–Fort Worth PBS affiliate, and won a $71,000 grant to air a show created, written, and produced by women for women to highlight "new possibilities, alternatives, and choices."[104]

During the summer of 1973, producers decided the pilot would include short documentaries on everyday women and selected Crystal Lee as one of them. The resulting segment thoroughly extracted her from the larger context, and its emphasis on Crystal Lee as solitary union leader and defiant woman undergoing personal growth within a marriage signaled possibilities for future refinement of the story. *Ms.* staff did research and preproduction,

WOMAN ALIVE! producer Joan Shigekawa enjoys a light moment with textile union organizer Crystal Lee Jordan - the subject of a film profile in the one hour special produced by KERA-TV Dallas/Fort Worth in collaboration with Ms. magazine, to be seen _____ at _____ on Channel _____ over the Public Broadcasting Service. (6/19/74 8 p.m. ET)

Woman Alive! producer Joan Shigekawa on location with Crystal Lee in 1974. | Woman Alive! Collection, Schlesinger Library, Harvard University, Cambridge, MA, reprinted by permission of the WNET Group.

KERA provided camera crews, and a joint team traveled to Roanoke Rapids in October 1973 and January 1974 to interview Crystal Lee and get footage. They tried to talk to a J.P. Stevens representative and film inside a mill, but the company did not respond.[105]

In February 1974, as Zivkovich pushed for a union election and arguments between Crystal Lee and Cookie escalated, the team edited the first video version of a Crystal Lee story. Studying the production of the *Woman Alive!* pilot uncovers the mechanisms beyond creative imagination that shape a final media product, even one for public television. These shows do not compete in the advertising market, but their outcomes—viewership, audience response, critical success, awards—determine funding for future productions within a capitalist economy. Such considerations guided the team's extraction of Crystal Lee's story and its subsequent circulation.

Before finalizing the pilot, the team conducted focus group screenings. Only two previewers had negative reactions to the Crystal Lee segment: one disliked the use of children as cheerleaders, and another thought the depiction of what one woman could do was "unrealistic." Most attendees, however, enjoyed the "North Carolina Union Organizer" segment and many mentioned Crystal Lee by name. They used the words "real" and "courageous" and liked that she and Cookie got along. One woman appreciated that Crystal Lee presented her husband in a "favorable way," like he was "a real man" who helped around the house. Consultants recommended ending with this segment because viewers thought it was the most positive.[106]

During the same month as the focus groups, disagreements between Crystal Lee and Cookie evolved into hostile arguments. Crystal Lee took the children and moved in with Syretha. "I just didn't need that kind of crap," she said.[107] Meanwhile, Zivkovich told his regional supervisors that it was time to call for a union election. In April, Zivkovich invited them to a rally, where leaders saw the enthusiasm and agreed to file for an NLRB vote. The regional supervisors, who had not spent much time in town, became more involved, and differences over tactics and union roles prompted Zivkovich to resign. In May 1974, he returned to his wife in West Virginia, and when he left, Crystal Lee resigned and went to stay with her mother in Burlington. She thought she might find a good job away from her notoriety.[108]

A couple weeks later, the *Woman Alive!* pilot episode aired on PBS stations.[109] Although the version the focus groups watched is not available, it is clear producers made changes based on the previewers' comments, because Crystal Lee's segment does appear at the end. Producers most likely edited the segment to further emphasize Crystal Lee and her husband as well. These creative business decisions served to extract a particular life story, and the television medium broadened its reach. Yet Crystal Lee and the children were still in Burlington because Cookie refused to leave their house. Crystal Lee had kept in touch with the producers, so they were aware that attorneys were trying to negotiate an agreement regarding her living arrangements.[110] This contrast between what was shown in the segment and reality, however, is not a simple fact-checking error. It illuminates the field of cultural production and the input and decisions of *Woman Alive!* participants, from the subject to the creative professionals.

The elevation of Crystal Lee to union leader aligned with the show's approach to women's liberation, which emphasized self-actualization over collective action. The episode starts with images of different women and a voice-over saying, "What does it mean to be a woman alive today, facing the excitement of change and the challenge of self-discovery?" This opening presents feminism through a liberal frame of personal growth and then cuts to a series of color shots of celebrities like Shirley Chisholm, Judy Collins, and Bette Midler. A close-up of Crystal Lee is the final image before the regular show begins.[111]

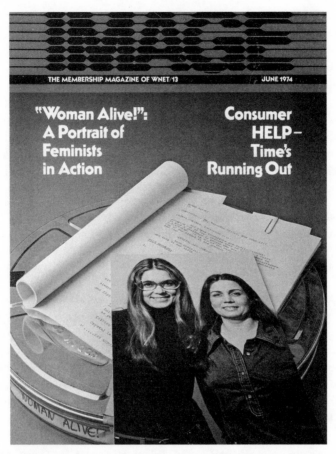

THE MEMBERSHIP MAGAZINE OF WNET/13 · JUNE 1974

"Woman Alive!": A Portrait of Feminists in Action

Consumer HELP— Time's Running Out

A 1975 PBS-WNET magazine cover with Gloria Steinem and Crystal Lee. | Woman Alive! Collection, Schlesinger Library, Harvard University, Cambridge, MA, reprinted by permission of the WNET Group.

The first segment follows a married couple in western Massachusetts who reversed gender roles after the wife took a job in the Everywoman Center at the University of Massachusetts, but the husband is ambivalent. *Woman Alive!* then presents Iowa women in a "rap session" about work and wages. After a comedic piece by Lily Tomlin, the show cuts to Steinem at the *Ms.* office speaking with members of the National Black Feminist Organization. The show transitions to the Crystal Lee segment via their conversation, in which they discuss her as a "new" blue-collar woman and not as one of many southern women and men who challenged mill owners and managers for decades.

Steinem: "The woman's movement is often stereotyped as white and middle class. In doing this, reporters not only ignore black and other third-world women, but they ignore the changes being made by blue-collar women as well."

Ronnie (*Ms.* staff member and one of the producers) responds: "There was a recent study done by Social Research, Inc. What it really showed was that blue-collar women, who had traditionally been the most stable unchanging voice, or one of the most stable and unchanging voices in society, has emerged as a very new political, economic, and social voice interested in the environment, consumerism, and in moving out and changing the world a little bit."

Nobody mentions the long history of southern organizing, the TWUA's eleven-year campaign, or the Black workers who joined in great numbers. Instead, the producers and Steinem construct Crystal Lee as the person who initiated the drive and pushed it forward.

Steinem: "There's a story that really says this in very human terms. It's Crystal Lee Jordan, who is a mill worker in North Carolina. She lives in the town of Roanoke Rapids. The influence of the company in the town is still so substantial that it's very difficult for workers like Crystal Lee to dare to even discuss a union. And yet the working conditions are, well, for instance the average work week is six days, you work eight hours a day and for those eight hours you are literally locked in the factory. You cannot leave. You get a twenty-minute lunch hour, which means you have to eat at your place of work. There's no seniority, there's one week of paid vacation. These conditions are really almost accepted out of fear, because even to discuss a union is such a challenge to people who are so dependent on J.P. Stevens. It's one of the major textile manufacturers, one of the oldest in the country. They really dominate the town. Crystal Lee Jordan is trying to break that domination, trying to unionize, and this is her story."[112]

Producers open the segment with images of a small-town street with old signs and a worn wooden church that evoke the fascination with the South. The remainder foregrounds Crystal Lee as an individual. She first appears in a wide shot of a mill gate, where she is handing out material and singing, "The union makes us strong, solidarity forever." Other women are also offering membership cards and pamphlets, but the producers center Crystal Lee and use a voice-over of her saying, "I got involved because it gives me the opportunity to be the woman I always wanted to be, because I can stand up and fight. And I know I'm gonna win this fight."[113]

Like Leifermann's article, the segment leads with the issue of Crystal Lee telling her children about their fathers but frames it as a labor tactic. Crystal Lee describes an "an older white woman" who stopped to take a card and said she only wanted to say, "I feel sorry for you. You have no respect for yourself." Viewers then see Crystal Lee in her little kitchen with three children at the table. She tells the off-camera interviewer, "I said, 'Ma'am, please don't feel sorry for me.' And I pointed to my son, and I said, 'That's my son and I love him.' I didn't want J.P. Stevens to have any weapon to use against me, and I thought they might dig into my past, and they might use it to try to shut me up." She gives the kids their meal and concludes, "The word 'illegitimate' is still a bad word, but to me it's not. . . . I don't have anything to worry about anymore."

Crystal Lee walks into an interracial gathering at the motel-room union office, where the camera catches a brief background chat about trying to get signatures at the plant. In accordance with the focus groups, however, producers decided to explore Crystal Lee's marriage rather than these union members' efforts at solidarity. The result funnels commentary on the union through the couple's personal views. The couple sits in their living room and Cookie expresses his apparent respect for her actions. "She is just not afraid," he says. "And her rights, she's gonna get them. And I'm proud of her for that. I wouldn't want it any other way. . . . They will not stop her." This attention to their marriage fits with *Woman Alive!*'s emphasis on heterosexual women's self-discovery.

Producers include Crystal Lee's analysis of local people as if other workers had not launched the membership drive. "People are not afraid of the union," she says. "They are afraid of J.P. Stevens, because J.P. Stevens owns six plants in Roanoke Rapids. . . . The people are afraid that if they are for the union, and the union comes in, that J.P. Stevens will shut the plant down." She mentions that banks and lending agencies have board members from the company, so it controls those too. Using this clip without additional context portrays Crystal Lee as a lone brave white woman rallying the town.

Several short scenes follow Crystal Lee working at TWUA headquarters and sewing letters onto a cheerleader jacket. In a voice-over, she provides more analysis, this time regarding gender politics. She argues that getting out makes her a better mother and expresses annoyance that men from the unionized paper mill refuse to let their wives organize for the TWUA. Viewers see her speaking to the camera: "A lot of men tell me . . . 'I can't wash dishes and cook for my wife' . . . like it would take away from his manhood. . . . I am proud of the fact [Cookie] wants to help me around the house and making the children's breakfast and even washing the clothes . . . 'cause I couldn't hold up." Crystal Lee asserts a clear critique of class and gender in mill town society. "Since I was a child, it seemed to me the man, he could do what he wanted, but the woman, she couldn't do nothing," she says. "And I don't believe a woman's place is in the home."[114]

The next shot shows Cookie making sandwiches, yet it hints at antagonism in the household. Viewers hear Cookie say, "I do what I feel is right and know that when a man and a woman both work, I mean, she gets tired . . . and it's a marriage and it's a partnership." But he adds, "Not that it wouldn't be really nice, I mean, to come home from work and fall down in the chair and holler for your wife to come in and put these slippers on and draw me a mug of coffee." He has the same ambivalence as the husband in western Massachusetts.

The segment, however, does not display the toll of organizing on their marriage, Cookie's discomfort with the public exposure, or the pressure on Crystal Lee to take responsibility for the home as mother, wife, and caretaker. The marriage appears to adapt to her activism and absence from the house without contestation, as she defies social taboos and becomes a public figure for the union. In this story, she expands the boundaries of her femininity and Cookie maintains his masculinity.

The historical record does not make clear who or what fueled this depiction. Editors on the PBS-*Ms.* team could have decided to formulate this impression through selective use of footage, especially after the focus groups. Zivkovich could have asked Crystal Lee and Cookie to avoid airing their disagreements because he needed more men to support their wives' activism. Zivkovich also could have suggested they appear cooperative to avoid negative publicity. In the spring of 1974, for example, he asked Crystal Lee to return to the house after she had moved out because Cookie was threatening to go to a newspaper with the accusation that "the union had taken his wife and children."[115] Perhaps Cookie agreed to participate only if producers portrayed him in a positive light. Or affirmative images of the household could have arisen without any self-conscious decisions, from an intuitive effort to perform like "a good family." The motivation most likely did not come from Crystal Lee. In a variety of other sources, she openly expressed her dissatisfaction with the marriage and Cookie's response to her organizing.[116]

Throughout the segment, she describes the union as a collaborative effort and uses the pronoun "we," undercutting the narrow focus on her. In the final scene, the interracial cheerleading squad and Crystal Lee stand at a union hall, and she says, "We are serious about this organizing campaign, and we are proud to be part of the union, and the union is the people." She stands with a man who calls the union meeting to order, and her voice-over declares that workers of all races and ages are gathering. The camera pans over Black and white millhands in the hall. "A lot of people don't understand why I am acting like I am. They think I just don't care about myself, but I do," the voice-over continues. "But I want the entire town to know I believe that strongly in the union. We are organizing in Roanoke Rapids." Her "we" together with these visuals consistently place her within a collective drive, which undermines the singular-hero narrative.

Crystal Lee emphasizes that the union is "the only answer" for workers, especially older people without options and children whose parents cannot afford college. She leads a song as her voice-over says, "They aren't gonna get me. They'll have to kill me first." The final tracking shot spans the crowd singing from TWUA booklets, and viewers hear Crystal Lee: "The union is behind us, we shall not be moved. Just like a tree that's planted by the water, we shall not be moved." The camera pauses on a group of three white men and pair of Black men sitting in rows as they sing with her, but the segment ends with a close-up on Crystal Lee's smiling face, and the show cuts to Melissa Manchester singing while credits roll.[117] The final moments associate two individual women, singing with uplifted faces, as embodiments of feminism.

Because Steinem was looking to refute the dominant narrative of women's liberation as middle class, producers ignored working-class women's complex relationship to feminist activism. Throughout the twentieth century, Black and white wage-earning women had advocated for issues related to employment and triggered debates over which strategies advanced women's equality. Many factory women wanted specific benefits, such as limits on heavy lifting and maternity leave. Black women in service work demanded access to better jobs, pay, and leisure and sought acknowledgment of their spousal and childcare obligations. Union women often viewed organizing and shop-floor leadership as activism for women as well as for labor. But these perspectives were frequently ignored by white middle-class feminists or Black club women.[118]

Even though Crystal Lee's comments subvert *Woman Alive!*'s individualist framing, the potent editing presents her as a singular force and constructs a story that overlooks women's organizing along the US Atlantic. Substantive regional resistance—generations of people who had lived with and navigated exploitation and derision; years of protests and walkouts; hundreds of arrests, beatings, and deaths; civil rights demonstrations, lobbying, legislative acts, and lawsuits; and the TWUA campaign to build a strong national union inclusive of southern workers—was subsumed in the segment's affect, the feelings of poignant virtue associated with good poor, white southerners. Its class, individualist, and setting simplifications infused Crystal Lee with the spirit of authentic outsider rebelliousness.[119] She became an underdog acting in a righteous oppositional way, an emblematic woman of courage and conviction diversifying *Ms.*'s pantheon of feminist heroes.[120]

Ms. paid for Crystal Lee to fly to New York to meet Steinem, do interviews with city radio and television stations, and visit tourist sites such as the Rainbow Room.[121] The pilot was a success, and New York PBS affiliate WNET/13 joined *Ms.* to produce ten thirty-minute episodes for 1975 and five sixty-minute episodes for 1977.

In August 1974, six weeks after *Woman Alive!* aired, Crystal Lee returned to Roanoke Rapids because Cookie had signed a thirty-day agreement promising to move to an apartment so she and the children could have the house.[122] Two weeks later, NLRB officials monitored an election in the J.P. Stevens plants, and Crystal Lee went to Delta #4 to submit a ballot. It went into a separate pile with seventy-one others because the company was contesting those from terminated employees. Zivkovich drove to town to watch the results with the millhands, and they stood in and around the plant as the NLRB counted: 1,448 for the company and 1,685 for the union. Millhands began shouting, and TWUA members cheered, including Crystal Lee.[123] J.P. Stevens recognized the union vote and acknowledged the requirement to bargain for a contract but said it would continue with its "operational decisions."[124] Union organizers knew the fight would linger through tough negotiations for an actual collective agreement.

During these chaotic months, Leifermann had been visiting Roanoke Rapids to conduct additional research for a biography of Crystal Lee, which he was pursuing despite threats from J.P. Stevens and editorials in southern newspapers accusing him of turning his back on his own kind by selling himself to the northern press.[125] The *New York Times* article had caught the attention of editors at Macmillan Publishing, who followed standard practice and offered him a contract to write the biography without offering Crystal Lee anything. She, Cookie, and Zivkovich met Leifermann at a law office in Roanoke Rapids to sign a release stating that he owned his version of their stories. Throughout 1974, Leifermann gathered more content about Crystal Lee's and Cookie's childhoods, first marriages, and jobs. The couple and Zivkovich, along with relatives and friends, were his major sources, but TWUA members and J.P. Stevens employees also contributed.[126]

Crystal Lee expressed dissatisfaction with how Leifermann discussed her marriage during their conversations for the book. She appreciated that he met with her, even when union leaders were disrespectful, but thought he believed Cookie's version of the marriage too easily. Crystal Lee wrote, "I'll admit I was concentrating a lot on what I was planning to do [about my marriage] when Hank [Leifermann] was down, and, I wasn't myself. But, then

The 1975 cover for *Crystal Lee: A Woman of Inheritance.* | Image courtesy of the author with the University of North Carolina Press art department

again, Hank is just another man in my book. He's got a lot to learn about life himself yet."[127] Crystal Lee participated in Leifermann's research anyway, because Zivkovich said the book would be important for working people. She believed in union education and hoped, she said, "to see something I believe in do people good."[128]

In October 1975, Macmillan released *Crystal Lee: A Woman of Inheritance*, a crucial step in the refinement of a Crystal Lee life story. Macmillan had revenues to pay for advertising, command book reviews, and get copies into mainstream stores and libraries, all of which circulated the story to new audiences. For other commercial producers, such an investment from a trade press was also an indicator of a story's ability to sell. In addition, *Crystal Lee* provided more substantial, distilled material for future productions. It formulated a dramatic personal arc for an unexpected poor mill girl becoming a modern woman, and it had the amount and type of detail screenwriters needed.

The book's epigraph, "According to the tribes of your fathers ye shall inherit," gives readers some insight into why Leifermann chose the title *Crystal Lee: A Woman of Inheritance*. The quotation comes from the Book of Numbers, part of the Jewish Torah and the Old Testament, and describes the Israelites' journey out of Egypt and the way families pass on titles and belongings. Leifermann's emphasis on inheritance reiterates a theme from his article: the supposedly unchanging quality of mill towns. It taps into the fascination with the peculiar South and the notion that it does not change, which relies on and reiterates vague understandings of poverty and social customs. In a later essay, he says the title refers to "the inheritance of failure which is their birthright" as poor millhands.[129] Like most stories of working-class households, the characters in *Crystal Lee* lack aspiration that change can or should be made in "the general pattern of life." Work schedules are the driving force in their existence, which refuses to manifest complicated thoughts or ambitions.[130] Rather than conveying a deep socioeconomic study or a rich psychological exploration, the book tells a tabloid-style life story of an intriguing, sensual woman who pushes against (but does not break) the constraints of mill town monotony.

Crystal Lee follows the formula for a girl's coming-of-age story. A cohesive personal strand about Crystal Lee and Cookie pulls the book together, which ends with a paragraph wondering whether they will maintain their marriage. Within this formula, her jobs and union activities are framed as impacts on her personal life and marriage. Parts 1 and 2 of the book describe Crystal Lee's and Cookie's families and childhoods. Their brief courtship and simple wedding and the death of Crystal Lee's father fill much of part 3, and the remainder follows Crystal Lee's tribulations in search of contentment, ending with her departure from the hostessing job.

The first mention of her interest in the TWUA appears in part 4, more than halfway through the book. Leifermann includes Zivkovich here and ends part 4 with Crystal Lee joining the union. Part 5 covers the weeks that Crystal Lee was active in the union drive and describes Cookie's reactions, Crystal Lee's attempt to copy the letter, and her arrest. Part 6 follows the drive from the summer of 1973 to 1974 and closes with Crystal Lee and Zivkovich leaving the TWUA when it is on the verge of the vote. A brief afterword covers the August 1974 victory in Delta Plant #4 without mentioning any other mills and ends with words from Crystal Lee: "'See, I was a daddy's girl. My daddy loved me too much. He did. Too much,' she says. Crystal Lee told Cookie she would try. Perhaps, she told herself, they could start all over again." The biography leaves readers with this comment on her personal relationships with men, not on exploitation or the union.

Although Leifermann includes descriptions of TWUA organizing and Zivkovich's and Banks's outreach to millhands prior to Crystal Lee, these are plot points driving the coming-of-age story. The formula emphasizes her relationships with men—her father, Junior, the college boy, Cookie, the town ladies' man, and Zivkovich—and culminates with a crisis in her marriage conflated with the union election. The organizing drive, instead of functioning as a tremendous social force advocating for the working class and calling for economic redistribution, becomes a vehicle for Crystal Lee's maturity and marital conflict. The successful vote returns her to the marriage.

Reviews of *Crystal Lee*, even critical ones, carried the life story further into popular culture. The most common criticism argued that it oversimplified histories of women in labor organizing to make an entertaining story about one interesting woman. Postwar Hollywood moviemakers, however, would not have worried about this lack of historical or social depth. They looked for straightforward stories that converted complexities into the triumph of an underdog hero. They probably appreciated reviews that described the book as "the true story of a woman's involvement with the Textile Workers Union in a small Southern mill town . . . [and] her commitment to the union [that] becomes the vehicle for her self-realization," or "[a woman's] union organizing [and how it] advanced both her social and personal goals by providing a kind of consciousness-raising."[131]

But as national media capitalized on the refined life story, Crystal Lee faced difficult conditions. Her 1973–74 TWUA activism had caused her to be blacklisted at the mills, and regional union leaders did not step up to assist her.[132] They were focused on contentious contract negotiations with J.P. Stevens, and many still saw Crystal Lee as an insubordinate woman who did not respect their authority.[133] She firmly believed unions were the best option for workers and continued to support them, but she admitted leadership had ostracized her and did not always have a good plan.[134]

From 1975 to 1976, Crystal Lee attempted to find a job in Roanoke Rapids and eventually worked in fast food and motel cleaning. Her marriage to Cookie deteriorated, with ongoing arguments about the children and money, and they went through a prolonged separation and turbulent divorce during 1976 and 1977. Their daughter Elizabeth often stayed with Cookie and blamed the TWUA for their family problems. Crystal Lee became so overwhelmed with bills and sad about Elizabeth that she contacted the *Woman Alive!* producer Joan Shigekawa in October 1976. *Ms.* staff sent her a typed response in November that said they were looking for "not just a lawyer—but someone with a practice and contacts that can give legal help and also personal support. As soon as we can get some help to you—we will." They told her to call the office collect if she needed to talk, and a handwritten note from Steinem asked Crystal Lee not to grow hard and assured her Elizabeth was "a whole person" who would survive the tough situation.[135]

Despite these grim circumstances for Crystal Lee, the unpredictable refinement of her popular-culture life story continued. A pivotal step was taken around this time when two independent women producers decided to turn the story into a Hollywood movie. Alexandra Rose, one of the first women producers in Los Angeles, had read Leifermann's 1973 *New York Times Magazine* article and was captivated by a mother facing jail and needing to tell her children about their different fathers. "My heart went out to her," Rose said, "and that's how it started for me." But she was still working for Roger Corman's distribution company and did not believe the moment was right for this movie. Three years later, in 1976, she teamed up with Tamara Asseyev to form their own company, Rose & Asseyev Productions, and they wanted the "Crystal Lee story" for their first project.[136]

CHAPTER FOUR

From Crystal Lee to "Crystal Lee" to *Norma Rae*

Making and Capitalizing on the Movie

[Sally Field] deserved that award but she could have talked
about the union or the boycott or the workers who made it
possible for her to get that award. I don't see how she could have
forgotten to say something in front of a million people.

—**Crystal Lee Sutton**

In November 1977, Crystal Lee walked into the law offices of Alexander & McCormick in downtown Chapel Hill, North Carolina, to sign a movie contract, but not with Rose & Asseyev Productions. Crystal Lee had received letters from several directors and producers, and Gloria Steinem had phoned her to introduce the filmmaker Barbara Kopple. Kopple wanted to produce a feature film about the TWUA drive, with Crystal Lee as a lead character, and had recently won an Academy Award for her 1976 documentary *Harlan County, USA*. It told a nuanced history of the 1973 coal miners' strike at Brookside Mine in eastern Kentucky.[1]

Crystal Lee was wary from losing friendships, fighting with Cookie, and being blacklisted by the mills. But Kopple was determined to build trust and acknowledged that some people in the movie industry might try to take advantage of her. To show good faith and exhibit her approach, Kopple suggested a private showing of *Harlan County, USA* and brought a copy to Chapel Hill, where Sydenham Alexander reserved a hall in the church he attended, Chapel of the Cross.[2] Alexander and John G. McCormick had defended Crystal Lee in an ugly civil lawsuit Cookie filed during the acrimonious divorce, and she stayed in touch with them. She introduced them to her third husband, Lewis Sutton Jr.—who went by "Preston"—and called them with updates about the children and questions about potential media.

Over the same weeks, Rose & Asseyev Productions and the film director Martin Ritt were also communicating with Alexander, but these exchanges became tense when they learned Crystal Lee did not like their screenplay and insisted on some type of approval. As a result, she gravitated toward Kopple, who invited her, Alexander, and McCormick to New York City to outline a contract for her film. Crystal Lee did not go, but the law partners scheduled two days to discuss a deal. When they returned, they explained the agreement and said Kopple was serious about the film and about including Crystal Lee in the creative process.[3]

Ritt again called the law office and said Crystal Lee was refusing to speak with him, so he and Tamara Asseyev wanted to fly to North Carolina to show their passion and explain why Crystal Lee should support his movie and sign their release. Crystal Lee declined to meet in person but said she would be available by phone. Ritt and Asseyev immediately traveled to Alexander & McCormick's bigger law office in Durham as a last-ditch effort to get her on board.[4]

At the same time as these convoluted conversations, Rose & Asseyev, which had purchased the film rights to Henry Leifermann's *Crystal Lee*, instructed its attorneys to investigate how to go ahead without a release. Crystal Lee had participated in Leifermann's *New York Times Magazine* article, the *Woman Alive!* television segment, and the biography published by Macmillan, and she had appreciated these opportunities to promote the union and take action beyond the bounds of white working-class femininity. She had met with Leifermann and the television producers multiple times to share her experiences, help the campaign against J.P. Stevens, and support the labor movement. But the terrain changed as soon as Rose & Asseyev acquired the film option.

Although the previous collaborations with mainstream media had served Crystal Lee's purposes in some way, they had also allowed writers, editors, producers, and directors to select, order, and frame events to create a story of personal growth and individual heroism. They had extracted and filtered a life story, which generated convenient content for creative professionals considering a Hollywood movie. The question was, who would make it happen and how? The movie development, which was combative and unpredictable, occurred from 1976 to 1979 within the system of Los Angeles studios and their mastery of intellectual property, copyright, contract law, and entertainment finances.[5] In this system, Crystal Lee was not an employee providing labor. Her experiences provided the cultural material, yet her low capital as a poor worker without assets and her low status as an outsider without a position in the movie industry meant she did not have much leverage. She fought anyway and contested not her conditions as labor but her ability to influence a popular-culture product about the American working class derived from her experiences, which she understood as bound with thousands of southern millhands.

Crystal Lee's maneuvering through the interconnected creative, financial, and legal experts—producers, directors, writers, studio executives, accountants, attorneys, and actors—reveals how capitalist mechanisms like copyright, liability releases, corporate accounting, contracts, and insurance requirements, even in the hands of well-intentioned professionals, marginalize working people. Studying movies as expensive high-risk industrial products clarifies the mechanisms and their power. Their relevance to history does not lie with a futile measure of accuracy and imaginative compression, because, as noted, films cannot be assessed simply for having abridgements and composites. Neither are the mechanisms a straightforward case of cosmopolitan professionals taking advantage of a "country bumpkin." Crystal Lee was an active combatant, despite the ways in which Ritt and Leifermann portrayed her.

Capitalist mechanisms have profound influence in the arena of cultural politics, especially regarding who contests and shapes the visibility and meanings for "worker" and "American working class." The movie *Norma Rae* reiterated the cultural narrative of the American working class as white individuals struggling in local gritty industries. It omitted disconcerting complexities of a global working class with diverse migrating women, and it obscured decades of contentious yet reciprocal labor and civil rights activism. Even though Crystal Lee's vision for a story of collective worker activism, without false sensationalism, did not appear on-screen, it drove her fight for influence in the field of cultural production. Over months of discussion and negotiation, Crystal Lee held her line and forced the production team to change its product. She also gained a better understanding of Hollywood industry and made tactical adjustments as a result.

In early 1977, Alexandra Rose and Tamara Asseyev put their development of a Crystal Lee movie into motion because *Rocky*, released in December 1976, had found enormous popular and critical success. *Rocky* was the first "negative pickup," an independent movie made without a studio green light or budget, to become a huge hit. Even more relevant, *Rocky* tells the story of a working-class white man who transforms his life and becomes an unexpected hero, a "paean to an underdog-triumphant white identity."[6] Both Asseyev and Rose had worked in multiple jobs with major studios and with Roger Corman, a producer and director well known for projects inside and outside the studios.[7] This experience drove their culture business logic that a movie about a working-class white mother who achieves personal liberation by fighting at a southern J.P. Stevens mill in a precarious US industry would appeal to a wide audience.

Launching the movie development involved tackling several issues. On one front, Rose & Asseyev approached Leifermann and Macmillan to buy the film rights to *Crystal Lee*. When Leifermann learned of their interest, he wrote to Crystal Lee to get her signature on a full release for a token one-dollar payment. Trusting him and misunderstanding the offer, she sent Leifermann a dollar with her signature.[8] Rose & Asseyev paid Leifermann $35,000 for the story rights, but the exchange ended because Ritt wanted known Hollywood professionals to adapt the screenplay.[9]

While they made appointments with studio executives to pitch "Crystal Lee" as a female *Rocky*, Asseyev and Rose started looking for a director and targeted Ritt because he was a white man with economic and social capital in Hollywood and a reputation for movies about working people.[10] By 1977, Ritt had found steady if measured success and talked about his films in terms of their "affirmation of the human struggle," "moral note," and interest in "the human equation."[11] A reviewer described him as "a veteran director of commercial films with a conscience. His pictures show a humanitarian concern and often focus on American classes and cultures otherwise seldom seen in Hollywood."[12]

Ritt had come out of the 1930s Popular Front scene in New York City with the Workers Laboratory Theater/Theatre of Action.[13] These young leftist creative professionals had cultivated a "proletarian tradition" of telling stories about working people, and the depiction of poor white southerners became a subgenre. Short stories and novels about millhands, including Mary Heaton Vorse's *Strike!* (1930), Sherwood Anderson's *Beyond Desire* (1932), and Erskine Caldwell's *God's Little Acre* (1933), helped establish it.[14]

Ritt had also fallen in love with the South while at Elon College in 1932–34, outside Burlington, North Carolina, where Crystal Lee lived in the 1950s. He would have seen the 1958 movie *God's Little Acre* with its sentimentalized image of millhands, taken from the Depression era and spun through the contemporary fascination with the troubled South for a new generation.[15] Although Ritt's first big movie, *Edge of the City* (1957), is about New York longshoremen, his commercial breakthrough came with *The Long, Hot Summer* (1958), which starred Paul Newman and was written by the couple Harriet Frank Jr. and Irving Ravetch (a.k.a. the Ravetches) as an interpretive amalgamation of three William Faulkner stories from the 1930s.[16] For the next three decades, Ritt made many movies set in the South—usually constructed as a place out of time, current yet eternal.

Asseyev and Rose knew attaching him to the movie would give it legitimacy. Ritt agreed to consider the "Crystal Lee" project if Frank and Ravetch wrote the script. They were already known for multiple box office successes and their awards for adapting books into screenplays, and Ritt had also worked with them on *Hud* (1963) and *Hombre* (1967) starring Newman, as well as *The Sound and the Fury* (1959), *Sounder* (1972), and *Conrack* (1974).[17]

Rose & Asseyev needed to contract with a studio to attain the millions of dollars necessary for production. They started at Columbia Pictures, where an executive, unable to introduce two businesswomen as "the producers," intentionally stumbled on the *p* in p-p-producers. Columbia said no. Asseyev, Rose, and Ritt then went to Twentieth Century-Fox for the investment because it had distributed and promoted *Rocky*, garnering commercial revenues and Academy Award accolades, including Best Picture and Best Director.[18] The women assured the executives that Crystal Lee was a "female Rocky," a determined working-class underdog.

Rose & Asseyev reached out to Crystal Lee to procure her support but did not invite her creative participation or offer payment. She spoke with the producers, as she had spoken to others wanting to make a movie from her life story. It was still unclear whether any might move forward.[19] Meanwhile, Ritt offered to cut his own salary in half, from $595,000 to $297,497, a financial gesture that paved the way for Twentieth Century-Fox to propose $5 million for the movie.[20] Although the producers needed to fulfill legal, insurance, and logistics requirements to secure the full investment, the movie development advanced, quantified through incremental agreements and invoices. A Hollywood film had become more likely.

Ritt needed to guarantee this "Crystal Lee" movie would be entertaining for a broad audience and earn big box office. He was a respected director, but his recent movies had not been financial successes. *The Great White Hope* (1970) and *Sounder* had received decent revenues and critical acclaim, but they were not blockbusters, and Ritt had mistakenly told his wife during postproduction on *Conrack* that their grandchildren would "live off" the movie.[21] His results with *The Molly Maguires* (1970) starring Sean Connery and *Casey's Shadow* (1978) starring Walter Matthau proved even celebrity actors did not ensure financial success. Ritt had predicted *Casey's Shadow*, with Matthau as a horse trainer raising an orphaned colt, would earn higher box office than all his other movies and was very disappointed.[22]

He believed Frank and Ravetch were crucial, and an incremental agreement designated partial disbursement of their $158,903 salary for a first draft of "Crystal Lee." Two of their creative choices prompted much of Crystal Lee's criticisms. First, to refine the life story from the article, television segment, and biography into an accessible commercial movie, Frank and Ravetch relied on the postwar Hollywood consensus that dictated the "conversion of all political, sociological, and economic dilemmas into personal melodramas" with the emotional redemption of a reluctant hero.[23] Scripts recycled this formula of a captivating, if unexpected, individual working to solve a complex political, social, or economic problem and achieving personal transformation.[24] Frank summed up how it applied to their script: "We couldn't believe how people survived in [those southern mills]. Then suddenly there's this ballsy woman who says she's going to get a union in there. She was at risk. Her economic life, such as it was, could be utterly swept away. But that woman stood up and said, 'This far and no more.' That was dazzling. More than dazzling. It was spectacular."[25]

The screenplay, while not predetermined, was limited by this established tendency, which depended on making Crystal Lee the only millhand pushing the union drive.[26] Although all movies compress time and characters, Frank and Ravetch did it in this particular way, eliminating not only the global context and longer southern history but even local worker organizing. They also selected moments and words from Crystal Lee's personal experiences to provide the stamp of the authentic folk rebel and distinctive details for the hero's emotional redemption, which gave the script a requisite gloss of newness.

The possibility exists for viewers to have divergent readings of a movie, yet this Hollywood conversion of knotty situations, events, and issues into a single internally motivated act of defiance is important for two reasons. One, it obscures the deep and intricate histories of diverse women in the global working class. Two, the reduction to the individual exemplifies a postwar cultural process by which rebellion became loosed from particular contexts, communities, or ideologies and transformed into a free-floating affective stance.[27] This structure of feeling was crucial to the 1980s mainstream cultural formation of neoliberal individualism and the refinement of the Norma Rae icon.

The second problematic choice was the creation of a flirtatious, if unconsummated, sexualized dynamic between the characters of Crystal Lee and Eli Zivkovich as a way to appeal to viewers looking for romance. Ritt wanted an added enticement, so he and the Ravetches "came up with the relationship between the organizer and the girl," which inflected the movie with heterosexual desires without undermining the Crystal Lee character as a dignified woman hero who stays admirable in her appropriate marriage.[28]

Before signing the release for Rose & Asseyev, the real Crystal Lee read the script, which the producers sent her in the summer of 1977. She thought they would consider her feedback, especially regarding these two creative decisions. Her response emphasized the years of effort by workers and organizers and the history of southern union members, and she said Zivkovich was like a second father, someone she respected for his guidance on labor issues. For her, the script was a betrayal of the union campaign and of her trust.[29]

She and Zivkovich, who joined some of the movie negotiations, had a legal foundation for script control. Unlike New York and California, North Carolina stipulated that a subject cannot be portrayed on-screen without explicit agreement, regardless of out-of-state contracts like the releases Crystal Lee had signed for Leifermann.[30]

When the conversations with Rose & Asseyev grew oppositional, she asked Alexander & McCormick to serve as her intermediary. The two men agreed but were only in their second year of general practice and were not knowledgeable about entertainment or intellectual property law. The production team was not deterred and forged ahead with its plans and the imperative to secure the full budget from Twentieth Century-Fox. In search of locations, Rose & Asseyev contacted Sol Stetin. He had been TWUA president at the start of the J.P. Stevens campaign in 1963 and had arranged a 1976 merger with the ACWA to form the ACTWU. When the producers wrote to Stetin, they said, "We are planning to produce a film for Twentieth Century-Fox based on the book CRYSTAL LEE: A WOMAN OF INHERITANCE by Henry P. Leifermann and to be directed by Martin Ritt. As you know Crystal Lee Jordan was instrumental in organizing the J.P. Stevens mill in Roanoke Rapids, North Carolina. We would appreciate your cooperation in locating a mill which would be amenable to a pro-union motion picture being shot on its premises."[31]

Ritt worked on the screenplay and wrote to Paul Newman in October for feedback, saying, "Here is the first draft of CRYSTAL LEE. I am curious to know what you think."[32] He also hired Warner Bros. to time the script. The studio sent him the bill with a note: "Dear Marty: Enclosed please find Betty Abbott Griffin's invoice for timing of script *CRYSTAL LEE* which we have paid. Please send this to Twentieth Century Fox so we can be reimbursed."[33]

Despite Crystal Lee's concerns and the producers' unsuccessful efforts to win her compliance, the creative professionals were still using "Crystal Lee" as a tentative title. A November 1977 rush invoice for "'Crystal Lee' - #558 Martin Ritt," confirmed movie development was under way with an incremental payment from Twentieth Century-Fox to Ritt. The invoice stated, "We have entered into a development deal with Martin Ritt as director of this picture, if made. He is to receive a Development Fee of $50,000 (against his Director's Fee) and the entire Development Fee has now accrued upon delivery of the first-draft screenplay of the Ravetches."[34] They were moving ahead and expected to assert full creative, financial, and legal control over the production.

But Crystal Lee did not give up. With disproportionate positions and assets in the field of movie production, Hollywood professionals and Crystal Lee jockeyed for access to resources and influence in the creative process and its product. She exerted the leverage she had by refusing to grant a free simple release, using her attorneys as mediators, and repeating her concerns, which had expanded beyond the two plot choices. She and her family were also anxious about the production using their names, given rampant blacklisting by local employers.[35]

Throughout that fall, Crystal Lee was also communicating with Kopple, who wanted to maximize the mainstream attention she had earned with her 1976 Academy Award.[36] Rather than pressure Crystal Lee for a release, Kopple was working to build a collaborative opportunity. She traveled to Chapel Hill to meet with Crystal Lee and show her *Harlan County, USA*, which follows several men and women over the course of a coal miners' strike in eastern Kentucky. Scenes include strategizing, debating, and adjusting tactics and a confrontation outside a mine with anti-union townspeople yelling and threatening union miners. Interviews with miners' wives highlight generational histories and family dedication to the labor movement, even with its problems.[37] Crystal Lee liked this approach.

Alexander and McCormick did not have experience with movie contracts, so they prepared for their November trip to meet Kopple by checking out the only two books on the topic from the local law library. Following constructive deliberations regarding rights, finances, and the scope of Crystal Lee's script review, Kopple took them to an elegant lunch. There was a clear difference in her approach to production: she agreed to grant Crystal Lee a $1,000 payment, script approval, and a percentage of the profits.[38] Crystal Lee would be a limited partner, not a source. Kopple finished by wooing the attorneys with tickets to the Broadway show *For Colored Girls Who Have Considered Suicide / When the Rainbow Is Enuf* and entrée to the hot disco Studio 54.[39]

Outside of Crystal Lee's purview, however, a decisive moment occurred in late November with Twentieth Century-Fox. The studio would not disperse funds beyond early preproduction until Rose & Asseyev acquired errors and omissions (E&O) coverage, meant to reduce the production's liability. Tensions came to a head when an assessment from the Fireman's Fund Insurance Company, one of the largest insurers in Hollywood, included a warning about Crystal Lee's potential future claims against the production, especially given her rumored project with Kopple. It refused to underwrite E&O coverage without a new release signed by Crystal Lee and Zivkovich—and Twentieth Century-Fox made its full investment contingent on this coverage.[40] Rose & Asseyev and Ritt, in coordination with the studio, applied increasingly coercive means to get Crystal Lee's compliance.

Attorneys for Rose & Asseyev put together a thorough release with precise conditions, including a token ten-dollar payment.[41] The lead attorney, Lawrence P. Mortorff, met with Alexander and McCormick to present the proposal as the best possible outcome. Mortorff insisted that the name J.P. Stevens and the legend "based on a true story" were "essential to this project" and urged Alexander and McCormick to get Crystal Lee's signature.[42] He also pressured them, saying there were several ways the production could get around her participation yet still use details from her life. He said that there were other women with "stories basically similar to Crystal Lee's" and that Crystal Lee "did not see the unionization fight through to its conclusion."[43] The negativity of this meeting spread into other discussions and spoiled possibilities for compromise.

Ritt decided to make a conciliatory offer because he did not like that Asseyev and Rose had not paid Crystal Lee. He asked Alan Ladd Jr., president of the film division at Twentieth Century-Fox, to approve a $25,000 payment for Crystal Lee.[44] Ladd agreed to this line item, and Ritt forwarded the offer to Alexander & McCormick. He flew with Asseyev to North Carolina to meet the attorneys, who repeated Crystal Lee's request for script approval, which Ritt again rejected. In a mix of subsequent letters and calls, Crystal Lee did not get a clear resolution. Without signing the release, she did not receive the payment, and Ritt had the capital to refuse to relinquish control and still go forward.[45] In a win-lose framing, it would appear Crystal Lee lost—but in the field of cultural production, the contest continued.

To deflect Crystal Lee while retaining control and addressing the E&O insurance issue, Ritt worked with Frank and Ravetch to create new character names. The mill became O.P. Henley, and the first documented use of the tentative title "Norma Rae" appears in a December 30, 1977, letter from Ritt to Dustin Hoffman asking for comments.[46] Rose & Asseyev added a qualifier for the closing credits that stated the "events, characters, and firms depicted in this photoplay are fictitious. Any similarity to actual persons, living or dead, or to actual events or firms is purely coincidental."[47]

Meanwhile, Mortorff and his legal staff tracked down every release Crystal Lee and Cookie had signed between 1973 and 1977. They had two releases from Leifermann, as well as others from 1974, 1976, and 1977. Rose & Asseyev presented these to the insurance company and Twentieth Century-Fox and sent a notice to Alexander & McCormick.[48] Crystal Lee contested the past releases, particularly one that had a special rider prohibiting its transfer. This did not change Mortorff's plan.

Fireman's Fund Insurance accepted the elimination of the title "Crystal Lee," the script revisions, and the movie credits disclaimer, plus the past releases, to approve E&O coverage.[49] Acquisition of this coverage formally ended Crystal Lee's direct participation in "Crystal Lee/Norma Rae," and she would not meet Sally Field until months after the movie appeared in theaters.[50] Although Crystal Lee was now excluded from the film production, it did not end her disputes in the overall field.

Twentieth Century-Fox confirmed that the requirements had been met and notified Rose & Asseyev that it had authorized the full $5 million. Capitalist mechanisms, including copyright, contracts, and releases, wielded by entertainment lawyers and studio accountants had been rallied to restrict Crystal Lee from the initial investments, future revenues, and creative process. A life story had already been extracted from the global working class, national labor movement, and southern organizing drive, but this separation from Crystal Lee was a definitive step in the refinement. Rose & Asseyev, Ritt, and Frank and Ravetch had established a separate entity, "Norma Rae," through which they could further simplify and consolidate the story of a rebellious woman hero from the working class.

In addition to the standard business expectation that they surpass $5 million in earnings, Rose & Asseyev, Ritt, and Field all felt additional pressure for a big commercial success. They needed to prove they could bring in solid sales if they wanted to reach a certain level of income and status. For Asseyev and Rose, if "Norma Rae" got made and distributed, it would be their first independent project. As two of the first women producers, they had to demonstrate they could make money. Ritt needed to show he could earn box office revenue and not just respectful accolades, and Field had to prove she could attract audiences as a serious film actress, to break from her youthful starring roles in two television comedies, *Gidget* (1965–66) and *The Flying Nun* (1967–70).

All four were experienced insiders who understood the Hollywood tendency. Ritt had also decided he did not want to make a union movie. His experience with *The Molly Maguires*, about a labor collective of Irish coal miners who sabotaged unsafe mines in 1870s Pennsylvania, directly impacted how he handled "Norma Rae." *The Molly Maguires* had flopped, and he described it as "the most painful experience of my professional life" because the movie "cost a lot of money" but was "a total failure."[51] Ritt resolved that union films did not have broad appeal.[52] That pain strengthened his pragmatism about making movies for a solid net profit if he wanted to keep getting hired. As a result, Ritt decided "Norma Rae" would not make an explicit statement about labor activism. "I've been overtly polemical before, but not in this film," he told a journalist. "[We didn't] want a union or labor film; we wanted an entertaining commercial one."[53]

Ritt assured Ladd that he "didn't want to start a film that had no chance of making money." Ritt said the movie would not be a "downer" because it was "about a girl who turns into a woman who can work, who can love, who can fight, who is as close to a complete woman of superior dimensions as any in film history."[54] He promised a recognizable name for the lead, which Kopple tried to block. Through her network, she learned who Ritt was contacting and sent the information to Alexander & McCormick. Alexander called the actresses to explain that they should not do the picture because the story had been taken from Crystal Lee, who wanted Kopple, a woman director, to make her story. After several stars, including Jane Fonda and Jill Clayburgh, turned him down, Ritt approached Sally Field, who was not receptive to Alexander's reasoning when he tried to talk her out of starring in the movie. She said yes, and Ritt pushed the studio to accept her.[55] He said she was "that kind of feisty little girl who would defend her kids with every drop of blood, somebody Middle America could relate to."[56] He had the racialized gender framing needed to achieve commercial success, positioning Norma Rae as a normative white girl and mother experiencing personal growth.

Field really wanted the part. In the early 1970s, she had made a decision to raise her status in the movie business and acknowledged she "had a desperate, very personal need to establish [her]self as a serious actress." Field had grown up in a family with ties to television and movies. As a teenager, she got the lead in *Gidget*, became a member of the Screen Actors Guild (SAG), and bought a house in the Hollywood Hills with income from the show, which became a hit in reruns and paid steady royalties.[57] Following three situational comedies, however, Field stopped taking roles and committed to studying drama, voice, and dance at the Actors Studio.

For three years, she focused on technique and auditioned for roles that would demonstrate her credibility, even though casting directors had to push against typecasting to get her seen.[58] By January 1978, Field had starred in the dramas *Sybil* (1976), *Stay Hungry* (1976), and *Heroes* (1977) and had joined her high-powered boyfriend, Burt Reynolds, in the blockbuster action-comedies *Smokey and the Bandit* (1977) and *Hooper* (1978).[59] She also became more serious about business and incorporated a company, Fogwood Films.

Although she was not a top-tier film actress, she had the name recognition Ritt needed for Twentieth Century-Fox. Her career, guild union membership, and agency representation, as well as her celebrity, gave Field the tools to demand not simply fair pay but proportional pay aligned with that of the producers and director. In acknowledgment of her contribution, something Crystal Lee did not have the leverage to demand, Field asked for the salary and credit reserved for high-status actors.

Field's February 1978 contract highlights the industry knowledge and legal skill required for an agent to secure maximum compensation for an actor and for producers to acquire a valuable actor as an asset. The contract permitted the "borrowed" use of Field from Fogwood to the "Norma Rae" production, based on specific criteria: $150,000 for two weeks of rehearsal, two months of principal photography, and three looping days; $25,000 deferred payment; an additional $15,000 if the film reached $30 million net profits; transportation to the location for herself, two children, and another adult; $1,000 per week for expenses while away from Los Angeles (approximately $8,000 total); "first star onscreen credit" (meaning her name would appear alone); and "full screen card with 100% of title" (meaning her name would appear the same size as the title).[60] This extensive contract stands in stark contrast to the ten dollars or even $25,000 offered to Crystal Lee, whose actions as a millhand and as a mainstream media subject and contributor provided the material.

While the production team negotiated with Field, they searched for a location. Ritt insisted on the South, despite knowing that political leaders and industry executives would not appreciate a movie about a millhand in a union. He had a vision based on his imagining of "the South," and by using a southern location with southern background actors and extras, Ritt would be able to claim his production was genuine. He hoped to work in Georgia, where he had shot Conrack with the encouragement of Governor Jimmy Carter. When Georgia's textile commission learned that he was planning a movie about Crystal Lee and the TWUA, however, it sent letters advising managers not to allow the production on their properties.[61]

Sol Stetin tried to connect Rose & Asseyev and Ritt with a mill, but the owners and managers were not receptive because of the ACTWU campaign. Managers in Pennsylvania and New Jersey were interested, because their factories already had unions and a site payment would counteract declines in orders.[62] Ritt said no, so the team turned to Alabama, where Governor George Wallace was recruiting moviemakers to increase revenue and tourism and to raise his own profile.[63]

Phil Cole of the Alabama Film Commission called textile executives and encouraged them to negotiate with Rose & Asseyev. He was a transplant from Los Angeles who had worked to establish the commission in 1978 after success with Steven Spielberg's Close Encounters of the Third Kind. Cole had helped draw 40 percent of that movie's 1976–77 filming to Mobile and then documented and publicized the economic benefits for the city. Cole flew the "Norma Rae" production designer, Walter Herndon, and production manager, Jack Terry, around the state to scout sites and meet with mill executives.[64]

Cole was determined to "nip in the bud any trouble, like what went on in Georgia," by explaining the film to executives and managers "before anyone had a chance to overreact." He took the line from Ritt that "Norma Rae" was "about a girl who turns into a woman." If executives and managers reiterated their opposition to the ACTWU or concern about the movie's favorable depiction of a union, Cole was ready with another answer about the business the movie would bring to the state.[65]

A unionized plant in Opelika welcomed Herndon and Terry for a visit, and Wallace encouraged the deal. But finalizing details with the mill manager, Oliver Smith, required "negotiations and a lot of PR work." After multiple phone calls, Rose & Asseyev and Ritt raised their site payment from $25,000 to $100,000—something they never offered to Crystal Lee—and Opelika Manufacturing agreed to permit shooting full interior and exterior scenes. Smith said he had the option to turn the parent company down, but the executives and chamber of commerce persuaded him the production would "be good for the community."[66] The additional payment probably helped as well.

With E&O coverage, a celebrity lead, and a location, Rose & Asseyev and Ritt's Saugatuck Productions received final approval from Twentieth Century-Fox in March 1978 for their budget. The detailed budget forms illuminate Hollywood moviemaking as an industry, with every aspect quantified like in Taylorized manufacturing. The studio approved the filming dates as May 1 to July 7, 1978, clearly noting the time span as fifty-seven production days and two holidays, all in Opelika. The forms enumerate dozens of expenses categorized under story rights, producer, director, cast, extras, staff, art costs, set costs, operating labor and materials, and miscellaneous. Each category includes cost subsets, plus possible taxes and tax reductions from local or state waivers.

Ritt was listed with the highest salary, at $297,497, and then Rose & Asseyev Productions with $150,036. Field received the top actor salary at $150,000, and Beau Bridges earned $85,000, more than the primary supporting actor, Ron Leibman, who accepted $70,000 to play the union organizer. Bridges was an established Hollywood asset with a recognizable family name, while Leibman was a New York stage actor with minor movie credits. The final allotted budget tallied $4,447,791 for explicit items plus $533,735 for overhead, totaling $4,981,526. Ritt prided himself on coming in under budget and believed it allowed him to keep working.[67]

The pitches, incremental agreements, negotiations, and conflicts had made this decisive capitalist mechanism possible: the elaborate, explicit process for distributing large sums of money. The probability that a "Norma Rae" movie derived from Crystal Lee's life story would get made increased exponentially. The budget, however, did not mention Crystal Lee or Zivkovich. Although they had provided value, they did not have the capital or leverage to access the means of production through this official allocation of finances. Crystal Lee would find other ways to make her claims on the production but not through the studio budget.

Crystal Lee did not hear from Rose & Asseyev or Ritt in early 1978, when they were calculating these line items. In April, as they went ahead with logistics for filming in Alabama, the ACTWU did notify her of the NLRB decision for her and several other fired J.P Stevens employees. After four years of company obstruction, the NLRB had awarded them their jobs and back pay. Crystal Lee and Preston Sutton had moved to Burlington in 1977, but she joined the other workers returning to the Roanoke Rapids mills. She claimed her position and her check for $13,000 after taxes, quit two days later, and went home, where Preston worked in the shipping department of a unionized Cannon Mills plant.[68]

Crystal Lee and Preston used her back pay to catch up on bills, and Ritt used the budget to finalize a script, commission storyboard drawings, and put together crews. Although rehearsals and filming on location often elicit unforeseeable changes, most directors require a revised screenplay before actors arrive. Drafts show how Ritt depended on popular fascination with the South, "women's lib" self-actualization, and the narrative of the American working class to make the script appealing.

Frank and Ravetch joined him on a visit to Opelika to plan for changes to scenes and dialogue.[69] Ritt said he "fell in love with Opelika" the moment he saw it and that people had "that certain stamp of southern pride on their faces." He described it as "typical Americana," like a Norman Rockwell cover for the *Saturday Evening Post* that would "proffer some of the most exciting photography ever captured on film."[70] Ritt understood the value of the southern location and its residents for his imaginative process and as cultural assets that carried meanings and emotions that would make the movie more marketable and increase sales.

Carrying on from the *Woman Alive!* segment, Ritt, Frank, and Ravetch emphasized a woman's self-actualization. They deployed the core technique of "women's lib" films: signifying liberation via a heterosexual white woman's consideration of sexual options. A potential higher-status sex partner, rather than collective activism, political organizing, or cultural resistance, serves as the catalyst to transformation. Even though the hero appears to have sexual options, "women's lib" scripts end with the woman constrained by marriage—either drifting alone outside it or repositioned inside it, often with motherhood.[71]

Ritt, Frank, and Ravetch broke from the Crystal Lee life story in four indicative ways.[72] These were not the only changes, and they were not aberrant prerogatives, because all writers and directors make changes. They are evidence, however, of Ritt's priorities as he enacted his creative control over the means of cultural production and sought that blockbuster return. Since Ritt needed the flirtation between Norma and the organizer to be a driving plotline, he invented their initial contact. Unlike Crystal Lee and Zivkovich, who met at a union event in a Black church after he had been in town for weeks getting membership cards, Norma meets Reuben Warshowsky at her parents' house. Reuben knocks and asks her father for recommendations on a place to stay. Reuben is alone, wandering an unnamed but unmistakably southern town. Her father tells him to hit the road. Later, Norma sees Reuben at the motel where she is meeting an older man for a tryst. Norma ends the affair, and the man smacks her and calls her a "hick." Reuben sees Norma and offers her some ice, and they chat in his room, a close private setting. It sets up the romantic possibility that envelops them throughout the movie—which Ritt considered an important element for commercial success.[73]

The second major script change represents Ritt's take, as a midcentury New Yorker, on the American fascination with the peculiar South. The TWUA organizer is not a fifty-five-year-old former United Mine Workers (UMW) organizer from West Virginia with a family, but rather a thirtysomething Jewish intellectual from New York with a love for poetry and an offscreen feminist girlfriend. Marginalia and script notes do not explain this change, but it clearly serves the cultural narrative of the problematic South in need of outside help. Reuben's secular Jewishness marks him as an external savior, someone coming to rescue poor millhands. He also mirrors Ritt, a Jewish New Yorker and lyrical filmmaker drawn to the timeless South, troubled yet redeemable.

In addition, Norma works on an older cotton textile loom in a mechanical space filled with banging machines and lint. The earliest available script places Norma, like Crystal Lee, at a folding table with towels flowing toward her on a moving line, but a handwritten note in the margin says "weave room." Frank and Ravetch liked the drama of the looms, which participated in and perpetuated the fascination with southern millhands. All subsequent scripts have Norma on the looms. Even with the relentless monotony, a millhand standing at a clean table folding towels for retail packaging did not induce the popular cultural familiarity with the South.[74]

The fourth change involves the man Norma marries, renamed Sonny. Instead of working in a unionized paper mill and serving as shop steward, Sonny labors in the same textile mill as Norma but does not join any aspect of the union. They meet when she's a stop-checker and he jokes and runs from her. The creative decision to put them in the same mill compressed time and space, a necessity for Hollywood movies. The more fascinating aspect of this modification is Sonny's complete indifference to unionizing. Rather than having Sonny, like Cookie, support unions but not his wife's participation, he does not express any prolabor ideas. He just wants their marriage to succeed. Perhaps Ritt understood, like the producers of *Woman Alive!*, that viewers would not feel much sympathy toward a husband who supported a union for himself but undermined his wife's efforts.

Having used status and capitalist mechanisms to evade and eliminate obstacles to his creative control of the script and production, Ritt had his assistant make arrangements for the ten-week stay in Opelika. Production managers were already on-site, because even on a genuine location, moviemaking involves scouting, leasing equipment, manufacturing sets, and finding props. The budget allocated tens of thousands of dollars for renting and redesigning locales.[75] Ritt's quest for popular authenticity did not depend on leaving the places and people as they were—quite the opposite. It required intensive management of their appearance and activities. The southern location and working people provided cover for Ritt to make the necessary changes to achieve his vision of an authentic peculiar South. He observed each site through the camera and ordered changes to construct his version of a typical southern mill town. For example, he had the effects crew blow cotton dust into the weaving room for ambience, and costumers dressed the extras, all local residents, using techniques that made the clothes appear worn.[76]

Actors arrived last and started rehearsing while Ritt made notes for each shot. He wanted to come in under budget and below fifty-seven days, so he used a handheld camera that would not require dolly tracks and asked the actors to prepare so that he might be able to print the first or second take.[77] Even as he directed the cinematography and acting, Ritt had to handle the business side. He welcomed Governor Wallace to the set on June 13 in appreciation of his support for the Opelika deal. During his visit, Wallace presented cast and crew with commemorative belt buckles, watched a scene, and posed for photos, including two with Field. He also invited the cast and crew to a dinner, which Field did not want to attend because of Wallace's past defense of segregation. Ritt told her to "quit being so childish" about the movie business and argued that Wallace's power was dwindling anyway. Although she did not change her opinion, Field went to the dinner. Frank and Ravetch, on the other hand, refused to interact with Wallace. They were award-winning writers who had the leverage to do so, and Wallace most likely asked for Field, a cute celebrity woman. An event with her would burnish his status.[78]

Principal photography wrapped the last week of June, and a party was arranged at the Sportsman's Inn. Ritt thanked the people of Opelika for their warmth and cooperation, which allowed the shoot to end two weeks ahead of schedule.[79] At that point, he went into postproduction with the editor to cut the movie and add sound. Twentieth Century-Fox executives were satisfied with the early print and finalized a budget for distribution that covered contracts with national theaters and a marketing campaign for a March 1979 release.[80]

The early poster deployed the notion of southerners as dignified, if parochial, poor working people. A gray shot of Field with a worried look hovers above a black-and-white image of rundown houses clustered together, dominated by a mill with a smokestack. The graphic artists used this mill village photograph even though it was from 1910, not the 1970s. The original photographer had described it as "Hell's Half Acre at Avondale Mills"

Governor George Wallace meets Sally Field on the *Norma Rae* movie set in Opelika, Alabama, during the summer of 1978. | Alabama Department of Archives and History, Montgomery, AL

in Birmingham, Alabama, where the most destitute people lived.[81] On the *Norma Rae* poster, however, the image became sentimental and reinforces the notion of the timeless troubled South—but only as flat atmosphere. The tag line emphasizes the emotional story of the individual hero: "The story of a woman with the courage to risk everything for what she believes is right."

In the 1970s, Hollywood movies had tremendous physical and cultural power. Radio only had local AM/FM stations, and television offered three networks that had to be watched in real time. Most people in a community read the same newspaper or viewed the same nightly news. Cable channels, VCRs, DVDs, TiVo, and the internet were not yet fragmenting the mainstream audience. Going to the movies was an affordable, casual leisure activity, and people watching *Norma Rae* in 1979 sat together in dark theaters with a big screen and surround sound. It swept them into a sensory experience and became a topic of media coverage at a time when movies were a broadly shared phenomenon made to engross US, not international, audiences. *Norma Rae* drew viewers into its melodramatic story of one white woman's transformation.

It was routine at that time for the sensory experience of a movie to start with opening credits. *Norma Rae* begins with complementary music and images that speak to the American fascination with the South and the poignant virtue of poor rural whites. A woman's voice sings a mellow country song, "It Goes Like It Goes," while a series of evocative images appear. Ritt gave the sequence a sepia tone, paired with folksy lines like "So it goes like it goes, like the river it flows," "Maybe what's good gets a little bit better, and maybe what's bad gets gone," and "Bless the child of a working man, she knows too soon what she is."[82] Interior shots of an archaic textile mill, where wizened men and elderly women monitor industrial spools, alternate with photos of Norma: posing as a little girl, graduating high school, holding a baby, smiling in a waitress uniform.[83] The nostalgic ambience encourages a sentimental distance between viewers and the realm of bad, old-fashioned southern labor in *Norma Rae*.

The quiet opening ends abruptly as the movie cuts to the loud noise of a weaving room, all clanging and bangs, where Norma threads multiple machines. When the women go to the canteen for lunch, the movie establishes Norma's personality. Her mother cannot hear her, so Norma rushes her to the company doctor. He says hearing loss happens all the time. Norma leans toward him and snaps, "Well, it doesn't happen to my mama!" He offers to give her mother a note for the day, and Norma says, "Come on, Mama. They don't care anything about you." The audience sees Norma is a feisty woman with attitude.

The next scene establishes Norma's father as the traditional patriarch who stands in regressive contrast to her conspicuous defiance. Norma arrives at her parents' house after work with her two young children, one from a deceased husband and another from an indifferent local man. She encourages them to do homework, then goes to change into a clean t-shirt. Norma wears tiny, form-fitting t-shirts throughout the movie, consistently emphasizing her petite figure and breasts. When her father says he will drive her where she needs to go, she dissuades him in a sarcastic voice, saying she is going to get a bra and Kotex—the first of three references to menstruation. During the 1970s, many feminists pushed to normalize menstruation, which mainstream culture had treated as an embarrassing private burden. The way a man responded to the topic became an indicator of his modernity. Her father ignores it and answers a knock at the door. He finds Reuben with an unbuttoned shirt and unkempt dark hair, another stark contrast to his traditional southern patriarchy. Her father sends him away, saying unions get people thrown out of jobs. Although she does not say anything, Norma looks intrigued.

The next three scenes unfold at the motel, extending Norma's ineffectual rebelliousness and appointing Reuben as her Pygmalion. Reuben sees Norma in the lobby and says hello. The movie cuts to Norma in a dim room in her bra and underwear breaking off the affair with a brawny older man. He shouts disparaging comments and slaps her, and Norma joins Reuben in his room to get ice. They are each in their thirties and make a lot of eye contact. She notices his books, and he talks about poetry and his girlfriend, a "hotshot labor lawyer out of Harvard." After apologizing for her daddy, Norma asks, "Are you a Jew?" Although surprised, Reuben answers in a positive tone, and she says ingenuously that she had heard they "all had horns." This exchange, which has no precedent with Crystal Lee, presents both the South's need for outside enlightenment and Norma's openness to new things. Reuben's kindness pivots to mentoring her in the world's opportunities. A man serves as the conduit for Norma's consciousness-raising and personal liberation—without Reuben, she might have continued funneling her defiance into unproductive sexual affairs.

Norma's and Reuben's daily lives increasingly overlap. Unlike Zivkovich, who worked with Margaret Banks, organized for weeks with Black and white members, and made contacts throughout the region, Reuben struggles alone until Norma. She sees him at the edge of the mill lot, trying to get workers to take pamphlets. Norma suggests he change the words so millhands can understand them better, again marking him as an outside influence on the backward South. Black millhands pass in the background but do not take an active role.

Bossmen notice Norma's interest in Reuben and discuss her demands for longer breaks and Kotex machines—the second reference to menstruation as an indicator of Norma's rebelliousness. One bossman says she has the biggest mouth and needs more responsibility, so he promotes her to stop-checker. A young man, Sonny, races around the machines, smiling and forcing Norma to chase him. The scene is a reference to Crystal Lee's job as a stop-checker, which allows a subtle comment on management's effort to monitor labor to be compressed into Norma and Sonny's introduction. Sonny stops by her parents' house and asks Norma for a date. They go to a dive bar, but she invites Reuben to join them when he enters. He is in their relationship from the start.

Reuben approaches her at a baseball game, where she also bumps into the father of her illegitimate child and derides him for his lack of interest in his son. Reuben tells Norma she is too smart for what is happening to her, and she looks appreciative. His role erases Crystal Lee's agency in deciding on her own to seek state-mandated child support and relocate rather than marry the college boy. Sonny and Norma take their kids on a picnic, where he says he wants a wife and she needs a husband, so they should get married. She seems hesitant, again erasing Crystal Lee's agency in pursuing Cookie. The movie cuts to their wedding at a small office. Meanwhile, Norma's job as stop-checker leads to friction with coworkers and an uncomfortable scene when she has to push her father to work faster. This reversal of strong patriarch and defiant girl-child uses gender norms to heighten the dramatic tension in preparation for a key turning point. Norma returns to weaving because it was so disconcerting to have authority over her daddy.

These situations with two white men—Reuben's mentoring and her father's vulnerability—rather than a lifelong resentment of class prejudice, awareness of union history, and analysis of white working-class femininity, push Norma to the TWUA. After weeks of flirtatious chatter, Norma reads a TWUA flyer about a meeting in a Black church. At the church, Reuben shares the experience of his grandfather in a New York union, unlike Zivkovich who emphasized TWUA's successes in mills. Reuben again functions as the outside savior, educating ignorant southerners on the history of labor activism. In the next scene, taken directly from Zivkovich's experience before he met Crystal Lee, Reuben arrives to inspect the bulletin board. Norma watches him striding in with confidence, and she smiles. He finds flyers covered by large barrels, but the bossmen grow tense until Black men step forward to assist Reuben. Their sudden allegiance to him for his assertive display proves he is a good white man, rather than demonstrating that Black workers were the crucial foundation for the TWUA.[84]

This performance of white masculinity, not the meeting at the Black church, leads Norma to go to the motel-room office and sign a union card. "You got me," she declares. Norma wears a union pin, talks to coworkers in the canteen, and asks her minister to use the church, but he says no, a scene that derived from Crystal Lee's comment that she never knew a white church that supported the TWUA.[85] Reuben and Norma hold a meeting at her house, which is in a cluster of cottages where a bossman also lives. Sonny expresses concern about having Black men in mixed company, but Norma says she does not care. They discuss workloads, standing for hours, and working while menstruating. The idea for the scene came from Crystal Lee hosting the interracial workers committee, but instead of a meeting for millhands to coordinate a strategy for TWUA membership, it is a complaint session with Reuben as the paternalist authority.

A montage deploys the popular fascination to beckon viewers into the increasing intimacy between Norma and Reuben. On farms and dirt roads, they speak with recognizable archetypes, like the aged white farmer by a rusty tractor and old white men in overalls whittling on the porch of a general store. The imagery harkens to an earlier time, and the imaginative nostalgia fosters a sentimental distance from the parochial South in which labor exploitation is a remnant of "bad" early industry disconnected from contemporary practices.[86] This framing separates the South from the global conditions in which mills operated.

The montage stops on a hot day, when Norma and Reuben decide to skinny-dip in a stream. Their flirtation reaches its titillating peak when Reuben says, "You're the fish I wanted to hook," and Norma swims closer to him. Reuben repeatedly floats away, refusing to touch her. Before filming, Ritt had directed Field to tantalize Leibman, without mentioning anything to Leibman, to create a voyeuristic look.[87] Norma and Reuben leave without consummating the coquetry, verifying he is a responsible Pygmalion who does not take advantage of the woman he is uplifting. It also endorses a particular stance on a woman's proper liberation: heterosexual, facilitated by and focused on men, but monogamous.

After one trip around the back roads, Norma stands in her kitchen wearing a nightgown and making phone calls. Sonny shows up angry, asking about dinner and laundry. Norma yells, bangs the pans, and throws dirty clothes into the sink. She tells him if he wants "to make love, then get behind" her while she irons. Sonny calms down and laughs. Their marriage stays intact, which contains Norma even as she funnels her defiance into a limited labor activism.

In the next scene, she is in the motel room at night, typing memos and putting together files. Reuben arrives upset and lonely. They talk about his girlfriend, and Norma asks, "How come she's so smart?" "Books," Reuben answers. He gives Norma an anthology by his favorite poet, Dylan Thomas. The flirtation continues, yet Reuben has set the boundaries as platonic. Despite their efforts, the Black church is empty for the next meeting, again making it appear as if Reuben and Norma are the only stable active contributors. When they go door to door, they discover the mill has everyone on a stretch-out, making them tired and afraid. Neighbors, kids, and old folks watch them but slam their doors.

In the key turning point, Norma's father dies after a bossman refuses to give him a break for chest pain. As in the movie *God's Little Acre*, the death of a strong working man prods people to action, and the TWUA motel-room headquarters fills with people, including Black men. Although Norma had supported the union and tried to rally coworkers, the patriarch's death prompts the membership surge. It is personal, and Norma's intensity escalates. When a man shows up late for an activity, she yells at him. Reuben tells her to shut up and get out, an adaptation of an incident in which Zivkovich asked Crystal Lee to take a break after arguing with another full-time organizer. Reuben tells Norma that she "can't come down that hard on a man and leave him his balls." She says the union is the only way workers can get their "own voice," a line taken directly from Crystal Lee and the most political statement in the movie.[88]

The following scene transfers the 1973–74 gossip about Crystal Lee's sexuality onto Norma but resolves the controversy in a way that elevates Reuben. In *Norma Rae*, two regional union leaders, their status indicated by their suits, arrive at the motel at night. Norma is there working, and the men advise Reuben to limit her activity. They tell him that she has an illegitimate child and sleeps around. He responds, "She's broken her ass [for the union], what the hell do I care if she's got round heels?" Norma hears this conversation and offers to quit, a disappointing choice because Crystal Lee never expressed any interest in quitting. Quite the opposite, in *Woman Alive!* she said she knew people tried to silence union women by calling them "whores," but that was not going to stop them.[89] In the movie, Reuben refuses to let Norma go, heightening both his good white masculinity and his role as catalyst for her self-actualization. Norma and Reuben emerge as a chaste pair, now united against four opponents: exploitative management, the southern racial divide, millhand fears, and sexist union leaders.

The movie advances toward its dramatic climax when a letter appears on a bulletin board saying the union will put Black workers above white. Five white men assault a Black millhand outside the delivery doors and say, "You want a union, you'll get a union." Three Black men and Norma break up the fight, and Reuben arrives at the fence to support her, a further marginalization of the fortitude of Black workers and interracial organizing.[90] *Norma Rae* does not develop any of the Black characters. They function to provide a simplistic racial visibility that creates a shallow contrast to reinforce the positive quality of Norma and Reuben. The Black characters are a vehicle for the white characters to become saviors—ideal white selves, brave and generous.[91]

Reuben tells Norma through the fence that she has to get him the letter. Norma and her friend try to memorize it and write it in the bathroom, but when she hands the toilet paper to Reuben, he asks, "Where's the rest of it?" Then he shouts that he needs the exact words. The movie cuts to Norma in the mill with a firm grimace marching to the bulletin board and using a pencil to write down the exact words. Two bossmen appear behind her as she copies, then three more, then the plant manager, and she refuses to stop. There is no safety supper; the plant manager and five bossmen escort Norma directly to the manager's office, where he asks about her phone calls on company time. Unlike Crystal Lee's experience, no forelady appears. The gender dynamics

Sally Field as Norma in the TWUA headquarters at the motel. She is foregrounded as the lead with Black supporting characters in the background. | *Norma Rae*, 1979

heighten the perception of Norma as a small solitary woman fighter against the lingering "bad" old industrial exploitation, resistant to modernity, feminism, and racial integration.

The manager fires her, so Norma asks for everyone's name and starts writing in her notebook. The manager gets angry and shouts, "Out!" Norma stomps to her weaving machine, but no coworker approaches or talks to her. A security guard tells her to move, so she goes to a worktable and sees police arriving. On her own, without speaking to a coworker, she writes UNION on a piece of cardboard and stands on the table. The camera lingers on this action for over two minutes, with shots cutting between an upward angle on Norma's emotional face and close-ups of her mother and other coworkers with upturned eyes. Her mother first, then a Black woman, and then all the other workers turn off their machines one by one until the room is silent. The sheriff arrives and tells Norma to get down. She asks where they will take her, and he says off the property. When she reaches the fence, however, she sees a police car. Norma fights, lunging against the men's grip on her arms. They lift her into the car as she yells, "No, you promised!"

She walks into the local jail and sits weeping in a cell. Reuben bails her out, and she cries in his truck on the way home. Once there, she wakes her two

Sally Field as Norma in an upward shot during the dramatic termination scene. The camera and editing emphasize the emotion of her solitary defiance rather than a shared expression of solidarity. | *Norma Rae,* 1979

children and Sonny's daughter and gets a box of papers and photos. Reuben and Sonny watch from another room as she tells the children about their fathers. Sonny steps into the kitchen with Reuben and expresses concern. Unlike Zivkovich, who encouraged Crystal Lee and Cookie to stick with their marriage, Reuben speaks as the voice of her personal liberation: "She's a free woman. Maybe you can live with it, maybe you can't." When Norma gets into bed, Sonny asks if she slept with Reuben. She says no, "but he's in my head." Sonny tells her he wants to grow old with her, and they hug. The three white men in her life, her father, Reuben, and Sonny, are the participants in and influences on the fulfillment of her potential, rather than other women or union members.

Norma Rae ends with the ballot count in the one mill, without any explanation of the longer NLRB process. The camera pans across workers standing and sitting close in stacked rows around a large room—but not Norma or Reuben. In 1974, Crystal Lee had voted inside the mill. During the shoot in 1978, however, Ritt made a last-minute decision regarding the final scene. Multiple script drafts and charcoal drawings for the storyboard and set design show Norma in a crowd of TWUA workers cheering outside the mill. On location, Ritt opted to have Norma and Reuben standing as a pair outside the fence.[92]

In a potent visual, workers inside the mill represent different ages, genders, and races, as well as people against the union. But their appearance harkens to the 1930s rather than the 1970s, which intensifies the scene's affective impact. They wear dusty work clothes, bandannas, and tatty caps, familiar indicators of poignant southern virtue, instead of dresses, skirts, collared shirts, and sports jackets like union members often wore to elections.[93] The shots cut between Norma and Reuben waiting outside the chain link fence and the millhands inside. A Black man wearing a backward cap and tank undershirt sits next to a white company man in a collared shirt as they count, race and clothing marking the opposition of good versus bad. The yes votes win, and workers chant, "Union!" When the distant cheer goes up, Norma smiles at Reuben. Inside the mill, dozens of workers shout and hug. Nobody mentions that a certification vote is the first step in a process that often takes months, or even years, to reach a contract.

Norma and Reuben turn to leave rather than joining the jubilant people streaming from the mill, again pulling the audience toward their relationship rather than toward labor movement solidarity. The camera follows Norma and Reuben into a vacant lot and side street, an emptiness that erases the communal aspects of mill town society and union drives, when organizers, coworkers, family members, and neighbors always gathered to hear the news.

Instead, Reuben asks Norma, "What are you gonna do now?" "Live, what else," she replies, declaring the end of her activism and allowing viewers to feel closure, buffered from any political-economic complexities. When Reuben offers to send her a Dylan Thomas book, she answers with a smile, "I bought one." His role as Pygmalion has come full circle: Norma gave up her aimless sexual liaisons, committed to an admirable goal, relied on him as a platonic mentor, bought a poetry book, and stayed in her marriage. The camera moves closer. He smiles and says, "Nobody can do anything for you," expressing his approval. But no kiss.

Norma looks at him and says solemnly, "You've done something for me. A lot."

"Well, you did something for us," he replies, referring to the union like it is separate from her, though organizers like Zivkovich and Crystal Lee always said the workers are the union.

The conversation ends *Norma Rae* on a personal note. "Thank you for your companionship, your stamina, horse sense, and a hundred and one laughs," Reuben says. "I also enjoyed looking at your skin, your hair, and your shining face." Their flirtation lingers.

Norma gives a big smile and replies, "Reuben, I think you like me."[94]

"Norma, what I've had from you has been sumptuous." They shake hands, and the mellow theme song plays as Reuben drives away in a packed dilapidated car. The final wide shot shows Norma at the end of the side street, small in front of the industrial mill. She stands alone, wrapped within a benign marriage and isolated from ongoing activism or even coworkers. She has reached self-actualization via a masculine white savior, achieving liberation without peers or community, while remaining contained and unthreatening. Viewers leave the theater uplifted by her stand and its triumphant outcome, knowing she stays safe with husband and children.

Despite this Hollywood refinement of the Crystal Lee life story, movies are not perfectly coherent texts. Different viewers might see potential for actions beyond what appears on-screen; others might bring their knowledge of unions or collective organizing to their interpretations of *Norma Rae*. Viewers might read Norma's individual rebelliousness in ways that draw them toward the complex political, sociological, and economic issues rather than away, and scenes of defiance might prompt a viewer to make changes within a household or look into unionizing. Although Norma remains contained in heteronormative marriage, she has hints of ambivalence, and a viewer might conclude that marriage seems imperfect or unfulfilling and imagine possible alternatives. For other viewers, the movie might be a portal that leads them to Crystal Lee and the deeper history.[95]

The press quickly found her, and Crystal Lee's interviews launched the construction of another entity, "the real Norma Rae." She cultivated and deployed this identification to her own purposes, using it to critique the movie, advocate for unions, present her ideas, and make claims against the revenues of Twentieth Century-Fox. It is uncertain how reporters learned about her, but Ritt's reaction makes clear he did not share the information. Most likely Kopple told press contacts about her November 1977 contract with Crystal Lee. The contestation had shifted terrain, from moviemaking to distribution, promotion, and sales, but Crystal Lee and Kopple remained in the field of cultural production and shifted tactics accordingly.

Eighteen months had passed since Ritt flew to North Carolina to try to woo Crystal Lee's compliance, and she no longer had the ability to influence the script or on-screen images. She could, however, jam the means of production by usurping media attention, disrupting the team's plans for a smooth release, and hampering the possibility of straightforward positive reviews. Crystal Lee was not simply complaining about differences in creative choices; her critique was her leverage in an industry dependent on ticket sales, reviews, and awards.

A national release of the movie moved these struggles into newspaper and magazine coverage of *Norma Rae*. While Twentieth Century-Fox, Ritt, and Field had great influence in these media, Crystal Lee had an opportunity to capitalize on the movie's success. She quickly took advantage of reporters' interest, which was critical, because as *Norma Rae* grew more popular and Field received more positive reviews, the media spotlight tilted away. The earliest articles centered the creative disagreements and contested legal rights, and Crystal Lee commented most about the narrative, not style or celebrity. She said to one reporter, "I wanted [the movie] to be about more than two people, because it took more than two people to win a campaign involving over 3,000 workers."[96] These criticisms were crucial to her creation of "the real Norma Rae."

Crystal Lee's descriptions of what happened with Rose & Asseyev and Ritt raised uncomfortable questions about creative responsibility and ethical culpability. They exposed Ritt's inability to resolve the inherent contradiction of his position as both a director interested in telling humanist stories of poor working Americans and a businessman in an industry that manages risk by avoiding complexities and repackaging the familiar in multimillion-dollar products. He reacted with defensiveness rather than apology, recognition, or payment. At different times, he justified the movie because producers had purchased the rights to Leifermann's biography; argued it was a fictionalized composite of several southern women; stated the film was not about the labor movement but about a woman's personal growth; or defended *Norma Rae* as a positive treatment of the labor movement. In a paradox, although Ritt's ego took a hit, box office sales most likely benefited from people thinking *Norma Rae* was actually a "true story." Even as the production team and studio stayed the course, deploying legal and financial instruments to maintain Crystal Lee's exclusion and deflect any obligation or liability, her experiences continued to serve their product.

A substantial *Los Angeles Times* article coincided with the release of *Norma Rae* in March. It provided a detailed description of the conflict over story and rights, presenting the situation primarily from Kopple's and Ritt's points of view, with a few lines from Crystal Lee and Alexander. It is not a flattering impression of Ritt, who argued the movie was a "fictionalized" version of Crystal Lee's story. The reporter describes Ritt as "embittered, even condescending toward his once-beloved subject." Although Kopple was moving ahead with a script approved by Crystal Lee, she told the reporter, "I think the film [*Norma Rae*] stands on its own, but I think the story of Crystal Lee has yet to be told." In the center of the article, editors set a close-up photo of Crystal Lee next to one of Norma talking to someone off-camera—the image with the UNION sign had not yet become the primary representation from the movie.[97]

Ritt did acknowledge that Leifermann and Rose & Asseyev had given Crystal Lee an "inequitable deal." He asserted, however, that when he came on as director, he knew Crystal Lee had signed the rights to Leifermann, so Twentieth Century-Fox had a legal right. Rose told the reporter she thought

Leifermann was going to split his payment with Crystal Lee, but Leifermann could not be located for comment and his representative at Sterling-Lord Agency hung up when questioned. The reporter notes that Crystal Lee refused invitations from Twentieth Century-Fox to attend a screening and applaud the film, still denying them her uncompensated acquiescent support. The only quotation in the article from Crystal Lee expresses concern that commercial movies exploit "the sexual aspect of life," when she wanted "to see a strong union film." She hoped Kopple's film would be a chance to get "the importance of the union struggle" out to people in the South.[98]

A couple weeks later, *People* ran the first use of "the real Norma Rae," in its headline for an article that centers Crystal Lee. The opening paragraph celebrates the movie, stating it is "one of the year's heartwarming Hollywood success stories." The reporter says *Norma Rae* is already getting enthusiastic reviews with calls for an Academy Award for Field, plus an impressive box office with $8 million gross in less than two months. The rest of the article contrasts this success with Crystal Lee's conditions, such as her trouble finding work and her current job as a motel maid. She confirms her commitment to unions and love of labor organizing, even though she acknowledges ACTWU representatives were cool toward her when she won reinstatement and back pay in 1978. The reporter also calls Ritt "bitter" about Crystal Lee's reaction to the movie and her plans for a project with Kopple. In both the *People* and the *Los Angeles Times* articles, Ritt is quoted calling Crystal Lee "a middle-class bourgeois woman who doesn't want anyone to know about her life."[99]

Ritt's willful disinterest in Crystal Lee's actual circumstances added cruelty to the defensiveness. Crystal Lee had been and remained open in multiple sources about her early relationships, the affair, and her unhappy marriage to Cookie. After such transparency, she said, it was dishonest to portray the TWUA organizer as a solitary man who had a sexual flirtation with Norma. To foreground activism over sensationalism, Crystal Lee told another reporter, "And remember, I didn't swim naked in no pond."[100] She knew opponents used sexuality and gossip to diminish the reputation of unions and the power of women activists. As an eminent creative professional and affluent businessman with tremendous economic and social capital, Ritt's deployment of class ideology to attack Crystal Lee is particularly revelatory. In this case, class functions as a cultural hammer rather than as an accurate marker of their income and wealth or their relationship to the means of production.

Feminist magazines including the liberal *Ms.* and radical *Off Our Backs* also raised questions about Ritt. *Ms.* ran an article, "'Norma Rae': The Story They Could Have Told," about the movie's divergence from Crystal Lee's experiences. The author applauds the depiction of Black workers, millhands, and a union but says the movie is "popcorn politics" and misleading. "Ritt and Company want to *use* Jordan's story rather than *tell* it," so Norma's motives "are trivialized, stemming only from sexual attraction that the noble Reuben resists and channels into activism." The reporter notes that without the context of union history and the industry, "Norma's character loses dimension. Ritt was left, then, with a sublimated love story, and the camera . . . gapes interminably at Sally Field's nipples, as they bob under her V-necked T-shirts."[101] The reporter was clearly unaware that Ritt, Frank, and Ravetch intentionally built the script around this sublimated love story to guarantee commercial success.

Ritt again responded with contradictory and defensive justifications. He even questioned Crystal Lee's activism, demeaning her while presenting himself as more politically conscious. "If [Jordan] is as interested in women and the working class as I am . . . she will see 'Norma Rae' as one of the singular films of our time," he said. "Besides, how many times can a girl turn you down? I went down to North Carolina and met with her lawyers. . . . I wanted to explain that [her demand for script control] was irrational. . . . I'm sorry I hurt her feelings, but I don't feel I did anything that was wrong."[102] Ritt was criticizing her challenge by equating it with sexual refusal and by categorizing her requests as driven by irrational or emotional femininity rather than political and creative motivation.

A reader's letter in *Off Our Backs* also emphasized the lack of realism and "truth" in the movie. She says she appreciated that *Norma Rae* is "a story about a woman, and her character is not succumbed to the development of male characters." Yet she found it lacking attention to the issues behind the J.P. Stevens campaign, the importance of Black workers, and conflicts with the husband. Without mentioning Crystal Lee by name, this reader agrees that the movie watered down working people's struggles, whitewashed the role of Black union members, and gave a false image of men.[103] Such commentary served Crystal Lee's development of "the real Norma Rae."

The media terrain changed as Field and her dramatic chops became the center of attention. The next string of articles fostered a perception of her as a serious professional and liberated woman, with the two often intertwined. The change is obvious in a new poster produced for the movie, which kept the tag line—"The story of a woman with the courage to risk everything for what she believes is right"—but removed the somber elements and centered a smiling Field on a plain white background. The pose does not appear in the movie, so the studio's marketing department mostly likely called Field for a photo shoot. In a bright celebratory shot, Norma stands on tippy-toes with arms uplifted, her tiny shirt revealing her belly button above her jeans.

Although the Academy Award season from January to April 1980 would revive media interest in Crystal Lee, coverage of Field would remain consistent throughout the 1980s.

The further refinement of the popular Crystal Lee life story into *Norma Rae* and eventually the Norma Rae icon depended on the expanding media frenzy around Field. The image of her as Norma became linked not only to the movie but also to her transformation from television cutie to dramatic film star. This association further removed *Norma Rae* from southern millhands and Crystal Lee, who were left behind when Field and Norma merged in the determined and liberated actress working her way to venerated success.

Many newspapers and magazines declared *Norma Rae* a women's lib film, often with a take similar to that of *Woman Alive!* and its celebration of individual women achieving personal transformation, without any complicated history of working-class women and feminism. The *New Leader* said the movie was "really a post–woman's lib love story" because a man of superior culture and education enlightens a downtrodden woman without having sex with her. It was "Cinderella with a truly liberating ending" as Norma is freed from her chains and from Reuben—notably missing the fact she is married with three children. In *Senior Scholastic*, a reviewer said *Norma Rae* was not a labor film but "the story of a woman learning that she can make her life count." A media scholar in *Cineaste* tempered her admiration for Norma's liberation with concern that Ritt made it dependent on a move toward "sexual purity."[104]

Writers who discussed women's liberation often knitted this interpretation to Field's elevation to serious actress. *Teen* said there were "great parallels between the fictional character and Sally herself."[105] The famous *New York Times* reviewer Vincent Canby said Norma had her consciousness raised in a platonic affair with Reuben. He liked that despite her flaws, Norma was capable of learning and growing, and he applauded Field for coming into her own as a serious actress. *MacLean's* announced that Field got tough and won, and European critics were congratulating her on portraying a young woman who "discovers her social conscience in the labor struggle."[106] Kenneth Turan, a nationally syndicated reviewer, wrote that Field's Norma "is that most unusual of screen personae, someone who matures and changes before our eyes in a way that is neither cute nor forced." He said her performance was the one superb asset of *Norma Rae* and proved Field had forcefulness.[107] Even years later, a 2002 book about women in Hollywood said, "*Norma Rae* liberated Field from the flying nun and from television."[108]

Most journalists emphasized *Norma Rae* as a decisive pivot for Field's career. Canby said the movie provided Field "with the plum role of her career, an opportunity to demonstrate once and for all that she is an actress of dramatic intelligence and force." In a longer piece a few days later, Canby argued that Field's Norma "represents a number of triumphs," especially her own performance. He described it as "the kind of complete performance one associates with theatrical films. . . . There's nothing held back here, no reserve of the public personality . . . one of the more common problems when television personalities switch to films."[109] The reporter for *Teen* declared Norma the vehicle for Field's "personal and professional achievements," and *MacLean's* said "*Norma Rae* was her lifesaver."[110]

Field, like Ritt, contended the movie was not political but about a woman and "her immediate environment." They each insisted "the character of the woman," not the labor movement, was the impetus, and Field said she did not base her performance on Crystal Lee but on how she related to Norma as a "small-town woman."[111] Field and the character of Norma rarely received criticism in the mainstream press, but several reviewers did take issue with Reuben's solitary and "unassailable" presence, his Pygmalion role, and the lack of attention to the number of millhands and organizers needed for a union vote. Some pieces even noted that the ending was like a "fairy tale" and ignored the procedures and negotiations that must continue after a vote. The most common complaint, however, involved Ritt and his habit of pushing messages right to the surface, with a simplistic and naïve liberalism that harked back to 1940s films. Turan said Ritt was "an old hand at this kind of movie-making," and though his sentiments were sincere, there was a "paint-by-the-numbers approach."[112]

Cineaste was the first outlet to use the photo of Field/Norma with the UNION sign as the primary representation from the movie, and it appeared in *International Musician* a month later.[113] The earliest germination of the Norma Rae icon comes into view with these May and June 1979 publications. The photo was a wide shot that included the industrial scenery, yet she stands alone. The image allowed public audiences—unexpected and unanticipated by Crystal Lee—to conceive of the stand with the UNION sign as a front-stage performance by Field/Norma rather than as a communal backstage gesture by a millhand with fellow union members, coworkers, and neighbors. Readers could see one self-possessed person, Field defying those who wanted to typecast her, which then transformed the act from a vernacular, unifying signal between coworkers aware of decades of activism into a highly individualistic iconic performance of rebellion.[114]

When awards season arrived in January 1980, Field had done dozens of interviews and the studio had promoted her through Oscar advertisements placed in trade magazines including the *Hollywood Reporter* and *Variety*. Field won more prizes in a year than any other American actress at that time, with Best Actress awards from the National Society of Film Critics, New York Film Critics, National Board of Review, Los Angeles Film Critics, Golden

Globe organization, and Cannes Film Festival, where the movie got a standing ovation.[115] Field then won the Academy Award in April, beating Jill Clayburgh in *Starting Over*, Jane Fonda in *The China Syndrome*, Marsha Mason in *Chapter Two*, and Bette Midler in *The Rose*.

Norma Rae and the awards elevated Field's career to the highest echelon of the movie industry, which opened the way for her to ask for hundreds of thousands of dollars above union scale while keeping the protection of SAG. The production and its massive commercial success also bonded Ritt and Field, and she sent him an effusive thank-you note. Sounding like Norma, she wrote, "Dear Marty, Thank you for believing in me. Thank you for teaching me. Thank you for appreciating me, as an actress, and a person."[116] In multiple interviews, Field expressed disappointment that Ritt had not been nominated for an Academy Award and told a reporter that she had to talk Ritt into attending the ceremony. It upset her that Crystal Lee had not acknowledged "her debt to Ritt." She told a reporter, "It's a shame it hasn't occurred to her that she can thank Marty Ritt for much of the recognition she's receiving," disregarding that Crystal Lee's activism and previous media participation had made Ritt's and Field's recognition possible.[117]

Leifermann also attempted to capitalize on the movie by publishing a 1980 essay with an Atlanta magazine. For the photo, he lounged in jeans and boots by an in-ground pool, with his *Crystal Lee* book and a can of beer next to his legs. Leifermann presented himself as an advocate for the working class and portrayed Crystal Lee as an innocent who was used by the union, Zivkovich, Kopple, and the *Norma Rae* producers. He blamed her for the fact that his name and book title were removed from the movie, which cost him the large payment he would have split with her. He also mentioned a couple of book ideas he was working on.[118]

The movie development from "Crystal Lee" to *Norma Rae* is not a straightforward tale of exploiting a poor woman to make the inevitable film. Differences over the script played out in the capitalist system of Hollywood production, and elite creative professionals brought its mechanisms to bear on Crystal Lee. But she refused to capitulate, because she had ideas about how to represent working-class people. She recognized the cultural stakes and used the leverage at her disposal to demand a role in the production as a creative contributor who had provided value and assets to the movie—her experiences, her "life story." Although Crystal Lee did not succeed in this round, her resistance and claims continued.

The ultimate script, locations, and movie costumes were not reflexive reproductions of stereotypes either. Rose, Asseyev, Ritt, and Field all wanted a major commercial success so they could advance in the industry. They read Leifermann's biography and they knew Crystal Lee's contentions, but the team recognized that a white woman underdog hero on a personal journey infused with heterosexual desire would attract the biggest audience. Ritt also understood the fascination with the South and enhanced the Opelika mill, the locals, and the clothing to appeal to it.

These capitalist maneuvers and creative business choices for the highest return on investment had consequences beyond the loss of Crystal Lee's vision, because they served a particular notion of industrial workers and its meanings for the American working class. But the contests in the field of cultural production carried on. Crystal Lee, Zivkovich, and Kopple persevered in their efforts to produce and exhibit their versions and challenged the asymmetrical power of Twentieth Century-Fox and Ritt. Their efforts did not stop *Norma Rae*, but they changed its trajectory. At the same time, Gloria Maldonado and Puerto Rican needleworkers were joining a public history project about their jobs and stories. *Norma Rae* dominated popular culture representations of industrial working women, but "Nosotras Trabajamos en la Costura" offered another narrative for the American working class, one in which women of color worked and migrated as part of a US colonial labor force and organized in a vibrant union movement.

PART III

CHAPTER FIVE

Norma Rae Stands Alone

Eliminating Alternatives

I'm not concerned that people know about my personal life,
but I wanted people to see a strong union film. I'd hoped
Leiferman's book would get the point across and it didn't. And
I thought Barbara's film would offer just one more chance to get
the importance of the union struggle across to the people.

—Crystal Lee Sutton

Thousands of listeners who tuned in to New York public radio in 1987 heard Gloria Maldonado's words quoted in an audio documentary about Puerto Rican needleworkers. She had done three oral history interviews in 1984 and 1985, sharing experiences from the factories, ILGWU, Central Labor Council, and Rutgers University Labor Center. Maldonado had also expounded on the difficult global conditions impacting women workers in textiles and apparel. Scholar Rina Benmayor produced the radio segment as part of a bilingual public history project, "Nosotras Trabajamos en la Costura." A few days after it aired, however, a friend called Maldonado to let her know some ILGWU members were upset because they thought she had said she was the only Puerto Rican in leadership. Their reaction worried Maldonado because she knew trust and solidarity were hard to build, so she called Benmayor to question the use of her words.[1]

Benmayor developed "Nosotras Trabajamos" to center needleworkers like Maldonado in new studies of the Puerto Rican diaspora and to share their stories as women in a collective history of colonial currents, communities, and labor activism. During the 1970s, Benmayor played an active role in establishing El Centro de Estudios Puertorriqueños at Hunter College–CUNY, or Centro. Its mission was to promote the study of the diaspora and experiences that connected the island and mainland.[2] At "the intersections of scholarship and activism," Centro set out to reclaim community histories, counteract reductionist or derogatory writing about Puerto Ricans, and develop innovative modes of analysis including a theoretical approach to migration.[3] "Nosotras Trabajamos" grew from this ambition, and the women scholars and needleworkers intended it as an alternative cultural production. They created it to puncture mainstream representation of Puerto Rican women and complicate meanings for the American working class, even if "Nosotras Trabajamos" could not saturate popular culture the same way as Norma Rae.

Although "Nosotras Trabajamos" did not have the capacity to compete with Norma Rae for national attention, a feature film by Barbara Kopple did have potential. In the early 1980s, wielding her 1976 Academy Award, progressive filmmaker bona fides, and connections with Hollywood distribution companies, Kopple continued to pursue her "Crystal Lee" project. A movie about the TWUA drive with Kopple's name attached had the possibility to reach a broad audience and shift popular conversation. Her previous creative choices indicated a likelihood her film would push against Norma Rae's narratives of the circumscribed white American working class and personal individualist rebellion.

The ease and extent of Norma Rae's popular triumph depended on the outcome of these contests within and between related fields of cultural production. The exceptional dominance of Norma Rae and the generation of a potent icon were not guaranteed—Kopple's alternative production had to be eliminated. Once again, elite Hollywood professionals collaborated with union leadership, but they modified their strategy with Crystal Lee.

The partnership between Twentieth Century-Fox and ACTWU leaders exposes how elites in national unions have multiple and incongruous alliances. Struggles over media production play out across these overlapping hierarchies of class and status, which conduct the access to and use of power.[4] Leaders such as Sol Stetin identified as "union men," with a commitment to the working class and its right to fair wages, yet they were also elites with income, wealth, and status above their institutional class alliance. Stetin viewed executives at Twentieth Century-Fox as peers and threw the ACTWU behind their movie, a decision that seemed like it would enhance the union's capital. However, giving unconditional support to Norma Rae and the individualist hero narrative worked to undermine the union's public significance and mainstream acknowledgment of its organizing.

Crystal Lee and Sally Field each sought to capitalize on the movie's cultural dominance as well. Crystal Lee marketed herself as "the real Norma Rae" for public speaking and sued the studio. When opportunities to make money as "the real Norma Rae" dwindled, she was again forced to pursue low-wage service jobs. The person who benefited most was Field. In the 1980s and '90s, she starred in blockbusters such as Places in the Heart (1984), Steel Magnolias (1989), Soapdish (1991), and Mrs. Doubtfire (1993) and did dozens of interviews and magazine covers. Norma Rae elevated her to the most exclusive echelon of actors, with the highest income and culture business clout.

Without national competition from a comparable story of the TWUA campaign and Crystal Lee, *Norma Rae* had the space to circulate in many venues and forms, further and further detaching from the longer industrial history and even from the overall context of work. In the 1980s and '90s, the Norma Rae icon emerged through repeated use, across diverse media, of the image of Field with the UNION sign and variations of the phrase "having a Norma Rae moment" or "going Norma Rae."

A facile perspective on Hollywood studios (i.e., *Of course they make what they make, since studios have an unambiguous drive to produce predetermined blockbusters*) misses the fights that occur throughout development, filming, distribution, and circulation.[5] Although capital plays a formidable role in every contest in the arena of cultural politics, Crystal Lee continued to push against and utilize *Norma Rae*, and Maldonado joined Puerto Rican needleworkers and scholars in an alternative production to articulate their version of the American working class.

In March 1979, when *Norma Rae* hit theaters, the ACTWU was sixteen years into a national campaign with J.P. Stevens that had stalled at contract negotiations for five years. Union leaders were overseeing a range of tactics: the southern membership drive, NLRB and EEOC grievances, and civil rights lawsuits. They also wrote policy, lobbied state and federal offices, and testified at congressional hearings about domestic employment, imports, and anti-union activities. In 1976, the ACTWU had launched a consumer boycott to support the contract negotiations and ramped up outreach to activist and student groups. It added a "corporate campaign" in 1977 to pressure J.P. Stevens's financial partners, from investment banks and insurance corporations to the board of directors.

The 1977–80 ACTWU corporate campaign fused financial tactics developed by civil rights, anti–Vietnam War, antiapartheid, and labor activists, who had swapped how-to pamphlets during the 1960s.[6] Ray Rogers, a boycott strategist, adapted the practices because J.P. Stevens sold few products direct to consumers and marketed products under many brands. A boycott was difficult to maintain. Rogers recognized that financial tactics provided a means to leverage J.P. Stevens's relationships with major investors, corporate directors, banks, and insurance companies.[7]

In 1977, Rogers started with conventional shareholder activism. He coordinated more than 600 individuals and organizations to purchase a share of J.P. Stevens stock and scheduled dozens of people to attend the shareholder meeting or allow proxies. Beyond this, Rogers targeted board members and corporate allies. ACTWU staff investigated the largest stakeholders, corporations and banks, such as Metropolitan Life Insurance, which had interlocking directorships and multimillion-dollar loans. The union sent letters to the executives and rallied outside their offices to demand that they "restrict the availability of financial or credit accommodations," because J.P. Stevens was not bargaining in good faith. This pressure triggered the resignation of corporate officers from the boards of Manufacturers Hanover Trust (the fourth largest US bank at the time), New York Life Insurance, and J.P. Stevens.[8]

While achieving success with this corporate campaign, the ACTWU helped promote *Norma Rae* and block Kopple. Leadership decided the movie was a boon, without questioning the possible consequences of a simplistic story set in an imagined nostalgic South. They did not offer countervailing, or even complementary, imagery or use the movie to spark wider discussions of global manufacturing, trade, and interracial domestic employment. This decision to completely hitch onto *Norma Rae* and its popular image of one woman's rebellious triumph sacrificed collective history and identity for a narrative of personal defiance. But as far as national leadership was concerned, the ancillary mainstream interest was satisfactory. They helped *Norma Rae* stand alone.

Stetin and other leaders arranged showings for labor audiences and sometimes synchronized with Twentieth Century-Fox. Anne Rivera from ACTWU's publicity department and its monthly magazine, *Labor Unity*, requested material from the studio's national coordinator of marketing for an April 1979 issue dedicated to *Norma Rae*. In one article, a union representative said, "As far as the ACTWU is concerned, 'Norma Rae' could not have been any more effective if they had produced it themselves." The reporter did note that a few unionists complained about the happy ending, which made it appear as if the certification vote corrected all the wrongs when it merely moved the process one step forward. ACTWU headquarters, however, sent director Martin Ritt a thank-you note, and the AFL-CIO gave him an award.[9]

ACTWU leaders invested more than indirect promotional support. They joined Twentieth Century-Fox to eliminate Kopple's alternative production, even though she had honed her techniques for representing intricate histories, efforts, and identities with the prolabor *Harlan County, USA*. ACTWU leaders did not want Kopple to make her "Crystal Lee" movie.[10]

Since November 1977, Kopple had hired Stuart Werban and Todd Merer to work on the feature film screenplay. They developed a "Crystal Lee" script that depicts the complications of organizing hundreds of workers and foregrounds the civil rights labor activism that sparked the successes in Roanoke Rapids. It exemplifies Kopple's technique for engaging labor history and displaying coordinated activism, just as Crystal Lee had hoped. The union drive appears as a collective effort to address the historic exploitation of millhands and as a vulnerable interracial alliance of committed workers. Kopple does not avoid the tensions inherent to any endeavor with so many people and so much at stake, but the workers persist.

Her 1979 screenplay does not start with Crystal Lee but with the character of Eli Zivkovich speaking at a Black church to an African American audience, rallying them to become TWUA members. The next scene cuts to the union's motel headquarters, where Zivkovich talks with Margaret Banks about Roanoke Rapids and the history of southern mills. In the third scene, three African American men, Joseph, Lester, and Jessie Williams, arrive at the motel room to give Zivkovich sixty signed cards and join the organizing efforts.[11]

The Crystal Lee character does not appear until the seventh scene, after the TWUA drive has launched and Zivkovich has received steady support from several Black workers and inspected all the mill bulletin boards. Crystal Lee and Cookie sit at home, discussing household bills, but when her oldest son offers to get a job, she says she will not let him go into the mills. Scene 8 follows Joseph Williams as he hands out TWUA pamphlets and cards, and scene 9 shows women at the mill doctor seeking treatment for nerves and hearing.

Crystal Lee's first interaction with the union comes in the tenth scene, when she walks away from her conveyor belt and folding station to view the bulletin board. She stands with a Black woman reading the J.P. Stevens apology letter required by the NLRB and a notification for another meeting at the Black church. When Crystal Lee mentions the TWUA to her sister, Syretha says, "That Union meeting is at a n—— church. No whites are gonna go there."[12]

The remainder of the screenplay closely follows the events from 1973 to 1974 and includes the conflicts at the motel about Crystal Lee and the arguments between her and Cookie. One of the last scenes shows Zivkovich and Crystal Lee driving to Joseph Williams's house to say goodbye in late spring 1974, after they each quit their organizing jobs—Zivkovich because of disagreements with leadership and Crystal Lee because of her deteriorating marriage. An on-screen paragraph notes that the TWUA wins the certification vote but still has to cope with multiple grievances for worker reinstatements and years of antagonistic contract negotiations. In the final scene, Crystal Lee enters the J.P. Stevens mill in 1978 to accept her reinstatement and back pay before quitting two days later to return to Burlington.[13]

In the fall of 1979, executives at Twentieth Century-Fox got a copy of Kopple's screenplay and sent one to ACTWU leaders, who expressed criticism among themselves and to the studio. They saw it as a negative portrayal rather than a complicated and interesting one. In the union's defensive opinion, the script focused on "inter-staff rivalries and animosities rather than basic issues. It portrays some staff as heroes and others as incompetent and disloyal. . . . The script is largely personalities with vendettas against others."[14] Stetin tried to persuade Kopple to revise the script, and when he failed to do so, he decided to cooperate with the studio executives to derail her. For different reasons, the studio and union each wanted to block her nuanced representation of a fraught but successful union drive, with a main character who goes through the collapse of a marriage and long wait for reinstatement.[15]

Twentieth Century-Fox and the ACTWU agreed they needed to drive a wedge between the two women, because Kopple was pitching her project to investors and donors as the one approved by Crystal Lee. In December 1979, while Kopple was talking to actors and researching locations, Twentieth Century-Fox executives again turned to capitalist mechanisms, drawing up a new contract for Crystal Lee. Two years after eliminating her from its production and changing the title to "Norma Rae," the studio reached out to Crystal Lee, Zivkovich, and Cookie to garner their cooperation. The contract offered to *jointly* pay the "principals of the story line of 'Norma Rae'" an initial $70,000, with the possibility of two more staggered payments of $35,000 if the movie earned net profits of $1 million and $2 million. A fourth payment of $30,000 was possible if the movie reached $3 million.[16]

The final April 1980 contract promised additional money if a *Norma Rae* television series was produced, and NBC had already paid for the television option and approved the budget for a one-hour pilot. Producers pitched the series as a "sequential television project" that focused on Norma's "struggles to fight a reputation as a free-living and unconventional woman in her small, industrial Southern town." In the pilot, the father of one son attempts to take custody by claiming this fictional Norma had an affair with an eighteen-year-old Black mill worker.[17] Although many pilots do not lead to a series, the possibility of more episodes held out the lure of more money: if a network picked it up, the three principals would receive $450 for each thirty-minute episode, $825 for each episode longer than thirty minutes, and $1,300 for each episode over ninety minutes.[18]

This Twentieth Century-Fox contract, however, was contingent on Crystal Lee's, Zivkovich's, and Cookie's ability to "break the assignment of their rights in an exclusive contract to Kopple." It was not simply a matter of interfering in Kopple's creative process; studio executives hoped this would "mess up" her $750,000 National Endowment for the Humanities grant and halt production.[19] ACTWU leaders were on board and said Kopple's script was "nonsense" and had the potential to damage the campaign. They did not want a movie that represented unsettling complications, like internal TWUA politics or years of conflict over employee reinstatements. Stetin and Harold McIver asked labor colleagues to persuade Crystal Lee that the *Norma Rae* movie was having positive results, and some friends called her to say it was bringing good publicity to unions despite its deficiencies. After numerous calls from studio executives and friends, Crystal Lee decided to rescind her approval of Kopple's script. Zivkovich, who continued to support Kopple, called to see what had happened, but Crystal Lee did not respond.[20]

As an interlocking tactic, the ACTWU hired Crystal Lee to do a speaking tour with radio and television interviews and lectures at union events and universities including Harvard, Columbia, and UCLA. The goal was to reinforce union support for *Norma Rae* and solidify Crystal Lee's split from Kopple, and it included a public relations specialist, Gail Jeffords. Jeffords contacted reporters ahead of time to try to agree on a set of prepared questions and advised Crystal Lee on making statements that avoided movie criticism and promoted the ACTWU. The entire tour was carefully planned to help eliminate Kopple's version, constrain Crystal Lee's critiques, celebrate *Norma Rae*, and garner media attention for the ACTWU. To document her effectiveness, Jeffords compiled reports with details about the radio and television stations, excerpts from interviews, and clips of local newspaper coverage.[21] The tour was a success that brought more audiences to the movie, deterred investors from Kopple, and helped *Norma Rae* to stand alone.

Despite public relations coaching, Crystal Lee remained noncompliant and shared her own ideas, criticizing the film's lack of attention to workers as a whole and to the systemic exploitation by mills. She told one photographer who asked her to smile, "I'm not an actress. I don't put on airs to have my picture taken."[22] But she usually added that she appreciated the movie's educational value. At a benefit showing in Ohio, Crystal Lee told the audience, "If that movie taught one person what a union is, it was well worth it," noting that even with its faults, it was the best prolabor motion picture ever made.[23]

The tour also revealed that Crystal Lee had adjusted her gendered class identity to challenge prejudice in a different way. In Boston, she said to a reporter, "I'm a woman. Not a lady. A woman."[24] Seven years after telling the Roanoke Rapids police to treat her like a lady—an industrial woman worker demanding respect through classed femininity—Crystal Lee had reframed her identity based on women's liberation. Her interactions with *Ms.*, Steinem, and Kopple had changed her sense of self and her idea about how to best assert her dignity as a working-class woman.

In March 1980, Crystal Lee and Field met briefly for the one and only time. The powerful SAG union arranged a benefit at the Berwin Entertainment Complex in Los Angeles to support the J.P. Stevens boycott, and Field agreed to make a quick appearance. It was an arranged photo opportunity to associate Crystal Lee, the J.P. Stevens campaign, Field, and *Norma Rae*. Despite Ritt's and Field's repeated statements that the film was not about Crystal Lee, and their insistence that it used a composite of women to tell a woman's

Sally Field and Crystal Lee make an appearance for the cameras at the 1980 SAG event in Los Angeles to benefit the ACTWU campaign against J.P. Stevens. | Bettmann Collection, Getty Images

story, not a labor story—Field stood with Crystal Lee at a union rally.[25] She shared a few words, grabbed Crystal Lee's hand, and raised it overhead in a familiar gesture of solidarity that did not extend beyond the SAG-ACTWU event. Ritt and Field continued to insist the movie was not about Crystal Lee, contradicting the 1976 purchase of film rights, the studio's 1980 offer to the "principals of the story line," and this photo.[26] Just a month later, when Field accepted her Academy Award, the solidarity was gone.

Prior to the ceremony, Crystal Lee's only concern about Field was her distracting relationship with Burt Reynolds. "She portrayed me well," Crystal Lee said, "but I wish they had cast an unknown actress—someone who wasn't known for being Burt Reynolds's girlfriend." In most statements about *Norma Rae*, Crystal Lee described Field as an entertaining actress. She argued the movie focused too much on one woman and created an erroneous, misleading sexual tension with the labor organizer, but she liked Field's depiction. Field's speech at the Academy Awards, however, truly disappointed Crystal Lee. Field said *Norma Rae* was "a gift given" to her by Alan Ladd Jr. and Twentieth Century-Fox, Alexandra Rose and Tamara Asseyev, Irving Ravetch and Harriet Frank Jr., the other actors, and, mostly, Ritt. "Marty Ritt is Norma Rae," Field said. "He has fought all his life to put on films that are courageous . . . that have the box office potential of seventy-five cents." She conflated an affluent white man and elite creative professional who owned a production company with a poor rural working woman because they were each defiant.

Crystal Lee had hoped for a comment on the labor movement, the union, or at least the mill workers. She told a reporter, "[Field] deserved that award but she could have talked about the union or the boycott or the workers who made it possible for her to get that award. I don't see how she could have forgotten to say something in front of a million people. She didn't take the chance to help when she could."[27] Years after her experience with the movie development, Crystal Lee remained committed to these ongoing contests in the field of cultural production and advocated for the millhands who were the raw material for Norma Rae.

As part of her tour, Crystal Lee also participated in a July 1980 march into Sperry Corporation's annual meeting. Seven hundred demonstrators, including public figures like Michael Harrington, held the floor for hours because the CEO served on the J.P. Stevens board. These events were having an effect. In the fall of 1979, the chairman of Seaman's Bank reached out and said he wanted to facilitate meaningful negotiations. After the Sperry demonstration, more executives became involved, and it all came to a conclusion in October 1980. The cumulative seventeen-year union effort—including six years of contract negotiations, five years of a consumer boycott, and three years of a corporate campaign—finally coerced J.P. Stevens to sign a fair contract. It included a retroactive pay raise, seniority protection, a check-off provision for union dues to be directly deducted from workers' paychecks, and a grievance procedure with independent arbitration. In return, the ACTWU agreed to end the corporate campaign.[28]

But when the ACTWU finally signed this contract, many mainstream articles ignored the years of labor activism and gave Norma Rae the credit.[29] Although the movie had amplified the attention, when asked what prompted the contract, J.P. Stevens's vice president of corporate and industrial relations said the corporate campaign was the tactic that finally forced executives into fair negotiations. He said the NLRB litigation, EEOC grievances, and boycott tapped company resources but had less effect than disrupting J.P. Stevens's access to millions of dollars in investment and credit.[30] He did not mention Norma Rae.

Throughout these months, Kopple remained in the arena of cultural politics, pursuing possible ways to produce her story, her imagining of the TWUA drive. Despite their split, Kopple continued with her movie project because Crystal Lee had granted initial script approval and Kopple had raised some money and scouted locations. She started to cast in early 1981, which vexed the Twentieth Century-Fox executives. They advised Stetin to talk to an entertainment lawyer about "possible controls which could be exercised by Crystal," particularly finding a legal means to terminate her contract assigning rights to Kopple.[31]

These maneuvers had their anticipated effect. The business rift with Crystal Lee and subsequent lack of major investors forced Kopple to fictionalize the script, reduce the scope of her project, focus on two Black workers as the leads, and change the title to "Keeping On." In 1982, PBS helped produce it as a seventy-five-minute episode for the series *American Playhouse*; it aired in 1983 with an impressive cast that included the respected theater actors Trazana Beverley, James Broderick, Danny Glover, and Carol Kane. Kopple sent a printed announcement to Crystal Lee with a warm handwritten greeting. "Keeping On," however, did not garner a large audience, positive reviews, or media attention. Even Zivkovich found it missed the mark and "lacked sparkle" despite Kopple's good intentions.[32]

Successful Hollywood movies involve more than the immediate theater distribution and ticket sales. They spark further circulation, exchange, and reproduction—which means people associated with the film can accrue more social capital and status and discover more opportunities for economic capital. It can be an upward spiral. Although she did not use such scholarly terms, Crystal Lee recognized the potential for capitalizing on her association with *Norma Rae* and filed a suit against Twentieth Century-Fox with a petition for revenues that garnered $52,000.[33] She also parlayed it into opportunities for travel and professional development, similar to what Maldonado had pursued in the 1970s. These activities expanded her outlook while strengthening bonds with the labor movement.

The paid tour covered travel to multiple cities and time with leaders and organizers from a variety of unions and fields. When the tour ended, Crystal Lee went a step further and launched her own public-speaking venture, promoting herself as "the real Norma Rae." She did not give blanket praise or mimic the movie. The business was a strategic decision to deploy the famous name as a means to reclaim her life experiences, raise her own profile as a labor activist, and earn income for her expertise as a worker and union organizer. She bent the movie's distribution and success to her purposes. Richard Koritz, a postal union representative she met at a labor event in Boston, helped her design a brochure. It led to more travel, including invitations from the national Coalition of Labor Union Women for parades and conferences.[34]

Several regional colleges, including Muskegon Community College in Michigan, invited her to speak, and the Quad Cities Peace and Justice Coalition of Davenport, Iowa, gave her its Peace and Freedom Award. However,

Crystal Lee speaks at an unnamed labor event in 1996. | Crystal Lee Sutton Collection, Alamance Community College, Graham, NC

when Crystal Lee attempted to directly affiliate with the movie, requesting a 35 mm print to show at her 1984 speaking events, Twentieth Century-Fox staff decided it was "not feasible." The studio still enforced her financial and legal exclusion from the *Norma Rae* product.[35] This did not stop Crystal Lee from following other opportunities. An international affairs representative for a Soviet trade union invited her and Koritz to attend a 1984 youth symposium in Moscow. Koritz went with Crystal Lee to get a visa and make travel plans for the USSR, where they toured textile and garment factories and served as delegates at the symposium, sponsored by the Textile and Light Industry Workers' Union. Crystal Lee saw that workers in Soviet factories had day care, medical care, and vocational training.[36]

After four years, Crystal Lee's ability to capitalize on *Norma Rae* contracted as Field's expanded. In 1985, when Crystal Lee sent out 250 "the real Norma Rae" brochures, she received only three bookings. The *Norma Rae* television series was not picked up, and the 1980 payment from Twentieth Century-Fox had gone to expenses, loans, and a used car for her husband. The couple was living off Preston's job, where he earned six dollars an hour in the shipping department at the unionized Cone Mills plant in Haw River, near where Crystal Lee had taken her first job. As her gigs dwindled, she was forced to return to low-wage work. She inspected women's garments in a nonunion mill for about a year in 1984, took orders at a drive-up film and photo booth in 1985, and worked as a guard for Burns Security in 1986, but the jobs did not last. Crystal Lee was laid off from the nonunion mill just before Christmas and heard the supervisor hired other women, but he would not give her another job. Like Lucy Sledge, she believed that as soon as managers recognized her or heard gossip about her union organizing, they got her out.[37]

Crystal Lee tried to balance the local hardship of notoriety with the benefits of a larger public platform. She made another demand on Twentieth Century-Fox in the field of cultural production. When executives no longer responded to her letters, she filed a second lawsuit in 1985 for invasion of privacy and said movie people were in "their own world" and "forget."[38] The studio settled and required a confidentiality clause—even her adult children were not aware of the details—but Crystal Lee received enough remuneration to finalize the purchase of her small house and pay bills. When speaking opportunities came, including a trip to join Ray Rogers at a 1987 demonstration with American Airlines flight attendants, she still requested travel reimbursement and payment. In need of steadier income, she enrolled in a nurse's aide certification program at Alamance Community College in 1988 but did not like the physical strain. Instead she opened a day care in her house, where photos of Martin Luther King Jr. and Nelson Mandela hung on the playroom walls until she closed it in 1994.[39]

She remained strategic about the media and her role as a labor activist. Her lawyer John McCormick monitored regular accounting statements from Twentieth Century-Fox regarding her and Zivkovich's participation percentage based on the 1980 contract. In 2001, when he requested $17,500 owed to Zivkovich, the studio said it was changing its accounting practices to include interest in the annual film costs, which would total $4 million and cause a net loss and end any payment owed. Crystal Lee retained another attorney, Alan McSurely, who litigated a $75,000 settlement for her if she signed an agreement releasing Twentieth Century-Fox from all claims based on that April 1980 contract. When the producer for GB Productions sent Crystal Lee a letter about obtaining the rights to make a musical based on her life and *Norma Rae*, she gave him lawyer Sydenham Alexander's number.[40]

Crystal Lee did speak to journalists but first asked about the purpose of their article or segment and who might see it. She talked with union leaders requesting campaign endorsements or attendance. If working people called for advice about bosses or steps to organizing, Crystal Lee always answered. She offered guidance about methods to get coworkers to sign membership cards or write affidavits for the NLRB, but she did not work again as a paid union employee.[41]

While Kopple had to shrink her project and Crystal Lee worked hard to contest and capitalize on *Norma Rae*, Maldonado joined Puerto Rican needleworkers and Centro scholars in their cultural production about the American working class. Very few products achieve *Norma Rae*'s level of accessibility and dominance, but all endeavors—especially those that create both temporary mainstream media and more permanent collections—inject wonderings, sounds, stories, images, and examples into the arena and modify it to some degree.

In 1973, Benmayor was one of several scholar-activists, community leaders, and students determined to establish a Puerto Rican Studies Program and El Centro, a repository for collections related to the diaspora.[42] Once they had an institutional base at Hunter College–CUNY, she and her colleagues submitted applications to the National Endowment for the Humanities, Ford Foundation, and New York Council for the Humanities for a sweeping project, Puerto Ricans in New York: Voices of the Migration. It built on fifteen years of research, and Benmayor spearheaded the Oral History Task Force.[43] The public and philanthropic funding allowed for the retrieval of primary sources and three years of interviews with pioneros, garment workers, and community leaders.[44]

From 1981 to 1982, Benmayor developed a public history project dedicated to the migration, labor, and activism of Puerto Rican needleworkers. She wanted as many interviews as possible, and proposed a media collage titled "Nosotras Trabajamos en la Costura" with public exhibits and a radio program. Benmayor, Celia Alvarez, and Blanca Vázquez, all needleworkers' daughters, conducted interviews in 1984 and 1985. Alvarez articulated the significance of these voices and Puerto Rican working women as a group. "In the collective space we created, we have publicly been able to validate ourselves, learn from each other and gain strength in our struggle to fulfill our human potential," she wrote. "In moving beyond our own individual lives we can come to appreciate the connections between us, the continuity and the change, and dispel fears which keep us apart."[45] It celebrated the women and their communities of work, migration, and labor organizing.

Maldonado also emphasized the importance of sharing this collective history. She was not just enjoying the attention or telling a personal story; she was offering political education and making sure future generations knew about the struggle. For Maldonado, it was utterly intersectional: the labor union fight as a woman working in an industrial manufacturing job caught in the tensions of global trade and her Puerto Rican identity were all bound together. She said most Puerto Rican needleworkers vowed their daughters would not go through what they had to endure, but she also said, "Our coming generations like my grandchildren and their children, we have to instill in them the pride of being a Puerto Rican and not to lose it. And that's what we're here about."[46] Her work, the union, her family, and the needleworkers' legacy were intertwined.

Maldonado spoke with all three scholars in August 1984 and February 1985 and discussed her jobs, labor activism, and issues of solidarity, organizing, trade, quotas, migration and immigration, and global exploitation. She explained ILGWU roles: organizers who recruit members, colonizers who infiltrate nonunion shops, and business agents who handle member issues with management. She celebrated labor history, including the Wagner Act and the ILGWU in the 1930s and '40s, and mentioned "other elements" that interfered with organizers, even threatening their families, if they tried to get into a shop used by the mafia.[47]

The transcripts of interviews with Maldonado, Louise Delgado, Eva Monje, and others share facets of their work, overlapping concerns, and nuanced details in similar anecdotes about generations of Puerto Rican women in textiles and apparel. They do more than having provided content for the "Nosotras Trabajamos" media collage. The women's involvement, appearances, and enduring presence in the archive, with easy availability at a public university, altered the arena of cultural politics and provided the foundation for and substance of this history and its interventions. Maldonado recognized that possibility.

In September 1984, Benmayor and Centro sent out posters promoting the initial events: a running slide show with narration, a photography display, and a bilingual panel with needleworkers. Benmayor, Alvarez, and several needleworkers also presented a workshop on oral history, "Interviewing Ladies Who Worked in the Garment Industry," again deploying the term "ladies" to claim dignity and respect for working-class women rather than to signal middle-class aspiration.[48] The events were participatory and transitory but also partially recorded for the archive.

Within the arena of cultural politics, the radio documentary "Nosotras Trabajamos" had its own field of production, where scholars, funders, university staff and administration, and needleworkers interacted, contesting their access to capital, the production, and its results. The investment stakes were lower than a Hollywood movie's because it was not a multimillion-dollar commercial product expected to return the biggest sales possible. As with *Woman Alive!*, however, the nonprofit institutions, philanthropic agencies, and universities funding "Nosotras Trabajamos" also had interests driven by quantifiable outcomes and financial expectations. The radio documentary was also the project's most refined and far-reaching cultural product. Benmayor, Alvarez, and Vázquez wrote English and Spanish scripts that brought women's shared stories together with scholarly research and theorizing about colonial migration. After weeks of writing, Benmayor worked

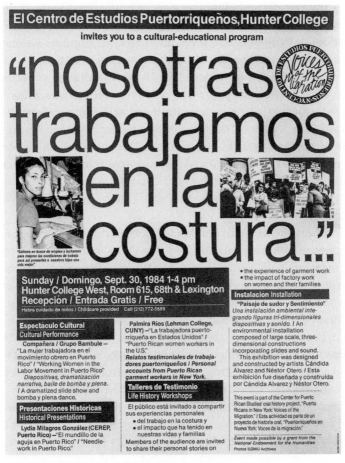

A poster promoting the 1985 public history series. Scholars used Spanish and made minimal effort to translate event titles and descriptions into English. | Centro de Estudios Puertorriqueños Records, "Nosotras Trabajamos en la Costura" poster, Centro Library and Archives, Center for Puerto Rican Studies, Hunter College–CUNY, New York, NY

with audio technicians to record and edit the documentary, and she mailed a cassette copy to each woman for feedback. She could not eliminate the disparities between herself and the needleworkers but wanted to make the field of production as transparent and interactive as possible. In 1985, local community radio stations broadcast the documentary, and listeners heard a narrator explaining the history and quoting women needleworkers.[49]

This broadcast did not close the field of production, however, because "Nosotras Trabajamos" went on to an extended period of promotion and distribution. In early 1986, out of 140 programs, the National Federation of Community Broadcasters selected "Nosotras Trabajamos" as one of five winners for best community broadcast. The National Federation of Community Broadcasters said the radio program typified "the unique contribution community radio makes to the American airwaves." At the Women at Work Broadcast Awards, the National Commission on Working Women gave the documentary third place for Radio Public Affairs/Documentary. These accolades led Benmayor to write Donna Shalala, president of Hunter College (1980–88), to encourage university support for more academic work with media and the public. They also prompted Radio WADO to contact Benmayor to re-air the documentary in spring 1987.[50]

This later broadcast led to Maldonado questioning the use of her words when someone called her after it aired. The caller told her that when some ILGWU members had heard the documentary, they thought it hurt the labor movement because she seemed to say that the union caused problems for workers and that she was the only Puerto Rican woman in leadership. It was not the first time colleagues had been annoyed by her assertiveness or public attention, but it was the first time her comments were part of a public radio show heard by thousands of people. Maldonado contacted the Oral History Task Force and said she was receiving criticism from other Puerto Rican organizers and told the scholars they had misused her words.

Benmayor sent Maldonado a letter expressing the task force's concern. She believed the negative response derived from confusion and assured Maldonado the radio program placed full responsibility for the difficulties of garment workers on "those who move jobs and capital around the world, with federal support and sanctions." Benmayor thought the misunderstanding about women in union leadership might have arisen from listeners conflating "*our* statement that Puerto Rican and Black women have not risen to the top ranks of leadership" with Maldonado's statement that she was the only Puerto Rican woman leader in her local. If listeners combined the two comments, they might have concluded that Maldonado said she was the only Puerto Rican woman leader in the whole ILGWU, "but neither you nor we say this." After mentioning where the task force had sent the cassette copy for her approval, Benmayor asked Maldonado to let them know if there was "anything you feel uncomfortable with" so they could change it before the next broadcast.[51]

In the field of cultural production, even for alternative media supported by public and philanthropic funds, people had different levels of economic and social capital, status, and access to creative decisions. The distinction between *Norma Rae* and "Nosotras Trabajamos" was not a lack of contestation but the degree of money, transparency, interaction, and hostility. Maldonado and the needleworkers had their names and words included throughout the project, participated in public events, and were invited to give feedback. They did not, however, have creative control or participate in the writing, distribution, and promotion. Given society's capitalist structures, they also did not have the economic and social capital or status to capitalize on "Nosotras Trabajamos" for future funding and media productions like Benmayor, Alvarez, and Vázquez did.

Hollywood professionals had tremendous opportunities to capitalize on *Norma Rae*'s commercial dominance for extraordinary career advancement. For the first time as director, Ritt traveled to six cities on a press junket and met with reporters, chasing the exclusive opportunities that would come if *Norma Rae* earned high net revenue and awards.[52] On the junket, he appealed to each audience by the mode he thought appropriate: celebrating *Norma Rae* as a movie about a Rocky-style loser who becomes a winner, a liberated woman who finds her inner strength, a mother who wants something better for her children, or a union member fighting for fair treatment. Although Ritt continued to say in most interviews that *Norma Rae* was not a union movie, when speaking to a labor audience or magazine, he was willing to highlight the TWUA.[53]

As women's liberation gained traction in the mainstream, *Norma Rae*'s circulation on television capitalized on and converged with feminist events in Hollywood. Before the proliferation of VHS cassettes, DVDs, and online streaming, popular films cycled through network television as a "movie of the week" or "midnight movie," and *Norma Rae* had multiple showings on ABC into the late 1980s.[54] At a Los Angeles dinner for women activists and professionals, Betty Friedan celebrated *Norma Rae* and told Alexandra Rose that it was a "watershed film." Ritt and his wife received an invitation to attend a dinner for Bella Abzug with the Hollywood Women's Political Committee.[55] Among such audiences, Ritt said the movie was a feminist film about a "liberated woman." He declared, "I was not interested in the story of trade unions; I wanted to tell the story of this one woman. . . . 'Norma Rae' is a pro-feminist film, not a pro-union film."[56] Like many male union members, Ritt viewed feminism as separate from labor activism.

As Ritt anticipated, the success of *Norma Rae* led to more opportunities for him, including five Hollywood movies with celebrities like Barbra Streisand, Richard Dreyfuss, Jane Fonda, and Robert De Niro. He worked again with Frank and Ravetch, who wrote his last film, *Stanley & Iris* (1990), also adapted from a book. Organizations invited Ritt to receive honorary and lifetime awards, including an appointment as the 1985–86 UCLA Distinguished

Director in Residence, a 1988 tribute at Boston University, and a 1989 Great Director Award from the USA Film Festival.[57]

Norma Rae launched Field into the most exalted tier for actors in the movie business. Fogwood Films and Ritt began development under a Paramount contract for *Back Roads* (1981), in which Field portrayed a feisty southern prostitute who hits the country roads with a drifter played by Tommy Lee Jones. In her 1981 negotiations for the legal thriller *Absence of Malice*, Field was able to demand the same title credit size, credit placement, and stills approval as her costar, Paul Newman, who had been acting since the 1950s, and Fogwood was entitled to 5 percent of gross proceeds after breakeven.[58]

Field won her second Best Actress Oscar in 1985 for portraying Edna Spaulding in *Places in the Heart*. The character is a single mother in 1930s rural Texas struggling to raise two boys and save her farm—another defiant, individualistic southern woman. Through Fogwood, Field acquired the script for *Murphy's Romance* (1985), which Frank and Ravetch adapted from a 1980 novella, cast herself as the lead, and hired Ritt as director. James Garner costarred as a small-town pharmacist who helps Field's character, a divorced mother, succeed at a southwest horse ranch after a bad divorce. She was also the lead in *Steel Magnolias*, playing a strong southern woman with costars Dolly Parton, Shirley MacLaine, Daryl Hannah, and Julia Roberts.

Field and her agent capitalized on the spiral of attention and got her multiple magazine covers. *Playboy* chose her for March 1986, and Field posed in a bunny costume and fishnet stockings, looking over her left shoulder with her buttocks tilted out and a come-hither look.[59] In this coverage of her soaring career, the photo with the UNION sign appeared in articles and talk-show segments. Editors often cropped the still photo to emphasize Field over the scene's industrial setting. In this form, the image was detached from the movie's already vague historical context to become a marker of Field's advancement, and the combined repetition and cropping propelled the image toward icon status.

As the edited photo circulated and became more decontextualized, its cultural impact changed. When readers or viewers—who may or may not have watched *Norma Rae*—saw the image, they could imagine the stand as a frontstage performance by Field. In *Norma Rae*, the stand had relied on but displaced Crystal Lee's communal backstage gesture. It was transformed from her vernacular message into a pivotal personal moment for one woman leading a drive in one mill. The 1980s circulation of the photo further refined it into a highly individualistic performance of one woman's grit and defiance.[60] The photo did not completely lose its deepest roots in collective labor union resistance to exploitation—the history imbues the image with its enduring marrow of authenticity—but audiences could easily see it as Field making her own stand.

The linguistic component of the Norma Rae icon also germinated in the early 1980s, in an episode of *Archie Bunker's Place* (1979–83), a continuation of *All in the Family* (1971–79). In season 2, Archie's wife Edith dies, and he hires a domestic servant, a Black woman named Mrs. Canby. In the October 1981 episode "Norma Rae Bunker," he makes an unsuccessful individual stand on her behalf. When Mrs. Canby needs money for her daughter's tuition, Archie suggests she sew piecework and gets her an address (neither character mentions a raise). Mrs. Canby goes to the sweatshop, where the women speak Spanish and the Latino shop manager asks if she is from Jamaica. When she says she was born in America, he makes a joke about everyone being born in America. He offers her $140 for a box of finished blouses but hands her $80 when she returns them. She argues the money is short, and he says the manufacturer demanded a lower rate or the contract would go to Taiwan. "If they cheat me, then I cheat her," he says. "I don't like it, but that's the way it is."

When Mrs. Canby complains to Archie, he says the top guy "ain't gonna talk to anybody that ain't a top guy," and it would help if "that guy is also white." Mrs. Canby implies he should go, and the conservative bigot becomes the good white savior, his decency confirmed by this personal effort to help a hardworking African American woman.[61] Archie goes to the office, demands sixty dollars, and threatens to talk to the union, but the manufacturer laughs and says the shop is not union. Archie returns home and gives Mrs. Canby sixty dollars as if it came from the manufacturer. She says the garment workers should have more "spunk" like Archie and announces she is starting a side business altering clothes.[62]

The episode does not mention any possible organized action with the Latinas, who perform a paradoxical role as exploited workers who deserve pity but not full attention, because they are "not American." Even in a show with Spanish-speaking factory labor, Puerto Rican women migrating as US industrial workers dissolve into a homogenized notion of undocumented Latina immigrants. Despite the episode's nod toward the significance of unions and unfairness of a racialized gendered labor system, the solution to Mrs. Canby's problem involves a white man using his personal money as an act of charity (even though he is her employer) and Mrs. Canby taking on the personal effort and risk to start her own entrepreneurial enterprise.

In an illuminating transplantation, the writers used the term "Norma Rae," a reference derived from the shared experiences of poor women labor activists in southern mills, for a white working-class man helping a woman of color deal with a northeastern sweatshop that has Latina workers in the background. It is the first example of the name being used to signify another person's defiance that is fully detached from the movie, Field, and Crystal Lee. The 1981 episode's reliance on an ambiguous association with women garment workers to transfer "Norma Rae" onto a man was a key cultural bridge for propelling the linguistic reference toward icon status. As with the image cropping, this transference set up the phrase "Norma Rae moment," fully releasing it from the movie and allowing it to be bound to any individual stand against anything deemed unfair.

The ACTWU, on the other hand, was unable to capitalize on its association with *Norma Rae*, and some suggested the movie actually hurt the domestic industry. ACTWU actions could not match the Hollywood limelight surrounding the movie and Field and how it outshone rather than spotlit labor history in the political economy. As facets of the movie circulated and became further detached from the raw source material, the ACTWU was severed from it just when leaders were fighting to stabilize domestic employment. And *Norma Rae* did no cultural work to weaken the opponents extending global supply chains and attacking union proposals as backward protectionism.

Throughout the 1980s, discount retail, branding and logistics technology, and financialization all converged with foreign economic policy and its support of imports and capital migration. Journalists' and pundits' focus on the bordered metropole, usually with attention to a particular corporation or city, has encouraged a tendency to blame unionization or high wages for late twentieth-century relocations and the collapse of domestic manufacturing and employment. Unions and workers shaped these currents as they navigated and contested terms and conditions, but they were not the driving force behind the reconfigurations. Trade offices, diplomats, international organizations, investors, and corporate executives made agreements and decisions that accelerated the disaggregation of manufacturing.

After Ronald Reagan's presidential election in 1980, his administration expanded incentives for EPZs and trade that opened US markets to the wider Caribbean. The malleable lines of sovereignty, citizenship, and extreme exemptions that US and insular governments, manufacturers, and financiers had experimented with in Puerto Rico came full circle. Mexico and the BIP maquiladoras had adapted them in the 1960s, and EPZs appeared in the Dominican Republic, Haiti, and Jamaica in the 1980s and 1990s. The 1983 Caribbean Basin Economic Recovery Act established the Caribbean Basin Initiative (CBI), a unilateral trade agreement with provisions that were amended but carried into the twenty-first century.

The CBI offered Caribbean nations a "mini–Marshall Plan" and a "Puerto-Rico style special relationship" with the United States. To qualify, countries could not have a communist government or property nationalized from a US citizen or corporation.[63] In return, they received subsidies and loans for export manufacturing, with trade preferences and duty-free access. Supporters claimed this diversification would reduce the region's vulnerability to fluctuations in its traditional raw-material exports, but Puerto Rican officials and managers worried the CBI placed Puerto Rico at a disadvantage because it had to comply with limited aspects of US labor and environmental regulations.[64] In 1985, to insert Puerto Rico into the CBI and reinvigorate Section 936, Governor Rafael Hernández Colón promised to use much of the $700 million in the PRIDC to fund investment in CBI nations.[65] The Reagan administration further tied colonial industrialization to the Caribbean in 1986 when it modified Section 936, mandating that $100 million of the $15 billion in Puerto Rican banks go to loans in CBI countries.[66]

As in Puerto Rico and Mexico, government offices and investors targeted textiles and apparel. Although the Caribbean Basin Economic Recovery Act appeared to bow to the domestic textile and garment industry's historical political clout by excluding particular items from preferential treatment, the act contained loopholes transnational corporations could manipulate.[67] Then the 1990 CBI Textile Program allowed garments manufactured in eligible Caribbean nations with US yarns and fabrics to enter the United States "free of quota and duty"; the program later expanded the allowance to include yarns and fabrics from designated CBI nations. Apparel and clothing accessories exported from the Caribbean to the United States grew from 5.5 percent of CBI trade in 1984 to 48 percent in 1998.[68]

By 1984, 50 percent of clothing sold in the United States was imported, and China was already the world's biggest textile producer and the fourth largest exporter of textiles and garments to the United States. If trade offices tried to restrict its imports, China refused US cotton, soybeans, and chemical fibers. Factories throughout New York City increasingly functioned like warehouses for managers who traveled and returned with items for finishing or distribution. A set of shirts could use fabric from China and be cut in New York, sewn in Taiwan or Jamaica, finished in Puerto Rico or Mexico, and sent to New York and London for distribution. Most managers no longer hired sewing machine operators; they sought floor girls and packers, and Puerto Rican needleworkers bore the brunt of this job deskilling.[69]

In the contests over the terms of globalization, a new player took a forceful role: discount retailers such as Kmart and Wal-Mart. The ACTWU, the ILGWU, and women workers were already fighting to constrain disaggregation, reduce cheap imports, and confront legalistic anti-union tactics when discount retailers gained an impressive economic stake that strengthened their political leverage. They asserted interests that directly contradicted those of domestic manufacturers and workers and instead aligned with policymakers, trade representatives, investors, and corporations that supported open US consumer markets and capital currents.[70]

In addition, more apparel companies emulated Liz Claiborne, which exploded in the 1980s by emphasizing brand identity and avoiding manufacturing. Its model maximized revenues via targeted marketing and offshore contracting dependent on logistics technology. Satellite transmission and containerization were important, and barcodes with computer scanners were especially transformative. Introduced by Wal-Mart in the early 1980s, computerized inventory control made reliance on contractors easier to manage and monitor, reducing theft and other inventory loss. Even Manhattan designers that had prided themselves on the quality of their domestically sewn clothing started to use offshore manufacturing.[71]

Quality declined, but prices stayed high because of the persuasive psychological and affective appeal of brands, which drew celebrities to sell their names to clothing lines. Maldonado was upset about Joe Namath partnering with a men's clothing line made in China. "The thing is that, even though [all of Joe Namath's clothing] is made there for less money," she said, "it's not sold here for less money like years back. The cut up is four times as much, or maybe ten times." When Robert Riley, a top designer since the 1940s and head of the lab at the Fashion Institute of Technology, retired in the 1980s, he criticized this new habit of holding name above craftsmanship.[72]

Domestic financial practices exacerbated this deterioration of work conditions and employment. Even when sites along the US Atlantic produced reliable earnings, financial "restructuring" with closures produced greater short-term returns and tax windfalls than manufacturing. In the 1980s, leveraged buyouts (LBOs) became widespread, and the Reagan administration made the deals easier via banking deregulation and the reduction of Securities and Exchange Commission (SEC) oversight.[73] The practice started in the 1970s with Michael Milken's promotion of "junk" bonds, low-rated bonds of small or moderate companies. His firm, Drexel Burnham, underwrote LBOs to produce high yields for investors and massive advisory fees for itself and even hosted an annual Predators' Ball in Beverly Hills. In an LBO, an investor group forms to buy a small or moderate company by borrowing against the assets of that company, which usually generates a spiked payment to shareholders. Even when the strategy fails and share value collapses, scavenger investors such as Warren Buffet at Berkshire Hathaway buy the cheapened company to sell off assets and implement tax-beneficial closures.[74]

In many LBOs, the acquired manufacturing company is compelled to pay "consulting fees" to the shell finance company created by the investor group. This payment structure evades the SEC income-disclosure reporting requirement for the senior management of public companies. In spring 1986, for example, a primary investor partnered with Drexel to attempt a hostile takeover of Warnaco, a garment manufacturer earning steady profits with Hathaway shirts, Olga bras, and WhiteStag sportswear.[75] The investor group provided 1 percent of the financing, with Milken raising the rest with junk bonds. The primary investor became chairman of the Warnaco board of directors, but he had no interest in leading an apparel corporation and drew no salary. Instead, he cashed in his equity stake and received a monthly consulting fee. Between 1986 and 1989, this investor paid himself $9 million in fees, which made him one of the highest-paid US executives without any SEC income reporting, all while gutting Warnaco assets.[76]

More than 250 home goods and garment factories closed between 1980 and 1985. In an attempt to save remaining businesses, the Fiber, Fabric and Apparel Coalition for Trade promoted its plants as "the nation's greatest manufacturing employers of women and minorities."[77] Crystal Lee and poor millhands in the South, especially Black women who had most recently entered the industry, faced a loss of reliable full-time jobs. Maldonado and Puerto Rican needleworkers in the Northeast lost the industrial employment that had served as a foundation for their income and their household survival since the turn of the century.

The American Thread Company case study exemplifies this situation for needleworkers. In the early 1980s, it reduced its overall workforce and closed distribution points in Puerto Rico. Although Puerto Rican women in Willimantic, Connecticut, were represented by ACTWU Local 460T, the union had little leverage after decades of disaggregation and mechanization. Many workers said the local did not fight enough for grievances and was unable to prevent management from raising quotas, lowering piecework rates, and using time-motion studies—which all constituted a stretch-out. Some women said they distrusted the union because representatives made promises they did not keep. Many Puerto Rican women, however, appreciated it and said conditions would have been worse without it. A woman named Lupe believed older workers were afraid of losing their jobs so they held the union back, choosing not to confront management and voting to accept company offers. In fact, most women did not want to strike due to possible violence and loss of earnings. "We have this economy that is hard to find jobs," a woman named Ligia said. "What is the use of losing four weeks of work to end up signing the same contract? The money workers lose in a strike is never recovered."[78] The ACTWU's support of *Norma Rae* and its narrative of self-actualization meant nothing to these women's work conditions.

In July 1984, American Thread announced its plan to close the Willimantic mill.[79] When it proceeded in 1985, Puerto Rican unemployment increased. Kendall Company, which produced synthetic fabric for diapers, had closed in 1983, and Brand Rex had reduced the number of its employees from 800 to 650 in 1981 and to 460 in 1983.[80] Similar conditions played out in other small New England cities. In 1989, the Gemini Mill in Springfield, Massachussetts, closed after the president tried two years of financial arrangements, and Irma Medina's mother took a job as a janitor in the city school district.[81] After Elco Dress Company in Holyoke, Massachussetts, closed, Maria Salgado-Cartagena's mother started her own hustles, such as cooking food in her kitchen for takeout. People in the neighborhood knew the days she cooked and ordered ahead of time.[82] Thousands of Puerto Rican women turned to jobs in service fields, including nurse's aide, office cleaner, and home attendant, when they could not find new industrial jobs. Others applied for unemployment insurance or Aid to Families with Dependent Children (AFDC) welfare payments, and older women often had to try to survive on Social Security.[83]

Even during these years of closure, "Nosotras Trabajamos" made inroads in the arena of cultural politics, reaching scholars and teachers. Two academic articles by Alvarez and Vázquez appeared in a 1988 issue of *Oral History Review*, where they discussed family members in garment factories as well as interview practices. In 1994, Benmayor published *Pioneras: Women's Voices of the Early Puerto Rican Migration* with Temple University Press. It was the "first book of women's testimonial accounts of the Puerto Rican migration experience in New York from the 1920s to the present."[84] A New York State–sponsored curriculum also used "Nosotras Trabajamos" in a 1995 set of lesson plans for K–12 students.[85]

Although needleworkers were losing jobs in the archipelago and mainland, and US agencies no longer promoted Puerto Rico for textile and apparel manufacturing, colonial industrialization continued—fully repackaged as EPZs and marketed as modern business. In 1985, WEPZA reorganized as an independent entity, separate from the UN, and the Flagstaff Institute, under Richard Bolin and his son, took over its administration. The new WEPZA allowed mixed membership with government and nongovernment members, including private EPZ developers, operators, and consultants. It offered trainings and workshops dedicated to EPZs as "vehicles for development" and published a journal with rationales and corroborating statistics. Membership covered sixty-six countries by the late 1980s.[86]

The 1985 fight for the Textile and Apparel Trade Enforcement Act (H.R. 1562) exposed how reconfigurations and concomitant splintering of the domestic industry left its advocates without resources to bring pressure. Descriptions of the failure to pass H.R. 1562 often blamed a weak industry and dying unions in ways that made their situation appear inevitable. But intentional labor and manufacturing manipulations with colonial and foreign economic policy, contracting and EPZs, anti-union consultants, discount retailers, brand companies, and financialization had impaired domestic companies, jobs, and unions. Resulting market systems granted transnational investors and major corporations even greater influence over globalization.[87]

Even though multiplying bilateral agreements nullified most congressional legislation to control imports and stabilize US employment, advocates still hoped H.R. 1562 might hinder transnational corporations' circumvention of the Multi-Fiber Agreement quotas via transshipments through third countries.[88] Unions emphasized the domestic labor force's racial diversity and the importance of protecting jobs for women, and flyers for H.R. 1562 represented white, Black, Latino/a, and Asian workers in various jobs. The National Puerto Rican Coalition supported the bill, arguing Puerto Rican communities were suffering due to cheap imports from Asia.[89]

The ACTWU, ILGWU, and remaining local and regional companies contacted political allies like the Congressional Textile Caucus, yet domestic managers continued to undermine their own allies with anti-union obstruction. Unions still decided to partner with the American Fiber, Textile, and Apparel Coalition, coordinating with this group of textile, hosiery, knitwear, and sportswear manufacturers with whom they also fought regarding contracts.[90]

Representative Edgar "Ed" Lanier Jenkins (D-GA) advocated for H.R. 1562 for political reasons and because domestic companies were modernizing. He argued they were becoming more efficient and clean but needed a fair chance to compete when Asian, Mexican, and Caribbean manufacturing facilities had fewer safety and pollution regulations and paid lower wages. Jenkins knew it would be a difficult fight but wooed several Democrats because their districts still had factories. They understood the domestic textile and garment enterprises were linked in success or failure.

Jenkins also consulted with executives including those at Harmax, which had thirty-three factories throughout the United States. Harmax had a history of advocating at local and state levels for its businesses and for the employees and towns it supported via pay, benefits, and a stable tax base. Secondary suppliers, companies that provided parts, machine repair, and water testing, also participated in H.R. 1562 lobbying.[91]

They were up against strong opposition and a growing tendency to frame Americans as consumers rather than workers. Transnational corporations and brands, such as Liz Claiborne and Esprit, argued H.R. 1562 was not in the interest of consumer prices. The largest domestic manufacturer, Levi Strauss, which was in the process of dispersing all its production into Asia in a bid to become a global brand, joined them. Retailers also attacked H.R. 1562, with Kmart and the National Retail Merchants Association reiterating the word "protectionist" in the narrowest terms and warning of price hikes. The

American Farm Bureau Federation and agricultural lobbies opposed the bill because they feared trade retaliation.[92]

The Reagan White House and its economic advisers used a rhetoric of "free trade" and "free markets" to criticize H.R. 1562. After months of talks and compromises, however, H.R. 1562 passed. Reagan vetoed it a week before Christmas 1985. Workers, union leaders, and domestic executives joined in a massive effort to override the veto. Norman Kominsky, CEO of Eastland Woolen Mills in Maine, enlisted employees in a letter-writing campaign. The ACTWU and ILGWU intensified their efforts at demonstrations, publicity, and lobbying. Then five days before the override vote, the Reagan administration announced it had negotiated a tougher Multi-Fiber Agreement with expanded import coverage and mechanisms to prevent import surges— without acknowledging all the ways international trade offices and transnational corporations evaded such criteria. Reagan trade representatives argued negotiation, not legislation, was the way to address the trade deficit, and on the day of the vote, Reagan contacted congressional Republicans to warn them that the party would be undermined by an override. In August 1986, the override was defeated, and by 1987, imports accounted for 57.5 percent of apparel sales in the United States.[93]

Some experts tracking unsuccessful legislation during the 1980s criticized *Norma Rae.* Unlike national ACTWU leadership, these regional company owners and business journalists argued the movie had portrayed southern mills as backward and covered in cotton lint, even though executives had invested in modernization, air systems, and automation throughout the 1970s and '80s. They complained that regressive stereotypes and anachronistic conceptions inhibited managers' ability to promote the industry, recruit young workers, and advocate for their employees, even after investing $1.5 billion per year in safety and computerization.[94] Although this argument failed to acknowledge that automation undermined the workers and unions, it did foreground the significance of cultural politics in debates over political economy.

Subsequent closures and job losses hit throughout the Northeast, the South, and Puerto Rico, rather than in a linear relocation. That dominant narrative veils the accelerating multivalent shifts with the reassurance of teleology—even one that ends in a gloomy outcome. It allows contemporary workers to conceive of a point in a linear series of events to which they might return, a goal that is much more convenient than scrutinizing and intervening in tax, finance, colonial, and foreign economic policies in addition to labor and employment legislation.

The decline in employment and union membership instigated an increasing number of sweatshops. These were not leftovers from the early 1900s, but rather new sweatshops that violated contemporary regulations. Although sweatshops never vanished, their number had dramatically decreased by the mid-twentieth century, when the ILGWU, TWUA, and ACWA organized workers, hired business agents to monitor mills and shops, raised public awareness, and pressed for labor legislation. As membership declined, however, so did funds, and the unions' ability to help sweatshop workers eroded. The downward spiral meant remaining domestic producers could turn to a sweatshop model with little resistance. In such conditions, managers used fear to exploit undocumented immigrants and prevent attempts at unionization.[95]

In the late 1980s, Maldonado understood the ILGWU's deteriorating position but remained adamant about its importance for Puerto Rican women. "There's a lot of beautiful things about the ILGW," she said. When her daughter was unhappy doing social work for the Board of Correction, Maldonado helped her become a business agent. She also encouraged and celebrated Rosa Mejías, a young woman born in Puerto Rico who became an ILGWU education director in New York.[96] Maldonado retired in the 1990s, and the archival fragments disappear. The ILGWU and ACTWU merged in 1995 to form the Union of Needletrades, Industrial, and Textile Employees (UNITE). A 2004 merger with the Hotel Employees and Restaurant Employees (HERE) union created UNITE HERE, because UNITE had funds but declining membership, whereas HERE had expanding membership but little cash.

"Nosotras Trabajamos" provided an alternative narrative for the American working class in which women of color in colonial migrations were part of industrial labor in a globalized workforce. As a regional public history project, however, it could not compete with *Norma Rae*, with its reach far beyond theater distribution. Rose & Asseyev Productions, Ritt, and Twentieth Century-Fox protected their creative property, eliminated alternatives, and earned royalties for years. They worked to maximize their accumulation of economic and social capital, and with Kopple's depiction of a collective interracial TWUA membership drive obstructed and marginalized, *Norma Rae* stood alone.

A single film is not responsible for thousands of job losses, but successful commercial movies intercede with outsized influence in the arena of cultural politics. As a secondary partner without rights to the creative property, ACTWU leadership tried to capitalize on *Norma Rae*'s popular success even though the narrative of individual defiance in a remote mill eclipsed the union's years of efforts to fight disaggregation and organize J.P. Stevens. The short-term flurry of media interest in 1980 did little to advance the goals of its members, the union as a political-economic institution, or the active solidarity required for a labor movement.

This conclusive *Norma Rae* cultural triumph was not guaranteed. It required intensive efforts. Once achieved, the film became a recognizable circulating element interacting with other texts across many media. *Norma Rae* remained an inspiration for many labor and women activists, and unions often showed it at events as well. But propagation of the movie, as a whole and as clips and stills, also generated a cropped image and variations of the phrase "Norma Rae moment." This stripped-down icon converged with texts constructing meanings for a white American working class and for an ascendant cultural formation of neoliberal individualism.

CHAPTER SIX

The Norma Rae Icon

Inspiring Neoliberal Individualism

They believe in free trade, that's what they tell us. . . .
We're not saying we don't want imports, because we have to
have imports to have exports . . . but not to the extent
that our people are gonna be out of work.

—Gloria Maldonado

The president stood in front of Congress to give his State of the Union address to an anxious society grappling with the oil embargo, withdrawal from Vietnam, resignation of a president, and combination of unemployment and inflation reporters had dubbed "stagflation." He called for a common purpose but said, "This sense of unity cannot be expressed in programs or in legislation or in dollars. It's an achievement that belongs to every individual American." In proposing a path forward, he declared, "Government cannot solve our problems, it can't set our goals, it cannot define our vision. Government cannot eliminate poverty or provide a bountiful economy or reduce inflation or save our cities or cure illiteracy or provide energy. And government cannot mandate goodness. Only a true partnership between government and the people can ever hope to reach these goals."

When the former navy lieutenant, peanut businessman, and Georgia governor Jimmy Carter took the podium in January 1978, two Democrats sat behind him. Vice President Walter Mondale and Speaker of the House Tip O'Neill had served in Congress for years and supported Great Society legislation. But Carter, a southern business owner and evangelical Christian, favored another approach to the economic crisis and resurging financial disparities, saying, "Private business and not the government must lead the expansion in the future."[1]

Three years later, when the former radio sportscaster, Hollywood actor and SAG president, GE spokesman, and California governor Ronald Reagan took the stage for his first presidential inauguration, the country remained entangled in those ordeals as well as the hostage crisis at the US embassy in

Iran. Standing above red, white, and blue bunting, Reagan offered an even more curt and disparaging assessment of government. "In this present crisis, government is not the solution to our problem; government is the problem," he declared.

Reagan's speech presented an unequivocal notion of the private individual as the means for addressing the nation's problems. Instead of looking to government, he suggested an end to the neglect of "the men and women who raise our food, patrol our streets, man our mines and factories, teach our children, keep our homes, and heal us when we're sick—professionals, industrialists, shopkeepers, clerks, cabbies, and truck drivers."[2] These people were not groups of investors, owners, management, and labor with a tense mix of coinciding and conflicting goals regarding access to wealth, income, resources, or power. They were individualized yet equivalent Americans who worked in different ways, yet did not have significant distinguishing characteristics to be considered. And government was not an intricate and contentious amalgam of elected officials, agencies, programs, and central banks that facilitated, protected, and distributed funds, resources, and power in hundreds of ways. It was a monolithic establishment blocking private individuals from their potential.

When Reagan announced this generic private individual as the solution, he was articulating an ideology that had gained momentum from the concerted efforts of wealthy businessmen, corporate lobbyists, Cold War anti-Soviet organizations, suburban voters in the South and West, and politically active evangelical leaders.[3] Although celebration of the individual was not new in the United States, this crystallization was distinct and extreme even as it drew on the longer history. Reagan's election was a watershed for the Republican Party that helped push a larger cultural shift throughout the 1980s and '90s. Over the previous two decades, internal pressure from right-wing members and interest groups had worked to direct the party away from moderate conservatism. In 1980, they succeeded in electing their preferred candidate in the primary, and Reagan went on to beat the incumbent Democratic president.

Norma Rae entered this milieu as it circulated through periodicals, television, and eventually the internet. Refinement of the icon image and phrase shows that it did not cohere in a vacuum as a freestanding object. Its potency came not only from its accessible and pleasing visual and linguistic compression, with its affective punch, but also from how it spoke to other cultural texts. As diverse texts interact, fostering entwined thoughts and emotional patterns across a general population, they forge mainstream cultural formations. These combinations of cognition and affect do not predetermine people's ideas but help constitute how people know the world and, as a result, how they participate in the constant reconfigurations of the political economy.[4]

Although often used with humor, the Norma Rae icon is not simple fun—it performed intricate cultural work that served an ascendant formation of neoliberal individualism. As an icon of ambiguous individualist rebelliousness loosed from the sources and record of its production, the Norma Rae image and phrase could be adapted for many purposes. Starting in the 1980s, the icon converged with multiplying texts from radical libertarian economists, right-wing politicians, and evangelical activists who were producing channels of discourse, imaginaries, sound bites, and images with narrative and affective emphasis on the generic private individual and defiance. This timing meant the icon contributed to an aspirational discourse of the individual made free by combative self-sufficiency and did cultural work to make neoliberal political and economic projects more rationalized and alluring. Even as a totally different type of text with roots in unionizing, the icon merged with expressions of hyperindividualism in a cultural process that pulled on their overlapping facets. When its appearances multiplied in the 1990s, it carried this meaning and feeling of individualist rebellion to new audiences immersed in the neoliberal turn.

For four decades, video and text media have used the Norma Rae icon to elicit audience responses. Television shows are especially interesting because they usually deploy the icon to accentuate, yet mock, someone's personal stand. In this paradox, the character recognizes a just grievance, their individual opposition serves as the only attempt at rectification, but it is marked as humorous, even futile. If limited cooperation with peers does occur, it is short lived or off-camera. In text media, on the other hand, writers have deployed the icon for a greater variety of purposes. Most general websites and blogs use it to applaud an individual stand, whether about office snacks or a spin class. Newspapers and magazines usually include the icon as a hook for a serious report on worker issues or labor organizing. In several instances, union web pages and flyers have used the image to catch people's attention and call them into an organized campaign or labor event. Even these latter uses, however, draw on the audience's understanding and feelings about individual defiance rather than collective action.

As the number of US textile and garment workers and locals declined, the Norma Rae icon sprouted in American popular culture. It fully cohered in the late 1980s and '90s, after the image and phrase were untethered from Sally Field and her career. The process was similar to that of a photo of Ernesto "Che" Guevara at a funeral service in Cuba, as it became cropped and compressed into the Che icon. Both Guevara as revolutionary and Field as Norma appeared in numerous photos available for recirculation. Media professionals, however, chose the funeral photo and the UNION still for their narrative and affective appeal and transformed them into adaptable icons.[5] The cropping, as much as the facial expressions, infused each photo with individualist appeal, and digital mass media allowed for repetitive appropriation.

Studies of the Che icon have outlined the popular culture process. Alberto Korda (a.k.a. Alberto Díaz Gutiérrez) took the photo at a 1960 funeral for people killed on a Belgian ship carrying explosives for the new Cuban government. Guevara, with his long wavy hair, strong jawline, and revolutionary's beret, stepped forward on a podium filled with emissaries. Korda snapped two dozen frames, two centered on Guevara's face, handsome and gazing intently into the crowd. As Korda developed the photos, he noticed the allure of Guevara's face in one of the closer shots and cropped it to eliminate distractions: a man in a suit and palm fronds. He knew how to find "the image within the image," to refine the composition with no concern for removing historical details. The Che icon germinated in this creative decision. Just before Guevara's 1967 assassination, Korda gave a copy of the cropped print to a leftist Italian publisher, who then used it for a poster to honor the dead man.[6]

Guevara became the revolutionary martyr Che through the announcements of his death that circulated around the world, many featuring the cropped print. People began adapting the image for all types of defiance, often associated with 1960s leftist politics and 1970s student activism. In the 1980s and '90s, however, transnational brands, seeking to mark themselves as "rebellious," appropriated the Che icon to sell sunglasses, clothing, and vodka. Corporations wanting to develop "radically individualistic and perpetually new" identities usurped the Che icon "to inoculate themselves against accusations that they were in fact selling sameness." The Marxist revolutionary who had traveled to support movements for the destruction of capitalist and imperial governments became an icon for individualist consumerism. Even knowledgeable consumers, aware of the gap between radical political action and brand commerce, buy such products because they take pleasure in the irony.[7]

Popular uses of the Che and Norma Rae icons constitute an "experimental negotiation" between buried but consequential political-economic content and the expanding mass commercial context of consumer societies. Their transmission opens "the possibility of endless visual mutation, of stylistic regeneration without ever losing the essence of what the face expresses."[8] Each icon remains tied—in unarticulated intuitive ways that must be uncovered, but tied nonetheless—to their roots in profound collective struggles. They do not usually represent the movement of their origin, but without that deeper moral resonance of historic shared action, overexposure would have emptied even these attractive representations of paradigmatic rebels. The icons manifest and illuminate this captivating tension between leftist collective activism, triumphant individualism, and the ubiquity of commercialization and consumerism.[9]

Although the deeper marrow of authenticity did not dilute as the Norma Rae icon cohered in popular media, the movie's embedded narrative was further reduced. It condensed from "the American working class is white individuals in gritty industries" to "individual defiance is the way." Like a palimpsest, affective traces of the expansive raw material endured under the simplistic cultural narrative. Unlike the Che icon, however, the Norma Rae icon's realization in the late 1980s and the '90s coincided with the ascendance of neoliberalism and its juggernaut of political, economic, and cultural projects.

Historical analysis of the Norma Rae icon with the mainstream cultural formation of neoliberal individualism highlights the incongruous and slippery relationship between American pop culture and the overall neoliberal turn of the 1980s and '90s. This turn occurred as a thorough shift in the global political, economic, social, and cultural milieu but did not have a core movement, precise political party, or exact year. Multiple forces built on, arose from, responded to, and countered earlier structures, while interacting in unpredictable ways—sometimes coordinated but also oppositional—that propelled changes and funneled their impact. Since widespread transformations like the neoliberal turn are neither predetermined nor random, cultural formations are a key element to understanding how they develop and become dominant.[10]

Broad social changes in the 1960s and '70s created rudimentary conditions for a possible genesis of hyperindividualism. Since the 1950s, youth, celebrities, pundits, and politicians at all levels, from left and right perspectives, were taking on the pose of outsider or rebel.[11] This defiant cool, as a standard pose, requires the constant appearance and tone, if not substance, of rebellion. At the same time, groups and constituents across the spectrum came to focus on a version of "individual freedom" as the essence of American liberty.[12] Organizations, consciousness seminars, spiritual and religious congregations, and books and magazines increasingly prioritized individual rights, self-actualization, or personal fulfillment.

During these years, three groups in the New Right—radical libertarian economists, right-wing politicians, and activist evangelicals—strove for public influence and worked in purposeful, often integrated, ways that helped neoliberal individualism to crystallize.[13] Their successful writers and speakers engaged popular media using plain language to reach the widest audience and emphasized individual freedom infused with aspirational defiance. Even institutional insiders and recognized leaders presented themselves as outsiders rebelling against the "real" insiders: liberal elites and their pernicious status quo.[14] They tied the message and sentiment of their individual freedom to phrases such as "choice in the market," "liberty from government," and "personal salvation," which were casual versions of ideological principles.[15]

As with all coalescing cultural formations, the swirl of interacting texts included white papers, legislation, and congressional debates. For decades, economists and theorists in discussions and disputes at the Walter Lippmann Colloquium, Mont Pèlerin Society, and University of Chicago had been developing concepts and relationships that established an apparatus of elite neoliberal expertise. They provided lengthy arguments with intricate rationales and formulas that undergirded specific proposals, while appearing to refute any contrary analysis.[16] Scholars and intellectuals presented at conferences for the top echelon of finance, business, and government, and their notions of the "free market" circulated through sites such as the American Enterprise Institute, World Bank, and World Economic Forum.

This apparatus of elite expertise played two roles in the overall neoliberal turn. First, its proposed legislation, regulatory reform, and policies for trade, finance, taxes, and employment reconfigured political-economic systems and governance. When the 1970s and '80s economic crises and subsequent collapse of Keynesian structures induced political muddling, the breach opened the way for neoliberal expertise. These scholars and intellectuals recognized the opportunity to implement policies and practices via their positions and connections in world conferences, think tanks, and government offices.[17]

Second, the apparatus of expertise contributed to the mainstream formation of neoliberal individualism. Public-facing writers and speakers translated the terms and concepts into appealing discourse, imaginaries, sound bites, and images for general audiences. Papers and propositions from the elite involved technical language most Americans did not read but supplied substance refined by both specialists such as Milton Friedman and followers such as Reagan—people savvy in narrative and affect who became catalysts for spinning extreme ideology from the elite apparatus into the coalescing cultural formation of neoliberal individualism.

In this way, neoliberal expertise and mainstream neoliberal individualism were not equivalents, but they were symbiotic rather than hierarchical. Cultural formations are not executed by a series of rational choices in a regimented plan. They are not enforced by mechanical top-down manipulation as ruling elites direct propaganda, stereotypes, and spectacles to steer the masses—such absolute, totalizing hegemony does not exist.[18] To be effective, a cultural formation "has to extend to and include, indeed to form and be formed from," the whole of a society's representations and interactions. It is an unpredictable combination of imaginative, discursive, social, and material processes constituted through many channels—some intentional, some not.[19]

Several libertarian economists, right-wing politicians, and activist evangelicals were especially charismatic and astute at adapting American terms like "liberty," "freedom," and "choice" to their proposals to appeal to general audiences. As veneration of the individual intensified in the 1970s and '80s, these three groups succeeded in binding it to their policies and practices through phrases such as "free market," "free enterprise," "entrepreneur," "deregulation and freedom from government," and "religious freedom."

Even though cultural formations appear stable, the most effective are supple rather than rigid. Meanings and notions processed (and reprocessed) in the formations do not reside sealed and static in separate articles, images, and phrases. They are generated and tweaked by the constant interactions between texts, discourses, and activities, including popular media and conversations about them. Through these recurring exchanges and their bonds, cultural formations coalesce and endure.[20] Structures of feeling are an especially potent element of formations because they percolate below conscious cognition. Texts, images, audio, and video that do not appear obviously connected to each other, or to any established institution, can share a constitutive affect, a structure of feeling. Instead of dogma, they share meanings and values actively lived and felt with emotional elements of impulse, inhibition, and tone.[21]

A cogent structure of feeling imbued neoliberal individualism with glorification of the private individual and aspirational defiance, entwined and filled with an emotional richness Americans could "inhabit imaginatively in their everyday lives."[22] The Norma Rae icon served the cultural formation in this capacity. Its narrative and dramatic affect aligned with this aspect of nascent neoliberal individualism, converging with its cultural work to naturalize the neoliberal turn.

Neoliberal individualism was neither monolithic nor absolutely consistent, but it taught and affirmed simple justifications and feelings that worked to sustain popular support for actions that did little to provide stability for working people. The apparatus of neoliberal expertise drove changes to redirect government agencies and funding away from public services and employment oversight, toward private investors and corporate assets. It pushed redistributive tax policies that favored individuals accumulating capital over the proportional collection of taxes to serve shared public goods like clean water and education.[23] This drastic restructuring of society thrust obligations, responsibilities, and risks onto the most vulnerable people, including wageworkers and average taxpayers. The cultural formation, however, imbued the projects with common sense and aspirational emotions, while helping shift the blame for increasing income and wealth inequality onto notions like individual passivity and government obstruction.

Neoliberal individualism also circulated rhetoric, narratives, and emotions that did vital work to rationalize political and economic practices that did not always match the stated principles. Such contradictions include an intellectual emphasis on limited government with financial deregulation versus the actual facilitation of global capital currents and its dependence on interventionist government, bailouts, and intricate regulation of bond markets, currency rates, and international banking. In another example, free-market visions of freedom and liberty do not correspond to the daily operation of corporations such as GE, Wal-Mart, and Amazon that manage through overbearing top-down hierarchies and demands for uniformity.[24]

The cultural formation worked to move veneration of the individual beyond legal protections for private property, respect for personal achievement, and celebration of one's creativity. It stripped away traditional notions of social obligations and the public good and defined rights and responsibilities solely via the private individual's position in "the market"—a blanket term that encompassed, in order to elide, all the socially constructed complexities of jobs and wages, consumer prices, medical care, education and training, transportation, real estate, banking, insurance, tax policies, inheritance, and currency. The result contributed to an "erosion of the idea that there is a difference between private wealth and the public interest."[25]

As this neoliberal individualism permeated society, people came to feel, as well as believe, that their difficulties arose from the sum of their personal choices, without any relation to larger structures or even local circumstances. The individual and the market were imagined as impartial and free if left to their own devices, and proponents presented massive social crises or inequitable economic distributions as private problems.[26] Abstracted collectives like the government, bureaucracy, and unions were obstacles that interfered with the market and its inherent solutions, and the successful individual was signified by an aspirational defiance, fighting against these abstractions. The combative individual stands alone.

The Norma Rae icon did not initiate the cultural formation, but it inadvertently helped because of its virtuosity as a condensed narrative and emotional experience.[27] It reinforced the reductionist rhetoric and defiant structure of feeling as neoliberal individualism congealed through mainstream imaginative and discursive axioms, images, and texts. Libertarian economists and right-wing politicians were particularly intentional in constructing cultural channels that would serve their political-economic efforts. The third group, activist evangelicals, contributed to neoliberal individualism with varying degrees of intention regarding overt policies, but all emphasized an individual relationship with God and personal salvation as the solution to life's problems, including jobs and household finances. Like the Norma Rae icon, their contributions to the cultural formation were often cognitive and affective, without an evident doctrinaire tie to the political economy.

Three white men demonstrate these cultural channels that helped form neoliberal individualism during the 1970s and '80s: Milton Friedman, Ronald Reagan, and Billy Graham. Their prominence—like that of the Norma Rae icon—works to obscure histories, organizations, and collaborative efforts that made their celebrity possible. Their popularity bloomed from decades of clubs, businesses, and media, and their contributions converged with many others. But Friedman, Reagan, and Graham were especially talented at disseminating narratives and emotions through discourse, catchphrases, and imagery. These men were not malicious dictators or members of a confidential sect. They were charming, articulate performers on behalf of nationwide groups of economists, politicians, and evangelicals that participated in mutually reinforcing, and often joint, conferences and meetings. Their amiable yet commanding appeal allowed them to reach a global audience with ideas that had extensive sources.[28]

Radical libertarian economists were crucial contributors who translated cerebral theory and extreme practices—austerity budgets, regressive income taxes, tax cuts for wealth and inheritance, elaborate regulation of monetary policy and currency, open global capital and trade markets, deregulation of employment conditions and financial oversight, anti-union rules—into appealing popular rhetoric. They built on previous efforts by conservative groups, including the National Association of Manufacturers, US Chamber of Commerce, and Business Roundtable, to undermine worker organizing and labor's political power and to further orchestrate government programs for private business. In some locations, they had allies among white workers who thought unions were socialist or viewed the labor movement as corrupt.[29]

In the 1960s, Friedman, a University of Chicago economist, emerged as a national business leader. In support of Barry Goldwater's 1964 presidential campaign, he wrote a piece for the *New York Times Magazine* stating that his philosophy was committed to the "freedom of the individual to pursue his own interests."[30] In the 1970s, business elites and organizations such as the American Enterprise Association shifted their identities with Friedman, from "economic royalists" to "protectors of individual liberty."[31] The narrative embedded in their mainstream appearances, speeches, and books celebrated choice in the market as the most intoxicating and valid form of rights and responsibilities—and the entrepreneur as its zenith.[32]

When the combined deep recession and rocketing inflation triggered anxiety and anger, more public attention than usual turned to economic discourse. Friedman became a popular figure recognized for speaking in short sentences and accessible terms like "free-market economics." He presented himself as an insurgent populist who believed in freedom and choices. As a result of his rhetorical style, Friedman received a column in *Newsweek* and made regular appearances on *Firing Line* with William F. Buckley (1966–71 local, 1971–99 PBS) and *The Phil Donahue Show* (1967–70 local, 1970–96 national).[33] He described the market as a complex but inherently logical set of systems better left to work on its own so the individual could succeed—a zealous oversimplification that appealed to viewers looking for an answer while mystifying the market as beyond their understanding.[34] After receiving the 1976 Nobel Prize in Economic Sciences for his research on consumption analysis, monetary history and theory, and stabilization policy, Friedman gained even more attention.

In 1977, a PBS station manager in Pennsylvania persuaded Friedman to do a series based on his book *Capitalism and Freedom* (1962). In the introduction, Friedman states that capitalist markets freed the serfs, preserved Jews in Europe, and helped overcome discrimination against African Americans in the South, as if these were proven historic facts rather than his interpretation. He emphasizes individualist self-sufficiency with an affect of combativeness throughout the book and says, "To the free man, the country is the collection of individuals who compose it, not something over and above him."[35] This language did more than present his economic theory of free-market capitalism. It promoted a holistic worldview.

After reading *Capitalism and Freedom*, the station manager left the Democratic Party to become a "free-market evangelist." His Friedman project converged with relentless Republican criticism about the supposed liberal bias of PBS, and his proposal for the series, *Free to Choose*, declared it would be a neutral, objective show about the "free market," even though Friedman was transparent in his advocacy of particular tax, trade, and currency policies. The manager and staff also assembled a new funding stream with the cooperation of corporate foundations and donors, all of which earned the series an appearance of "balance" and a budget.[36]

Episodes aired in 1980, with Friedman declaring that "freedom is the ultimate goal and the individual is the ultimate entity." He articulated a seductive if imaginary level playing field, an economic utopia where individuals make choices in a natural and neutral market as they progress through its complicated but logical systems. In this utopia, individuals who work hardest and make the best choices succeed by earning financial rewards. He also proposed cutting public services and government oversight of banking, corporations, and employment, because individuals would then have the ability to make "free choices." Whereas economists such as John Kenneth Galbraith, who narrated the BBC series *The Age of Uncertainty* (1977), discussed a collapse of certainties, Friedman offered new certainties as a rebel economist.[37]

Viewers wrote PBS to express appreciation for Friedman's "spontaneous" ideas and simple points that eluded elite academics, missing the fact that he was an elite research academic with extensive ties to universities and institutes. To carry his ideas further, Friedman dedicated time and resources to get videotapes of *Free to Choose* to as many high school and higher education students as possible.[38] Friedman also worked with his wife, economist Rose D. Friedman, to publish a book based on the television series, and they conscientiously refined the episodes' vernacular language. They took several months to travel, and he gave talks based on the episodes, using audience feedback to hone the text to potent and succinct points.

The book *Free to Choose* (1980) asked readers to "turn the issues over in your mind at leisure, consider the many arguments, let them simmer, and after a long time turn your preferences into convictions." It culminated with the notion that "human freedom and economic freedom working together came to their greatest fruition in the United States. . . . Fortunately, we are waking up. We are again recognizing the dangers of an overgoverned society."[39] This soaring rhetoric and emotion called readers to stand in defiance, and the book became a bestseller. It made Friedman an exemplar of the narrative and affective work libertarian economists did to constitute mainstream neoliberal individualism. Even Galbraith conceded that Friedman was the most influential economic figure of the 1980s, despite what he saw as extremist economic ideas.[40]

Others carried the concepts into public conversation as well. Speakers with less celebrity, including Friedrich von Hayek, Ron Paul, and Thomas Sowell, appeared on television. Right-wing philanthropy funded the spread of ideas through groups such as the Americanism Educational League. The league bought several sets of *Free to Choose* and loaned them to universities. In the 2020s, a freetochoose.tv website kept Friedman's series in circulation and produced new shows, hosted by contemporary libertarian economists, that continued to distill his ideas for mainstream viewers.[41]

College groups including Students in Free Enterprise took up the rhetoric, distributing pamphlets from institutions such as the Foundation for Economic Education. One pamphlet declared, "Collectivism as a way of life is a manifestation of the abyss into which men sink when not motivated by the pursuit of truth and justice." Students in Free Enterprise carried Friedman's language and emotion further into the mainstream with public service announcements and booths in malls. In the 1980s, the group popularized an elementary school version of *Free to Choose* with skits, and its "business superhero" SIFE-Man appeared in a cape with a dollar sign on his chest. He was not based on researched economics or intensive policy debates; he was created from the students' perception of a desperate need to defend US society, as understood in market terms, from powerful villains like the state.[42] They entered adulthood, national party politics, and think tanks trained in the rhetoric and affect of neoliberal individualism.

Libertarian economists and their followers, however, remained silent on the question of protecting individuals from people and organizations that seek to enrich themselves at the expense of their fellow citizens and neighbors.[43] Because they argued that the market took care of everything, they did not discuss how to prohibit corporate activities that seriously damage shared resources, like air, water, and soil, that every individual depends on. Such concerns about the individual and corporations or firms as abstract organizations remained outside the formation of neoliberal individualism and its making of meanings and dispositions.

Although centrist Republicans and New Democrats in the 1990s and 2000s advocated policies and projects in the overall neoliberal turn, right-wing politicians were crucial to the coalescing cultural formation in the 1980s. Their channel of discourse, imaginaries, sound bites, and images often intersected with libertarian economists, and Reagan relied on Friedman as an unofficial adviser.[44] British prime minister Margaret Thatcher is a notable example, and her most famous contribution appeared in a 1987 magazine interview. "They are casting their problems on society and who is society? There is no such thing!" she said. "There are individual men and women, and there are families and no government can do anything except through people, and people look to themselves first." She criticized the idea of teaching children that society is at fault. "There is no such thing as society. There is a living tapestry of men and women and people . . . and the quality of our lives will depend upon how much each of us is prepared to take responsibility for ourselves."[45] Thatcher often spoke in this mode of the combative individual, an outsider taking on insider Labour elites, wasteful government, and orthodox Conservative men.

Reagan was also a dynamic, assertive speaker who contributed concision and vitality to neoliberal individualism. As governor and president, Reagan worked with his staff to craft staged photo opportunities and press conferences, as well as his pithy narrative about government. He was extremely effective at this cultural work after decades in broadcasting, acting, and public speaking.[46] He had developed a welcoming style that drew viewers to his messaging, which instigated a sense of encroaching doom before pronouncing glorious individualist and free-market solutions.

His time as GE spokesman allowed Reagan to perfect his genial persona while soaking up and practicing the company's sharp rhetoric about communism, capitalism, and the conflict between freedom and government. GE corporate literature emphasized the primacy of the individual in the free market as the site of liberty and progress. In the 1950s, when an employee complained about not receiving a Christmas bonus, the company response stated, "We feel that every time the state, an employer, or anyone else takes over one of our individual responsibilities completely, we are one step further along the road to socialism and a halt to progress."[47] Reagan did not create such ideas, but he was an ardent and aspirational persona on their behalf.

Like the GE literature, Reagan's political speeches presented audiences with a simplistic binary of good capitalism / bad communism. Like Friedman, he conflated capitalism with free-market economics: if people did not support free markets as defined by radical libertarian economists, they supported the horrors of communism. In sweeping language, Reagan held up the United States as the archetype of freedom and free enterprise, in contrast to the authoritarian Soviet Union.[48] His 1964 speech for Goldwater announced that Americans were faced with the choice between freedom and totalitarianism. In a radio address he wrote for September 1976, Reagan quoted the London *Daily Mail*: "The US is the first nation on earth deliberately dedicated to letting people choose what they want and giving them a chance to get it. For all its terrible faults, in one sense America still is the last, best hope of mankind."[49] In this worldview, neoliberal policies offered the only alternative to communist dictatorship.

Throughout his political career, Reagan used grand emotion and idealism to applaud the individual risk-taker. He celebrated the United States as the center of triumphant individual liberty and joined a growing discourse of the entrepreneurial mind-set.[50] "Freedom and the dignity of the individual have been more available and assured here than in any other place on earth," he said. In his 1985 second inaugural address, Reagan announced that the time had "come for a new American emancipation—a great national drive to tear down economic barriers and liberate the spirit of enterprise." He declared that Americans had decided to "strive with all our strength toward the ultimate in individual freedom."[51] These declarations infused his comments with oppositional certainty.

When discussing economic programs, Reagan spoke as if all jobs were equally good, with the dignity of work standing in for working conditions, and said workfare reforms were an attempt at "salvaging human beings."[52] For inheritance tax cuts, Reagan turned attention away from "the wealthy" as an aggregate group and instead highlighted struggling family farms.[53] Then efforts by elite experts to restructure wealth taxes appeared to help working farmers rather than intensify the concentration of assets for the richest people.

Reagan's most repeated sound bite was the accusation that government caused the nation's problems, so it could never be the solution. In his Goldwater speech, Reagan tied this narrative to a compelling alarm when he said, "The government can find some charge to bring against any concern it chooses to prosecute. Every businessman has his own tale of harassment. . . . Our national inalienable rights are now considered to be a dispensation of government, and freedom has never been so fragile, so close to slipping from our grasp."[54] Reagan announced his fear that private property rights were "so diluted that public interest is almost anything that a few government planners decide."[55]

Responding to the second oil crisis in 1975, Reagan announced, "Our problem isn't a shortage of oil. It's a surplus of government." This catchy axiom served three purposes: it removed blame from petroleum corporations previously seen as greedy gougers, directed blame toward government intervention in the market, and celebrated deregulation as the only solution (done selectively, without ending subsidies). In his first inaugural address, in 1981, Reagan applied this narrative to the United States as a whole. "In this present crisis, government is not the solution to our problem. Government is the problem," he stated. "[It is time to] check and reverse the growth of government which shows signs of having grown beyond the consent of the governed." His second inaugural address grandly proclaimed, "For the first time in history, government, the people said, was not our master, it was our servant."[56]

When Reagan was not blaming government in the abstract, he was ignoring the decisive contributions of actual government programs and agencies. He spoke fondly of *Little House on the Prairie* (1974–83), a television series that erased both the federal services provided to ameliorate the poverty of most plains settlers and the collective efforts they needed to survive. Instead, the show celebrated the individual work ethic in a Christian family. In a 1976 radio address, Reagan said, "Farms and small businesses are really the backbone of our free enterprise system—millions of individuals making their own way," without acknowledging the subsidies and public systems that supported most contemporary farms and industries.[57] He omitted federal and state land grants, army attacks on indigenous peoples, real estate surveys, railroads, construction of ports and highways, water and sewer lines, and waste management that government offices and programs had provided from public tax revenues and enforced and protected with the US military for two centuries.[58]

Reagan used the bully pulpit to "spread the faith of the free market," and his boosters took up the emotional call.[59] T. Boone Pickens Jr., who had made millions in petroleum and finance, wrote in *Fortune* magazine, "The American free enterprise spirit is something we will be able to maintain only under a Reagan Administration. . . . At stake in this election is the future of the free enterprise system."[60] Reagan's boosters argued the nation was endangered, suffering from a lack of investment because tax rates sapped the willingness of individuals to invest and work, which led reporters to popularize the term "supply-side economics."[61]

Throughout his presidency, Reagan equated secularism with overbearing government, stating that "those who have discarded the time-tested values upon which our very civilization is based . . . proclaim they are freeing us from superstitions of the past. They have taken upon themselves the job of superintending us by government rule and regulation." He entangled Christianity and freedom in phrases that coincided with those of activist evangelicals, such as his friend and adviser Billy Graham. At the 1983 National Association of Evangelicals meeting, Reagan said, "Freedom prospers when religion is vibrant and the rule of law under God is acknowledged. . . . We will never give away our freedom. We will never abandon our belief in God."[62]

Activist evangelicals furnished another cultural channel that helped forge neoliberal individualism through a variety of media.[63] *Newsweek* even declared 1976 "The Year of the Evangelical" because of their increased involvement in national as well as state politics, including Carter's run for president. Most American Protestantism grew from and participates in long-running theological debates about pietism, which envisions personal transformation through a spiritual rebirth derived from individual devotion and reading the Bible as a private and literal experience. Evangelicals did not initiate this Protestant emphasis on the individual, but activism in the 1970s and '80s adapted the theology to assert its worldview in more public forums, with the intention of impacting policy and legislation.[64]

Evangelical activists built on Christian endeavors that had grown during the twentieth century. Since World War I, conservative evangelicals articulated a rigid opposition to communism and the Soviet Union and equated these with any collective movement, like worker organizing, which they said destroyed the individual. Fundamentalists believed that only individual salvation and biblical interpretation provided life answers, and conservative evangelicals such as the 1930s proselytizing manufacturing executive Robert G. LeTourneau agreed that "an individualistic application of the problems of the Christian gospel will solve the problems of contemporary industrial society."[65] Unions were not just communist; they were profane.

Starting in the 1940s, evangelicals and corporations formed more official relationships. General Motors employees received *Guideposts*, founded by the minister Norman Vincent Peale and his wife, with its inspirational mix of Christianity, anticommunism, individualism, and free enterprise. Evangelicals joined work sites as industrial chaplains, especially in the South, to fight communism and protect individual freedom by obstructing labor unions. They offered personal religious solutions for the concerns of workers and downplayed worker solidarity or collective organizing. As with the human resources departments that emerged in the postwar period, industrial chaplains believed workers should interact as individuals with managers and administrators. When union membership shrank in the 1970s, some chaplains remained, emphasizing salvation and free enterprise as the solution to worker issues.[66]

As early as the 1950s, Graham contributed to the spread of evangelical activism when he traveled to revivals and warned that America needed a spiritual renewal of born-again Christians for its fight against the Soviet Union. He sought politicians to talk to about individualism, freedom, and free enterprise linked to Christianity and God. In 1953, Graham and Dwight Eisenhower partnered to launch a Presidential Prayer Breakfast based on state-level events. Renamed the National Prayer Breakfast in 1970, it attracted more and more politicians from both major parties.[67]

During the 1970s, activist evangelicalism gained momentum. More ministries, radio personalities, and religious organizations pressed the idea that personal salvation must be part of politics. Organizations that originally served a set fundamentalist community in its own church sought to broaden membership and assert a public voice for evangelicals as a whole. The minister Jerry Falwell founded the Moral Majority in 1979 to bring evangelicals into national politics, pronouncing it was not sinful.

Activist evangelicals connected salvation to specific policies and practices, particularly free-market capitalism, and spread their discourses, imaginaries, sound bites, and images through revivals and partnerships with Christian colleges and corporations such as Wal-Mart. Falwell founded Lynchburg Baptist College in 1971 but changed the name to Liberty University in 1985 to capture his vision of "a world filled with doctors, lawyers, teachers, entrepreneurs, and professionals from all walks of life who loved God." In 1982, Oklahoma Christian University helped develop Enterprise Square USA, a tourist attraction for free-market capitalism that warned of the horrors of government control.[68]

Freedom with an emphasis on the saved individual was a galvanizing concept for activist evangelicals. Evangelical groups equated premarital sex, homosexuality, women who did not have children, and alcohol and drug use with personal bondage and the "compulsions" of modern secular life. They promoted freedom from these "fixations" through salvation and reading the Bible. In this worldview, personal freedom did not derive from bodily autonomy or the ability to make decisions about medical care, marriage, sexuality, and gender. It derived from one's free and open connection to Christ. This

Christ-centered liberty denounced behaviors, from smoking cigarettes to having gay and lesbian relationships, that threatened a person's freedom by giving these compulsions the control.

Because they viewed certain behaviors as bondage, activist evangelicals did not recognize a conflict between individualism, freedom, the golden rule, and their drive to criminalize birth control, abortion access, and sex education; proscribe homosexuality; and severely punish drug use. Some conservative evangelicals even argued that the broad liberal idea of freedom, with its pluralism and tolerance for diversity, was a devil's mask for sinfulness and selfishness.[69]

As with Friedman and Reagan, Graham excelled at circulating popular discourse and imaginaries through the evangelical channel and advanced cultural contributions to neoliberal individualism. By the 1960s, Graham was a celebrated personality with newspaper interviews, radio and television shows, appearances with famous performers and politicians, and best-selling books.[70] He did not invent Christian media but was proficient at using them all to present the evangelical worldview.[71] Graham reached mainstream audiences and gave millions of people repeated opportunities to absorb the narrative certainty and aspirational affect.[72]

Graham emphasized the individual as the site of salvation and salvation as the solution to all problems in every household and in the world. In his best-selling 1978 book *How to Be Born Again*, he said, "I have had countless people tell me, in person and by letter, how they were born again and their lives were changed. . . . The central theme of the universe is the purpose and destiny of every individual. . . . Lives can be remarkably changed, marriages excitingly improved, societies influenced for good—all by the simple, sweeping surge of individuals knowing what it is to be born again." Graham describes a man named Joe, a thief who had learned that stealing and lying were "good." Rather than providing social or economic analysis of the whole context, Graham argues Joe must recognize his sin and have faith in Christ to become free as a born-again individual. "Salvation is by Christ alone, through faith alone, for the glory of God alone" without attention to systems, situations, or even good deeds.[73]

In this worldview, circumstances derive not from social, political, and economic structures or even community but rather from an individual relationship with God, assisted by the Holy Spirit. Graham was not a deviant authoritarian minister manipulating unthinking audiences. He was participating in a common American evangelical discourse to provide encouragement and "guidance to those who are frustrated by the events of our generation."[74] Graham's radio, television, magazine, and book preaching, however, distilled and enriched an economic and political as well as religious dedication to the individual. His narrative was so successful, Reagan even recirculated it when he announced, "There is a great spiritual awakening in America, a renewal of the traditional values that have been the bedrock of America's goodness and greatness."[75]

Confronted by knotty world conflicts and complicated economic crises, which hit households that had envisioned prosperity and security for generations to come, radical libertarian economists, right-wing politicians, and activist evangelicals offered firm assurance in the face of angst. They said each individual could improve his or her situation and save the nation through defiant aspiration, choices in the market, hard work, and a relationship with Christ. They shared these ideas in impressions and tones people could inhabit imaginatively in their everyday lives.

A fourth channel, American pop culture, produced shows, catchphrases, sound bites, and representations that inadvertently served neoliberal individualism in this way. Their individualist images and dialogue were rich with emotion and closure, and new technologies allowed for rapid media replication. As discussed, Hollywood writers and directors do not usually conspire to reproduce political-economic policies and practices. Neither do their products simply reflect society around them or function as single free-floating texts. Popular media exist in active relation to all other aspects of society, and based on the historical contingencies of each time period, specific cultural products join into conversation with specific political-economic discourses. At the "messy intersections" of different sets of texts and their repetitions, the cultural work of making sense of the world happens.[76] This sense is made via linguistic, cognitive, imaginative, and emotional bonds soldered at key fusible points. It is constructed, contingent, social, and emotional.

The Norma Rae icon that cohered in the 1980s and '90s illustrates how American pop culture served neoliberal individualism without contributing an overt slogan, political aphorism, or economic theory. Instead, the icon provided narrative validation and affective inspiration.[77] Rose & Asseyev Productions, Martin Ritt, Twentieth Century-Fox, and the writers, editors, showrunners, and bloggers who circulated the icon had no intention of supporting a neoliberal turn. The icon's sharp individualist narrative and affect of defiance, however, aligned with the mainstream cultural formation of neoliberal individualism, which worked to naturalize and veil policies and procedures promoted by the apparatus of neoliberal expertise. The icon bolstered the notion that discrete but generalized individuals are responsible for big social, political, and economic problems and solutions. More significant, the sensations of its enchanting heroic posture blended with the cultural formation's potent structure of feeling—a pattern of tones, attitudes, and impulses of personal demand and defiance.[78]

Three features distinguish the Norma Rae icon from other recirculated fragments of pop culture and make it extraordinary. Although many Hollywood stars, like John Wayne and Marilyn Monroe, become iconic celebrities and sell millions of posters, t-shirts, and knickknacks for many years, the Norma Rae icon served the notion of individual combativeness for various causes. It was not a commodification of Sally Field's celebrity.

Second, even though Hollywood specializes in rebellious heroes solving big problems, few movies produce one moment that endures as a reference for over four decades. Almost none generate an icon in a visual and linguistic combination that can be adapted to carry a consistent notion and feeling across an assortment of purposes. Other 1970s movies about the working class—*Joe* (1970), *Dog Day Afternoon* (1975), *Rocky* (1976), *Saturday Night Fever* (1977), and *The Deer Hunter* (1978)—had memorable depictions of volatile blue-collar white men but did not generate an icon. *Dirty Harry* (1971) and *The Godfather* (1972) established catchphrases: "Go ahead, make my day," and "I'm gonna make him an offer he can't refuse." Martin Scorsese's *Alice Doesn't Live Here Anymore* was one of the few movies about working-class white women on the job, and it received critical acclaim but not a singular circulating image.[79]

Lastly, the Norma Rae icon is remarkable because it originated in historic raw material—low-wage workers in a complex labor movement—that directly opposes the concepts and projects of elite neoliberal expertise. Key moments from Crystal Lee's life story, extracted and ordered by previous media, allowed Ritt to create a movie that derived from the labor movement without foregrounding its collective principles or history of organizing. The production team understood capital investment, and Ritt promised box office success. He knew to focus on one character's transformation. As a result, even a left-leaning director produced a movie that personalized systemic problems and reified the individual. *Norma Rae* did not guarantee the inception of an icon but made it possible. Analysis of how the icon cohered illuminates its convergence with neoliberal individualism and its ability to draw people into accepting and even valuing extreme policies and practices that erode their political-economic position.[80]

Since the 1980s, video and text media have developed and deployed the icon in both visual and linguistic form. Through these uses, the icon has fused with its combined narrative of *individual defiance is the way* and affect of rebelliousness, which mingled with discourse, imaginaries, sound bites, and images from libertarian economists, right-wing politicians, and evangelical activists. On television, writers often used the icon to comment on an individual stand but with a hint of comic relief. Because of television's dependence on three interrelated revenue sources—capital from investors to produce shows, sales for advertising slots during shows, and either time or subscription fees from viewers wanting to see shows—it cannot afford to alienate people. In text, the icon appears in two venues: general blogs, websites, and social media; and newspapers and magazines. The labor movement also reappropriates and deploys the Norma Rae icon for flyers, social media posts, and online campaigns. Even in this last category, however, the icon appeals foremost to individual rebelliousness rather than to solidarity in action and still transmits the divisive notion of the white American working class in industry.

Starting with the 1981 episode of *Archie Bunker's Place* and running through a 2020 episode of *Gentefied* (2020–21), the Norma Rae icon has reached millions of people through beloved series. Over time, its usage rarely had an overt relation to the industrial working class but retained the narrative and affect of individual defiance, undercut by an inflection of comic relief to avoid audience agitation. Several illustrative examples track the icon's emergence and solidification and how television stripped it down to bare individual rebelliousness.

The first season of *Roseanne* (1988–97) has two Norma Rae allusions, which served as a bridge to the icon's coherence. Like *Archie Bunker's Place*, the sitcom portrays a working-class character with a valid grievance about a manufacturing job. Roseanne works at Wellman Plastics, where she and three coworkers become frustrated at the lack of women's room supplies. When the foreman chastises her for going into the men's room for paper towels, she laughs, holds one overhead, and calls out, "Union." The foreman smiles and tells someone to get paper towels. This scene captures the contradictions of the icon on television: the women share a complaint and express awareness that Wellman uses small worries to distract them from serious concerns, such as benefits and safety. Their conversation, however, ends with laughter.

The second allusion occurs in the season finale, which *Vulture* magazine listed in 2018 as an essential episode with the comment, "Roseanne has her own Norma Rae moment."[81] Roseanne quits after a new manager raises quotas, and some friends leave with her but without collective organizing. In a dive bar during the show's last seconds, Roseanne laughs and calls herself "Sally Field" while she and her friends drink, without jobs in a town with few options.[82]

The icon solidified when writers had a character comment on another's defiant stand by calling it a "Norma Rae moment" or "going Norma Rae." One of the first instances of this appeared in a 1988 episode of *Who's the Boss?* (1984–92) in reference to a male housekeeper. The series relies on this gender-norm reversal played for comedy: Tony, an Italian American man and former boxer, works for Angela, a WASPy high-powered corporate executive. When housekeepers in her affluent Connecticut neighborhood find out Tony makes more money than they do, they refuse to work.

The Norma Rae Icon on Television

Linguistic form except where noted with an asterisk

Television Series	Episode	Date
1980s		
Archie Bunker's Place	"Norma Rae Bunker"	Season 3, Episode 4, 1981
Roseanne	"The Memory Game"*	Season 1, Episode 7, 1988
Who's the Boss?	"Housekeepers Unite"	Season 4, Episode 19, 1988
Roseanne	"Let's Call It Quits"	Season 1, Episode 23, 1989
1990s		
Frasier	"Sleeping with the Enemy"	Season 3, Episode 6, 1995
2000s		
The West Wing	"The Lame Duck Congress"	Season 2, Episode 6, 2000
Dawson's Creek	"To Green, with Love"	Season 3, Episode 16, 2000
Friends	"The One Where Rachel Goes Back to Work"	Season 9, Episode 11, 2003
Queer as Folk	"Poster May Lead to the Truth"	Season 3, Episode 11, 2003
Dead Like Me	"Reaping Havoc"	Season 1, Episode 5, 2003
Gilmore Girls	"Welcome to the Dollhouse"	Season 6, Episode 6, 2005
Lost	"S.O.S."	Season 2, Episode 19, 2006
Gilmore Girls	"Introducing Lorelai Planetarium"	Season 7, Episode 8, 2006
King of the Hill	"Bobby Rae"	Season 12, Episode 2, 2007
2010s		
Glee	"The Substitute"*	Season 2, Episode 7, 2010
18 to Life	"In Sickness and in Health"	Season 1, Episode 11, 2010
The Office	"Whistleblower"	Season 6, Episode 26, 2010
Parks and Recreation	"Bowling for Votes"	Season 4, Episode 13, 2012
Commercial for Las Vegas Convention and Visitors Authority	"Norma Rae"*	2012
Madam Secretary	"Another Benghazi"	Season 1, Episode 2, 2014
2 Broke Girls	"And the Zero Tolerance"	Season 4, Episode 16, 2015
Orange Is the New Black	"We Can Be Heroes"	Season 3, Episode 11, 2015
Orange Is the New Black	"We'll Always Have Baltimore"	Season 4, Episode 5, 2016
Pose	"Access"	Season 1, Episode 2, 2018
2020s		
Shameless	"O Captain, My Captain"	Season 10, Episode 9, 2020
Gentefied	"Protest Tacos"	Season 1, Episode 9, 2020

Tony insists he cannot stop because Angela is a good boss. The show implies he has higher pay because of her generosity, not because he is a man or had made a demand. Angela encourages Tony to support the housekeepers in their strike because those who are "more fortunate" cannot turn their backs on those who are deprived, which makes his work stoppage charity, not solidarity. Angela is fine until she does not have Tony's labor for an unexpected dinner party.

A few hours before the client dinner, Angela wears a bandanna as a babushka and cleans the living room. When a housekeeper comes to the door, Angela calls out, "It's for you, Norma Rae," and pauses for the laugh track. The housekeeper announces the offscreen strike has ended, and Angela removes her babushka in an immediate return to the upper class. The show closes with Angela giving Tony another raise and toasting, "To solidarity."[83] The housekeepers' effort was brief, but Tony's alliance with his boss sustains him.

The icon expanded beyond sitcoms in the 2000s, and the dramedy *Gilmore Girls* (2000–2007) exemplifies how it became more individualistic, without any association to labor or an offscreen group. In season 6, the main character, Lorelai, argues with town officials when they want to rename the street where she co-owns a quaint New England inn. The town tourism board plans to rename her street "Sores and Boils Alley" because it had a nineteenth-century hospital. Lorelai tells her co-owners that she stood on a bench "all Norma Rae" to demand the town keep the current name. She did not succeed, however, because a selectman patted her head and said, "Good girl," and she overreacted.[84] Lorelai rises in defiance but stands alone without success.

A Las Vegas Convention and Visitors Authority "Norma Rae" commercial was part of a 2012 "Take Back Your Summer" advertising campaign that circulated through cable television and early streaming services. The campaign targeted viewers as consumers affected by the mortgage recession who were feeling pressure to not take vacations. The commercial starts with people in an office at gray computers on repetitive gray desks. Phones ring softly and keyboards click. Then a woman gets on her desk. Her wrinkled khaki skirt and bland casual shirt and cardigan mark her as a regular worker. She announces that she has saved forty-seven vacation days, smiles, and holds up a sign that reads, VACATION NOW! A fun star dots the exclamation point.[85]

None of her peers join her or even show interest. The lack of solidarity and the woman's lonely stand make her defiance the brunt of a joke rather than a radical act. The commercial argues that the "real" act of rebellion is not labor solidarity or collective action but the private consumer's willingness to go on vacation. It ignores the union movement and decades of violent confrontation that made employment benefits possible and elides the constant

The "Norma Rae" commercial for the 2012 Las Vegas Convention and Visitors Authority "Take Back Your Summer" advertising campaign. | Made by R&R Partners for the LVCVA, screenshot courtesy of the author

labor fights in Las Vegas over fair pay and conditions for hotel, hospitality, and sex workers.

Like the icon's use on television, most of its appearances on blogs, websites, and social media accentuate someone's personal stand yet defuse it, even when referring to a serious, if fleeting, moment of rebellion. An angry Wal-Mart shopper, who dislikes self-checkout because it eliminates jobs and forces customers to do the retail labor, complained loudly to a manager in a 2004 "Norma Rae moment" she described on a discussion board. In 2014, a man shared on his blog that he "went Norma Rae" by announcing his dissatisfaction to a spin instructor who was always late, and a 2020 Facebook user posted "Trump is having a Norma Rae moment" when he refused to accept the election outcome.[86]

Newspapers and magazines, which combine journalism standards and editorial oversight with efforts to catch limited attention spans in an ocean of digital options, most often deploy the icon as a hook for an earnest article about unions or exploitation of workers. Even when writers and graphic artists consciously use the icon as a marker for US workers, it perpetuates the individualist narrative and the racialized, industrialized meaning for the American working class. Two newspaper pieces illustrate this point. A 2001 *Los Angeles Times* review of *Nickel and Dimed: On (Not) Getting By in America* by Barbara Ehrenreich is titled "Calling Norma Rae," despite the book's focus on expanding retail and service labor with many people of color.[87] The icon might hook readers, but its individualist white hero from an old factory controverts Ehrenreich's reporting. A 2013 *New York Times* article, "At Cablevision, Norma Rae's Been Escorted Outside," refers to members of Communications Workers of America (CWA) being fired while attempting to speak to an executive about dragging contract negotiations. In the accompanying photo, a worker, La'kesia Johnson, appears in a stylish cape and hat at a dapper angle with seven men of color gathered for solidarity.[88] The article explains a messy

Using the Norma Rae icon, a woman argues Nilla Wafers are a respectable office snack, and a father demands better libraries for his children. | *Love This Space* and *Long Distance Dad* blogs, screenshots courtesy of the author

situation in which some workers discussed decertifying the union and Johnson worried about impacts on coworkers and her family. The title exemplifies the limits of having such a dominant icon with its narrative of individualist rebellion based on a notion of a poor white worker in a midcentury factory.

Some mainstream media, as well as a southern country band, deploy the icon as a generic representation of the American working class, transmitting the notion that it is white and industrial. Without intention, these uses maintain the historic racial fragmentation of US workers and the racialized notion of the white working class. In this way, long-standing, intersecting divisions of race, gender, ethnicity, and citizenship that served elites throughout the twentieth century continue to serve the apparatus of neoliberal expertise into the twenty-first century.

A 2015 *Salon* piece about the limited news coverage of workers and increasing coverage of entrepreneurs provides an example. At the top of the online article, the moderator for NBC's *Meet the Press* is superimposed on the Norma Rae icon. The author writes, "Working people, meanwhile, find themselves lavished with much less attention. And forget about unions, which, even in their diminished state, still represent millions and millions of people." Yet editors cropped the icon to cut off the UNION sign, eliminating the visual reference to labor organizing while perpetuating the racialized and industrialized meaning for the American working class.[89]

The 2017 website for Norma Rae, a country band from Athens, Georgia, included their photo: three white men and a white woman in casual jackets and t-shirts standing over a pool table in a dim honky-tonk. The description said, "Like the heroine from the famous movie, Norma Rae gives a voice to the working class; to the people struggling to make ends meet; to the folks who work hard; to you and me. Norma Rae gets down to the nitty gritty of life, love, and social concerns and blends original lyrics with raw, inescapably Southern harmonies into its American sound. The stories told are inspired from real life struggles and indelibly sown to the unpretentious and unpredictable, soggy part of the real South."[90] The band conflates the South and its white industrial workers with the American working class as a whole. The result racializes and simplifies the meaning and emphasizes toughness in remote struggles to live day to day, rather than unions or long-term movement building.

In the arena of cultural politics, unions and labor activists have also claimed the Norma Rae icon, just as Crystal Lee reappropriated the movie. Their flyers and posts often have the same contradiction as newspapers: they might grab attention and spark a sense of recognition, but they inadvertently perpetuate the individualist defiance and working-class whiteness embedded in it. The best outcomes happen when workers or members dig beyond the icon and discover their bond to histories of collective labor activism.

A 2011 blog post titled "Last Night's PEP Meeting on Verizon Contract and Its 'Norma Rae' Moment" exemplifies the dilemma. It describes a rally before a meeting of the New York City Panel for Educational Policy regarding a Verizon contract. The author explains the exhilarating situational allegiance between parents, teachers, and striking CWA Verizon workers. She emphasizes that a new technology contract benefited the corporation at the expense of both schools and Verizon employees. A video clip spotlights one woman: "Amy Muldoon, a passionate Verizon striker and mom, calls out the DOE." Muldoon, a white woman, is surrounded by Asian, Black, and white parents, teachers, and workers, with a young Black woman behind her for the microphone. Muldoon declares herself a striking worker, parent, and taxpayer, which makes her "different than Verizon"—inciting applause.[91] People shout and wave signs as she articulates a shared message, but use of the icon both lauds and reduces her action, celebrating its force while marking it as singular instead of a link in a bigger effort.

In a 2015 New York State United Teachers (NYSUT) post, a photo from a community forum directed toward Governor Andrew Cuomo shows a female teacher holding a large sign overhead. The sign declares "98% teacher effectiveness" and blames state testing, designed by corporations, for the district's low scores. To her right, a man is clapping, and the caption reads, "Vice President Paul Pecorale (right) applauds South Seneca teacher Cindy Brewer's 'Norma Rae' moment during the Lansing Community Forum," again praising her but labeling her stand as individual and brief.[92]

The Norma Rae Icon in Text Media

Visual and linguistic forms

Media Type	Creator, outlet	Icon appearance(s)	Date
Social Media, Blogs, and Websites			
Blog	Dolo Amber, Democratic Underground forum	*Linguistic:* "'Norma Rae' moment at the Mall-wart"	2004
Blog	Monica Crowley, "Norma Rae . . . Or Norma Desmond?," *Monica Memo*	*Linguistic:* "Hillary has spent her entire adult life as Norma Rae: the fighter who defies authority and the naysayers by muscling her way to the top."	2008
Blog	Denise Wymore, "Tellers: Not Just for Balancing Anymore," *Denise Wymore*	*Visual:* Norma Rae icon with sign digitally edited to read "Tellers Rule!"	2009
		Linguistic: "I'm the Norma Rae of tellers. I'm the gal standing in the lunchroom with a sign that says 'You CAN'T be SERIOUS!'"	
Blog	"Protesting Prop 8," *Shakesville*	*Visual:* comedian Kathy Griffin holds large sign with UNION crossed out and MARRIAGE written above it to support marriage equality in California	2009
Blog	"Lian: My Norma Rae Moment at the Eye Doctors," *Satellite Sisters*	*Linguistic:* "Norma Rae would have been proud of me. Satellite Sister Sheila would have joined me. I took a stand yesterday in my (former) eye doctor's waiting room."	2010
Facebook post	Donna Whitfield	*Linguistic:* "My Norma Rae moment was taking hold of my life and moving into ministry."	2010
Blog	"Long-Distance Advocacy," *Long Distance Dad*	*Visual:* Norma Rae icon with sign digitally edited to read BETTER LIBRARIES	2012
		Linguistic: "When I get into my Norma Rae mode, my advocacy isn't limited by miles!"	
Blog	Peter Hanlon, "Another Cruel, Cruel Summer for Power Plants," *GraceLinks*	*Linguistic:* "It was as if Illinois fish had a Norma Rae moment, standing together in solidarity!"	2012
Blog	Will Pollock, "Wisconsin Recall," *Ascribe*	*Linguistic:* "Time for a 'Norma Rae' Moment"	2012

The Norma Rae Icon in Text Media (*continued*)

Media Type	Creator, outlet	Icon appearance(s)	Date
Blog	Daphne Ashbrook, "My Norma Rae Moment at Gally 2013," *Daphne Ashbook*	*Visual:* Ashbrook holds sign overhead that says OCCUPY GALLIFREY!	2013
		Linguistic: "My Norma Rae Moment"	
Website	Peter Amsel, "NagaWorld Staff Go Norma Rae," *CalvinAyre*	*Visual:* Norma Rae icon digitally edited with NagaCorp logo	2013
		Linguistic: "NagaWorld Staff Go Norma Rae"	
Blog	"Political Scientists Attempt Political Activity," *Mischiefs of Faction*	*Visual:* Norma Rae icon with sign digitally edited to read NSF	2013
Blog	Kevin Maher, *ThisKevin*	*Visual:* Norma Rae icon with sign digitally edited to read CHAOS REIGNS	2013
Blog	Kevin Maher, *ThisKevin*	*Visual:* inflatable Christmas penguin with sign overhead digitally edited to read SANTA'S THE COOLEST	2013
Blog	"Office Snacks," *Love This Space*	*Visual:* Norma Rae icon with sign digitally edited to read NILLA WAFERS	2014
		Linguistic: "I did not get the job and I knew that's what would happen when I defended the Nilla Wafer but for some reason, this was my Norma Rae moment. . . . I'd like to say I'm fighting for the little guy but the truth is, I just like to be contrary."	
Blog	Alan Greenblatt, "How Millennials Can Make Their Mark on Unions," *Governing*	*Linguistic:* "That led to what Fisher describes as a 'Norma Rae moment.' A couple of grad students sent out an email to some friends, raising the idea of joining a union."	2014
Blog	Dougall Fraser, *Dougall Fraser*	*Linguistic:* "I'm the Norma Rae of Spin Class."	2014
Blog	Lauren Lipton, "Norma Rae Moment," *Lauren Lipton*	*Linguistic:* "For the moment, I seem to be a bit of a Norma Rae figure to mistreated journalists everywhere."	2015

The Norma Rae Icon in Text Media (*continued*)

Media Type	Creator, outlet	Icon appearance(s)	Date
Facebook post	DeeDee Marcelli	*Linguistic:* "Really really great Email!! A Norma Rae moment and now . . . #HappyMakeUpGirl"	August 2015
Reddit entry	"DAE have a Friends quote they regularly use?"	*Linguistic:* "I now regularly use, 'calm down, Norma Rae.'"	2016
Blog	"Joy (****) - Norma Rae Can Stuff It," *coolpapae*	*Linguistic:* "Understandably, they threw the corn fed dramatic twists in there to give [Lawrence] something more to stand up against, just like Norma Rae."	2016
Blog	Michael Logan, "Bob's Burgers," *TVInsider*	*Linguistic:* "'He goes on a one-boy crusade to get the candy company to change back to the original formula,' says Dauterive. 'It's his Norma Rae moment.'"	2016
Website	Norma Rae, country music band, Athens, Georgia	*Linguistic:* "Like the heroine from the famous movie, Norma Rae gives a voice to the working class; to the people struggling to make ends meet; to the folks who work hard; to you and me."	2017
Blog	"Breaking News—Multi," *CHEEZburger*	*Visual:* Norma Rae icon with sign digitally edited to read NO TAGS *Linguistic:* "Multi has Norma Rae Moment"	2018
Facebook post	Alison Mahoney	*Linguistic:* "You guys I had a serious Norma Rae moment today at an audition #micdrop"	2018
Facebook post	Lee Ann Huntley	*Linguistic:* "Trump is having a Norma Rae moment it will take the National guard to get him out of there"	2020
Facebook post	Evanthia Hill	*Linguistic:* "My Norma Rae moment. Happy Labor Day! Join your union." *Visual:* woman with sign overhead reading WE SUPPORT OUR STATE EMPLOYEES! VERMONT STATE EMPLOYEES' ASSOCIATION	2021

The Norma Rae Icon in Text Media (*continued*)

Media Type	Creator, outlet	Icon appearance(s)	Date
Newspapers and Magazines			
Book review	Stephen Metcalf, *Los Angeles Times*	*Linguistic:* headline, "Calling Norma Rae," review of *Nickel and Dimed: On (Not) Getting By in America* by Barbara Ehrenreich	2001
Article	Stefan Fastis, *Wall Street Journal*	*Linguistic:* headline, "Norma Rae of Jocks Leads Push vs. NCAA"	2001
Article	Brian Lowry, *Variety*	*Linguistic:* headline, "SAG Misses Its 'Norma Rae' Moment: No Reason to Believe Studios Will Capitulate"	2008
Cover article	*Memphis Flyers*	*Linguistic:* cover headline, "The *Norma Rae* Moment: A Look Back at the Grizzlies' Magical Season of Heart, Grit, and Grind"	2011
Op-ed	Kyle Smith, "Inequality for All," *New York Post*	*Linguistic:* "In his 'Norma Rae' moment, [former labor secretary Robert Reich] nudges us all toward a solution."	2013
Article	Michael Powell, *New York Times*	*Linguistic:* headline, "At Cablevision, Norma Rae's Been Escorted Outside"	2013
Essay	Leonard Nalencz, "Kafka and the Nurses," *Al Jazeera America*	*Linguistic:* "Elise's response struck me as a reverse Norma Rae moment. . . . I had assumed my class would put themselves in Gregor's position and say: Forget work—get me a doctor! But they all seemed willing to accept that work had dehumanized Gregor."	2014
Article	Aurora Snow, *Daily Beast*	*Linguistic:* headline, "Porn's Norma Rae Moment"	2015
Article	Jack Mirkinsin, "The Media vs. the American Worker: How the 1 Percent Hijacked the Business of News," *Salon*	*Visual:* Chuck Todd, host of NBC's *Meet the Press*, imposed on the Norma Rae icon	2015
Article	Pat Ferrier, "N. Fort Collins Bustles with New Homes, Businesses," *Coloradoan*	*Linguistic:* "In a collective Norma Rae moment, they raised their voices, formed a business association and advisory group, supported a city urban renewal authority, and made officials take notice."	2015

The Norma Rae Icon in Text Media (*continued*)

Media Type	Creator, outlet	Icon appearance(s)	Date
Article	Carlos Santoscoy, "Sally Field Speaks in Support of Houston's LGBT-Inclusive Equal Rights Ordinance," *On Top Magazine*	*Visual:* Sally Field holds large sign overhead that reads VOTE YES ON PROP 1 PROTECT HOUSTON'S EQUAL RIGHTS ORDINANCE	2015
		Linguistic: "On Wednesday, Field channeled a scene from her Oscar-winning *Norma Rae* performance."	
Union Flyers and Labor Posts			
Blog	Mike, "Scenes from the Strike Front, Day Three," *Franklin Avenue*	*Visual:* man with UNION sign overhead	2007
		Linguistic: caption, "'The Riches' creator Dmitry Lipkin has a 'Norma Rae' moment."	
Blog	"With Record Profits, IBM Workers Face Pay Cut," *Daily Kos*	*Visual:* the comic strip character Dilbert holding a UNION sign overhead	2008
		Linguistic: "But watch out, because the labor rights that Norma Rae had are scarcely enforced."	
Blog	Leonie Haimson, *NYC Public School Parents*	*Linguistic:* "Last night's PEP meeting on Verizon contract and its 'Norma Rae' moment."	2011
		Linguistic: caption, "See [video] below, for a 'Norma Rae' moment, as Amy Muldoon, a passionate Verizon striker and mom, calls out the DOE for their contempt for workers, kids, and NYC taxpayers."	
Blog	Kevin Mahoney, *Raging Chicken Press*	*Visual:* Norma Rae icon digitally edited to stand over a Blu Home	2012
		Linguistic: headline, "I Can See Norma Rae from Here: Blu Homes Re-opens Union-Busting Wounds"	
Blog	Marty, "Norma Rae, Jimmy Hoffa, JFK," *Saint Marty*	*Linguistic:* "I didn't mean to go all Norma Rae on you guys this morning. It's just that I've been doing this adjunct work for so long (close to 20 years), and I really had hopes that this whole union thing was going to make a difference."	2012
Flyer for Women's History Month panel about women workers and labor organizing	North Carolina Women United, North Carolina AFL-CIO	*Visual:* Norma Rae with UNION sign	2015
		Linguistic: event title, "Norma Raes, Past & Present"	

The Norma Rae Icon in Text Media (*continued*)

Media Type	Creator, outlet	Icon appearance(s)	Date
Blog	"NYSUT Teachers Union at Community Forum," *NYSUT*	*Visual:* Cindy Brewer holds sign overhead about state testing	2015
		Linguistic: caption, "Vice President Paul Pecorale (right) applauds South Seneca teacher Cindy Brewer's 'Norma Rae' moment during the Lansing Community Forum"	
Blog	Doktor Zoom, "Congratulations, Grad Students! NLRB Says You're Employees, Now Raise Hell!," *Wonkette*	*Visual:* Norma Rae icon digitally edited to stand in front of a chalkboard with advanced mathematics	2016
Button	unknown	*Visual:* Norma Rae icon with sign digitally edited to read BERNIE	2016
Blog	"A Life of Joyful Resistance," *AFT Voices*	*Linguistic:* "In 1934, while she attended Hunter College in New York City, the college tried to increase milk prices in its cafeteria, leading to Lumpkin's first 'Norma Rae' moment, she told People's World. The 16-year-old freshman led a milk boycott."	2018
Flyer, protest of Supreme Court decision in *Janus v. AFSCME*	AFL-CIO	*Visual:* Norma Rae with UNION sign	2018
		Linguistic: directions to "make your own sign with the word UNION and have your picture taken holding the sign (stand on a desk at work like Sally Field in the iconic movie Norma Rae or do your own thing)" and post	
Op-ed	Paul Mulshine, "The Upcoming Union Rally: Will this be Murphy's Norma Rae moment?," *NJ.com*	*Linguistic:* "When Corzine got up before that crowd in 2006 and shouted 'We're gonna fight for a fair contract' that became known as his 'Norma Rae Moment.'"	2019

In the wide photo, however, Cindy Brewer stands amid a crowd of applauding union members and community partners. She wears a red t-shirt that says RESPECT PUBLIC EDUCATION, IT WORKS, and to her left, another teacher wears a red t-shirt that says UNION YES! Like Crystal Lee reappropriating her life story, this post tries to claim the icon for collective activism by using it to refer to a woman communicating with fellow NYSUT members, coworkers, and neighbors. If the caption read, "South Seneca teacher Cindy Brewer and union members stand together at the Lansing Community Forum," it would be more obvious as a vernacular gesture of solidarity in communal resistance. But it would not have the pop culture hook.

The third example involves a 2013 piece about the gambling industry that attempted to make light of Cambodian workers in Phnom Penh. When NagaCorp, which operates a dazzling resort casino for global customers, refused to give its workers raises or address workload, 90 percent of personnel went on strike. Women in housekeeping were a large, militant group, demanding an eighty-dollar raise to $150 per month. Casino security and police removed workers and arrested nineteen leaders, and NagaCorp terminated 413 employees. A gambling industry website, most likely written by publicists, superimposed the Norma Rae icon on the NagaCorp logo and deployed it for a piece describing the workers as "going Norma Rae."[93]

To undermine the women's effort to assert some control over their work conditions, the piece used the icon to mock their labor organizing and minimize the violent suppression. Yet it prompted some Cambodian women to research the name Norma Rae. On their own, they pushed through the icon to the movie and into its history. They found Crystal Lee and the TWUA campaign. Chhim Sitthar, the twenty-seven-year-old leader of a union with 3,000 workers at the NagaWorld Hotel, appreciated the comparison to Crystal Lee. She reclaimed the name Norma Rae and negotiated hard with NagaCorp to return the 413 workers to their jobs while pushing for higher pay.[94]

In 2018, the AFL-CIO asked members to make UNION signs, hold them overhead like Norma Rae, and take photos for a social media campaign against the Supreme Court's decision *Janus v. AFSCME*.[95] Even though many workers gathered in pairs or groups to take photos, the image still did cultural work to push emotional defiance over long-term and often grinding activism. The labor movement needs a new image that catches audience attention and sparks curiosity while sharing a message of long-term organizing with a diverse mobile working class.

Throughout these appearances, the icon's narrative—"individual defiance is the way"—and affect of personal ire converged with mainstream texts from libertarian economists, right-wing politicians, and evangelical activists. Their lingo, staged press conferences, axioms, and directives served the

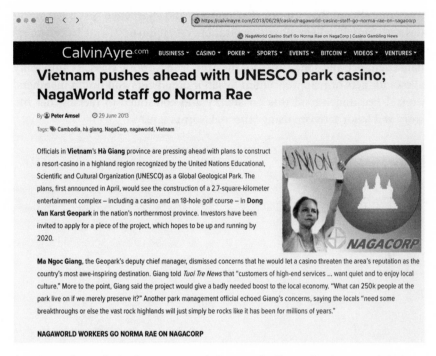

A casino and speculative investment website uses the Norma Rae icon to minimize a 2013 strike by NagaWorld hotel workers in Phnom Penh, Cambodia. It backfires and leads the women to learn about the TWUA, Crystal Lee, and her lifelong labor activism. | Calvin Ayre website, screenshot courtesy of the author

cultural formation of neoliberal individualism, which did work for the policies and practices of the apparatus of expertise. Together, they facilitated and naturalized an overall neoliberal turn—infusing it with seemingly logical values and emotional meanings. Struggling in a solitary stand, blaming an abstracted government, or complaining about an annoying situation shared the righteous realism of the underdog hero. But sometimes a viewer or union member asked about Norma Rae. They researched, and the icon opened a portal to the history of labor organizing, exposing traces of the rich context that made the icon possible.

The Norma Rae icon that cohered in the 1980s and '90s did not reiterate the exact words of radical libertarian economists, right-wing politicians, or activist evangelicals, yet it entwined with their narrative and affect. It served a mainstream cultural formation, which grew from several channels, some more intentional than others, that spoke to and sharpened historical affinities with individualism, liberty, aspiration, rebelliousness, and American exceptionalism. Although the icon appears as a marker most often for individualist defiance and sometimes for the American working class, its ambiguity allows for acts of reappropriation by labor organizers and union members. Crystal Lee understood this possibility and continued to reclaim her life story and labor activism using "the real Norma Rae."

EPILOGUE

Contesting Who Determines
the American Working Class

We were the first ones to start crying out, you know,
and nobody heard us. Until finally, now, the other industries
that are being affected, now they see what we were talking
about fifteen years ago. To us, it's very late.

—Gloria Maldonado

I did not want people to turn against joining a union because
of what had happened to me. Because I believe that a piece of a
union is better than no union at all. . . . I feel real good about the
things I have done to help other people have a better way of life.

—Crystal Lee Sutton

In 2014, 20th Century Studios started development for a new film version of *West Side Story*. Three years later, award-winning writer Tony Kushner took charge of the screenplay. The next year, Steven Spielberg signed a contract to coproduce and direct, and auditions began. The Hollywood production's full budget for writers, directors, music, choreographers, cast, rehearsals, costumes, locations, sets, crew, equipment, sound, and editing was $100 million. It opened in national movie theaters two years after a highly anticipated Broadway revival had been forced to close almost immediately because of the COVID-19 pandemic.

Six decades after the original *West Side Story*, these two reproductions—the February 2020 Broadway play by Ivo van Hove and the December 2021 movie release by Spielberg—presented new depictions of Maria and Anita. The wealthy, world-renowned white male directors selected Latina actresses to portray the Puerto Rican women, and revisions to each script updated references to address more contemporary perspectives. Van Hove moved the musical to a general present, abandoned the original Jerome Robbins choreography, and reframed the "Gee, Officer Krupke" number with anger and background video of police harassing people of color. Kushner and Spielberg kept the story in the 1950s but added dialogue about the demolition being done to build Lincoln Center, a sixteen-acre performing arts campus, and translated parts of the Sharks' dialogue into Spanish without subtitles. Yet neither production team decided to foreground Maria and Anita as needleworkers, as industrial labor in the US empire.

In the Broadway revival, as in the 1957 original, Maria and Anita work at sewing machines in a city shop, but the stage set minimizes the details by placing a couple machines and bolts of fabric into a niche in the background. The characters' primary performance remains as exotic beauties, not workers. Maria, Anita, and the other young women wear skinny jeans, leggings, and track pants instead of swirling dresses, but they carry on the narrative of beautiful, troubled urban youth. In the scene where Maria sees Tony at the dance, she wears a cute white dress that could have come from Old Navy or H&M, made in an EPZ sweatshop derived from the early twentieth-century colonial industrialization with Puerto Rican needleworkers.[1]

Spielberg and Kushner, on the other hand, transplant the Puerto Rican women to Gimbels department store as a late-night cleaning crew. Instead of manufacturing apparel, they sing and dance between racks of clothing and accessories they cannot afford but also did not make as skilled labor.[2] Women like Lucila Padrón, Louise Delgado, Eva Monje, and Gloria Maldonado had browsed department stores to see the prices on the nightgowns and dresses they produced; they were not simply poor consumer admirers in a retail wonderland. The revision reflects the idea of speaking to contemporary audiences familiar with women of color and immigrants in service jobs in a deindustrialized city.[3] But this creative decision eliminates the only reference, minor though it was, to the historic context of Puerto Rican needleworkers as manufacturing labor.

The tenacious power of popular representations of Puerto Rican women as exotic beauties or troubled youth, rather than migrating industrial workers, highlights the importance of creative contests in fields of cultural production. If Maldonado and ILGWU women had not expressed themselves via the public history project "Nosotras Trabajamos en la Costura," current scholars and writers would have to dig even harder to find their experiences and voices. Telling their stories and thoughts was a shared act of resistance, memory, and history making and produced the raw-material transcripts that can be used for many more representations in the arena of cultural politics, where disputes over meanings for the American working class play out. The Puerto Rican women staked their claim and impacted ongoing contests over who the public understands as a "worker," even though the *Norma Rae* movie and icon held a dominant cultural power.

Norma Rae also endured as a financial asset, licensed in deals that generate royalties for creative professionals and advertising, fees, and subscriptions for pay-per-view and premium channels such as Turner Classic Movies (TCM), a cable network dedicated to a collection of canonized films.[4] In this way, the movie persists as a wellspring for reengaging in contests over meanings for the American working class, activism, and unions, often pulling the public conversation back to the sentimental notion of isolated white individuals in localized industries.

The potent sentimentality still surrounds southern mills and shapes public understanding of "real work." In 2016, after sitting unused for seventeen years, the Alabama mill where *Norma Rae* was filmed burned down. The *Opelika-Auburn News* editor wrote a wistful piece with a photo of the mill shrouded in drifting smoke. It was shot at an angle that showcased old railroad tracks in weeds—melancholy with nostalgia. "Smoke lingered long after the fire," Troy Turner writes, "hanging in the air much like the memories themselves of a long-past way of life that once dominated the South." Pittsburgh had steel, Detroit had cars, and the South had textiles, he adds, reiterating America's industrial mythology with its vision of localized manufacturing and naturalized rusty decline.[5]

Like *Norma Rae*, the article's nostalgia includes a hard-edged acknowledgment of the exhausting work, sore bodies, and stretched hours.[6] People had tough stories, including Turner's grandmother who took a job in 1968 after losing her husband and often soaked her feet in hot water and Epsom salts. Turner celebrates *Norma Rae* for winning its acclaim by "candidly depicting some of the harsh conditions many mill workers faced as the main character fought to organize a union and create change." Turner also elides decades of worker resistance and labor activism and the thousands of millhands and union staff who participated in the interracial 1963–80 TWUA/ACTWU campaign. He completely misses the efforts of unions and workers along the US Atlantic to fight cheap imports and direct the parameters of globalization.

Turner relied on the recurrent and oddly comforting notion of the bad old days, with dirty industrial manufacturing, as a foil to the good present day, with clean office and service jobs that do not seem to exploit workers because the labor is not as filthy or physically debilitating in obvious ways. If the mills, old kings of the South, pass away from decay and fire, their practices of hard labor and cruel wages must go with them. Turner wishes mills could be reclaimed, renovated for apartments and shopping—again, contemporary good capitalism with its market-based consumer solutions rehabilitating bad old capitalism with its deprivations and deterioration. He does not mention that the 2008–10 mortgage recession, triggered by finance capitalism and its questionable investment instruments, ended plans to renovate the mill for upscale condominiums.[7]

The article maintains the practice of extricating the immediate experiences of industrial workers in a particular neighborhood from the shifting operations of transnational corporations and banks in the global economy.[8] The perspectives of local workers and studies of households, neighborhoods, and specific business hierarchies are unquestionably valuable—they capture important proximate circumstances and worker reactions. But mainstream media rarely acknowledge the complicated position of US workers in entangled larger systems, which means industries seem to naturally "die" or vanish because of local conditions. It misses the ways workers, factories, managers, government offices, and investors function as part of a broad, if not perfectly hegemonic, set of economic structures.

Like the movie, the Norma Rae icon appeared as a tight, accessible signifier into the 2020s. Writers for two television shows, *Pose* (2018–21) and *Gentefied*, applied the icon's narrative of righteous individual defiance to a Latinx woman of color, subverting the whitening of this stance. As in previous examples, however, a character uses the reference to undercut another's personal action, and neither episode uses it to address women as workers. This continuation of the neoliberal individualism and lack of confrontation with the notion of the American working class as white industrial labor underscores the importance of looking beyond straightforward diversity of representation and into the scope of storytelling devices and embedded narratives.

Yet both deployments hint at new possibilities for the icon. While it is used to mock a character's individual stand, the incident becomes a step toward stronger collective activism in the longer arc of the series. Rather than a closure, the incident becomes a learning experience for the character to better analyze the terrain and engage effectual partners the next time. In addition, although the women do not act as workers or union representatives, they do take action as community organizers. Throughout *Pose* and *Gentefied*, each woman is inextricably bound with a commitment to her community. Their intersectional identities and positions in society are not associated with the working class, but they are tied to the community's economic condition, as well as to their gender, sexuality, race, ethnicity, and citizenship. This economic condition is low-income and precarious, but the women seek community collaboration rather than worker organizing. Unlike in *West Side Story*, they participate in a mode of collective action, just not unionizing.

Community—the notion, its experience, and its realization—is a common catalyst for low-income and marginalized people of color to take action. The committee members who formed Centro at Hunter College–CUNY said in 1972 that they wanted to "articulate the social and intellectual problems of our community while reaffirming the intent to define and control our own intellectual agenda."[9] Grassroots nonprofits, neighborhood advocates, mutual aid groups, and event coordinators build on community to gather people for various purposes.[10] Their work often facilitates access to resources, but community organizers face many challenges when trying to forge these efforts into a larger movement. The pressures of reaching new migrants or immigrants; guiding neighbors through public housing bureaucracies; offering English language learning and adult basic education; helping applicants with job, Temporary Assistance for Needy Families (TANF), and electronic benefit transfer (EBT) paperwork; demanding multilingual options; and applying for foundation grants and state contracts can take all the organizers' time, energy, and creativity. There are cases, however, in which community organizing has launched into movement building, as with Clark County Welfare Rights/Operation Life in Las Vegas during the 1970s and SisterSong Women of Color Reproductive Justice Collective in Georgia in the 1990s.[11]

Pose explores the 1980s LGBTQ ballroom community in New York City. Creator and showrunner Ryan Murphy was in a stretch of successful series, including *Glee* (2009–15) and *American Horror Story* (2011–), when he approached Miramax to buy an eighteen-month option for its property *Paris Is Burning*, the famous 1991 documentary about ballroom.[12] Murphy and his business partner, Brad Falchuk, intended the series to be made with and about queer performers of color and trans people.[13] Over three seasons, the episodes focus increasingly on Blanca, the trans woman dedicated to her community as well as the "children of her house."

In season 1, Blanca lives and performs with House of Abundance, overseen by Elektra, a Black Caribbean trans woman. During the second episode, after a big ballroom win, house members go to a gay bar in the West Village frequented by white men, but the bartender refuses them service. Blanca repeatedly returns and demands to get served. Elektra finds this stand absurd and walks into the nail salon where Blanca works to say, "You're a regular transvestite Norma Rae. Don't get me wrong, I admire your determination. You have always been impossible to stop once you get an idea in your head. But take it from a woman of the world . . . these gay white boys don't want anything to do with you and never will." Rather than shrink, Blanca sets her jaw and eventually leaves House of Abundance to start House of Evangelista.

In her Norma Rae moment, Blanca stands alone at the gay bar and endures physical obstruction and verbal insults, and Elektra attempts to diminish the action. But the stand explicitly arises from and expresses Blanca's identity as a trans woman of color making a demand on gay white men. She shouts at the bartender and the customers, demanding fair treatment and unity for people who do not comply with heterosexual norms.[14]

Pose's first season focuses on personal relationships rather than the organizing that sustained ballroom or the political, social, and cultural activism of groups such as AIDS Coalition to Unleash Power (ACT UP). Murphy and

Falchuk made a concerted decision to highlight organizing in the second season. The series's plot maintains an emphasis on relationships and performances, but a middle-aged white lesbian who works as a nurse in an HIV/AIDS ward invites Pray Tell, the gay Black man who emcees the ballroom competitions, to an ACT UP meeting. He discovers people of various genders, races, ages, sexualities, and backgrounds leveraging collective power to demand changes to HIV/AIDS research and treatment. Blanca requires her Evangelista family to join him for a demonstration that includes a lie-in inside a Catholic church, a scene based on a 1989 action in St. Patrick's Cathedral. At the next ball, Pray Tell makes a furious public call for the Black, brown, and queer community to care for itself and get active.[15] Norma Rae is not in the building.

In *Gentefied*, the Latino and predominantly Mexican American community of Boyle Heights in East Los Angeles suffers the stresses of gentrification: the transition from artists seeking affordable rent to an influx of hipster investors who bring inflated real estate prices, the lure of upscale jobs and business opportunities, and the loss of neighborhood ties. The series tells intimate familial stories that personalize these overlapping issues.[16] Three main characters, the Morales cousins Ana, Chris, and Erik, have goals they try to balance against the needs of their grandfather Pop's taqueria, Mama Fina's, named for their beloved grandmother.

Chris wants to train as a chef and works in a fine restaurant until he gets fired. He goes to Mama Fina's, where Erik has worked for years, and encourages Pop to try new dishes, which Erik dislikes at first. Ana is an ambitious artist torn between the dismantling of her community and the new opportunities. She is in a relationship with Yessika, a queer Black Dominican woman who says that in five years, she "will still be working in the community." Yessika hopes the agency where she works, Hermanas Poderosas, will collaborate with the Centro for Latinx Equalidad and the Alliance for Pan-Latino Development to build a framework that they "can all plug into." Movement building is on the radar if only as a solitary atmospheric reference.[17]

When Chris convinces Pop and Erik to put the shop on a hipster food tour, Yessika declares there are other ways to raise money without "selling out the community" and promises to respond. Ana gets caught in the conflict because the episode, like the series, walks a fine line. It has to convert the complicated juggernaut of gentrification into personal melodramas to sell the show to Netflix and its viewers.

Erik develops a plan to lean into Yessika's threatened response. He suggests they promote the tour by playing on white liberal guilt, and Yessika becomes angry that Ana cannot stop it. Yessika walks to the taqueria ahead of eight unnamed people, who hold signs behind her when she stands as the focus and confronts Ana. At the end, Chris says to Erik, "Yo, even with Yessika acting all Norma Rae, we cleared three times what we expected."[18] As a forceful queer Black Caribbean woman in a historically Mexican American neighborhood, Yessika complicates and enriches the series, but it appears that she stands alone, even with friends hovering behind her. The show does not represent coalitions, such as Defend Boyle Heights, that emerged from coordinated opposition in the 2010s. The Norma Rae phrase marks Yessika as solitary and drains the intensity. In the second season, however, Yessika appears less as Ana's ex-girlfriend and more as a community organizer. Viewers see her in her office, with Latina and Latinx women busy with the activities of the agency.

Pose and *Gentefied* are sharp series with insightful writing, smart social commentary, and casts that magnify active intersections of gender, race, sexuality, and citizenship. Their scripts and sets make the economic conditions, the poverty and precarity, visible and dignified. Blanca and Yessika identify as low-income queer women of color who care for their communities, yet the labor movement, unions, and even worker activism remain invisible. Like *Norma Rae* and *West Side Story*, the shows miss the long histories of women of color in unionizing. The embedded narrative of women of color addressing poverty and its effects by caring for their communities is a potent one, but its elision of worker resistance and class identity inadvertently serves to sustain a split between poor people of color and the American working class.

This rift consistently erodes the power of low-income working people in the political economy. Raising awareness of the historic overlaps between labor activism and community organizing would help build a movement of working people through conscientious and respectful alliances between unions, which do not often address poverty or white privilege, and grassroots agencies, which do not often address wages, working conditions, or job benefits.

In the icon's dozens of media representations, despite occasional ripples of subversion and the latent potential to become a portal into history, complicated histories of southern millhands are buried and Puerto Rican needleworkers are missed, while the narrative of individual defiance endures. It is too easy to say, "Of course the rich historical context of women workers gets lost in Hollywood," but this outcome was not untroubled or inevitable. The asymmetrical capital and financial mechanisms of studios and elite creative professionals impacted the contests, yet working-class people fought—just like they did in industrial manufacturing. They did not simply tell their experiences and stories—they fought in the field of cultural production to share their interpretations and creative ideas, to shape the narratives. Erasures and reductions were not a straightforward result of myopic imaginations or predictable sexism, racism, and bigotry either. They were a result of decisions and actions in capital formations with the culture business prerogative to earn the biggest box office, advertising sales, subscriptions, and clicks.

In the nexus of commercial cultural production, the capitalist mechanisms of finance and property distribution command budgets and revenue expectations. Studio hierarchies, contract details, and nuances of intellectual property vary over time, but corporations and investors continue to prioritize the accumulation of capital. During the 1980s, independent producers like Tamara Asseyev and Alexandra Rose and creative professionals like Martin Ritt and Sally Field became more involved with the capitalist mechanisms, demanding greater percentages of profits and becoming assertive partners in movie development and production.

Field has continued to thank Ritt for *Norma Rae*, and two chapters of her memoir *In Pieces* (2018) discuss the movie and Ritt without mentioning TWUA organizing, the *Crystal Lee* biography, the 1977–78 movie negotiations, or her meeting with Crystal Lee Sutton at the 1980 SAG event. For the first time, however, Field formally acknowledges her in print by stating, "The story was based on Crystal Lee Sutton, a heroic union organizer and advocate who in the early 1970s bravely stood up against the J.P. Stevens mills for the mistreatment of their workers." Yet when promoting the memoir on *Literary Hub*, Field described her 1980 trip to Cannes with a focus on Burt Reynolds, Ritt, Harriet Frank Jr. and Irving Ravetch, and the standing ovation the movie received.[19]

Sutton persisted with her reclamation of *Norma Rae* for targeted purposes such as union organizing, but not for the 2003 closure of the Roanoke Rapids mill. Following financial battles within J.P. Stevens during 1988, another conglomerate, West Point-Pepperell, acquired the corporation. Just a year after that acquisition, Michael Milken and Drexel Burnham Lambert used junk bonds to take 95 percent of West Point-Pepperell in an LBO.[20] During the dispersal of assets for maximum financial extraction, Delta Plant #4 became part of a spin-off, WestPoint Stevens. In 2003, the plant closed for a Chapter 11 bankruptcy restructuring, shuttering the last textile and home goods factory in Roanoke Rapids.[21]

UNC-TV invited Sutton to participate in a segment about the closure, but she wrote on an envelope, "Note: 6/17/03 Tuesday I decided not to do this interview," which shows she still weighed media options and did not accept public appearances if she did not think they furthered labor's interests.[22] A sentimental melancholy retrospective about a closure was not an activist piece, and Sutton was focused on unionizing.

She also deployed "the real Norma Rae" to demand fair treatment after doctors diagnosed her with a brain tumor called meningioma, a usually benign cancer that unfortunately threatened her life. The neoliberal turn included more business practices that honed "efficiencies" in extracting value for investors by orienting corporate procedures toward financialization, even in medical care. The apparatus of neoliberal expertise promoted deregulation of health insurance and employer policies, and billing became stacked with layers of fees, copays, and deductibles. Sutton had to file multiple appeals for payment, until regional and national press learned "the real Norma Rae" was fighting her health insurance company. She gave interviews, and the company finally approved payment for the surgeries, follow-up drugs, and chemotherapy. Her husband Preston took a second job to cover the remaining expenses, and the North Carolina AFL-CIO asked members to donate to a fund.[23] The labor movement, even with its internal tensions, acted in solidarity.

The illness prompted Sutton to leave her papers at Alamance Community College because of its record of providing education for all people. "Thank God for ACC, where even the working poor can come, get financial assistance, and get a new start in life," she said at the 2007 opening of her collection. The papers include little about her personal life but many TWUA documents and clippings about her labor activism.[24] When she felt well, Sutton still contributed her name and time to labor events. She made a 2008 appearance with a Haitian labor organizer and supported the global labor campaign to organize Coca-Cola factories.[25] In one of her last interviews, Sutton reflected, "It is not necessary I be remembered as anything, but I would like to be remembered as a woman who deeply cared for the working poor and the poor people of the U.S. and the world. That my family and children and children like mine will have a fair share and equality."[26] Years of collective activism and travel had expanded Sutton's perspective, and she had joined in the larger struggles over the terms of globalization.

Puerto Rican workers like Maldonado had long recognized these struggles—not because they were more tied to globalization but because as colonial needleworkers following pathways of imperial industrialization, their ties were more apparent. In Puerto Rico and the metropole since the turn of the twentieth century, they had migrated a range of distances and loops to pursue job opportunities and wages. They were almost as mobile as the manufacturing, relocating in multiple directions and working in homes and factories at the same time. Thousands of these Puerto Rican women, including Maldonado, also made demands in political-economic contests and the arena of cultural politics.

Many of Maldonado's concerns regarding globalization came to fruition in the 1990s. When President George H. W. Bush endorsed the Caribbean Basin Economic Recovery Expansion Act (1990), it pulled Puerto Rico further into US imperialism by permitting materials made in Puerto Rico to be used in CBI

In 2009, Preston and Crystal Lee Sutton show support for global labor organizing at Coca-Cola factories. They stand in their living room, in front of a *Norma Rae* poster. | Corporate Campaign, Inc., website, photo provided by Crystal Lee Sutton during the last months of her life

exports to the United States. It further linked CBI nations to Section 936 by allowing Puerto Rican banks to lend to investors at one to two points below market rate for enterprises in the Caribbean.[27] By the end of the 1990s, apparel and accessories, both knitted and non-knitted, became the largest US import from Caribbean nations.[28] In 1996, however, Congress legislated a ten-year phaseout of Section 936, and corporations began reducing and closing enterprises in Puerto Rico before the extreme exemptions were to end in 2006.[29]

The EPZ model that was developed in Puerto Rico during the first half of the twentieth century, formalized in Mexico in the 1960s, and cultivated by WEPZA in the 1970s and '80s flourished around the world. Enclaves appeared under new names such as "special economic zones" (SEZs), because the conditions of low-wage, low-safety export manufacturing received criticism. But EPZ/SEZs still complicate and blur sovereignty, invent borders, and manipulate import/export to facilitate the lowest taxes and wages, broadest exceptions, and most fluid currents of capital and durable goods. The Chinese government has used SEZs to push into South Asia, particularly with the China Pakistan Economic Corridor, and the World Bank remains an advocate and has launched SEZ expansion in Africa.[30]

As the textile and garment industry sprawled into more countries, Puerto Rican needleworkers lost their position in the labor markets. In the 2000s, technologies of subcontracting became so agile, Chinese manufacturers and their sewing machine operators even moved to Italy. They set up fleeting mobile sweatshops in old buildings to make products that had to contain the label "Made in Italy" to garner high retail prices.[31] With such nimble contracting, labor, and shipping systems and thousands of poor women workers and light sewing machines moving on every continent, the colonial template has become the global arrangement for lowest-wage manufacturing, while the histories of Puerto Rican needleworkers who were part of its development remain marginalized in mainstream culture.

When Sutton died in September 2009, the *New York Times* obituary mourning the loss of "the Real-Life 'Norma Rae'" exemplified the contradictions of attaining popular attention from a movie that distorted her experiences. It features a haunting 2001 Associated Press photo of Sutton at sixty on her living room couch, under a poster of Norma Rae holding the UNION sign. While Sutton has grown older and heavier—an actual woman worker who bears the physical tolls of repetitive work, low-income stresses, tense labor activism, and aging—Norma Rae stands young, timeless, and eternally defiant above her. Sutton smiles, appearing pleased about her association with the icon.

This rare honor of a *New York Times* obituary came at a price: the newspaper's stature formalized and entrenched a certain set of facts while erasing others. The obituary celebrates Sutton, describing her as the inspiration for Field's character in the Academy Award–nominated movie, but implies that her stand on a folding table is what led to the successful vote to unionize a few months later. She had fought this very act of erasing the histories and people involved in southern organizing and civil rights labor activism. The writer does not mention Sutton's critiques of the movie, let alone the deeper conflicts with Rose & Asseyev Productions, Ritt, and Twentieth Century-Fox. The consequential decision not to use her name for the movie title is explained simply as a "legal necessity," wiping away Sutton's fights in the field of cultural production.[32]

Activists, worker groups, and regional newspapers published memorials as well. Most have "Norma Rae" in the title, as a hook and acknowledgment of where the movie came from, but they commemorate the dedication of Sutton's activism. In these pieces, she becomes an outstanding organizer among many people building an ongoing labor movement.[33] Bruce Raynor, president of Workers United and executive vice president of the Service Employees

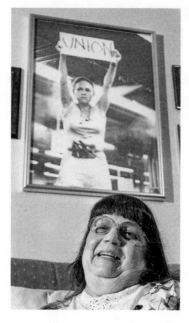

A 2001 photo of Sutton on her couch, under a poster of Norma Rae. The *New York Times* used the image for its initial obituary in September 2009. | Photograph by Joseph Rodriguez, Associated Press Photo/News & Record, 2001

International Union (SEIU), had worked on the J.P. Stevens campaign. "Our nation lost a great hero and champion of working people," he wrote in his remembrance. "She . . . is an inspiration to every worker who holds out hope and is prepared to fight for justice and respect at work." The *New York Times Magazine* end-of-year memorials included a more insightful profile as well, titled "The Organizer," with a photo of Sutton from 1974, the peak of the TWUA drive.[34]

Eight years later, the cultural dominance of *Norma Rae* was still strong enough that Bespoke Theatricals and Fox Stage Productions began development for a musical based on "the iconic 1979 film." A "talented roster of creatives" signed contracts, including Rosanne Cash as composer. Producers, however, ran into a union issue with Cindy Tolan, a respected casting director, who wanted them to contribute to her Teamsters health and pension fund. Tolan and other creative professionals had been pressing the producers' trade organization, the Broadway League, to recognize them as Teamsters with Local 817, which represented them when they did casting for television and movies. Rather than give in to this request, producers canceled the "special 29-hour reading," the final step in deciding if a show will go into full production.

An article about the conflict noted that Sutton inspired the "fictionalized version of a real-life union organizing drive" and criticized the hypocrisy of obstructing unionization while making a musical about it. Field even tweeted a selfie holding a printed flyer under her chin that announced I SUPPORT CASTING DIRECTORS, but the production stalled. Bespoke Theatricals and Fox Stage Productions, which had earned $1.5 billion the previous year, did not comment, and the Broadway League said casting directors were independent contractors, not employees. It filed a lawsuit claiming they were operating as a cartel to inflate prices.[35]

Interrogating the contentious phases of cultural production, from the raw material to the generation of an enduring popular icon, reveals the complications of gender, race, class, and citizenship in constructing both labor markets and dominant representations. Each phase involves conflicts over who attains access to the massive financial and technological resources of mass media production. Even producers and directors with a humanistic or left-leaning point of view must operate within the capitalist nexus that sifts access, ranks contributors' value, demands revenues for investors, and directs the distribution of billions of dollars. The result has cultivated stories of the individual underdog hero in a personal melodrama for major commercial products that enter the arena of cultural politics, where they earn millions of dollars and influence the reconstitution of narratives and their circulation and meaning-making. In this framework, the quantity of gender, racial, ethnic, sexual, and citizenship identities in big cultural productions does not necessarily challenge intrinsic narrative or affect, alter meanings, or disrupt cultural formations and their structure of feeling.

In mainstream American popular culture, secure revenues depend on simplification and repetition with a gloss of novelty, and slight differences or subversions of gender, racial, ethnic, sexual, or citizenship norms can provide that gloss. Even as the bodies attached to cultural representations diversify, it is possible to legitimize and sentimentalize an inequitable distribution of resources in society and to marginalize the collective power necessary to challenge such systems. From this vantage, *Norma Rae* was extraordinary for centering a white working-class woman as the heroic underdog and showing a union drive in a positive light. Yet it conveyed a continuity with previous narrow notions of who are legitimate "American workers" and what constitutes "real work." It also had a potent convergence with neoliberal individualism and its personalization of complex social problems. In these ways, *Norma Rae* and its icon influenced popular understanding of who is the American working class and served the overall neoliberal turn from the 1980s to the early 2000s.

PREVIEW

Making Christian Smalls

You're focused on me I'm focused on We.
—**Christian Smalls, ALU Provisional President**

All that time, we were getting our coworkers' phone numbers—
and we'd compile all of them into one big list . . . so that we
could follow up over the regular phone banks we held out
of the [UNITE HERE Local 100] office in Manhattan. And
as organizers, we stayed coordinated; for example, we kept
schedules for who of us would be in the building.
—**Angelika Maldonado, ALU Workers Committee Chair**

Dozens of women and men exited the Staten Island JFK8 Amazon distribution warehouse and gathered along the sidewalks and edges of the parking lot. Most had masks or bandannas to cover their noses and mouths. Many took photos with cell phones and chatted as they held signs protesting management's response to COVID-19. It was March 2020 and the rate of infection was exploding, but epidemiologists did not yet understand how it spread. Workers wanted better protective gear and transparency regarding testing, infections, and quarantining. Christian Smalls, a management assistant, held a handmade sign with cut-out letters that said OUR HEALTH IS JUST AS ESSENTIAL. After hearing workers' angry concerns, he and Derrick Palmer had coordinated the walkout and even announced it to media ahead of time. Later that day, a company official called to tell Smalls he was fired for breaking quarantine. Palmer received a warning.[1]

Over the next year, a dedicated group started the Congress of Essential Workers to talk about COVID-19 and labor organizing. Smalls and Palmer, two vocal young Black men, were key members. In April 2021, after workers at an Amazon warehouse in Bessemer, Alabama, who had affiliated with the Retail, Wholesale and Department Store Union did not receive a clear yes majority in an NLRB certification vote, several JFK8 employees in communication with Smalls decided to start an independent union. Smalls and Palmer did not have labor organizing training, but they were a solid team as the Amazon Labor Union (ALU) provisional president and vice president. Smalls, who had skills in performing and public speaking from an earlier career in hip-hop, organized on the outside. He talked to workers at bus stops, did interviews, and appeared at events. He was also effective in the "union drip" trend, which hyped the labor movement by celebrating labor folks with sexy and cool styles. Palmer organized on the inside, recruiting Angelika Maldonado to chair the Workers Committee, speaking to people about membership, facing down union-busting harassment, and coordinating break-room information sessions.[2]

In this arrangement, Smalls received a great deal more popular media attention than Palmer and Maldonado. In talks, interviews, and social media, however, he emphasized the ALU, solidarity, and momentum for the labor movement. He was not shy and did not deflect people's interest, but Smalls repeatedly used the pronoun "we" and explained the crucial activities of Palmer, Maldonado, and other employees still inside JFK8. Yet mainstream media wanted to center him as the unexpected singular underdog hero of ALU's successful NLRB certification vote in April 2022.[3]

The situation even sparked a Twitter debate with an indirect reference to Norma Rae after labor journalist Sarah Jaffe posted, "guys Chris Smalls did a hell of a lot of work and was personally targeted by Amazon but *no one wins a massive union election alone* and I'm seeing way too many 'this guy did . . .' and not 'these 2,564 workers did.'" In the arena of cultural politics, Jaffe was asserting the intensive collective aspects of union organizing, but some readers took her comment as a diminution of Smalls's role rather than as a celebration of all ALU organizers and members. Nicki Washington, a computer science professor at Duke University, responded by quoting Jaffe's tweet with her own post: "They made Oscar-winning movies about white women who did the same. Or was that more palatable for you."[4] Smalls issued his own retorts to the relentless headlines and posts that declared he had won the ALU vote, tweeting, "You're focused on me I'm focused on We." Like Crystal Lee Sutton and Gloria Maldonado, he shared his forceful voice but envisioned it within a collective effort.

The archival record for Smalls has just begun. Its form and quantity will be determined by these contests in the arena of cultural politics—involving many fields of cultural production—as well as by academic institutions and historical societies. He has advantages, including his use of social media, with the Twitter @Shut_downAmazon and Instagram @chris.smalls_ accounts. He posts daily, presenting his own interpretations without the filters of commercial producers and editors. During the summer of 2022, Smalls traveled the country to speak at labor events, and many union members posted photos with him that gushed about meeting the "labor legend." When Smalls posted, he usually emphasized bonding with other unions and

Left: Crystal Lee as "The Organizer" in a 1974 photo used for her 2009 end-of-year remembrance in *New York Times Magazine*. *Right:* Christian Smalls as "The Organizer" on a 2022 cover of *New York* magazine weeks after he participated in a successful union vote for Amazon Labor United in Staten Island. | Maggie Jones, "Crystal Lee Sutton: The Organizer," *New York Times Magazine*, December 2009. Wes Enzima, "The Organizer," *New York*, cover, July 2022.

sustaining the labor movement, like when he retweeted a photo with another worker fired for her labor activism who wrote, "They can fire us, but they CAN'T put out the fire inside us."[5] Sutton had expressed the same conviction in a 1986 oral history interview.[6]

In July 2022, however, Smalls already had a magazine cover with the sobriquet "The Organizer," a title Gloria Maldonado never got and Crystal Lee did not receive until her obituary.[7] The first major, and more permanent, production will be his memoir, contracted with Pantheon Books in June 2022 under the title "The Revolution Is Here." As with all commercial media, Smalls will not have total control over the contract, editing, packaging, and marketing, but he entered this field of production in a strong position. He has experience in hip-hop, with its bookings and contracts, and a national media presence he has consciously sculpted. He will be credited as the author and granted royalties, even if the publisher assigns a ghostwriter to work with him.[8] And perhaps there will soon be a screenplay tentatively titled "Christian Smalls."

ACKNOWLEDGMENTS

Librarians and archivists made this book possible. In museums and universities, they do the work historians depend on, often while struggling with annual budgets and competition from for-profit media companies. Special thanks to Melissa Holland, Patrizia Sione, Colleen Macklin, Pedro Juan Hernández, Juber Ayala, Lindsay D. Wittwer, Jane Ward, Shakti Castro, Penni Martorell, Jamie Eves, Jillian Maynard, Sarah White, Betsy Pittman, and Laura Smith.

My colleagues and friends Irma Medina and Maria Salgado-Cartagena shared the stories of their mothers and abuelas at a crucial stage of my research. Their trust and willingness to grant me permission to include their families transformed the project. Their camaraderie and humor got me through tough stages of writing.

At Central Connecticut State University, Robert Wolff, dean of the Carol A. Ammon College of Liberal Arts and Sciences, and Mark Jones, chair of the History Department, were vital advocates for the time and resources necessary for me to revise and prepare the manuscript. Without Brenda Lopez, assistant director of grants and funded research, all these images would not be here.

A wide-ranging history depends on conversations with scholars in a variety of fields—too many to list here. I appreciate all their guidance and openness to my traversing conventional academic boundaries. Women labor historians have remained a foundation and inspiration. Thank you to Annelise Orleck for years of support and commitment to the stories of working women. Eileen Boris, Marisa Chappell, Jennifer Guglielmo, Lisa Levenstein, and Jennifer Mittelstadt have been role models and mentors. Jorell Meléndez-Badillo, Eileen Findlay, Aldo Lauria-Santiago, Elena Rosario, Emma Amador, and especially Anne S. Macpherson were generous with their expertise in Puerto Rican history. As a mentor with the Organization of American Historians, Julie Greene shared her wisdom and encouraged me to pursue this project. Kim Phillips-Fein provided crucial feedback on an early draft of chapters 1–2 after hearing my paper at a conference for the American Political History Institute at Boston University. I am very grateful to Stephen Pitti for his insightful questions, thoughtful comments, and invitation to share my work at the Center for the Study of Race, Indigeneity, and Transnational Migration at Yale University.

This book would not have been possible without the determination of the Organization of American Historians and the Coordinating Council for Women in History to foster new scholars of all ages and backgrounds. I am indebted to them for the Lerner-Scott Prize and Catherine Prelinger Award, which sustained my research and writing.

I owe tremendous thanks to Mark Simpson-Vos for shepherding this book through publication. His patience, kindness, and dedication to publishing academic history shine a bright light. The editorial and art departments at the University of North Carolina Press, and especially Thomas Bedenbaugh, María Isela García, Erin Granville, Madge Duffey, and Lindsay Starr, as well as copyeditor Iza Wojciechowska, made this a better and beautiful book. The reader reviews from Jessica Wilkerson and a second historian provided invaluable critique and the wisdom of their scholarly and writing expertise.

I received invaluable feedback when I presented parts of the book at conferences for the Organization of American Historians, Labor and Working-Class History Association, Puerto Rican Studies Association, and *Film & History*, and at a Faculty Fellowship Seminar with the Center for the Study of Race, Indigeneity, and Transnational Migration at Yale University, History of Capitalism Seminar at the Newberry Library, Boston Seminar on the History of Women, Gender, and Sexuality cosponsored by the Massachusetts Historical Society and Schlesinger Library at the Radcliffe Institute, Moses Greeley Parker Lecture at Lowell National Historical Park, and Fellow's Talk at the UConn Humanities Institute. Sections of the book appeared with other research in the *Journal of Working-Class Studies* and *Journal of International Labor and Working-Class History*. I deeply appreciate the comments of their readers and editors.

The UConn Humanities Institute, El Instituto, and donors who support history research contributed essential time, space, and funds for travel to archives. Micki McElya encouraged my questions and offered incisive book and writing recommendations. Christopher Clark, Peter Baldwin, and Jason Chang shared much-appreciated guidance and encouragement.

Thank you to the family and friends who gave me care and support because of—and despite—my decision to write this book. I have to give a special shout-out to my parents, Kathleen and Richard Loiselle, and grandparents, Gladys and Woodrow Sylvia, for encouraging my two sisters and me to pursue education and adventures.

NOTES

Abbreviations

Centro	Centro Library and Archives, Hunter College–CUNY, New York, NY
CLS	Crystal Lee Sutton Collection, Alamance Community College, Graham, NC
Dodd Center	Archives and Special Collections at the Dodd Center, University of Connecticut, Storrs, CT
Kheel	Kheel Center for Labor-Management Documentation and Archives, Catherwood Library, Cornell University, Ithaca, NY
MHL	Margaret Herrick Library, Academy of Motion Picture Arts and Sciences, Los Angeles, CA
MR	Martin Ritt Papers, Margaret Herrick Library, Academy of Motion Picture Arts and Sciences, Los Angeles, CA
NYT	*New York Times*
Osborne	Osborne Library at the American Textile History Museum, Lowell, MA
RG	record group
RG 323	Reel 3 "Records of PRRA," RG 323: "N.A. Arrangement: Records of the Washington Office General Records, 1935–1945, Labor, 1937–1939, FLSA, 1938–1939, Needlework, 1938–1941"
Ross Papers	M. H. Ross Papers, Special Collections, Georgia State University Library, Atlanta, GA
Schlesinger	Schlesinger Library at the Radcliffe Institute, Harvard University, Cambridge, MA
SSC	Sophia Smith Collection, Smith College, Northampton, MA
SHLA	Springfield History Library and Archives, Lyman and Merrie Wood Museum of Springfield History, Springfield, MA
TD	ACTWU Textile Division, Kheel Center for Labor-Management Documentation and Archives, Catherwood Library, Cornell University, Ithaca, NY
WTHM	Windham Textile and History Museum, Willimantic, CT

Introduction

1. For the majority of the book, I use Crystal Lee's first name when referring to her. Patriarchal reliance on patrilineal surnames meant Crystal Lee Pulley had her father's name from 1940 to 1959 and became Crystal Lee Wood after her first wedding in 1959. During her 1973–74 TWUA activism, she used the name Crystal Lee Jordan from her second marriage (1962–78). She married a third time in 1978 and took the name Crystal Lee Sutton, which she kept until her death in 2009.

2. My use of "textile and garment industry" highlights interconnections between textile, home goods, apparel, and accessory manufacturing but is not intended to conflate or equate them.

3. "Bwy Local 66 class," March 5, 1971, no. 5780/102P, box 19, folder 2, ILGWU Justice Photographs, Kheel; "Maldonado," August 8, 1984, 11–13, box 229, folder 3, series XIX "Audio-Visual (1973–99)," El Centro de Estudios Puertorriqueños Collection, Centro.

4. Osburn, *Negro Employment*; Rowan, *Negro in the Textile*; Jacqueline Jones, *Labor of Love*; Byerly, *Hard Times*; Minchin, *Hiring the Black Worker*.

5. Crystal Lee Jordan, affidavit, State of North Carolina, June 21, 1973, drawer 2, CLS; Byerly, "Crystal Lee Sutton," in *Hard Times*, 207–8; Henry P. Leifermann, "The Unions Are Coming: Trouble in the South's First Industry," *New York Times Magazine*, August 1973, 26; Leifermann, *Crystal Lee*, 142–45; Cobb, *Selling of the South*, 257.

6. I use "bossmen" because millhands used this term for section managers who watched performance and tracked output. Supervisors had higher status and power, and foremen/foreladies were millhands with duties such as checking schedules and assignments.

7. Jordan affidavit, CLS.

8. Jordan affidavit, 5–7; Byerly, "Crystal Lee Sutton," in *Hard Times*, 209–10; Leifermann, *Crystal Lee*, 145–50.

9. Carbado et al., "Intersectionality"; Cho, Crenshaw, and McCall, "Toward a Field."

10. Lelia Carson Albrecht, "The Real 'Norma Rae' Is Anguished by the Hollywood Replay of Her Life," *People*, April 30, 1979, 11, 43.

11. For historians with this intersectional approach to labor, see Glenn, *Unequal Freedom*; Rockman, *Scraping By*; Greene, *Canal Builders*; and Hahamovitch, *No Man's Land*.

12. I use "current" as a critique of the dominant neoliberal discourse for trade and migration, with its emphasis on freely moving "flows." Currents move within water or air, constantly interacting with temperature, gravity, chemistry, and solid objects. Use of the term emphasizes factors that interact with migrations, relocations, and investments and is inspired by Woods ("Building Empire's Archipelago," 133), who questions the "uncritical and ambiguous language of migrant 'flows.'"

13. "We work in the garment industry."

14. "Maldonado," August 8, 1984, 38–39, Centro.

15. Hall, *Representation*, 1–15.

16. Ritt, *Norma Rae*.

17. The main character in the movie goes by "Norma." Crystal Lee usually used one name, but depending on the situation, people called her "Lee" or "Crystal."

18. Hale, *Nation of Outsiders*, 127–29. Hale describes Bob Dylan's 1960s lyrical

references to "change" in the same way. He emphasized change without ideology or imperative, so listeners could fill his lyrics with any emotion.

19. Local areas experience "deindustrialization." When a factory or mine that had employed thousands of residents closes, they experience the immediate results of deindustrialization, unemployment and dark empty buildings, and the ripple of secondary closures. This book studies workers within the broader reconfigurations of manufacturing, the relentless shifting of currents in many directions as regulations, resources, taxes, and technologies change.

20. Robbins and Wise, *West Side Story*.

21. Davine, "Could We Not Dye," 139–49; Foulkes, "Seeing the City"; Paredez, "'Queer for Uncle Sam'"; Acevedo-Muñoz, *West Side Story*; Silva, "'I Like to Live'"; Garebian, *Making*. The musical's success prompted two movies with Puerto Rican characters wielding knives in the streets, *Cry Tough* (1959) and *The Young Savages* (1961).

22. Tools from history of capitalism help to understand how capitalist practices and institutions impacted workers and changed over time. This analysis challenges the idea that capitalism functions in a teleological way, with a logic of advancement, rather than as a constantly shifting array of enterprises seeking any available means for increasing rates of return on investment. Most corporations and firms prioritize increasing their return, which is often tied not directly to costs or profits but to financial instruments. Cutting certain costs, such as labor and materials, earns accolades on its own for ideological, as much as financial, reasons. See Appleby, *Relentless Revolution*; and Beckert et al., "Interchange."

23. Bourdieu, *Field of Cultural Production*, esp. part 1; Williams, *Marxism and Literature*.

24. Bourdieu, *Field of Cultural Production*, 38–39, 44–46; Bourdieu, "Forms of Capital."

25. Bourdieu, *Field of Cultural Production*, esp. part 1; Bourdieu, *Distinction*; Jameson, *Postmodernism*, 58–59.

26. Williams, *Politics and Letters*; Williams, *Marxism and Literature*; Denning, *Cultural Front*, 27–28; Klein, *Cold War Orientalism*, 7, 16; Ahmed, *Cultural Politics of Emotion*.

27. Williams, *Marxism and Literature*; Klein, *Cold War Orientalism*, 7, 16.

28. McAlister, *Epic Encounters*, 8; Klein, *Cold War Orientalism*, 8–10. These scholars do not address neoliberalism, but they use movies and television, museum exhibits, speeches, and policy papers to show the convergence of cultural, social, and political structures in extending US imperialism.

29. Duggan, *Twilight of Equality*; David Harvey, *Brief History of Neoliberalism*, 40–41; Grewal, *Transnational America*; Ong, *Neoliberalism as Exception*; Steger and Roy, *Neoliberalism*; Rodgers, *Age of Fracture*; Appelbaum and Batt, *Private Equity at Work*.

30. Ray, *Certain Tendency*, 18, 47–59.

31. Kimble and Olson, "Visual Rhetoric," 553–54. Kimble and Olson studied Westinghouse factory posters commissioned by managers during World War II, one of which has become known as "Rosie the Riveter." Building on Erving Goffman's sociological concepts, they argue the iconic image's twenty-first-century embedded narrative of individualist empowerment derives from the imaginative process that resulted when the 1940s poster appeared outside its original context.

32. Hanagan and van der Linden, "New Approaches."

33. Bodnar, *Blue-Collar Hollywood*; Denning, *Culture*, 1–10.

34. Leifermann, *Crystal Lee*, 89, 95–96; Byerly, "Clara Thrift," in *Hard Times*, 110–11; Conway, *Rise Gonna Rise*, 125; Rooks, "Cowboy Mentality," 46.

35. Interviews with needleworkers, box 230, series XIX "Audio-Visual (1973–99)," El Centro de Estudios Puertorriqueños Collection, Centro; Korrol, *From Colonia to Community*, 108–12; Minchin, *Empty Mills*, 3–5, 99.

Chapter One

1. Bruce G. Harvey, *World's Fairs*, 66–68.

2. Hyde, *Empires, Nations, and Families*; Kiernan, *Blood and Soil*; Banner, *How the Indians*.

3. Dietz, *Economic History*, 83; Schoultz, *Beneath the United States*, chaps. 1–8; Whalen, "Colonialism," 5–6; McGuinness, "Searching for 'Latin America'"; Jacobson, *Whiteness*, esp. "Crucible of Empire," 203–22.

4. Ayala and Bernabe, *Puerto Rico*, 14.

5. Trías Monge, *Puerto Rico*, 28; Schoultz, *Beneath the United States*; Jacobson, *Whiteness*. The 1819 treaty for Florida, 1848 Treaty of Guadalupe Hidalgo for large parts of Mexico, 1867 treaty for the purchase of Alaska, and 1898 annexation of Hawai'i included rapid incorporation and citizenship rights.

6. Peter A. Schulman, *Coal and Empire*, 125–63; Whalen, "Colonialism," 6–8.

7. Carlos Sanabria, "Women's Labor and the Home Needlework Industry in Puerto Rico, 1898–1930," draft, May 1988, 9, 13, 15–17, folder 11; "Throughout the Century," paper, 1, folder 13; and "Worker Emigrations from Puerto Rico: A Historical Note," paper for PR Women in Garment Industry, [198?], 1–3, folder 13, all in box 139, series XII "Research Task Forces (1950–2001), History (1974–97)," El Centro de Estudios Puertorriqueños Collection, Centro; Summary of *Investigation of Minimum Wages and Education in Puerto Rico and the Virgin Islands: Hearings on H.R. 75, Before the Special Investigating Subcomm. of the Comm. on Education and Labor*, 81st Congress 150 (1949), in box 1, folder 5, Dorvillier News Letters (1952–64, 1973–78), ILGWU/UNITE Collection, Centro; Pesotta, *Bread upon the Waters*, 108; Korrol, *From Colonia to Community*, 20–25; Benmayor, "For Every Story," 6.

8. Korrol, *From Colonia to Community*, 19–28; Dietz, *Economic History*, 85; Sedgewick, "What Is Imperial," 313.

9. Sanabria, "Women's Labor," 15–17; "Worker Emigrations," 1–3; "Working Outline: Puerto Rican Women in Garment Industry," 2, box 158, folder 2, series XII, "Research Task Forces (1950–2001), History (1974–97)," all in El Centro de Estudios Puertorriqueños Collection, Centro; Baerga, "El género," 4–55; González, "La industria," 59–81; Pesotta, *Bread upon the Waters*, 103–24; Matías-Ortiz, "Ambivalent Solidarities," 25–28; Ayala and Bernabe, *Puerto Rico*, 33–47.

10. Korrol, *From Colonia to Community*, 13–14; Findlay, *We Are Left*, 28–29; Rodríguez-Silva, *Silencing Race*; Thompson, *Imperial Archipelago*; Thompson, "Representation and Rule"; Lanny Thompson, "The Colonialist's Gaze," *Southern Spaces*, September 5, 2017, video, 8:50, https://southernspaces.org/2017/colonialists-gaze; Duany, *Puerto Rican Nation*, 39–58; Duany, "Portraying the Other"; Garcia, "I Am the Other"; Lloréns, *Imaging*; Go, *American Empire*.

11. Also known as creole landowners; in Puerto Rico, these were usually light-skinned or white men of Spanish descent who owned large plantations and other assets.

12. Thompson, *Imperial Archipelago*; Go, *American Empire*; Ayala and Bernabe, *Puerto Rico*, 52–73; Briggs, *Reproducing Empire*; Trías Monge, *Puerto Rico*.

13. Santiago Iglesias, Pan-American Federation of Labor letter re: AFL ILGWU support in Puerto Rico, August 5, 1918, no. 5780/009, box 2, folder 1, Benjamin Schlesinger Records (1914–23), ILGWU Collection, Kheel; Meléndez-Badillo, *Lettered Barriada*; Ayala and Bernabe, *Puerto Rico*, 17, 61.

14. For related histories, see Silvestrini, "Women as Workers"; A. G. Quintero Rivera, *Patricios y plebeyos*; Findlay, *Imposing Decency*; Galvin, *Organized Labor Movement*; Matías-Ortiz, "Ambivalent Solidarities"; Macpherson, "Citizens v. Clients"; and Emma Amador, "'Women Ask Relief.'"

15. Stoler, *Along the Archival Grain*, 4, 105–7; Briggs, *Reproducing Empire*, 1–3, 20.

16. Woods does not use the notion of "scaffolding" but argues that postcolonial practices of the 1940s "set an important precedent in the development of the relationship between states, capital, and labor migration," which neoliberalism accelerated thirty years later. Woods, "Building Empire's Archipelago," 149–50.

17. Larner, "Neo-liberalism"; Duggan, *Twilight of Equality*; David Harvey, *Brief History of Neoliberalism*; Phillips-Fein, *Invisible Hands*; Mirowski and Plehwe, *Road from Mont Pèlerin*; Val Marie Johnson, "Introduction, Special Section"; Rodgers, *Age of Fracture*; Bockman, *Markets*; Burgin, *Great Persuasion*; Slobodian, *Globalists*; Ben Jackson, "At the Origins."

18. See Venator Santiago, *Puerto Rico*, for a history of US policy and Puerto Rican sovereignty and citizenship. See Canaday, *Straight State*, esp. chaps. 1 and 6, for an analysis of homosexuality as a means to change and restrict the obligations of the state.

19. Go, "Chains of Empire," 346, 352; Ayala and Bernabe, *Puerto Rico*, 24–30.

20. Cooper, *Colonialism in Question*, 91–112; Go, "Chains of Empire," 346, 352; Sassen, *Sociology of Globalization*; Ayala and Bernabe, *Puerto Rico*, 33.

21. For histories of the Insular Cases, see McCoy and Scarano, *Colonial Crucible*; Sparrow, *Insular Cases*, 79–110; and Burnett and Marshall, *Foreign*.

22. Edmunds, *Insular Cases*, 4–5, 9–10; Sparrow, *Insular Cases*, 79–110; Burnett and Marshall, "Between the Foreign," 6–18.

23. Go, "Chains of Empire," 357.

24. "Special West Indian Commissioner," *Exposition* 1, no. 4 (March 1901): 123; and "The West Indian Exhibit" and "Senorita Davila and Her Embroidery," *Exposition* 1, no. 9 (August 1901): 326, 329, all in Osborne.

25. "West Indian Exhibit"; "Senorita Davila."

26. Baerga-Santini, "Trabajo diestro," 158–62.

27. Bruce G. Harvey, *World's Fairs*; Chibbaro, *Charleston Exposition*; Perdue, *Race*.

28. "Exposition Flyer" trifold, *The Exposition: Bound* (1901), 1, Osborne.

29. "An Interesting Exhibit," *Exposition* 2, no. 4 (March 1902): 592, 595, Osborne.

30. R. M. Mitchell, "The American Manufacturers' Joint Cotton Mills," *Exposition* 2, no. 2 (January 1902): 545, Osborne.

31. Hall et al., *Like a Family*; Tami J. Friedman, "Exploiting the North-South Differential."

32. Ayala and Bernabe, *Puerto Rico*, 29–30; Thompson, *Imperial Archipelago*; Duany, "Portraying the Other"; Wilson, "Advantages of Obscurity."

33. Boris, "Needlewomen," 37.

34. Chomsky, *Linked Labor Histories*, 107; New York State Curriculum, "Old Voices, New Voices," 39. A group of manufacturers founded the Philadelphia Textile School in 1884 to train workers and managers because they wanted to compete with British quality. It became the Philadelphia College of Textiles and Science in 1961 and Philadelphia University in 1999. Susan Snyder, "Jefferson-Philadelphia University Merger," *Philadelphia Inquirer*, March 1, 2018.

35. A few executives, including Warren Coleman of North Carolina, tried to run Black-only mills at the turn of the century, but they were short-lived. Rowan, *Negro in the Textile*, 49.

36. Rowan, *Negro in the Textile*; Mitchell, *Rise of Cotton Mills*; "Frank Cosswaith Dead; Pioneer Negro Organizer," *Justice* 47, no. 13 (July 1, 1965): 11, in Kheel; "Mission to Montgomery," *Justice* 47, no. 7 (April 1, 1965): 1, in Kheel; Osburn, *Negro Employment*; Conway, *Rise Gonna Rise*, 10–56; Byerly, "Born a Womanchild" and "Black Workers, White Mill Town," in *Hard Times*, 43–74, 125–62; Jacqueline Jones, *Labor of Love*; Janiewski, *Sisterhood Denied*; Hall et al., *Like a Family*; Hunter, *To 'Joy My Freedom*; MacLean, *Freedom Is Not Enough*, 78–89; Minchin, *Hiring the Black Worker*.

37. Conway, *Rise Gonna Rise*, 158–97; Hall et al., *Like a Family*, 99–104, 211; Fones-Wolf and Fones-Wolf, *Struggle*, 93; Kuhn, *Contesting*, 83–90.

38. Kuhn, *Contesting*, 91–110.

39. Hall et al., *Like a Family*, 77–78.

40. Wilkerson, *To Live Here*.

41. Summary of *Investigation of Minimum Wages*, Centro; Grosfoguel, "Puerto Rican Labor Migration," 508.

42. Juarbe, "Anastasia's Story," 16–18; E. E. Pratt to William C. Redfield, in *Textiles in Porto Rico and Jamaica* (Special Agent Series 137), no. 47 (February 14, 1917), reel 1 "Records of BIA, 1900–34, N.A. Arrangement: Files 27184 Textiles," Bureau of Insular Affairs, Records of the PRRA 1918–1949 Microfilm Collection, Centro.

43. Ayala and Bernabe, *Puerto Rico*, 28, 46–47, 58.

44. For studies of the Jones Act, see Thomas, "'How They Ignore'"; del Moral, "Colonial Citizens"; and McGreevey, *Borderline Citizens*, esp. chap. 4.

45. Rowan, *Negro in the Textile*, 58–60; Hall et al., *Like a Family*, 186–89.

46. Rowan, *Negro in the Textile*, 55.

47. Stevenson conversation; English, *Common Thread*; Tami J. Friedman, "Exploiting the North-South Differential."

48. For histories of women and factories in New York City, see Orleck, *Common Sense*; Enstad, *Ladies of Labor*; Bender, *Sweated Work, Weak Bodies*; Guglielmo, *Living the Revolution*; and Gayle, "'Invaders.'"

49. Korrol, *From Colonia to Community*, 31; Boris, "Needlewomen," 37–38.

50. G. L. Jones, "Sweatshops," 163–64.

51. Jones, 165–66.

52. Sanabria, "Women's Labor," 21–22, Centro.

53. Muñoz Marín, "'Sad Case,'" 174–75.

54. "Int'l Garment, Textile Group Spurs Hong Kong Unionizing," *Justice* 47, no. 12 (June 15, 1965), 3, in Kheel; Beckert, *Empire of Cotton*, 379–426; Fones-Wolf and

Fones-Wolf, *Struggle*, 89–90; Ekbladh, *Great American Mission*, 159; Chomsky, *Linked Labor Histories*, 16, 117.

55. Alvarez, "El Hilo," 29–36; New York State Curriculum, "Old Voices, New Voices," 38–41; Whalen, "Colonialism," 41; Whalen, "'Day the Dresses Stopped,'" 122; Findlay, "Artful Narration," 164; Findlay, "Slipping and Sliding," 25; Thomas and Santiago, *Rethinking*, 18–19. For migration as an arena of struggle between workers, government officials, and recruiters, see Greene, "Movable Empire," 4, 8, 18.

56. The concept of "labor arbitrage" appears in Ong, *Neoliberalism as Exception*. The concept of "regulatory arbitrage" appears in Cerny, *Rethinking World Politics*.

57. "Eva Monje," July 8, 1984, box 230, folder 2, series XIX "Audio-Visual (1973–99)," El Centro de Estudios Puertorriqueños Collection, Centro; Alvarez, "El Hilo," 26; Whalen, "'Day the Dresses Stopped,'" 122; New York State Curriculum, "Old Voices, New Voices," 37–41.

58. Whalen, "Sweatshops Here and There," 45–68.

59. "Agency History," finding aid, Archives of Puerto Rican Diaspora, Offices of the Government of Puerto Rico in the United States Collection, 1930–93, Centro; Thomas and Santiago, *Rethinking*, 12–14.

60. Puerto Rican and Hispanic League and the Worker Alliance.

61. "Eva Monje," July 8, 1984, Centro; Alvarez, "El Hilo," 26; New York State Curriculum, "Old Voices, New Voices," 37–41; Whalen, "'Day the Dresses Stopped,'" 122.

62. Findlay, *Imposing Decency*, 152–73; Ayala and Bernabe, *Puerto Rico*, 66–68.

63. John Murray, "The Hispanics: The Fastest Growing Ethnic Community," *Waterbury Observer*, April 11, 1996, 4, box 1, folder 5 "Puerto Ricans in Connecticut, 1961–89" from Ruth Glasser: Research on Puerto Ricans in Connecticut, Hispanic Collection, Connecticut Historical Society, Hartford, CT.

64. "Corporate History," register of J.P. Stevens and Company, 1813–1989, pp. 2–3, finding aid, Special Collections, Clemson University, Clemson, SC; Byerly, "From Farm to Factory," in *Hard Times*, 11–42; Conway, *Rise Gonna Rise*, 13–20; Leifermann, *Crystal Lee*, 49.

65. Simon, "Rethinking Why." The two women who in 1931 leveled a false accusation of gang rape against the young Black men who became known as the Scottsboro Boys were southern millhands riding the rails for jobs.

66. Byerly, "Everything We Had," "Born a Womanchild," and "Black Workers, White Mill Town," in *Hard Times*, 3–43, 43–74, 125–62; Hall et al., *Like a Family*, 105–10; Fones-Wolf and Fones-Wolf, *Struggle*, 11–13; Hahamovitch and Halpern, "Not a 'Sack'"; Rowan, *Negro in the Textile*, 56–57; Conway, *Rise Gonna Rise*, 11–15; Padfield and Martin, *Farmers, Workers, and Machines*; McWilliams, *Factories in the Field*.

67. Byerly, *Hard Times*; Hall et al., *Like a Family*, 197–99, 212–18; Salmond, *Gastonia, 1929*, 1–9.

68. Hall et al., *Like a Family*, 201. The conglomerate was the Manville-Jenckes Company.

69. Salmond, *Gastonia, 1929*, 12–20, 28.

70. Hall et al., *Like a Family*, 301–2; Conway, *Rise Gonna Rise*, 3; Salmond, *General Textile Strike*, ix–x.

71. Vázquez Erazo, "Postscript," 44; Boris, "Needlewomen," 38, 44; Dietz, *Economic History*, 175.

72. Radiogram CK 132, 14th 0431, folder 3 "Needlework Amendments," in box 1, entry

601 Records Relating to the Needlework Industry (March 1934–January 1936), Puerto Rico Records, RG 009, NRA Territorial Office for Puerto Rico records; and Administrative Order No. 58, August 6, 1940, folder 6 "Special Investigation Case Files," in box 1, entry 18 Records of Industry Committees Investigations and Records of the PR Industry Committee (August 1940–January 1942), Cigarettes, etc. Miscellaneous Handiwork Division, Puerto Rico Records, RG 155, Records of the Wage and Hour and Public Contracts Division, both in National Archives in New York City; Ayala and Bernabe, *Puerto Rico*, 96; Boris, "Needlewomen," 39.

73. Baerga-Santini, "La defensa"; Boris, "Needlewomen"; Boris, "Organization or Prohibition"; Matías-Ortiz, "Ambivalent Solidarities," 61–87.

74. Angleró letter, December 4, 1934, box 1, folder 8 "Piece Rates Commission," entry 593, Office Files of Boaz Long (November 1933–November 1935), Puerto Rico Records, RG 9, NRA Territorial Office for Puerto Rico records, National Archives in New York City; Rose Pesotta, undated report on Needle Workers' Union Local 300 describing confidence in Angleró, ILGWU Zimmerman Papers, Kheel; Wm. D. Lopez to Charles Zimmerman, July 30, 1934, describing meeting between Pesotta and Angleró, no. 5780/014, box 30, folder 10 "Needle Workers' Union of PR Local 300," ILGWU Zimmerman Papers, Kheel; Teresa Angleró, "Folded-Arms Strike Wins in Puerto Rico," *Justice* 18, no. 7 (April 1, 1936): 11, in Kheel; Ayala and Bernabe, *Puerto Rico*, 96; Boris, "Needlewomen," 38–39, 48.

75. Salmond, *General Textile Strike*, 1, 8–9.

76. Salmond, 46–56.

77. Frederickson, "'I Know Which Side,'" 171–72; Salmond, *General Textile Strike*, 80.

78. Hall et al., *Like a Family*, 349; Biles, *South*, 84–86.

79. "Public-private" is used as an umbrella descriptor, denoting relationships between government offices and any private organization. The term "government-industry" indicates arrangements between government offices and business corporations. Differentiation makes visible the many forms of public-private activities and the ways in which the state partners with many types of private organizations: unions, nonprofits, churches, environmental groups, etc., as well as business corporations and investment banks, which have the lobbying power and staff to demand more.

80. Sullivan-González and Wilson, *South and the Caribbean*; Ring, *Problem South*, 58–94, 175–215; José Amador, *Medicine and Nation*.

81. "Mrs. Roosevelt Inspects 12 Towns: Hears Seamstresses' Plea," *Boston Globe*, March 13, 1934, 28; "Model Puerto Rican City Named Eleanor Roosevelt," *NYT*, June 15, 1936, 1; "San Juan's Poor Greet 'First Lady,'" *Los Angeles Times*, March 11, 1934, 1; Cook, *Eleanor Roosevelt*, 166–74.

82. Tugwell, *Stricken Land*; Rodríguez, *New Deal*; Beruff, *Strategy as Politics*, chaps. 5–7; Ekbladh, *Great American Mission*, 18–19; Whalen, "Colonialism," 15; Ayala and Bernabe, *Puerto Rico*, 97, 102–3; Robert David Johnson, "Anti-imperialism."

83. *Issues for Industry in Puerto Rico*, report, 1934, R.V.S. 18S36, 34, reel 1, 1935–70, Library of Congress Relating to Puerto Rico, Materials from the, Centro.

84. McConnell, *Economic Trends*, 8.

85. The Bureau of Insular Affairs in the War Department did not fully close until 1939. Ayala and Bernabe, *Puerto Rico*, 97, 102–3.

86. Earl Hanson, *Planning Problems and Activities in Puerto Rico*, preliminary report

to PRRA and National Resources Committee, San Juan, PR, November 23, 1935, 8, 15, RG 323, Centro.

87. Hong, *Ruptures of American Capital*, 70–100.

88. Lopez, *Matters of Choice*; Briggs, *Reproducing Empire*.

89. For a history of the FLSA debate, see Macpherson, "Birth."

90. Silvestrini, "Women as Workers," 69–71; Chomsky, *Linked Labor Histories*, 109.

91. Daniel Nadal to Franklin D. Roosevelt, September 26, 1938, no. 156; and Domenech to Roosevelt, October 26, 1938, no. 157, both in RG 323, Centro.

92. Leon to Charlotte Westwood, December 1, 1938, no. 154; and Edward Leon, *Puerto Rico and Fair Labor Standards Act of 1938*, undated report on needlework, no. 148, both in RG 323, Centro; "To Seek Wages Act Exemption," *NYT*, August 24, 1938, 4.

93. "Pay Plea for Puerto Rico," *NYT*, September 21, 1938, 9; "Wage Relief Sought," *NYT*, August 16, 1938, 20; "Confer in Puerto Rico," *NYT*, August 18, 1938, 8; "To Seek Wages Act," 4; "Needleworkers to Go On," *NYT*, October 26, 1938, 15; "Puerto Rican Industries Lay Off 21,343 of 27,457," *NYT*, November 16, 1938, 8; "Puerto Rico," *NYT*, November 27, 1938, 80.

94. "Urges Puerto Rico to Act on Wage Law," *NYT*, August 20, 1938, 4; P. Rivera Martínez, "Puerto Rico and the Wage and Hour Law," 1938, no. 151, RG 323, Centro.

95. "Labor through 1937–1938 in Puerto Rico," 1939, no. 153, RG 323, Centro; Macpherson, "Birth," 659–66, 673.

96. "Puerto Rico and the Virgin Islands," Fair Labor Standards Act proposed amendments, S. 2682, RG 323, Centro; McConnell, *Economic Trends*, 12–13; Macpherson, "Birth," 677–80.

97. Mr. Fairbank to Mrs. Graham, radiogram, September 25, 1938, no. 162; Department of Agriculture and Commerce, *The Needlework Industry and Its Crisis in the Year 1938*, undated report, p. 3 for reference to tariffs with Switzerland and China, no. 155; "Importations of Handkerchiefs into the United States with Exception of Puerto Rico," December 1, 1938, no. 153; and "Outline of Information Desired by the Tariff Commission on Handkerchiefs," 1939, no. 145, all in RG 323, Centro.

98. Hall et al., *Like a Family*, 308; de Jong, "'With the Aid,'" 230, 238–55; Honey, *Southern Labor*, 51; Biles, *South*, 125–52; Salmond, *General Textile Strike*, 207; Cook, *Eleanor Roosevelt*, 162–64; Suggs, *"My World Is Gone,"* 102, 145.

99. Hall et al., *Like a Family*, 7, 12–15; Conway, *Rise Gonna Rise*, 51–55; Cobb, *Selling of the South*, 64–95.

100. Honey, *Southern Labor*, 26; Salmond, *General Textile Strike*, 27–29, 33–35.

101. Biles, *South*, 83–102; Windham, *Knocking on Labor's Door*.

102. Rosen, *Making Sweatshops*, 58–60; Benton, *Fraying Fabric*, 37–44, 100–107.

103. Rosen, *Making Sweatshops*, 28; Beckert, *Empire of Cotton*, 403–8; Roberts, *Staying on the Line*, 1–42.

104. Tugwell, *Stricken Land*; Maldonado, *Teodoro Moscoso*; Dietz, *Economic History*, 207–9; Findlay, *We Are Left*, 9; Ayala and Bernabe, *Puerto Rico*, 142–46.

105. Arthur D. Little, Inc., *Report on New Industries*; Schmidt, *In Search of Decision*, 221–45; Magee, *Arthur D. Little, Inc.*, 10–16.

106. Dietz, *Economic History*, 207–9; Findlay, *We Are Left*, 9; Ayala and Bernabe, *Puerto Rico*, 142–46.

107. Cobb, *Selling of the South*, 35–95; Jewell, *Dollars for Dixie*.

108. "US Is Urged to Copy Puerto Rico Tax Law," *NYT*, May 18, 1951, 50; Bolin, "What Puerto Rico Faced," 1–2; Dietz, *Economic History*, 193–94, 209–10; Ríos, "Export-Oriented Industrialization," 322–24; Whalen, "Sweatshops Here and There," 47; Ayala and Bernabe, *Puerto Rico*, 179–89.

109. Dietz, *Economic History*, 209–10; Ayala and Bernabe, *Puerto Rico*, 189.

110. "Textron Building Puerto Rican Mill," *NYT*, December 8, 1948, 51. By 2018, Textron had become a transnational corporation with diverse holdings in materials, equipment, and finance.

111. Whalen, "Sweatshops Here and There," 47–48; Whalen, "Colonialism," 27–28; Ayala and Bernabe, *Puerto Rico*, 190–91.

112. Santiago, *When I Was*, 105–30.

113. Winslow telephone conversation; "En la union esta la fuerza," photograph, [195?], ILGWU Local 600 PR, ILGWU Justice Photographs, Kheel; "N.Y. Puerto Ricans Fight Island Sweatshops," *Justice* 37, no. 14 (July 15, 1955): 3, in Kheel.

114. Muñiz-Mas, "Gender, Work," 194–98.

115. Whalen, "Sweatshops Here and There," 50.

116. Korrol, *From Colonia to Community*, 30–46; Briggs, *Reproducing Empire*, 87–90, 111–14; Findlay, *We Are Left*, 98–103.

117. "Descriptive Summary," "Historical Note," and "Agency History," all in finding aid, Archives of Puerto Rican Diaspora, Offices of the Government of Puerto Rico in the United States, 1930–93, Centro; Meléndez, *Sponsored Migration*.

118. "Howard Clothes," April 20, 1951, no. 266; "Fairway Skirt," April 2, 1952, no. 213, reel 351, box 2054, folders 1–24; and "Employment Program Staff Meeting," June 4, 1964, no. 1100, reel 351, box 2055, folders 9–11, all in Easy Jobs?: PR Employment Program in NY, 1948–91, Offices of the Government of Puerto Rico in the United States Collection, 1930–93, Centro.

119. New York State Curriculum, "Old Voices, New Voices," 38–40.

120. Juarbe, "Anastasia's Story," 15; Whalen, "Colonialism," 1–2; Ayala and Bernabe, *Puerto Rico*, 180–81.

121. Korrol, *From Colonia to Community*, 35–47; Whalen, "Sweatshops Here and There," 49–50.

122. Ortiz, "'En la aguja," 64–67.

123. "Eva Monje," July 8, 1984, 10–13; "Emilia Giboyeaux," January 8, 1984, 27, box 228, folder 4, series XIX "Audio-Visual (1973–99)"; and unnumbered cassette *Puerto Rican Women in Garment Industry*, radio program, 1985, Oral History and Audiocassette Collection, all in El Centro de Estudios Puertorriqueños Collection, Centro; Galvin, *Organized Labor*, 157.

124. "Louise Delgado," August 15, 1984, 20, 26, box 227, folder 8, series XIX "Audio-Visual (1973–99)," El Centro de Estudios Puertorriqueños Collection, Centro.

125. Vázquez Erazo, "Stories Our Mothers Tell," 46–48.

126. Dietz, *Economic History*, 253; Ayala and Bernabe, *Puerto Rico*, 192.

127. New fabrics included nylon, Orlon, Acrilan, dynel, and Dacron, different from previous synthetics, rayon and acetate, made from natural polymers. Airov, *Location*, 2–8, 148–49.

128. Silk was no longer profitable due to synthetics. Ekbladh, *Great American Mission*, 91; Rosen, *Making Sweatshops*, 29–42; Koistinen, *Confronting Decline*, 193–94.

129. Stein, *Pivotal Decade*, 6–8.

130. Many in US government wanted to open American markets to Asian textiles—and eventually garments—to sustain anticommunist political and economic ties, as well as US military dominance, in the Pacific. From 1954 to 1956, the Trade Agreements Act reduced Asian textile tariffs each year, and imports to the United States grew. Shenin, *United States*, 49, 134; Rosen, *Making Sweatshops*, 29–42.

131. Ekbladh, *Great American Mission*, 77–113; Chomsky, *Linked Labor Histories*, 115–16; Shenin, *United States*, esp. 15, 28, 41, 67, 133, 162–64; Latham, *Right Kind of Revolution*, 1–63.

132. Rosen, *Making Sweatshops*, 154; Adler, *Mollie's Job*, 207–16.

133. Arthur D. Little, Inc., *Report on Ten-Year*, foreword; Magee, *Arthur D. Little, Inc.*, 10–16; Chomsky, *Linked Labor Histories*, 116; Schmidt, *In Search of Decision*; Bonacich and Waller, "Mapping a Global Industry," 28–30.

134. Conway, *Rise Gonna Rise*, 4–5; Cobb, *Selling of the South*, 171–74. Three research institutions, Duke University, the University of North Carolina at Chapel Hill, and North Carolina State University, anchored the eight-county region.

135. Frederickson, "'I Know Which Side,'" 173; Hall et al., *Like a Family*, 193–95; Clark, *Like Night and Day*, 143–66, 168–200; Simon, "Rethinking Why," 465–84; William P. Jones, "'Simple Truths of Democracy.'"

136. Frederickson, "'I Know Which Side,'" 173; Hall et al., *Like a Family*, 193–95; Clark, *Like Night and Day*, 143–66, 168–200; Simon, "Rethinking Why," 465–84; William P. Jones, "'Simple Truths of Democracy.'"

137. Henry P. Leifermann, "The Unions Are Coming: Trouble in the South's First Industry," *New York Times Magazine*, August 1973, 10; Leifermann, *Crystal Lee*, 4–20.

138. "Supplementary Unemployment and Severance Benefits," *Justice* 47, no. 16 (August 15, 1965): 6–7, in Kheel; Whalen, "'Day the Dresses Stopped,'" 133–38.

Chapter Two

1. Multiple interviews, esp. "Louise Delgado," February 17, 1985, 122, box 227, folder 8, series XIX "Audio-Visual (1973–99)," El Centro de Estudios Puertorriqueños Collection, Centro; Ortiz, "'En la aguja,'" 61; Korrol, *Pioneros II*, 9; Whalen, "'Day the Dresses Stopped,'" 121–50.

2. Unnumbered cassette, *Puerto Rican Women in Garment Industry*, radio program, 1985, Oral History and Audiocassette Collection; "Maldonado," August 8, 1984, 38–39, box 229, folder 3, series XIX "Audio-Visual (1973–99)," ; and "Eva Monje," July 8, 1984, box 230, folder 2, series XIX "Audio-Visual (1973–99)," all in El Centro de Estudios Puertorriqueños Collection, Centro.

3. Stevenson conversation; Rosen, *Making Sweatshops*; Collins, *Threads*.

4. Whalen, "'Day the Dresses Stopped,'" 133–38.

5. "Set N.Y. Dress Strike Machinery," *Justice* 40, no. 4 (February 15, 1958): 3–4; and "105,000 in 7-State Dress Strike," "Demand Pay, Enforcement Gains," and "N'East, EOT Gird for Dress Strike," *Justice* 40, no. 5 (March 1, 1958): 1–9, all in Kheel; Whalen, "'Day the Dresses Stopped,'" 130–37.

6. Whalen, "'Day the Dresses Stopped,'" 133–38.

7. "NLRB Upholds Union Rights," *Justice* 47, no. 5 (March 1, 1965): 8 (NYC handkerchief shop closed for vacation, during break equipment relocated to Amsterdam, NY);

"Eastern Region Hits at Racket Stronghold," *Justice* 41, no. 22 (November 15, 1959): 11 (Grace Dress in Bridgeport, Connecticut, does contract work for nonunion company in New York City); "East Region Wins Phoenix in Hartford Breakthrough," *Justice* 41, no. 17 (September 1, 1959): 10 (nonunion shop organized in Hartford, a center of contractors); and "Strike Won!," "The Terms of the Settlement," "An Historic Strike," "The Day the Dresses Stopped," and "On the Line in Seven States," all in *Justice* 40, no. 6 (March 15, 1958), 1–11, all in Kheel; Whalen, "'Day the Dresses Stopped,'" 125–26, 134–35; Korrol, *Pioneros II*, 9.

8. "Registration Trophy," *Justice* 40, no. 1 (January 1, 1958): 11; and "60th Anniversary: La Prensa," *Justice* 42, no. 13 (July 1, 1960): 12, both in Kheel.

9. Whalen, "'Day the Dresses Stopped,'" 121–50.

10. *Puerto Rican Women in Garment Industry*; "Maldonado," August 8, 1984, 38–39; and "Eva Monje," July 8, 1984, 101–8, all in Centro.

11. Wakefield, "Long Night's Journey," 273–74; Korrol, *Pioneros II*, 9, 41; Cardona, *History*, 97–98.

12. Labor Advisory Committee on Puerto Rican Affairs, 1952–57, box 30, folders 7–9, finding aid, ILGWU Zimmerman Papers, Kheel.

13. Glaessel-Brown, "Time of Transition," 348, 360–61; Ortiz, "Puerto Rican Workers," 105–16; Whalen, "'Day the Dresses Stopped,'" 133–38.

14. Winslow telephone conversation; "Puerto Rican Progress Report," *Bridgeport Post*, August 20, 1957, clipping, box 2, folder 1 "Bridgeport—Puerto Ricans," Ruth Glasser: Research, Hispanic Collection, 1961–89, Connecticut Historical Society, Hartford, CT; "N'East, EOT Gird," Kheel; "Nutmeg Chairladies Keystone of Strike," *Justice* 40, no. 5 (March 1, 1958): 4, in Kheel; "Conn. Sunbeam Sees Light on Minimums After Quicky Halt," *Justice* 46, no. 7 (April 1, 1964): 5, in Kheel; Glaessel-Brown, "Time of Transition," 348, 360–61; Hartford, *Working People of Holyoke*, 202–5; Glasser, *Aquí Me Quedo*, 93.

15. "Raises, Severance for N.Y. Sportwear Workers," *Justice* 40, no. 8 (April 15, 1958): 5, 11; and "'We Have Won More Than Ever in Our History,'" *Justice* 40, no. 6 (March 15, 1958): 7, both in Kheel.

16. Ortiz, "Puerto Rican Workers," 52; Vázquez Erazo, "Stories Our Mothers Tell," 48–50.

17. Studies in the 1950s marked Puerto Rican migrants as deficient and unable to form productive working communities on the mainland. Mills, Senior, and Goldsen, *Puerto Rican Journey*; Handlin, *Race and Nationality*; Handlin, *Newcomers*.

18. Notes about the Theater, *Chicago Daily Tribune*, July 4, 1957, E10; Dorothy Kilgallen, "What's in a Name?," *Washington Post and Times Herald*, July 24, 1957, B8; "New Musical Show Scores in Premier," *Los Angeles Times*, August 20, 1957, 23; Richard Coe, "'West Side' Has That Beat," *Washington Post and Times Herald*, August 20, 1957, B12; William Glover, "New Broadway Musical to 'Say It with Dancing,'" *Hartford Courant*, August 25, 1957, 12B; Louis Calta, "'West Side Story' Unfolds Tonight," *NYT*, September 26, 1957, 21; Brooks Atkinson, "Theatre: The Jungles of the City," *NYT*, September 27, 1957, 14; Albert Goldberg, "Critic Raves over 'West Side Story,'" *Los Angeles Times*, October 1, 1957, C8.

19. In *Capital Moves*, Cowie tracked an RCA electronics plant from New Jersey in the 1930s to Indiana, Tennessee, and ultimately Mexico in the 1990s.

20. Nuñez, "Poultry, Thread, and Whitewater." The English Sewing Company bought the Willimantic Linen Company in 1898.

21. "Annual Report: To Stockholders," 1953–69, box 1, American Thread Company Reports; and "Millworkers of Willimantic, 1979–1980," box 45, Center for Oral History Interviews Collection, both in Dodd Center.

22. Russo conversation; "Annual Report: To Stockholders," 1953–69, Dodd Center; "Millworkers of Willimantic," Dodd Center; Boujouen, "'Menea Esas Manos,'" 73.

23. The American Thread Building remains a Tribeca landmark with high-end apartments, and its facade was the setting for a 2015 photo shoot of celebrated designers. Mina Hochberg, "American Thread Building Penthouse," HGTV, August 14, 2015, www.hgtv.com/design/decorating/design-101/american-thread-building-penthouse-in-new-york-pictures; "A Great Day in Men's Wear," *Esquire*, August 13, 2015, www.esquire.com/style/mens-fashion/a37163/a-great-day-in-mens-wear-082015. For analysis of the "deindustrialization sublime," see High and Lewis, *Corporate Wasteland*, 1–20, 43–60.

24. "Annual Report: To Stockholders," 1953–69, Dodd Center; Windham, *Knocking on Labor's Door*, 115.

25. Lewis, "Puerto Rico"; "Democracy's Laboratory in Latin America," *Time*, June 23, 1958.

26. Ayala and Bernabe, *Puerto Rico*, 202.

27. Dorvillier News Letter, February 19, 1966, January 1, 1972, box 6, folders 1–3; Economic Development Administration, "Industrial Development Program," December 1959, box 6, folders 1–3; Commonwealth of Puerto Rico Planning Board, "Statistical Yearbook Trade Stats Supplement," 1951–52, box 4, folders 1–4; and "1964 Directory of Economic Development Admin Manufacturing Plants," box 4, folders 1–4, all in Dorvillier News Letters (1952–64, 1973–78), ILGWU/UNITE Collection, Centro; Ayala and Bernabe, *Puerto Rico*, 192.

28. "Dubinsky with Luis Munoz Marin," photograph, no. 5780/176P, box 18, folder 4, ILGWU Communications Department Photographs, Kheel.

29. Juarbe, "Anastasia's Story," 20; Boujouen, "'Menea Esas Manos,'" 53–55; Ayala and Bernabe, *Puerto Rico*, 193–94.

30. Santiago, *When I Was*, 105–30, 245–47.

31. *Price and Lee's Holyoke City Directory* (New Haven, CT: Price and Lee, 1958–85), in Research Archives at Wistariahurst Museum, Holyoke, MA; Hartford, *Where Is Our Responsibility*.

32. New York, Chicago, and Philadelphia had larger numbers but as a lower percentage of city population. Wagenheim, *Survey*, 58–60; Cardona, *History*, 100–104; Barreto, "Evolving State," 292–94; Hernandez, "Quiet Crisis," 151–53; Félix V. Matos Rodríguez, "Puerto Ricans in the United States," presentation given in Fajardo, PR, December 9, 2013; Ralph Rivera, "Latinos in Massachusetts"; Republican Newspaper Group, *Nuestra Historia*, 1–23; Sosar, "Tale of Two Cities"; Barber, *Latino City*.

33. Kathleen M. Butler to Nieves, [196?], in "Out of the Barrio: The Puerto Rican Migration beyond NYC," no. 0078, reel 151 "Regional and Field Offices: Hartford," boxes 2494–95, folder 1, Offices of the Government of Puerto Rico in the United States, 1930–93, Centro.

34. Camacho to Flavio Reverón, memorandum, December 23, 1964, in "Out of the

Barrio: The Puerto Rican Migration beyond NYC," no. 0095, reel 151 "Regional and Field Offices: Hartford," boxes 2494–95, folder 1, Offices of the Government of Puerto Rico in the United States, 1930–93, Centro.

35. "Olga Mele," June 26, 2000, 5, transcript, binder, Ruth Glasser Interviews, Nuestras Historias/Our Histories, Connecticut Historical Society, Hartford, CT.

36. Manufacturers handle all aspects of apparel production and sales; jobbers buy excess fabric to make small orders or overstock apparel for discount sales; contractors complete production and assembly only on order from manufacturers or jobbers. "N'East Ups Pay for 5,000 in New England," *Justice* 43, no. 8 (April 15, 1961): 4, in Kheel.

37. Norma Boujouen and James R. Newton, "The Puerto Rican Experience in Willimantic," blue booklet, [198?], 10–11, Windham Regional Community Council, WTHM.

38. Boujouen, "'Menea Esas Manos,'" 1–5, 35–63, 76–77, 97–98, 101–6; Boujouen and Newton, "Puerto Rican Experience," 13, WTHM.

39. Medina interview; Salgado-Cartagena conversation; Ramírez, "Puerto Rican Experience," 2–5; Boujouen, "'Menea Esas Manos,'" 1–5, 35–63, 76–77, 97–98, 101–6; Boujouen and Newton, "Puerto Rican Experience," 13, WTHM.

40. "Pact Averts Dress Strike," *Justice* 43, no. 5 (March 1, 1961): 1, 3, in Kheel.

41. "Pay First Nat'l Severance," *Justice* 43, no. 8 (April 15, 1961): 3; and "Begin 1st Nat'l Severance Fund," *Justice* 42, no. 21 (November 1, 1960): 2, both in Kheel.

42. Uptown Handkerchief 0802, multiple job orders, Easy Jobs?: PR Employment Program in NY, 1948–91; and Industrial Workers [Clerical, Farm, Household, Industrial, Professional, Service, Training] [1957–90], reel 314, box 1838, folder 6, to box 1839, folder 6, both in Offices of the Government of Puerto Rico in the United States Collection, 1930–93, Centro.

43. "Maldonado," August 8, 1984, 11, Centro.

44. "Maldonado," 11–13.

45. Zaragosa Vargas, "Latino Workers," section Latino Workers in the Postwar Years, *American Latino Theme Study: Labor*, National Park Service, https://www.nps.gov/articles/latinothemelabor.htm

46. "Maldonado," August 8, 1984, 12–24, Centro.

47. "Maldonado," 11–12.

48. "Maldonado," 11–12.

49. Boris, Hoehtker, and Zimmermann, *Women's ILO*.

50. "Maldonado," August 8, 1984, 12–14, Centro; "Bwy Local 66 class," March 5, 1971, no. 5780/102P, box 19, folder 2, ILGWU Justice Photographs, Kheel.

51. "Maldonado," August 8, 1984, 11–17, Centro; "Members of Local 66 Learn," October 1, 1973, box 19, folder 2, ILGWU Justice Photographs, Kheel.

52. Rosen, *Making Sweatshops*, 56–81; Stein, *Pivotal Decade*, xi, 6–8.

53. Minchin, *Empty Mills*, 49; Koistinen, *Confronting Decline*, 193–94.

54. Minchin, *Empty Mills*, 45–90; Rosen, *Making Sweatshops*, 77–118.

55. A. H. Raskin, "Organizing South and Fighting Job Loss From Imports," *NYT*, October 26, 1977, 81; Windham, *Knocking on Labor's Door*, 108, 115–22.

56. Rosen, *Making Sweatshops*, 55–118; Minchin, *Empty Mills*, 45.

57. "Maldonado," August 8, 1984, 29, and February 17, 1985, 41–55; and "Eva Monje," July 8, 1984, 110–11, all in Centro; Janet Salaff to Burt Beck [director of public relations at Amalgamated Clothing and Textile Workers Union], clipping of interview with Takashi Izumi, November 28, 1978, no. 5619/038, box 10, folder 17 "J.P. Stevens

Japanese Boycott 1970," room 515, TD; "300 Convention Resolutions," *Justice* 44, no. 13 (July 1, 1962): 8, in Kheel; "The Other Cheek: India and China Cartoon," *Justice* 41, no. 23 (December 1, 1959): 12, in Kheel; Richards, *Union-Free America*, 97–98.

58. Rosen, *Making Sweatshops*; Stein, *Pivotal Decade*, 37–40.

59. "Maldonado," August 8, 1984, 29, Centro.

60. Foreign Trade and Investment Act of 1973, H.R. 1056, 93rd Cong. (1973), www.congress.gov/bill/93rd-congress/house-bill/1056?r=301182.

61. Windham, *Knocking on Labor's Door*, 124.

62. Letters, fact sheets, and "Technical Explanation" cards, no. 5619/033, box 10, folder 12 "Burke-Hartke Trade Bill 1971," room 415, ACTWU Political and Legislative Department Records, Kheel.

63. "Burke-Hartke Bill Opposed by Chamber of Commerce," *NYT*, April 10, 1972, 57; Brendan Jones, "Javits, Hartke Debate Trade Bill," *NYT*, March 28, 1972, 59; Brendan Jones, "Business Leaders Assail Trade Bill," *NYT*, March 15, 1972, 65; "The Burke-Hartke Bill: A Return to Protectionism," draft, January 1, 1972, Legislative Files 1964–77, Heinz Collection, Carnegie Mellon University, Pittsburgh, PA.

64. Stein, *Pivotal Decade*, 8–13, 95, 156–58.

65. Rosen, *Making Sweatshops*, 66–76.

66. Stein, *Pivotal Decade*, 11–12.

67. Stein, xi, 25–32, 158–59; Krippner, *Capitalizing on Crisis*.

68. Multiple documents, no. 5619/032, box 1, folder 36 "Trade Adjustment Assistance 1979–83," room 515, ACTWU International Affairs Department, 1976–84, Kheel; Rosen, *Making Sweatshops*, 55–76; Stein, *Pivotal Decade*, 12, 37–40.

69. "Hong Kong Organizing World Garment Goal," *Justice* 46, no. 16 (August 15, 1964): 9; "Free Labor's Global Brotherhood," *Justice* 46, no. 1 (January 1, 1964): 6–7; "Upswing in Economy," *Justice* 46, no. 19 (October 1, 1964): 12; "ILG Chief Scans Critical World Situation," *Justice* 44, nos. 11–12 (June 1–15, 1962): 2, 18; and "Reach Pact on World Trade for Cotton Textile, Apparel," *Justice* 44, no. 6 (March 15, 1962), 5, all in Kheel; "Maldonado," February 17, 1985, 46, Centro; Minchin, *Empty Mills*, 3.

70. "Maldonado," February 17, 1985, 40–57, quote on 43, Centro.

71. Bonacich et al., *Global Production*; Rosen, *Making Sweatshops*, 1–12, 55–118; Collins, *Threads*, 27–61.

72. Pastor, "Sinking"; Glasser, "Mofongo Meets Mangú," 103–6; Windham, *Knocking on Labor's Door*, 51–55.

73. "Know Your Union in English, Spanish, Chinese," *Justice* 47, no. 16 (August 15, 1965): 5; photos celebrating Quebecois workers in Montreal and Asian workers in New York, in "Goals for 1965," *Justice* 46, no. 23 (December 1, 1964): 1; "First Class Citizens," *Justice* 46, no. 14 (July 18, 1964): 6–7; and "In Any Language . . . Moving Forward Together," *Justice* 44, no. 15 (August 1, 1962): 6–7, all in Kheel.

74. Whalen, "Sweatshops Here and There."

75. Flyers and posters in Spanish and Chinese, flyers ILGWU Locals 23–25, box 8, folders 2–9, Andrade Papers, Centro; flyers, no. 5619/034, box 9, folders 19 "Amalgamated Service and Allied Industries/ESL Spanish 1978–79," 21 "Amalgamated Service and Allied Industries/ESL Haitian-French," and 23 "Local 444/Brooklyn Quilting ESL Spanish 1978–79," room 515, in ACTWU National Textile Recruitment and Training Program Records, 1975–81, Kheel.

76. "Maldonado," August 8, 1984, 18, Centro.

77. Windham, *Knocking on Labor's Door*, 52–54.

78. "Delgado and Maldonado," February 17, 1985, 150, box 227, folder 8; "Delgado," August 15, 1984, 52, box 227, folder 8; "Juanita Erazo Lucret," November 3, 1984, 6–9, box 228, folder 1; and "María Rodríguez," undated mix of handwritten notes and partial typed transcript, box 232, folder 6, all in series XIX "Audio-Visual (1973–99)," El Centro de Estudios Puertorriqueños Collection, Centro; "Maldonado," August 8, 1984, 16–21, 29, and February 17, 1985, 56–59; and "Eva Monje," July 8, 1984, 111, all in Centro; number 60, "Hunter College/Palmira Ríos (A)," September 30, 1984, Oral History and Audiocassette Collection, El Centro de Estudios Puertorriqueños Collection, Centro; Whalen, "Sweatshops Here and There," 55–63.

79. "Maldonado," August 8, 1984, 12–13, Centro.

80. I use the terminology and identities workers or organizations used in their documents and interviews. Language is contested and changes over time, and "Hispanic" was a term of assertion in the 1960s and 1970s.

81. "Maldonado," August 8, 1984, 14–16, Centro.

82. "Maldonado," 14–16.

83. "Women's Labor Roles Highlighted in Exhibit," *Central New Jersey Home News*, December 7, 1975, 78; "Labor, Economy is Subject of Seminar," *Central New Jersey Home News*, November 3, 1974, 24; "1976 Festival of American Folklife: Working Americans," Smithsonian Folk Life Festival, https://festival.si.edu/past-program/1976/working-americans.

84. "Maldonado," August 8, 1984, 16–17, Centro.

85. Ronald Reagan, speech given to International Business Council, September 9, 1980, transcript in Boyer, *Reagan as President*, 106–9; Akram-Lodhi, "What's in a Name"; Wendy Brown, "Neoliberalism, Neoconservatism, and De-democratization"; Rodgers, *Age of Fracture*, 41–75, esp. 42–56; Krippner, *Capitalizing on Crisis*.

86. Joseph A. McCartin, commentary for the panel "Neoliberalism and Its Discontents" at the Labor and Working-Class History Association Meeting, Seattle, WA, June 26, 2017; Mike Collins, "Wall Street and the Financialization of the Economy," *Forbes*, February 4, 2015, www.forbes.com/sites/mikecollins/2015/02/04/wall-street-and-the-financialization-of-the-economy/#5209c3b65783; Palley, "Financialization," 2–4.

87. Stein, *Pivotal Decade*, 193–95.

88. Cruz, "Pushing Left," 70–72.

89. Phillips-Fein, *Fear City*.

90. "Maldonado," February 17, 1985, 49–50, Centro. Donald Trump benefited from this shift to financialization and commercial real estate speculation. John Bierman, "Posh Trump Tower Opens," *Boston Globe*, February 15, 1983, 4; Alan S. Oser, "New York Office Market Gains," *NYT*, June 23, 1980, D1, D6; Patricia Lynden, "Where the Donald Trumps Rent," *NYT*, August 30, 1979, C1; Alan S. Oser, "About Real Estate: Law to Change on Conversion of Buildings," *NYT*, June 30, 1978, A17; Alan S. Oser, "Hotel Dispute Focuses on Tax Abatement," *NYT*, April 27, 1976, 27.

91. Michael Abramson, *Palante: Young Lords Party* (New York: McGraw-Hill, 1971), 34–36, as quoted in Wagenheim and Jiménez de Wagenheim, *Puerto Ricans*, 348–52; Phillips-Fein, *Fear City*, 241–55; Ayala and Bernabe, *Puerto Rico*, 242–44; Perez, *¡Yo soy boricua!*

92. Fones-Wolf, *Selling Free Enterprise*; Rosen, *Making Sweatshops*, chaps. 4–6;

Collins, *Threads*, chaps. 1–2; Minchin, *Empty Mills*, introduction, chaps. 2, 4; Stein, *Pivotal Decade*, chaps. 5, 6, 8.

93. A. H. Raskin, "Organizing Obstacles Are Not Just Legal," *NYT*, July 24, 1977, E4; A. H. Raskin, "Labor's Textile Fight, an Echo of the 1930s," *NYT*, March 2, 1977, 75; Windham, *Knocking on Labor's Door*, 1–26.

94. Phillips-Fein, *Invisible Hands*, 16–17, chaps. 5, 6, 8, 9; Stein, *Pivotal Decade*, 189; Cowie, *Stayin' Alive*, 229–32; Waterhouse, *Lobbying America*; Windham, *Knocking on Labor's Door*, 57–81.

95. Lichtenstein, *Retail Revolution*, 200–201.

96. Dietz, *Economic History*, 264–65, 254.

97. Rafael Hernández Colón, "Message of the Governor before the Electronics Industry Association," speech given at Fundación Biblioteca, Puerto Rico, April 1976, https://rafaelhernandezcolon.org/index.php/mensajes-de-rafael-hernandez-colon-1976/; Ayala and Bernabe, *Puerto Rico*, 268–69.

98. Ortiz, "Puerto Rican Women Workers," 50–51.

99. Gautier-Mayoral, "Puerto Rican Model," 3–7; Dietz, *Economic History*, 264–65; Ayala and Bernabe, *Puerto Rico*, 268–73.

100. Imports: Import Demonstrations, April 12, 1977, box 4, folder 2, finding aid, ILGWU Justice Photographs, Kheel.

101. Letter about boycott stapled to ILGWU flyer, no. 5619/007, box 4, folder 2 "ACTWU Support Boycott Papers 1980," ACTWU Organizing Department Records, 1960–95, Kheel; Mary Thornton, "The Union versus the Mill," *Boston Globe*, March 19, 1978, A1; Haberland, *Striking Beauties*, 115–41.

102. Minchin, *Empty Mills*, 68–69.

103. Multiple job orders, Easy Jobs?: PR Employment Program in NY, 1948–91, reels 314–18 "Job Orders, Industrial Workers," Offices of the Government of Puerto Rico in the United States, 1930–93, Centro.

104. Medina interview; Martínez written interview questions.

105. Salgado-Cartagena conversation.

106. Medina interview; Carolyn Robbins, "Gemini Prospers in Century-Old Plant," *Springfield Sunday Republican*, February 17, 1985, B9; Kevin Claffey, "Clothing Maker Has Jobs, Needs Daycare, Parking Space," *Springfield Daily News*, September 1, 1979, 3, clippings, both in folder SPFD 670-Business, Gemini Corp., SHLA; Rumelt telephone conversation.

107. Salgado-Cartagena conversation.

108. Boujouen, "'Menea Esas Manos,'" 95–96.

109. "Annual Report: To Stockholders," 1970–78, Dodd Center; Ramírez, "The Puerto Rican Experience"; Boujouen, "'Menea Esas Manos.'"

110. Dietz, *Economic History*, 255.

111. "History," WEPZA, www.wepza.org/history; "Influencers," WEPZA, www.wepza.org/gallery-of-honor; Bolin, *Why Export Processing Zones*; Bolin, "What Puerto Rico Faced"; Tellew, "Private Foreign Investment," 8–11, 204–30; Alterman, "Egypt," 50–56.

112. Multiple documents with testimony and memoranda re: imports, adjustment assistance, unemployment, and changes in international economy, folder 2 "Trade Act of 1974"; and multiple documents related to types of apparel and Yugoslavia, Italy,

Japan, Hong Kong, Taiwan, Korea, and Uruguay, folder 1 "Import Statistics 1975," all in box 10, room 415, ACTWU Political and Legislative Department Records, Kheel.

113. Testimony of Calvin Siegal [president of Calvin Clothing Corp.] to Multi-Fibre Arrangement Task Force, Fall River, MA, July 24, 1978; William DuChessi [executive vice president of ACTWU], "ACTWU endorses exemption," July 10, 1978; letters and press releases from the American Textile Manufacturers Institute, *Textile News*, July 15, 1978; William A. Klopman, summary statement, Burlington Industries; "Joint Statement of Fifteen Fiber, Textile and Apparel Industry Associations and Labor Unions," n.d., folder 22 "Holland Tariff Bill 1978"; and multiple documents in folder 23 "Import Limitation 1978," all in ACTWU International Affairs Department Records, Kheel; Windham, *Knocking on Labor's Door*, 108.

114. Unions and workers were not complacent, and globalization did not have to cause weak collapsing unions. German unions remained strong due to national labor policy. But the drop in US textile and garment membership and confidence due to 1970s union busting—which included scaring workers with globalization rather than fully collaborating to address it—meant a weak counterbalance to the finance and retail sectors that lobbied to open US markets to cheap imports and outgoing capital currents. Windham, *Knocking on Labor's Door*, 108, 117, 120–26; Benton, *Fraying Fabric*, 6–18.

115. Corporations "dump" products by exporting them to another nation at below-market pricing. The goal is to ruin competition and take a bigger market share.

116. Lloyd Schwartz, "GAO Calls Antidumping Act Ineffective, Urges Overhaul," *Daily News Record*, April 3, 1979, folder 1 "Anti-Dumping, 1977–79"; testimony of Jacob Sheinkman [secretary-treasurer for ACTWU], February 7, 1978; US International Trade Commission, report to president on investigation, March 1978; and "Gloves, People's Republic of China," 95th Cong. 1st Session, Committee Print WMCP: 95-43, Subcommittee on Trade, July 19, 1977, box 1, folder 9 "Consumer Prices 1977," all in ACTWU International Affairs Department Records, Kheel; Stein, *Pivotal Decade*, 37–40.

117. Meyer Bernstein to Labor Advisory Committee members, memorandum, October 23, 1979, stapled to booklet "Federal Register: Monday Oct 15, 1979, Part II, International Trade Commission," box 1, folder 1 "Anti-Dumping, 1977–79," room 515, ACTWU International Affairs Department Records, Kheel.

118. Richard Wightman, "Mfrs. Pressured to Ease Opposition to Tariff Cuts," *Daily News Record*, August 18, 1978, 1, 13, folder 22 "Holland Tariff Bill 1978," ACTWU International Affairs Department Records, Kheel.

Chapter Three

1. Byerly, "Crystal Lee Sutton," in *Hard Times*, 201–2; Leifermann, *Crystal Lee*, 20; Hall et al., *Like a Family*, 60–65. These authors describe the phenomenon of children following parents and older siblings into mills during their free time, often watching the work or helping.

2. Byerly, "Crystal Lee Sutton," in *Hard Times*, 201–2; Leifermann, *Crystal Lee*, 20.

3. Caldwell, *God's Little Acre*.

4. Mann, *God's Little Acre*.

5. Marian Christy, "Crystal Lee—Tough as Steel," *Boston Globe*, January 28, 1980, 23–24; Byerly, "Crystal Lee Sutton," in *Hard Times*, 202–3. Other mill workers expressed a similar duality—with both an awareness of prejudice against "lintheads" and a strong pride in their work, strength, and cooperation. Hall et al., *Like a Family*, 179–80; Conway, *Rise Gonna Rise*, 10–57.

6. Byerly, "Crystal Lee Sutton," in *Hard Times*, 216–17; Leifermann, *Crystal Lee*, 106–10.

7. William Chapman, "White, Black Butt Heads in Danville," *Washington Post*, August 18, 1963, E2; Hall et al., *Like a Family*, 66; Conway, *Rise Gonna Rise*, 90–129; Salmond, *General Textile Strike*, 11; Roediger, *Wages of Whiteness*.

8. Hall et al., *Like a Family*, 157, 372–73; Conway, *Rise Gonna Rise*, 46–49, 184, 90–129; Salmond, *Gastonia, 1929*, 36, 49, 141; Salmond, *General Textile Strike*, 11–12, 15–16, 181; Kuhn, *Contesting*, 25, 34; Orleck, *Storming Caesars Palace*, 7–68.

9. Leifermann, *Crystal Lee*, 38. Censored by the author.

10. Hall et al., *Like a Family*, 65–66; Hunter, *To 'Joy My Freedom*; Leslie Brown, *Upbuilding Black Durham*; Glenn, *Forced to Care*, 1–87.

11. Hall et al., *Like a Family*, 66; Honey, *Southern Labor*, 20; Kuhn, *Contesting*, 217, 221.

12. Honey, *Southern Labor*, 52–58.

13. Fones-Wolf and Fones-Wolf, *Struggle*; Kuhn, *Contesting*, 217–18.

14. Lemann, *Promised Land*; Ownby, *American Dreams in Mississippi*; Cohen, *Consumer's Republic*; Hahn, *Nation under Our Feet*; Zieger, *For Jobs and Freedom*, 43–174; Sugrue, *Sweet Land of Liberty*; MacLean, *Freedom Is Not Enough*; McElya, *Politics of Mourning*.

15. Rowan, *Negro in the Textile*, 92–96, 119; Airov, *Location*; Fones-Wolf and Fones-Wolf, *Struggle*, 23–28; Cobb, *Selling of the South*, chaps. 5–7.

16. Byerly, "Crystal Lee Sutton," in *Hard Times*, 202–3; Leifermann, *Crystal Lee*, 20–27.

17. Glen Raven abuts the Elon College campus, where Martin Ritt, director of *Norma Rae*, attended college.

18. Hall et al., *Like a Family*, 208–9.

19. Byerly, *Hard Times*; Hall et al., *Like a Family*; Conway, *Rise Gonna Rise*.

20. Byerly, "Crystal Lee Sutton," in *Hard Times*, 204; Leifermann, *Crystal Lee*, 26–33; Hall et al., *Like a Family*, 164; Henry P. Leifermann, "The Unions Are Coming: Trouble in the South's First Industry," *New York Times Magazine*, August 1973, 25.

21. Byerly, "Crystal Lee Sutton," in *Hard Times*, 204.

22. Leifermann, *Crystal Lee*, 36–37.

23. Leifermann, 35–38; Roediger, *Wages of Whiteness*.

24. Hall et al., *Like a Family*, 156–57.

25. Leifermann, *Crystal Lee*, 40.

26. "Two rewettable 100 percent fiberglass fabrics have been introduced by the Glass Fabrics Division of J.P. Stevens & Co., Inc., for such insulation applications as shipboard lagging and jacketing materials"; "Two Rewettable Fabrics," 71.

27. Minchin, *"Don't Sleep with Stevens!,"* 70; Conway, *Rise Gonna Rise*.

28. MacLean, *Freedom Is Not Enough*, 84–87; Minchin, *Hiring the Black Worker*; Minchin, *"Don't Sleep with Stevens!,"* 70; Windham, *Knocking on Labor's Door*, 107–14.

29. "NAACP Files 96 Race Discrimination Charges," *Los Angeles Times*, August 19, 1965, 23; Ronald J. Ostrow, "US Sues and Is Sued on Job Discrimination," *Los Angeles Times*, April 9, 1969, 5; Byerly, "Corine Lytle Cannon," in *Hard Times*, 153; Conway, *Rise Gonna Rise*; Minchin, *Hiring the Black Worker*, 220–23; Minchin, *"Don't Sleep with Stevens!,"* 14–24.

30. Sledge v. J.P. Stevens, 585 F.2d 625 (1977); Conway, *Rise Gonna Rise*, 96–103, 106–13; Jacqueline Jones, *Labor of Love*, 303; Minchin, *Hiring the Black Worker*, 53, 61, 122, 135–37, 172.

31. *Sledge*, 585 F.2d; Conway, *Rise Gonna Rise*, 106–13; Jacqueline Jones, *Labor of Love*, 303; Minchin, *Hiring the Black Worker*, 53, 61, 122, 135–37, 172.

32. Reese Cleghornerwin, "The Mill: A Giant Step for the Southern Negro," *NYT*, November 9, 1969, SM34; Minchin, *Hiring the Black Worker*, 220–23; Minchin, *"Don't Sleep with Stevens!,"* 14–24.

33. Minchin, *Hiring the Black Worker*; Minchin, *"Don't Sleep with Stevens!,"* 2–3, 24–25; Leifermann, *Crystal Lee*, 109.

34. Conway, *Rise Gonna Rise*, 2–9, 130–57; Minchin, *"Don't Sleep with Stevens!,"* 1–69.

35. "Who Won the Marathon?," *Forbes*, May 25, 1981, 12–14. Managers did not completely abandon physical intimidation and harassment. But starting in the 1970s and increasing in the 1980s, "a new breed of management consultants began to teach employers" how to use coercive speech and legal tactics. Windham, *Knocking on Labor's Door*, 24–25, 32–33, 57–81.

36. Conway, *Rise Gonna Rise*, 2–9, 130–57; Minchin, *"Don't Sleep with Stevens!,"* 1–69.

37. Leifermann, *Crystal Lee*, 38–42 ("The most disapproving words were spoken when a child was born out of wedlock"); Hall et al., *Like a Family*, 157, 171; Cahn, *Sexual Reckonings*.

38. Leifermann, *Crystal Lee*, 75–77.

39. In Puerto Rico, women expressed similar concerns about working-class femininity and paternalism or sexual harassment by working-class men and union organizers. Matías-Ortiz, "Ambivalent Solidarities," 55–57, 76, 85.

40. Leifermann, *Crystal Lee*, 78–84.

41. Byerly, "Crystal Lee Sutton," in *Hard Times*, 204; Leifermann, *Crystal Lee*, 88–90.

42. Haberland, *Striking Beauties*, 17–56.

43. Byerly, "Crystal Lee Sutton," in *Hard Times*, 205; Leifermann, *Crystal Lee*, 94–97.

44. Leifermann, *Crystal Lee*, 98–99; Lawrence Glickman, "3 Tropes of White Victimhood," *Atlantic*, July 20, 2021, www.theatlantic.com/ideas/archive/2021/07/three-tropes-white-victimhood/619463.

45. Byerly, "Crystal Lee Sutton," in *Hard Times*, 205; Leifermann, *Crystal Lee*, 100–105.

46. Byerly, "Crystal Lee Sutton," in *Hard Times*, 205; Leifermann, *Crystal Lee*, 100–105.

47. Mary Thornton, "The Union versus the Mill," *Boston Globe*, March 19, 1978, A1; Minchin, *"Don't Sleep with Stevens!,"* 70; MacLean, *Freedom Is Not Enough*, 80–83.

48. Eli Zivkovich interview recording, parts 1–2, June 8, 1983, Ross Papers. The tumult that followed the 1969 murder of Jock Yablonski (a Miners for Democracy candidate) destabilized the United Mine Workers for several years. Kopple, *Harlan County, USA*; Cowie, *Stayin' Alive*, 23–27.

49. Leifermann, *Crystal Lee*, 115–16.

50. Windham, *Knocking on Labor's Door*, 107–18.

51. Conway, *Rise Gonna Rise*, 184–96.

52. Leifermann, *Crystal Lee*, 118–22.

53. Leifermann, 109–11; Conway, *Rise Gonna Rise*, 2–9, 158–97.

54. Fones-Wolf and Fones-Wolf, *Struggle*, 113–46.

55. Leifermann, *Crystal Lee*, 109–11.

56. Byerly, "Crystal Lee Sutton," in *Hard Times*, 206; Leifermann, *Crystal Lee*, 112–15.

57. Leifermann, *Crystal Lee*, 126–28.

58. Leifermann, 111, 130–31.

59. Byerly, "Crystal Lee Sutton," in *Hard Times*, 207.

60. Crystal Lee Jordan, affidavit, State of North Carolina, June 21, 1973, drawer 2, CLS; Cobb, *Selling of the South*, 257; Byerly, "Crystal Lee Sutton," in *Hard Times*, 207–8; Leifermann, "Unions Are Coming," 26; Leifermann, *Crystal Lee*, 142–45.

61. Jordan affidavit, CLS.

62. Jordan affidavit.

63. Jordan affidavit, 5–7; Byerly, "Crystal Lee Sutton," in *Hard Times*, 209–10; Leifermann, *Crystal Lee*, 145–50.

64. Jordan affidavit, 6; Eric Leif Davin, "Crystal Lee," *In These Times*, March 15–18, 1980, 15–16.

65. Tribute to Harold McIver, October 28, 1994, video cassette, drawer 1; and Pam Woywod, partial article clipping with Crystal Lee's handwritten comments, 1979, folder 7, drawer 2, both in CLS.

66. Zivkovich interview recording, part 1, Ross Papers; Kimble and Olson, "Visual Rhetoric," 553–54.

67. Jordan affidavit, 5–7, CLS; Byerly, "Crystal Lee Sutton," in *Hard Times*, 209–10; Leifermann, *Crystal Lee*, 145–50.

68. Jordan affidavit, 7, CLS.

69. Byerly, "Crystal Lee Sutton," in *Hard Times*, 211–12; Leifermann, *Crystal Lee*, 151–53.

70. Lelia Carson Albrecht, "The Real 'Norma Rae' Is Anguished by the Hollywood Replay of Her Life," *People*, April 30, 1979, 43; Byerly, "Crystal Lee Sutton," in *Hard Times*, 211–12; Leifermann, *Crystal Lee*, 161–63.

71. Leifermann, *Crystal Lee*, 163–65.

72. NLRB to J.P. Stevens, "Charge Against Employer," June 7, 1973; and McIver to Reed Johnston [regional director, NLRB], June 7, 1973, drawer 2, both in CLS.

73. Jordan affidavit, CLS.

74. By the 1970s, many corporations realized it was more cost effective to use legal and bureaucratic obstruction to block unions, even if they were fined. Windham, *Knocking on Labor's Door*.

75. Leifermann, *Crystal Lee*, 167–69; Conway, *Rise Gonna Rise*, 158–97; Fones-Wolf and Fones-Wolf, *Struggle*, 48–51, 95–96; Jewell, *Dollars for Dixie*, 202–41.

76. Henry P. Leifermann, "A Ride on the Hollywood Merry-Go-Round," *Atlanta*, 1980, clipping, binder 25, article 27, CLS; Mary Bishop, "The Diary of a Union Organizer," *Charlotte Observer*, May 7, 1978, D1–D3, drawer 2, CLS; "Henry P. Leifermann (1942–2016)," obituary, *North Augusta Star*, September 13, 2016.

77. "J.P. Stevens Sets Earnings Record," *NYT*, September 10, 1965, 45; "Labor Board Rules against Textile Firm," *Chicago Tribune*, March 23, 1966, B7; "Labor Asks LBJ to End Stevens Pact," *Chicago Tribune*, May 22, 1966, C9; "J.P. Stevens Acts to Reinstate 69," *NYT*, December 28, 1967, 27; Clare M. Reckert, "J.P. Stevens Plans Expansion," *NYT*, February 7, 1968, 7; Isadore Barmash, "J.P. Stevens Chief Expects Gain in the Need for Military Apparel," *NYT*, March 6, 1968, 74L; "J.P. Stevens Ruling Is Held Up in Court," *NYT*, January 4, 1969, 56; Walter Trohan, "Union Frustrated by Free Choice," *Chicago Tribune*, October 31, 1969, 18; John J. Abele, "Deficit Worsens at J.P. Stevens," *NYT*, May 26, 1972, 45; "J.P. Stevens Is Sued by Union for Allegedly Bugging Officers," *NYT*, August 16, 1973, 70.

78. Jerry Knight, "Death of a Company Town," *Washington Post*, September 19, 1988, BF1; Franklin Wallick, "The American Worker: An Endangered Species," *Washington Post*, September 3, 1972, C1; Herbert Koshetz, "A Southern Textile Recovery-Import Curbs Helped," *NYT*, June 18, 1972, F2; "Textile Workers Ask Protection," *Hartford Courant*, December 12, 1969, 41E; Herbert Koshetz, "Southern Mill Towns Feel Pinch of Textile Imports," *NYT*, May 9, 1969, 49; Zaretsky, *No Direction Home*.

79. Caudill, *Night*; Kirby, *Media-Made Dixie*; Campbell, *Celluloid South*; Cox, *Dreaming of Dixie*; Allison Graham, *Framing the South*; Harkins, *Hillbilly*; Barker, *American Cinema*; Ring, *Problem South*; Matthews, *Capturing the South*.

80. Jacobson, *Whiteness*; Jacobson, *Roots Too*; Roediger, *Working toward Whiteness*.

81. Cox, *Dreaming of Dixie*; Allison Graham, *Framing the South*, 147–93; Harkins, *Hillbilly*, 173–203.

82. "Work Safety Agency Revises Regulation on Cotton Dust," *Washington Post*, December 6, 1985, A25; "US Issues Amended Rules on Cotton Dust Exposure," *Wall Street Journal*, December 6, 1985, 8; Mimi Conway, "Brown Lung Increases among Cotton Workers," *Boston Globe*, November 27, 1975, 65; Judy Klemesrud, "Learning about Hillbillies First Hand," *NYT*, August 27, 1973, 32; "'Brown Lung' Bill Introduced," *Washington Post*, August 17, 1970, A20; Bruce Galphin, "Nader Cites 'Brown Lung' Peril," *Washington Post*, August 11, 1969, A4; Wilkerson, *To Live Here*, 34–39.

83. Colman McCarthy, "Slow Survival in the Back Hollows," *Washington Post*, August 5, 1969, A16; Hank Burchard, "Va. Poverty Unit to Decide VISTA Workers' Future," *Washington Post*, January 27, 1969, A15; Joseph A. Loftus, "Hostility Grows between Kentucky Businessmen and Poverty Workers," *NYT*, August 27, 1967, 71; Scottie Lanahan, "News to Me: VISTA Starts Craft Program," *Washington Post*, April 16, 1967, K8; David Gilbert, "Lyons Woman, 18, to Try VISTA Job before Taking Vow," *Chicago Tribune*, October 23, 1966, S1; "VISTA Worker Fights Poverty with Bulldozer," *Hartford Courant*, January 16, 1966, 15A; Marjorie Hunter, "West Virginians Near Start on Antipoverty Program," *NYT*, March 28, 1965, 79; Eve Edstrom, "First Urban Job Corps Sites Named," *Washington Post*, December 17, 1964, A1; "Begin 'Great Society' in Appalachia," *Justice* 47, no. 6 (March 15, 1965): 2, in Kheel; Caudill, *Night*; Elizabeth Barret, *Stranger with a Camera*; Harkins, *Hillbilly*; Korstad and LeLoudis, *To Right These Wrongs*.

84. Hale, *Nation of Outsiders*, 3, 60–61, 103.

85. Byerly, "Crystal Lee Sutton," in *Hard Times*, 216; Conway, *Rise Gonna Rise*, 58–89.

86. Byerly, "Crystal Lee Sutton," in *Hard Times*, 216; Bishop, "Diary," D1–D3, CLS; Leifermann, "Ride," 97–99, CLS; "Henry P. Leifermann (1942–2016)."

87. Loiselle, "Corpse, Lover, Mother," 26–38; Roth, *Separate Roads to Feminism*.

88. Loiselle, "Corpse, Lover, Mother," 39–93; Toplin, "Norma Rae."

89. Leifermann, "Unions Are Coming," 10–26.

90. Leifermann, 10; Simon, "Appeal of Cole Blease."

91. Leifermann, "Unions Are Coming," 25.

92. Leifermann, 25.

93. Ed McConville, "5 Years after Union Victory, Battle Goes on at J.P. Stevens," *Washington Post*, August 29, 1979, A2.

94. Schmidt, *In Search of Decision*, 146–302.

95. Elizabeth Jager to Andrew J. Biemiller, AFL-CIO memorandum (subject: "Bill authorizing appropriations for US section"), October 10, 1969; "Rock-Bottom Wages: Workers of US, Mexico Hurt," *AFL-CIO News*, April 12, 1969; Stanley Levey, "Unions Weigh Boycott of US-Mexican Firms," *Daily News*, April 14, 1969; and Lewis H. Diuguid, "Mexican Border Industries Thrive as US Firms Export Components," *Post*, October 12, 1969, clippings, all in box 10, room 415, folder 7 "Mexico Industrialization Sec 806–807," ACTWU Political and Legislative Department Records, Kheel.

96. "Japanese Fabrics Expected to Rise," *NYT*, December 3, 1952, 51; Elie Abel, "Chinese Exports Undercut India's," *NYT*, September 28, 1958, 5; "US-Japan Reach New Cotton Pact," *NYT*, September 9, 1961, 26; "US-Japan Accord Near on Textiles," *NYT*, August 7, 1963, 41; Paul P. Kennedy, "Mexico Starting Industrial Plan," *NYT*, May 30, 1965, F5; Philip Shabecoff, "Stans, in Japan, Firm on Textiles," *NYT*, May 13, 1969, 57; Herbert Koshetz, "Textile Leaders Abandon Hope Japan Will Reduce Export Flow," *NYT*, March 20, 1970, 69; Herbert Koshetz, "US Textile Makers See Profits Shrink, Japanese Worried," *NYT*, April 26, 1970, F1; Philip Shabecoff, "Sato and Cabinet Discuss Textiles," *NYT*, June 26, 1970, 59; Philip Shabecoff, "US Cool to Curb by Japanese Textiles," *NYT*, March 9, 1971, 59; Leonard Silk, "Textiles: Is Peace Here?," *NYT*, March 10, 1971, 59; "Mexico Is Pushing Border Projects," *NYT*, May 24, 1971, 47; "Strides Are Seen in Taiwan Textile Talks," *NYT*, June 10, 1971, 61; "US-Taiwan Talks on Textiles Fail," *NYT*, October 2, 1971, 43; Max Frankel, "'Japan Inc,'" and "'Nixon Shocks,'" *NYT*, November 25, 1971, 2; "US and Japan Sign Agreement on Textiles," *NYT*, January 4, 1972, 45.

97. Leifermann, *Crystal Lee*, 173–75.

98. Byerly, "Crystal Lee Sutton," in *Hard Times*, 215.

99. Byerly, 214–15.

100. Leifermann, *Crystal Lee*, 175–76.

101. Byerly, "Crystal Lee Sutton," in *Hard Times*, 214–15; Fink, "In Good Faith."

102. Byerly, "Crystal Lee Sutton," in *Hard Times*, 215–16; Leifermann, *Crystal Lee*, 178–80.

103. "Our History," Ms. Foundation for Women, http://forwomen.org/about/our -history (site discontinued); Farrell, *Yours in Sisterhood*, 1–99.

104. "Briefs on the Arts: Woman's Program Receives Grant," *NYT*, August 15, 1973, 28, clipping, folder 4 "Woman Alive! Clippings"; and Myrna Blyth, "'Woman Alive!': The New Feminism in Action," *Image*, June 1974, 6, in folder 1 "Woman Alive! 1974 Special General June 1974," both in box 7 "Special Proj," Ms. Foundation for Women Records, SSC; finding aid, MC 421, Woman Alive! Collection, Schlesinger.

105. Multiple newspaper articles, drawers 1, 3, CLS; Ellen Cohn, "Two TV Shows That Reflect the Changing Roles of Women," *NYT*, June 16, 1974, 23, 38; Liza Baskin,

"When Ms. Had Its Own TV Show," *Ms.*, January 31, 2013, http://msmagazine.com/blog/2013/01/31/when-ms-had-its-own-tv-show; Susan Lester to Paul Barrett [public relations manager for J.P. Stevens], March 12, 1974, box 7 "Special Proj," folder 7 "Woman Alive! 1974 Crystal Lee Jordan Segment," Ms. Foundation for Women Records, SSC.

106. Preview panel reports from Denver, Tallahassee, Dallas, and Lansing, box 7 "Special Proj," folder 12 "Preview Panels 1974," Ms. Foundation for Women Records, SSC.

107. Byerly, "Crystal Lee Sutton," in *Hard Times*, 216; Leifermann, *Crystal Lee*, 179–81.

108. Byerly, "Crystal Lee Sutton," in *Hard Times*, 215–16; Leifermann, *Crystal Lee*, 178–82.

109. *Woman Alive!*, video cassette, 1974, drawer 1, CLS; *Woman Alive!* pilot, June 19, 1974, MC 421, Vt-30, reel 1, Woman Alive! Collection, Schlesinger.

110. Crystal Lee to Joan Shigekawa, August 1974, box 7 "Special Proj," folder 2 "Woman Alive! 1974 Special Gen Jul 1–Dec 1974," Ms. Foundation for Women Records, SSC; Leifermann, *Crystal Lee*, 187.

111. *Woman Alive!* video cassette, CLS.

112. *Woman Alive!* video cassette.

113. *Woman Alive!* video cassette; *Woman Alive!* pilot, Schlesinger; transcript of Crystal Lee Jordan segment, n.d., box 7 "Special Proj," folder 7 "Woman Alive! 1974 Crystal Lee Jordan Segment," Ms. Foundation for Women Records, SSC.

114. Press releases and transcript, 1974, MC 421, folder 18 "Pilot," Woman Alive! Collection, Schlesinger.

115. Crystal Lee to Shigekawa, 12, SSC.

116. Crystal Lee to Shigekawa, 12; Byerly, "Crystal Lee Sutton," in *Hard Times*; multiple interviews and newspaper clips, drawers 1, 3, CLS; Leifermann, *Crystal Lee*.

117. *Woman Alive!* video cassette, CLS; *Woman Alive!* pilot, Schlesinger; transcript of Crystal Lee Jordan segment, SSC.

118. For histories of this relationship, see Cobble, *Other Women's Movement*; Cobble, *Dishing It Out*; Orleck, *Common Sense*; Gabin, *Feminism*; Jacqueline Jones, *Labor of Love*; and Leslie Brown, *Upbuilding Black Durham*.

119. Hale, *Nation of Outsiders*, 4, 126.

120. The suffrage and women's rights movement of the early twentieth century appropriated Harriet Tubman for the same purpose. Sernett, *Harriet Tubman*, 150–64.

121. Leifermann, "Ride," 99, CLS.

122. Crystal Lee to Shigekawa, 12, SSC.

123. Minchin, *"Don't Sleep with Stevens!,"* 73–74; Conway, *Rise Gonna Rise*, 2–9.

124. Leifermann, *Crystal Lee*, 186–90.

125. Leifermann, "Ride," 98–99, CLS.

126. Leifermann, *Crystal Lee*, acknowledgments; Leifermann, "Ride," 99, CLS.

127. Crystal Lee to Shigekawa, 12, SSC.

128. Byerly, "Crystal Lee Sutton," in *Hard Times*, 216, 218.

129. Leifermann, "Ride," 98, CLS.

130. Steedman, *Landscape*, 11–12. Steedman wrote her memoir using techniques of scholarly history and the analysis of gender and class across time to challenge conventional working-class biographies. Barrett, *History*, 1–32.

131. Patricia Goodfellow, review of *Crystal Lee: A Woman of Inheritance*, by Henry P.

Leifermann, *Library Journal* 100, no. 19 (November 1975): 2044; unsigned review of *Crystal Lee: A Woman of Inheritance*, by Henry P. Leifermann, *Kirkus Reviews*, October 1, 1975, www.kirkusreviews.com/book-reviews/henry-p-leifermann/crystal-lee-a-woman-of-inheritance.

132. Crystal Lee Sutton, "The Rest of the Story: Norma Rae," interview, *Reelz Time*, March 6, 2008, video cassette, drawer 1, CLS; Washington Post Service, "Real 'Norma Rae' Now Seeking to Organize Her Life," *Hartford Courant*, November 4, 1980, A2A; Susan E. Harrison, "'Norma Rae': Labor Organizer Lives Liberation," *Los Angeles Times*, December 13, 1979, L20.

133. "Who Won the Marathon?," 12–14; "Battlefield Truce," *Fortune*, November 17, 1980, 15–16; Harry Bernstein, "Union, J.P. Stevens Reach Accord, End 17-Year Fight," *Los Angeles Times*, October 18, 1980, A1.

134. Crystal Lee to Shigekawa, 12, SSC; Albrecht, "Real 'Norma Rae,'" 43; Davin, "Crystal Lee," 16; Vernon Scott, "'Norma Rae' Fortunes Cost Organizer Plenty," *Chicago Tribune*, March 19, 1980, B5.

135. Karin Lippert, Joanne Edgar, and Phyllis Langer [friends at *Ms.*] to "Crystal, Mark and Jay," November 11, 1976, drawer 2, CLS; Byerly, "Crystal Lee Sutton," in *Hard Times*, 215.

136. Borda, *Women Labor Activists*, 109; Gregory, *Women Who Run*, 146–47. Corman was a prolific director and producer who became known for his cult classics and worked with Peter Bogdanovich, Martin Scorsese, and Jonathan Demme.

Chapter Four

1. Kopple, *Harlan County, USA*.

2. Alexander telephone conversations.

3. Alexander to Larry Jordan and Eli Zivkovich, cc: Crystal Lee Jordan, October 28, 1977, binder 24, article 13, CLS; Alexander telephone conversations.

4. Alexander telephone conversations; Clarke Taylor, "The On-Camera, Off-Camera Drama of Crystal Lee Jordan," *Los Angeles Times*, March 4, 1979, T5.

5. Morton H. Smithline to Rose & Asseyev Productions, letter and contract, January 19, 1978, distribution list 1, subject "Norma Rae," basic property, box 23, folder 235 "Norma Rae, Legal 1977–1979," MR.

6. Roediger, *Working toward Whiteness*; Jacobson, *Roots Too*, 17, 96–98.

7. Borda, *Women Labor Activists*, 109; Gregory, *Women Who Run*, 146–48.

8. Lelia Carson Albrecht, "The Real 'Norma Rae' Is Anguished by the Hollywood Replay of Her Life," *People*, April 30, 1979, 43; Eunice Field, "Real Norma Rae 'Not Bitter' over Not Receiving Any Money," *Hollywood Reporter*, March 14, 1980, 28, clipping, no. 5619/038, box 10, folder 9, TD.

9. Twentieth Century-Fox Film Corp., "Prod Budget 'Norma Rae,'" March 17, 1978, box 22, folder 229 "Norma Rae Budget," MR.

10. White men with some training or education had most often worked on Hollywood movies. Smyth, *Nobody's Girl Friday*; Hill, *Never Done*.

11. Aljean Harmetz, "Martin Ritt Focuses on Labor Strife," *NYT*, February 25, 1979, D19.

12. Pat Aufderheide, "A Mensch for All Seasons," *In These Times*, April 16–22, 1980, 14.

13. Ritt said he never joined the Communist Party or received subpoenas, but in the early 1950s he dealt with a short period of FBI surveillance and blacklisting from television work. Carlton Jackson, *Picking Up the Tab*, 27–38.

14. Denning, *Cultural Front*, 64–65, 262.

15. Cobb, *Away Down South*, 1–33; Mann, *God's Little Acre*.

16. *Edge of the City* starred up-and-coming actors John Cassavetes and Sidney Poitier. Carlton Jackson, *Picking Up the Tab*, 10–38.

17. McGilligan, *Interviews*.

18. Borda, *Women Labor Activists*, 109; Gregory, *Women Who Run*, 146–48.

19. Lawrence Mortorff, "Norma Rae" Script Revis memorandum, December 30, 1977, folder 235 "Norma Rae Legal 1977–79"; and Ritt to Sidney E. Cohn, February 27, 1978, folder 232 "Norma Rae Corresp 1977–79," both in box 23, MR.

20. Twentieth Century-Fox Film Corp., "Prod Budget 'Norma Rae,'" MR.

21. Clipping, *L'Express Magazine*, June 1979, box 23, folder 240 "Norma Rae Publicity, 1979–81," MR; oral history transcript, 58, box 1, folder 392 "Ritt, Martin 1987," SMU Collection, MHL; Harmetz, "Martin Ritt Focuses," D1.

22. Harmetz, "Martin Ritt Focuses," D1; Ritt to Becky Wild, September 14, 1977, box 41, folder 522 "Wild, Becky 1966–82," MR.

23. Ray, *Certain Tendency*, 18, 47–59.

24. Ray, 47–59.

25. Gregory, *Women Who Run*, 149.

26. Maza, "Stories in History," 1498–1500.

27. Hale, *Nation of Outsiders*. Hale argues that when affluent and middle-class white youth performed the folk in an affective bid for connection and authenticity, they severed music, lyrics, and clothing from their historical context. They celebrated the emotional resonance of being an outsider without actually giving up the privileges and material benefits of being an insider.

28. Aufderheide, "Mensch for All Seasons," 14–15; Lou Gaul, "It's Now or Never," *Bucks County Courier Times*, March 25, 1979, clipping, box 29, folder 239 "Norma Rae Publicity, 1978–79," MR.

29. "'Norma Rae' Inspirer Tells Real Union Story," *News and Observer*, January 30, 1981, 26, clipping, box 23, folder 240 "Norma Rae Publicity, 1979–81," MR.

30. Eunice Field, "Real Norma Rae," 28, TD; Vernon Scott, "'Norma Rae' Fortunes Cost Organizer Plenty," *Chicago Tribune*, March 19, 1980, B5.

31. Asseyev and Rose to Stetin, August 1, 1977, box 23, folder 236 "Norma Rae Misc. 1977–81," MR.

32. Ritt to Newman, October 6, 1977, box 23, folder 232 "Norma Rae Corresp 1977–79," MR.

33. Warner Bros. to Ritt, memorandum, October 12, 1977, box 23, folder 236 "Norma Rae Misc. 1977–81," MR.

34. Morton H. Smithline to Susan McIntosh, invoice no. 000776, re: development deal for "Crystal Lee," November 23, 1977, box 23, folder 235 "Norma Rae Legal 1977–79," MR.

35. Lawrence Mortorff to Robert Dudnik, December 30, 1977; and to George Chasin, January 19, 1978, both in box 23, folder 235 "Norma Rae Legal 1977–79," MR.

36. Jordan and Jordan conversation.

37. Kopple, *Harlan County, USA*. For a commercial film that represents collective action in a southwest mining town with intersections of class, gender, and race, see Biberman, *Salt of the Earth*.

38. Alexander to Crystal Lee, Cookie Jordan, and Zivkovich, November 3, 1977, binder 24, article 25, CLS; Taylor, "On-Camera," T5.

39. Alexander telephone conversations.

40. Mortorff to Dudnik, MR; Mortoff to Chasin, MR; Henry P. Leifermann, "A Ride on the Hollywood Merry-Go-Round," *Atlanta*, 1980, 208, clipping, binder 25, article 27, CLS.

41. Ritt to Cohn, MR.

42. Mortorff to Rose & Asseyev Productions, November 16, 1977, box 23, folder 235 "Norma Rae Legal 1977–79," MR.

43. Alexander letters re: Los Angeles negotiations and Kopple preference, October 28, 1977, article 13; December 12, 1977, article 14; and December 14, 1977, article 16, all in binder 24, CLS; Taylor, "On-Camera," T5.

44. Aufderheide, "Mensch for All Seasons," 14.

45. Alexander telephone conversations; Eunice Field, "Real Norma Rae," 28, TD; Scott, "'Norma Rae' Fortunes," B5. Crystal Lee spent about $3,000 in legal fees during this time.

46. Leifermann, "Ride," 219, CLS; Ritt to Hoffman, December 30, 1977, box 23, folder 232 "Norma Rae Corresp 1977–79," MR.

47. Elizabeth Stone, "'Norma Rae': The Story They Could Have Told," *Ms.*, May 1979, 33; Ritt, *Norma Rae*.

48. Mortorff to Jeffrey L. Nagin, January 30, 1978, box 23, folder 235 "Norma Rae Legal 1977–79," MR.

49. Morton H. Smithline to Ritt, letter and contract, January 19, 1978, box 23, folder 235 "Norma Rae Legal 1977–79," MR.

50. Nancy Shryock, "Real Norma Rae Continues Her Fight," *Globe-Democrat*, 1980, clipping, box 13, folder 25, TD.

51. Oral history, 58, box 1, folder 392 "Ritt, Martin 1987," SMU Collection; Summary of Findings and Detailed Findings, "The Molly Maguires" focus group, 1969, 1–2, box 2, folder 11, Communikon Audience Test Reports; and "Current Cinema: Duds," *New Yorker*, February 7, 1970, 91, clipping, in box 9, folder 106 "Molly Maguires, Reviews 1968–78," all in MHL; Roger Ebert, "Director Martin Ritt Believes in 'Norma Rae,'" *Arizona Daily Star*, April 23, 1979, clipping, box 23, folder 240 "Norma Rae Publicity, 1979–81," MR; Aljean Harmetz, "Martin Ritt Focuses on Labor Strife," *NYT*, February 25, 1979, D19.

52. Taylor, "On-Camera," T5.

53. Taylor, T5.

54. Harmetz, "Martin Ritt Focuses," D19; Borda, *Women Labor Activists*, 109; Gregory, *Women Who Run*, 146–48; Carlton Jackson, *Picking Up the Tab*, 181.

55. Alexander telephone conversations; Thomas O'Connor, "Martin Ritt: Human Relationships and Moral Choices Fuel His Movies," *NYT*, January 12, 1986, H23; Gregory, *Women Who Run*, 148.

56. O'Connor, "Martin Ritt," H23; "Special Features: Backstory of Norma Rae," in Ritt, *Norma Rae* (2001).

57. Wil Haygood, "Sally Field: After a Long Struggle, She's Found a Place in the Heart of Hollywood Stardom," *Boston Globe*, December 10, 1985, 65–66.

58. Bob Dingilian, product info guide for "Norma Rae," Sally Field press release, 2–3, box 23, folder 241 "Norma Rae Publicity Press Kit 1979," MR; Haygood, "Sally Field," 65.

59. In *Sybil*, Field costarred with Joanne Woodward, wife of Paul Newman and close friend of Ritt. In *Stay Hungry*, she costarred with Jeff Bridges, brother of Beau Bridges, her costar in *Norma Rae*. *Smokey and the Bandit* was the second top-grossing movie of 1977.

60. Pink memo, February 20, 1978, box 23, folder 235 "Norma Rae Legal 1977–79," MR.

61. Carlton Jackson, *Picking Up the Tab*, 116–27, 180–83.

62. Stetin to Asseyev, October 14, 1977, box 13, folder 26, TD.

63. Lorraine LoBianco, *Norma Rae* blurb, Turner Classic Movies, www.tcm.com /this-month/article/480760%7Co/Norma-Rae.html (page discontinued); Ray Herbeck Jr., "Shoot 'Norma Rae' in Dixie? Martin Ritt's Film on Textile Workers Rankled Southern Industry," *On Location*, November/December 1978, 60–61.

64. "Cole Promotes Alabama Sites for Film Making," *Alabama Development News*, June 1978, 3–4, in Alabama Department of Archives and History, Montgomery, AL; Debbie Price, "Opelika Discovered by Hollywood," *Opelika-Auburn News*, March 23, 1978, 1.

65. "Cole Promotes Alabama Sites," 3–4, Alabama Department of Archives and History; Price, "Opelika Discovered by Hollywood," 1; Herbeck, "Shoot 'Norma Rae,'" 60–67; Gregory, *Women Who Run*, 148; Carlton Jackson, *Picking Up the Tab*, 181–82.

66. "Cole Promotes Alabama Sites," 3–4, Alabama Department of Archives and History; Price, "Opelika Discovered by Hollywood," 1; Herbeck, "Shoot 'Norma Rae,'" 60–67; Gregory, *Women Who Run*, 148; Carlton Jackson, *Picking Up the Tab*, 181–82.

67. Twentieth Century-Fox Film Corp., "Prod Budget 'Norma Rae,'" MR; O'Connor, "Martin Ritt," H23; Aufderheide, "Mensch for All Seasons," 14.

68. "North Carolina Now: Plant Closing," June 25, 2003, video cassette, drawer 1, CLS; M. L. Myrick for J.P. Stevens to Crystal Lee, faded letter with job offer for Kaumagrapher, March 22, 1978, folder 16, drawer 2, CLS; Jim Brady, "Struggles of Crystal Lee: Hard Times Continue for the Real 'Norma Rae,'" *Washington Post*, July 24, 1985, B1–B2; Susan E. Harrison, "'Norma Rae': Labor Organizer Lives Liberation," *Los Angeles Times*, December 13, 1979, L20; Eric Leif Davin, "Crystal Lee," *In These Times*, March 15–18, 1980, 15.

69. Undated sketches, box 24, folder 244 "Norma Rae Sketches–Undated," MR; Gregory, *Women Who Run*, 148.

70. Twentieth Century-Fox, press release, March 14, 1978, box 23, folder 241 "Norma Rae Publicity Press Kit 1979," MR.

71. Loiselle, "Corpse, Lover, Mother," 10–14; Hallam, "*Working Girl*," 173–98; de Lauretis, *Technologies of Gender*; Kaplan, *Women and Film*.

72. Irving Ravetch and Harriet Frank Jr., *Norma Rae*, box 22, folder 225 "Norma Rae Script–Undated," MR.

73. Transcripts of radio and TV reports, WNET NY, March 2, 1979, box 23, folder 242 "Norma Rae, Reviews 1979," MR; Anne Rivera, "Norma Rae Reel Life," Stevens Campaign News Service, *Labor Press*, March 26, 1979, box 23, folder 242 "Norma Rae, Reviews 1979," MR; and Lyn Goldfarb and Anatoli Ilyashov, "Ritt," transcript, Icarus

Films, November 26, 1985, 3, box 44, folder 560 "Interviews, Goldfarb and Ilyashov 1985–91," MR.

74. Ravetch and Frank, *Norma Rae*, 2 (mill description), 20, 38, 40, 44, 55, MR; Gregory, *Women Who Run*, 149.

75. Guy Rhodes, "When Norma Rae Came to Town," *Tuskegee News*, April 23, 2009, www.thetuskegeenews.com/opinion/when-norma-rae-came-to-town/article_85c7b6ce -05a7-5384-868a-254bb3406782.html (site discontinued); Debbie Price, "Filming Closed to Public," *Opelika-Auburn News*, May 1, 1978, 2; "'Norma Rae' Film Sets Off Limits to Star Gazers," *Opelika-Auburn News*, April 30, 1978, A2; "'Norma Rae' Funeral Scene to Be Shot at Rosemere," *Opelika-Auburn News*, April 19, 1978; "Child Actors' Casting Scheduled Monday," *Opelika-Auburn News*, April 16, 1978; "Preparing for Filming 'Norma Rae,'" *Opelika-Auburn News*, March 30, 1978, A2.

76. Herbeck, "Shoot 'Norma Rae,'" 64–65; Mary Kennamer, "Tricks and Talent Needed to Sew for Stars," *Opelika-Auburn News*, June 6, 1978; Carlton Jackson, *Picking Up the Tab*, 183.

77. "Norma Rae," AFI Catalog of Feature Films (website), reference to June 1979 issue of *Millimeter*, https://catalog.afi.com/Catalog/moviedetails/56122.

78. "Wallace Meets Sally," photo, *Opelika-Auburn News*, June 14, 1978, 1; Carlton Jackson, *Picking Up the Tab*, 182–83; LoBianco, *Norma Rae* blurb.

79. Herbeck, "'Shoot 'Norma Rae,'" 66; "Hollywood Bids Adieu," *Opelika-Auburn News*, June 25, 1978, A1–A2.

80. Herb Wallerstein, interoffice correspondence, Picture Cost Report, July 26, 1978, box 22, folder 229 "Norma Rae Budget," MR.

81. Lewis Wickes Hine, "Hell's Half Acre," November 1910, photograph, National Child Labor Committee Collection, Library of Congress, Prints and Photographs Division, www.loc.gov/item/2018674843.

82. Jennifer Warnes, vocalist, "It Goes Like It Goes," by David Shire and Norman Gimbel, recorded 1979, track 1 on *Norma Rae* (soundtrack), Varese Sarabande Club. The song won the 1979 Academy Award for Best Original Song over nominees like "Rainbow Connection" sung by Kermit the Frog in *The Muppet Movie*.

83. "Special Features: Backstory of Norma Rae," in Ritt, *Norma Rae* (2001).

84. Cripps, "Frederick Douglass," 154–63; Foster, *Performing Whiteness*, 1–46; Feldstein, *Motherhood*; Vera and Gordon, *Screen Saviors*, 263–66; McPherson, *Reconstructing Dixie*, 1–18, 205–56.

85. Leifermann, *Crystal Lee*, 113.

86. Stanton, "Performing the Postindustrial." Stanton argues that even when museums such as Lowell National Historical Park represent the economic tensions and exploitation of nineteenth-century mill girls, they often engage nostalgia, which creates a temporal distance between "bad" industrial capitalism and "good" postindustrial technological capitalism. As such, the exhibits enact this tendency of neoliberal capitalism and become a ritualized reconciliation of past and present, of exploitation and the insecurity of capitalism. For similar ideas of the deindustrial, see High and Lewis, *Corporate Wasteland*, 1–20, 43–60.

87. "Special Features: Backstory of Norma Rae," in Ritt, *Norma Rae* (2001).

88. Leifermann, *Crystal Lee*, 111; Henry P. Leifermann, "The Unions Are Coming: Trouble in the South's First Industry," *New York Times Magazine*, August 1973, 25.

89. *Woman Alive!*, video cassette, 1974, drawer 1, CLS; transcript of Crystal Lee Jordan segment, n.d., box 7 "Special Proj," folder 7 "Woman Alive! 1974 Crystal Lee Jordan Segment," Ms. Foundation for Women Records, SSC; *Woman Alive!* pilot, June 19, 1974, MC 421, Vt-30, reel 1, Woman Alive! Collection, Schlesinger.

90. Eli Zivkovich interview recording, part 1, Ross Papers.

91. Cripps, "Frederick Douglass," 154–63; Foster, *Performing Whiteness*, 1–46; McPherson, *Reconstructing Dixie*, 1–18, 205–56; Vera and Gordon, *Screen Saviors*; Vera and Gordon, "Sincere Fictions."

92. Ravetch and Frank, *Norma Rae*, MR; undated sketches, box 24, folder 244 "Norma Rae Sketches–Undated."

93. Black-and-white photograph of victory hand signs, n.d., no. 5981P, box 41, folder 29, Labor Unity Photo Files, ACTWU Collection, Kheel.

94. When Field won her second Academy Award in 1985, for *Places in the Heart*, she adapted this line for her famous speech, saying, "The first time I didn't feel it, but this time I feel it. And I can't deny the fact that you like me. Right now, you like me!"

95. Loiselle, "Corpse, Lover, Mother," 10–14; Hallam, "*Working Girl*," 173–98; de Lauretis, *Technologies of Gender*; Kaplan, *Women and Film*.

96. Davin, "Crystal Lee," 15.

97. Taylor, "On-Camera," T5.

98. Alexander to Kopple, re: film progress, October 4, 1979, binder 24, article 7, CLS; Taylor, "On-Camera," T5. Leifermann died in 2016 at his home in Georgia.

99. Albrecht, "Real 'Norma Rae,'" 43.

100. "'Norma Rae' Inspirer," MR.

101. Stone, "'Norma Rae,'" 25–26.

102. Stone, 33.

103. Marcy Rein, review of *Norma Rae*, *Off Our Backs*, April 1979, 23; Cathy Uccella, letter to the editor, *Off Our Backs*, July 1979, 29.

104. Pat Aufderheide, review of *Norma Rae*, *Cineaste* 9, no. 3 (Spring 1979): 42–43; Margaret Ronan, review of *Norma Rae*, *Senior Scholastic*, May 1979, 35–36; Robert Asahina, "Cinematic Delusions," *New Leader*, April 1979, 20.

105. "Sally Field: Gidget Grows Up," *Teen*, August 1979, 49–51.

106. Laura Deans, "Sally Field: The Girl Next Door," *MacLean's*, June 25, 1979, 4–5; Vincent Canby, "Sally Field's 'Norma Rae' Is a Triumph," *NYT*, March 11, 1979, D19, 24; Vincent Canby, "Film: 'Norma Rae' Mill-Town Story," *NYT*, March 2, 1979, C10; unsigned review of *Norma Rae*, *Seventeen*, March 1979, clipping, box 23, folder 242, Norma Rae-Reviews 1979, MR.

107. Kenneth Turan, "Anchored to Reality," *Progressive*, May 1979, 52–53.

108. Gregory, *Women Who Run*, 147.

109. Sally Field, interview by Lawrence Grobel, *Playboy*, March 1986, 49–57; Canby, "Sally Field's 'Norma Rae,'" D19, 24; Canby, "Film: 'Norma Rae,'" C10; and Richard Phillips, "The Escape from Acute Cuteness," *Philadelphia Inquirer*, April 5, 1979, C1, clipping; Frank Rizzo, "Sally Field Did What Couldn't Be Done," *New Haven Journal-Courier*, March 1, 1979, 40, clipping; and Jill Jackson, "Ex–Flying Nun Is Flying High," *Times-Picayune*, March 1, 1979, section 2, p. 8, clipping, all in box 23, folder 239 "Norma Rae Publicity 1978–79," MR; clippings, box 23, folder 242 "Norma Rae Reviews, 1979," MR.

110. Jerry Parker, "Gidget Goes Grownup," *Boston Globe*, February 3, 1980, C1; "Sally Field: Gidget Grows Up," 49–51.

111. Aimee Lee Ball, "Sally Field: Feeling Good about Being a Woman," *Redbook*, June 1979, 33; Deans, "Sally Field," 4–5.

112. Aufderheide, review of *Norma Rae*, 42–43; Peter Rainer, "Movies: A Blue-Collar Whitewash," *Mademoiselle*, May 1979, 60; Turan, "Anchored to Reality," 53; Asahina, "Cinematic Delusions," 20–21; Richard Schickel, "Strike Busting," *Time*, March 12, 1979, 76; David Denby, "Good Ol' Girl Meets David Dubinsky," *New York*, March 12, 1979, 72–73; David Ansen, "True Grits," *Newsweek*, March 5, 1979, 105; Donald J. Hutera, "Redneck Winner," *Twin Cities Reader*, March 23, 1979, clipping, box 23, folder 242 "Norma Rae Reviews, 1979," MR.

113. Aufderheide, review of *Norma Rae*, 42; photograph of Field with sign, in "'Norma Rae' Takes on the Textile Giant," *International Musician*, June 1979, 19–20, clipping; and photograph of Field with sign, in "Cannes 1979," *Film en Televisie*, 1979, 12–16, clipping, both in box 23, folder 240 "Norma Rae Publicity, 1979–81," MR; collection of photos and headshots, box 23, folder 241 "Norma Rae, Publicity Press Kit 1979," MR.

114. Kimble and Olson, "Visual Rhetoric," 553–54.

115. Fred Robbins, "Sally Field: Coming Up Clover," *Saturday Evening Post*, January/ February 1981, 66–69; Natalie Gittelson, "The Winning Ways of Sally Field," *McCall's*, April 1980, 17–18.

116. Field to Ritt, undated notecard, box 38, folder 477 "F—Miscellan, 1952–90," MR.

117. Vincent Canby, "Screen: Sally Field Stars in Ritt's 'Back Roads,'" *NYT*, March 13, 1981, C6; Kirk Honeycutt, "Sally Field Maps a Career on 'Back Roads,'" *NYT*, October 12, 1980, D11; Eileen Stukane, "Sally Field Revealed," *Ladies' Home Journal*, September 1980, 33–34; Marilyn Beck, "Field's Director 'Crushed,'" *Palm Beach Post*, April 18, 1980, B16.

118. Leifermann, "Ride," CLS.

Chapter Five

1. Benmayor to Maldonado, May 18, 1987, Hunter College, box 158, folder 1 "NTC: PR Women, 1985–89," series XII "Research Task Forces, 1950–2001," El Centro de Estudios Puertorriqueños Collection, Centro.

2. Most documents in archives from the 1970s and 1980s use the terms "island" and "mainland." At the time, this linguistic distinction was an act of assertion calling attention to the particular experiences and identities of Puerto Ricans in diaspora.

3. Whalen, "Radical Contexts," 221–55.

4. Bourdieu, *Field of Cultural Production*, 30, 37–41.

5. Hall, "Encoding and Decoding."

6. Grace Davie, "Severing the Ties: Strategic Research and the Making of ACTWU's J.P. Stevens Corporate Campaign, 1974–1980," paper presented at the Labor and Working-Class History Association meeting, Durham, NC, June 2019.

7. James L. Tyson, "Ray Rogers Hits J.P. Stevens Where It Hurts," *Harvard Crimson*, September 26, 1979, www.thecrimson.com/article/1979/9/26/ray-rogers-hits-j-p-stevens; A. H. Raskin, "The Stevens Settlement," *NYT*, October 21, 1980, A19; Ray Rogers, "How a Corporate Campaign Defeated J.P. Stevens," *Labor Educator* 8, no. 2 (April 1999),

www.laboreducator.org/stevens.htm; Ray Rogers, "The 'Corporate Campaign' Strategy," Corporate Campaign, Inc. (website), www.corporatecampaign.org/history_actwu_jp _stevens_1978.php.

8. Ray Rogers, memorandum and outline, April, May 1977, box 31, folder 4 "Corporate Campaign," ACTWU Legal Department Files, Kheel; "ACTWU vs. J.P. Stevens, 1976–1980: Birth of the Corporate Campaign," Corporate Campaign, Inc. (website), www.corporatecampaign.org/history_actwu_jp_stevens_1978.php.

9. Paul Swaity, letter, April 24, 1980, box 3, folder 15 "J.P. Stevens Norma Rae," ACTWU Organizing Department Records, Kheel; and Eddie Kafafian, memo re: "Workmen's Circle at studio theatre," March 5, 1979, box 23, folder 236 "Norma Rae Misc., 1977–81"; "'Norma Rae' Takes," *International Musician*, 19–20, clipping; Rivera to Hal Sherman, April 9, 1979; Anne Rivera, Metro Labor Press Council letter, April 9, 1979, box 23, folder 240 "Norma Rae Publicity, 1979–81"; copy of *Labor Unity*, April 1979, 65, 4, box 24, folder 243 "Norma Rae Reviews, 1979–80"; Murray Finley and Jacob Scheinkman to Ritt, April 11, 1980; and Howard D. Samuel, letter, July 16, 1980, box 41, folder 525 "A, Miscellan 1978–86," all in MR.

10. Union memo, re: concerns about Prime Time interview and Kopple film, box 3, folder 15 "J.P. Stevens Norma Rae," ACTWU Organizing Department Records, Kheel.

11. Barbara Kopple, script, 1–17, no. 5619/038, box 10, folder 8 "Roanoke Rapids," TD.

12. Kopple script. Censored by author.

13. Kopple script.

14. Paul Swaity, ACTWU interoffice memo, January 25, 1980, box 10, folder 8 "Roanoke Rapids," TD.

15. Stetin and ACTWU leaders, memos, letters, and attempts to coordinate phone calls re: Kopple, box 10, folder 6 "Kopple, Barbara 1978–79," TD.

16. HB to SS (Sol Stetin), January 22, 1980; Walter L. Swanson to Robert F. Levine, April 30, 1980; and Pam Woywod to "Officers, Status of Legal Repres for Crystal Lee Sutton/Kopple," memorandum, May 14, 1980, all in box 10, folder 8 "Roanoke Rapids," TD.

17. Cassie Yates played Norma Rae, and Gary Frank played Reuben. "Norma Rae: A Pilot for a Television Series," Carol Evan McKeand (Saracen Productions, Rose & Asseyev Productions, Twentieth Century-Fox Television, 1981), overview of "Norma Rae" (1981), television show, IMDb (page discontinued); C. Gerald Fraser, "Television Week: More Mileage," *NYT*, November 5, 1981, TG3.

18. Definition of net profits, Twentieth Century-Fox agreement, binder 13, article 7, CLS; HB to SS, TD; Swanson to Levine, TD; Woywod to "Officers," TD.

19. HB to SS, TD; Swanson to Levine, TD; Woywod to "Officers," TD.

20. Koritz telephone interview; Eli Zivkovich interview recording, parts 1–2, Ross Papers; Michael Sneed, "The Real 'Norma Rae' Proud of Victory," *Chicago Tribune*, October 25, 1980, clipping, box 24, folder 245 "Norma Rae, Sutton, Crystal Lee, 1980–85," MR.

21. Gail Jeffords, memos on "Norma Rae events," box 10, folder 2 "J.P. Stevens, Crystal Lee Jordan, Gail Jeffords-Public Relations, 1979–80"; Jeffords to ACTWU and studio leaders, memorandum, June 30, 1980; and press tour article clips, esp. Evan Kossoff, "The Real 'Norma Rae' Didn't Like Movie until She Found It Was Educating Folks," *Lifestyle*, March 27, 1980, and Judith Schultz, "The Real 'Norma Rae' Liked the Movie," *Dayton Journal Herald*, February 16, 1980, all in box 10, folder 9 "Gail Jeffords Reports," TD; Marian Christy, "Crystal Lee—Tough as Steel," *Boston Globe*, January 28, 1980, 24.

22. Stephen Beverly, "The Real 'Norma Rae' Fights On," *Los Angeles Times*, July 6, 1980, G10.

23. Gail Jeffords, memo and reports, no. 5619/017, box 31, folder 11 "Crystal Lee Sutton Media Coverage Report, 1980," ACTWU Legal Department Files, 1942–95, Kheel; Hodges, "Real Norma Rae," 251–72.

24. Christy, "Crystal Lee," 23.

25. Flyers, memo, and program of rally appearance, Los Angeles, March 16, 1980, box 14, folder 8 "Meet Crystal Lee Sutton Rally," TD.

26. In 2019, Field granted Crystal Lee a slight acknowledgment but still said the script for *Norma Rae* "was loosely based on Crystal Lee Sutton." Told to Jennifer Ferrise, "First Person: Taking a Stand," *InSTYLE*, March 2019, 126.

27. Washington Post Service, "Real 'Norma Rae' Now Seeking to Organize Her Life," *Hartford Courant*, November 4, 1980, A2A; Christy, "Crystal Lee," 24; Zoe Trachtenburg, letter to the editor, *Los Angeles Times*, April 27, 1980, O2.

28. "An Uneasy Peace Reigns at J.P. Stevens," *Business Week*, February 22, 1982, 116–20; "Who Won the Marathon?," *Forbes*, May 25, 1981, 12–14; "17-Year Labor Struggle Ends as Textile Workers Accept Contract," *Hartford Courant*, October 20, 1980, B11; Green, *On Strike at Hormel*, 16–19.

29. Harry Bernstein, "Film 'Nine to Five' Sparks Interest in Unionization of Office Workers," *Los Angeles Times*, March 6, 1981, B3; Harry Bernstein, "Union, J.P. Stevens Reach Accord, End 17-Year Fight," *Los Angeles Times*, October 18, 1980, A1.

30. "Uneasy Peace Reigns," 116–20; "Who Won the Marathon?," 12–14; "17-Year Labor Struggle Ends," B11.

31. Stephen Klain, "Kopple Eyes J.P. Stevens: Actors to Simulate Union Organizers," *Variety*, March 15, 1978, clippings, folder 6 "Kopple, Barbara 1978–79"; HB to SS, January 22, 1980, folder 8 "Roanoke Rapids," both in box 10, TD; Levine and Thall law firm to David Lubell (re: arrangement with Kopple), July 30, 1980, binder 13, article 13, CLS.

32. Announcement telecast of "Keeping On," February 8, 1983, binder 9, article 13, CLS; Zivkovich interview, parts 1–2, Ross Papers; *American Playhouse*, season 2, episode 4, "Keeping On," directed by Barbara Kopple, aired February 8, 1983, on PBS.

33. Jim Brady, "Struggles of Crystal Lee: Hard Times Continue for the Real 'Norma Rae,'" *Washington Post*, July 24, 1985, B1; Christy, "Crystal Lee," 23–24; Jordan and Jordan conversation.

34. Crystal Lee to Jim Renfroe, re: May 10–16, 1982, grievance for parade dress, July 17, 1982 folder 4, drawer 2, CLS; Crystal Lee letter offering services, March 23, 1984, black folder, drawer 3, CLS; "Norma Rae" Labor Associates, Inc., to Communications Workers of America president, re: NC AFL-CIO, March 23, 1987, binder 19, article 25, CLS; Koritz telephone interview.

35. Muskegon Community College letter, November 1979, folder 14, drawer 2, CLS; Marty Ritt letter, re: copy of film, November 2, 1984, binder 14, article 18, CLS; Walter Swanson to Crystal Lee, re: purchase of *Norma Rae* film print, July 1, 1985, binder 14, article 12, CLS; interoffice memorandum from Brooke (subject: Crystal Lee Sutton–Norma Rae Print), August 6, 1984, and several subsequent memos, box 24, folder 245 "Norma Rae, Sutton, Crystal Lee 1980–85," MR.

36. Koritz telephone interview; Cale Jordan, "Crystal Lee: Influence on Union in America," final paper, for college course HIS 218, March 21, 2011, in author's possession.

37. Crystal Lee interviewed at her home, "TNT Raw Interview: American Dreams," personal DVD, 1996, drawer 1, CLS; "Crystal Lee Sutton: The Real Norma Rae," timeline, in author's possession.

38. "Crystal Lee Sutton," timeline; Jordan and Jordan conversation; Cale Jordan, "Crystal Lee"; Brady, "Struggles of Crystal Lee," B1–B2.

39. "TNT Raw Interview," CLS; "Crystal Lee Sutton," timeline; Jordan and Jordan conversation; Cale Jordan, "Crystal Lee"; interoffice memorandum from Brooke, August 6, 1984, and several subsequent memos, MR; Patricia Sullivan, "Labor Organizer Was Inspiration for 'Norma Rae,'" *Washington Post*, September 16, 2009, B5, clipping, MR; Stephen Rebello, request for comment, March 1, 1985, box 45, folder 586 "R, Miscellany 1973–89," MR.

40. Levine and Thall law firm to Twentieth Century-Fox, re: deferred payments, April 24, 1984, binder 13, article 5; John McCormick to Zivkovich, re: keeping tabs on movie breakeven, February 8, 1990, binder 13, article 2; Chris Willett to Crystal Lee, re: Norma Rae rights, April 4, 2001, binder 13, article 10; Chuck Spellman to McCormick, June 14, 2001, binder 12, article 21; Granville Burgess to Crystal Lee, June 19, 2001, binder 12, article 25; and Fox Group to McSurely, re: Norma Rae settlement, November 15, 2002, binder 14, article 14, all in CLS.

41. "TNT Raw Interview," CLS.

42. Benmayor, "For Every Story," 3–5.

43. "Oral History Task Force: Alvarez et al.," report, supported by Frank Bonilla, Ricardo Campos, History Task Force, input from artists Cándida Alvarez and Néstor Otero, box 159, folder 7 "Stories to Live By: Continuity and Change in Three Generations," series XII "Research Task Forces, 1950–2001," El Centro de Estudios Puertorriqueños Collection, Centro; Whalen, "Radical Contexts," 250.

44. Pioneros are early community settlers. Undated handwritten notes re: oral history, trainings, timelines, most by Benmayor, box 158, folder 2 "Notes, nd, 1981–87"; oral history budgets, grant applications, and "Puerto Ricans in New York" proposal, box 158, folders 6–8 "Puerto Ricans in New York: Voices of Migration, 1982–87"; "Puerto Ricans in New York" proposals, box 159, folders 1–5 "Puerto Ricans in New York: Voices of Migration, nd, 1982–85"; and Benmayor et al., "Oral History Task Force," 1988, box 159, folder 7 "Stories to Live By: Continuity and Change in Three Generations," all in El Centro de Estudios Puertorriqueños Collection, Centro.

45. Undated handwritten notes, re: oral history, trainings, timelines, most by Benmayor, Centro; Alvarez, "El Hilo," 42.

46. "Maldonado," August 8, 1984, 39, box 229, folder 3, series XIX "Audio-Visual (1973–99)," El Centro de Estudios Puertorriqueños Collection, Centro.

47. "Maldonado," 18–22.

48. Number 61, workshop, "Interviewing Ladies Who Worked in the Garment Industry," September 30, 1984, box 3, Oral History and Audiocassette Collection; and "Nosotras Trabajamos en la Costura" poster, 1984, box OS IX, item 2, series XII "Research Task Forces", both in El Centro de Estudios Puertorriqueños Collection, Centro.

49. Multiple cassettes, Oral History and Audiocassette Collection; "Nosotras Trabajamos" poster; and Benmayor to Gloria Maldonado, May 18, 1987, box 158, folder 1 "Nosotras Trabajamos en la Costura: PR Women in Garment Industry, 1985–89," series

XII "Research Task Forces", all in El Centro de Estudios Puertorriqueños Collection, Centro.

50. Benmayor to Shalala, October 10, 1986; National Commission on Working Women letter, September 25, 1986; and National Federation of Community Broadcasters letter, July 15, 1985, all in box 158, Nosotras Trabajamos, series XII "Research Task Forces," El Centro de Estudios Puertorriqueños Collection, Centro.

51. Benmayor to Maldonado, May 18, 1987, El Centro de Estudios Puertorriqueños Collection, Centro. Underline in original.

52. Janet Martineau, "Ritt's Movies Bullish on People," clipping, box 23, folder 240 "Norma Rae Publicity, 1979–81," MR.

53. Roger Ebert, "Director Martin Ritt Believes in 'Norma Rae,'" *Arizona Daily Star*, April 23, 1979, clipping, box 23, folder 240 "Norma Rae Publicity, 1979–81," MR.

54. Patricia Brennan, "This Week's Picks," *Washington Post*, July 7, 1985, TV3; Kevin Thomas, "Movie of the Week," *Los Angeles Times*, July 7, 1985, Z5, February 22, 1981, P5; "Channel Scan: Evita and Norma Rae Dominate Week's Fare," *Hartford Courant*, February 22, 1981, R4; "Television: Top Weekend Films," *NYT*, February 20, 1981, C27; Hodges, "Real Norma Rae," 251.

55. Western Union letter, re: Hollywood Women's Political Committee, Jayne Meadows et al., [1986?], box 41, folder 525 "A, Miscellan 1978–86," MR; Gregory, *Women Who Run*, 147.

56. Lou Gaul, "It's Now or Never," *Bucks County Courier Times*, clipping, box 23, folder 239 "Norma Rae Publicity, 1978–79," MR.

57. Gaul, "It's Now or Never"; and Tom Topor, "Ritt on His 'Norma Rae,'" *New York Post*, March 2, 1979, clipping; "'Norma Rae': Martin Ritt's Newest," *On Location*, November/December 1978, 60–67, clipping, box 23, folder 239 "Norma Rae Publicity, 1978–79"; program, letters, congratulations from celebrities, and transcript of appreciation narration, box 42, folder 539 "Boston University Tribute, 1988"; Lyn Goldfarb and Anatoli Ilyashov, "Ritt," interview transcript, September 11, 1985, 3, box 44, folder 560 "Interviews–Goldfarb and Ilyashov, 1985–91"; Cliff Rothman, "Director Ritt Honored on 50th Anniversary," *Hollywood Reporter*, December 19, 1985, 4, clipping, box 47, folder 619 "Tributes 1985–86"; memos, letters, UCLA Distinguish Dir, box 47, folder 625 "UCLA Distinguished Dir in Residence 1985–86"; and letters, USA Film Festival Great Dir Award, February–March 1989, box 47, folder 628 "USA Film Festival 1978–89," all in MR.

58. Vikki Pamkowski to Sydney Pollack, March 31, 1981; paid ad billing, March 13, 1981; "To Ed, By Messenger," May 19, 1981; Columbia interoffice communication, June 4, 15, 1981, all in box 6, folder 44 "Absence of Malice Credits, 1980–81," Pollack Papers, MHL; Wil Haygood, "Sally Field: After a Long Struggle, She's Found a Place in the Heart of Hollywood Stardom," *Boston Globe*, December 10, 1985, 65.

59. Julie Calsi, "Sally Field and Life after Oscar," *Broward Times*, December 18, 1980, B1, clipping; and "Sally Field: A Change of Pace," Mirage Enterprises, 2, both in box 6, folder 46 "Absence of Malice, Sally Field, 1980–81," Pollack Papers, MHL; *Playboy*, March 1986, cover.

60. Kimble and Olson, "Visual Rhetoric," 553–54.

61. Roediger, *Working toward Whiteness*; Jacobson, *Whiteness*; Jacobson, *Roots Too*; Sugrue and Skrentny, "White Ethnic Strategy," 171–80.

62. *Archie Bunker's Place*, season 3, episode 4, "Norma Rae Bunker," produced by Tandem and Ugo Prod., aired October 18, 1981, on CBS, www.imdb.com/title/tt0078562.

63. Dypski, "Caribbean Basin Initiative," 103; Rosen, *Making Sweatshops*, 129–52.

64. Pastor, "Sinking"; Dypski, "Caribbean Basin Initiative," 101; Gautier-Mayoral, "Puerto Rican Model," 13; Polanyi-Levitt, "Origins," 229, 242–43.

65. Gautier-Mayoral, "Puerto Rican Model," 11.

66. Rosen, *Making Sweatshops*, 135.

67. Dypski, "Caribbean Basin Initiative," 105.

68. International Trade Association, *Guide*, 1–4, 8–10.

69. Transcript of radio program, typed with edits, n.d., box 158, folder 1 "Nosotras Trabajamos," series XII "Research Task Forces," El Centro de Estudios Puertorriqueños Collection, Centro; Minchin, *Empty Mills*, 68–69.

70. Rumelt telephone conversation; Vance and Scott, *Wal-Mart*, 57–135; Petrovic and Hamilton, "Making Global Markets," 107–42; Rosen, *Making Sweatshops*, 141; Lichtenstein, *Retail Revolution*, esp. chaps. 1, 2, 6, 8; Moreton, *To Serve God*, 248–63; Windham, *Knocking on Labor's Door*, 108, 123–27.

71. Bonacich and Hardie, "Wal-Mart," 163–88; Collins, *Threads*, 104–25; Moreton, *To Serve God*, 66, 130.

72. "Maldonado," February 17, 1985, Centro; Cline, *Overdressed*, 70–75.

73. MacLean, *Freedom Is Not Enough*, 312–13; Rodgers, *Age of Fracture*, 71–76.

74. Adler, *Mollie's Job*, 234–42; Rodgers, *Age of Fracture*, 80–81.

75. In a hostile takeover, a finance firm or group of investors attains a corporation by going to its major shareholders with promises of high rates of return rather than by purchasing the corporation.

76. Adler, *Mollie's Job*, 246–48.

77. Minchin, *Empty Mills*, 7; Lichtenstein, *Retail Revolution*, 202–3; Benton, *Fraying Fabric*, 8–12.

78. Boujouen, "'Menea Esas Manos,'" 118–20.

79. Boujouen, 118, 121–29.

80. Norma Boujouen and James R. Newton, "The Puerto Rican Experience in Willimantic," blue booklet, [198?], 30, 35–36, Windham Regional Community Council, WTHM.

81. Medina interview; Gregory Sandler, "All in the Family: Harvard MBA Karen Cmar Takes Over the Helm at Gemini," *Business Journal*, July 1988, 1, 19–20, vertical files/periodicals, SHLA; Carolyn Robbins, "Consultant Returns to Lead Family Firm," *Springfield Sunday Republican*, May 22, 1988, E1, clipping, folder "SPFD 670-Business, Gemini Corp.," SHLA; George O'Brien, "Gemini Project Set to Lift Off," *Business West*, May 1999, 27–28, SHLA. Paese Acquisition Group, a partnership of three investors, bought the Gemini Building in 1999, a year after Springfield seized it for unpaid taxes. The investor group paid $100,001, just a dollar above the minimum accepted payment. It did not develop the building; the plant burned to the ground in 2003. The city's Office of Planning and Economic Development remediated the site in 2009–10. "Gemini Site," Office of Planning and Economic Development, City of Springfield (website), www.springfield-ma.gov/planning/index.php?id=111.

82. Salgado-Cartagena conversation.

83. Boujouen and Newton, "Puerto Rican Experience," 30–36, WTHM; Boujouen, "Menea Esas Manos," 189–218; Benmayor, "For Every Story," 7–8; Juarbe, "Anastasia's Story," 23; Alvarez, "El Hilo," 32–34; Glasser, *Aquí Me Quedo*, 179–81.

84. Book prospectus, box 158, folder 3 "Pioneras: Women's Voices, nd, 1994," series XII "Research Task Forces," El Centro de Estudios Puertorriqueños Collection, Centro; Vázquez Erazo, "Stories Our Mothers Tell," 23–28; Alvarez, "El Hilo," 29–40.

85. New York State Curriculum, "Old Voices, New Voices," 36–42.

86. "History," WEPZA, www.wepza.org/history.

87. Rosen, *Making Sweatshops*, 119–28; Collins, *Threads*, 27–61; Minchin, *Empty Mills*, 91–158.

88. Transshipments occur when a nation has met its quota of, e.g., towel imports to the United States, so its trade office makes an agreement with another country on behalf of manufacturers to send excess towels to that country, which has not met its quota of imports. That country then ships the towels into the United States on behalf of the nation of origin for a fee.

89. Minchin, *Empty Mills*, 111.

90. Minchin, 95–104; Windham, *Knocking on Labor's Door*, 120–26.

91. Minchin, *Empty Mills*, 95–104.

92. Collins, *Threads*, 27–61, 104–25; Minchin, *Empty Mills*, 105–20.

93. Collins, *Threads*, 27–61, 104–25; Lichtenstein, *Retail Revolution*, 202–3; Minchin, *Empty Mills*, 105–20.

94. Minchin, *Empty Mills*, *Norma Rae* references on 134.

95. Rosen, *Making Sweatshops*; Whalen, "Sweatshops Here and There," 45–68; Minchin, *Empty Mills*, 126–59.

96. "Maldonado," August 8, 1984, 24–25, Centro.

Chapter Six

1. Jimmy Carter, State of the Union address, January 19, 1978, transcript, Jimmy Carter Presidential Library, www.jimmycarterlibrary.gov/assets/documents/speeches/su78jec.phtml.

2. Ronald Reagan, first inaugural address, January 20, 1981, transcript, Ronald Reagan Presidential Library, www.reaganlibrary.gov/archives/speech/inaugural-address-1981.

3. Bruce Schulman, *Seventies*; Bruce Schulman, *From Cotton Belt*; McGirr, *Suburban Warriors*; Moreton, *To Serve God*; Phillips-Fein, *Fear City*; Phillips-Fein, *Invisible Hands*; Dochuk, *From Bible Belt*; Worthen, *Apostles of Reason*.

4. Williams, *Politics and Letters*; Williams, *Marxism and Literature*; Couldry, *Media Rituals*; Ahmed, *Cultural Politics of Emotion*.

5. Ziff, *Che Guevara*; Eric D. Carter, "Where's Che?"; Michael Casey, "In Argentina, Che Guevara Finally Gets More Than a Lousy T-Shirt," *Wall Street Journal*, June 14, 2008, A1; Casey, *Che's Afterlife*; Memou, "Re-appropriating Che's Image," 449–51.

6. Charlton, introduction, 5–8; Casey, *Che's Afterlife*, 25–50. Casey presents evidence that Korda was also responsible for the iconic image of Fidel Castro, with rebel commander Camilo Cienfuegos, riding into Havana atop a military jeep. Korda's older brother, Luis, had taken the photo but had no interest in it until Alberto cropped it (Casey, 79).

7. Ziff, "Guerrillero Heroico," 8–10, 15–19; Casey, *Che's Afterlife*, 23–134.

8. Ziff, "Guerrillero Heroico," 8–10, 15–19.

9. Ziff, 12; Wallis, "Che Lives!," 24–25; Eric D. Carter, "Where's Che?," 1; Casey, *Che's Afterlife*, 32–33.

10. Williams, *Marxism and Literature*, 113. He notes that "dominant" is not "domination," because hegemony is never total or exclusive; alternative and oppositional politics and culture still exist.

11. McGirr, *Suburban Warriors*, 331–39; Hale, *Nation of Outsiders*; McGuigan, *Neoliberal Culture*.

12. Duggan, *Twilight of Equality*, 1–20, 22–42; Schoenwald, *Time for Choosing*, 247–48; Moreton, *To Serve God*, 145–71, 173–91; Dochuk, *From Bible Belt*, 51–77, 196–221, 223–56; Kruse, *White Flight*, 78–104, 161–79; Kruse, *One Nation under God*, 239–73, 275–94.

13. "Radical libertarian economists" go by several names, including free-market economists, market fundamentalists, and ultracapitalists.

14. Ronald Reagan, "A Time for Choosing," in Schweizer and Hall, *Landmark Speeches*, 44; Schoenwald, *Time for Choosing*, 245; Troy, *Morning in America*, 9; Crespino, "Civil Rights," 92–93; Suri, "Détente and Its Discontents," 241–42; Edward H. Miller, *Conspiratorial Life*.

15. I discuss these three cultural channels in broad terms, with emphasis on their general popular presence rather than on the subtle distinctions between different leaders, groups, and dogmas. The goal is to study their sweeping public statements and emotional accessibility rather than taking deep dives into the historical, social, and financial analysis of their development.

16. I highlight their collaboration and the overlap in the apparatus of expertise, not the intricacies of their internal esoteric discussions. Many economists, political theorists, and policymakers who are called "neoliberal" had keen internal debates and nuanced disagreements. See Bockman, *Markets in the Name*; and Slobodian, *Globalists*.

17. Larner, "Neo-liberalism"; Duggan, *Twilight of Equality*; David Harvey, *Brief History of Neoliberalism*; Phillips-Fein, *Invisible Hands*; Mirowski and Plehwe, *Road from Mont Pèlerin*; Val Marie Johnson, "Introduction, Special Section"; Rodgers, *Age of Fracture*; Bockman, *Markets in the Name*; Burgin, *Great Persuasion*; Slobodian, *Globalists*; Ben Jackson, "At the Origins."

18. Bourdieu, *Field of Cultural Production*, esp. part 1; Williams, "Hegemony," in *Marxism and Literature*, 108–14; Dean, *Governmentality*; Sennett, *Culture*; McAlister, *Epic Encounters*, xviii.

19. "Formations" are potent associations and tendencies in social life and cognition that have significant and even decisive influence on the development of a society, but they often have variable and oblique relations to formal institutions. Williams, *Marxism and Literature*, 117; Klein, *Cold War Orientalism*, 7–9.

20. Gramsci, *Prison Notebooks*; Williams, *Marxism and Literature*, 108–20, esp. 110–12; Klein, *Cold War Orientalism*, 7–9.

21. Williams, *Politics and Letters*; Williams, *Marxism and Literature*; Goldberg, *Antisocial Media*, 12.

22. Klein, *Cold War Orientalism*, 8.

23. Duggan, *Twilight of Equality*; David Harvey, *Brief History of Neoliberalism*; O'Connor, "Financing the Counterrevolution," 154–55; Steger and Roy, *Neoliberalism*; Connell, "Understanding Neoliberalism," 22–36; Luxton, "Doing Neoliberalism," 163–83.

24. Bockman, *Markets in the Name*; Panitch and Konings, "Myths of Neoliberal Deregulation"; Burgin, *Great Persuasion*; Krippner, *Capitalizing on Crisis*; Dobbin, Martin, and Sewell, "Book Symposium"; Val Marie Johnson, "Introduction, Special Section."

25. O'Connor, "Financing the Counterrevolution," 123.

26. Jack, "Producing," 515; Lichtenstein, *Retail Revolution*, 287; Luxton, "Doing Neoliberalism," 163–83; David Harvey, *Brief History of Neoliberalism*, 5–62.

27. Williams, *Marxism and Literature*, 113–14, 150. Works of art and media, by their "substantial and general character," are especially important sources of evidence for grasping the active, formative, and transformational processes of hegemony—particularly the processes of cultural formation; an important aspect of a work of art is its "power to evoke response."

28. Slobodian, *Globalists*; MacLean, *Democracy in Chains*; Phillips-Fein, *Invisible Hands*.

29. E.g., Roll (*Poor Man's Fortune*) traces the long history of white working-class conservatism among metal miners in the Tri-State district of Kansas, Missouri, and Oklahoma from the 1870s to World War II. Fones-Wolf, *Selling Free Enterprise*, esp. 74–94, 161–63, 259–62; Phillips-Fein, *Invisible Hands*; McGirr, "Now That Historians Know," 765–70.

30. Phillips-Fein, *Invisible Hands*, 137.

31. Moreton, *To Serve God*, 145.

32. O'Connor, "Financing the Counterrevolution," 154–65.

33. Milton Friedman, "Federal Reserve Must Stop Going from One Extreme to Another," *US News and World Report*, January 31, 1983, 66–67; "What Is America," *Saturday Evening Post*, October 1978, 16; "Answering the Big Questions," *Newsweek*, May 29, 1978, 80–81.

34. Richard Feloni, "The Economist Joseph Stiglitz Explains Why He Thinks the Late Milton Friedman's Ideas Have Contributed to Rising Inequality," *Business Insider*, March 13, 2018, www.businessinsider.com/joseph-stiglitz-milton-friedman-capitalism -theories-2018-3; Mimi Teixeira, "Why Milton Friedman's *Capitalism and Freedom* Is Still Relevant Today," *Acton Institute Powerblog*, July 29, 2016, http://blog.acton.org /archives/88316-why-milton-friedmans-capitalism-and-freedom-is-still-relevant-today .html; Ferrero, Hoffman, and McNulty, "Must Milton Friedman," 37–59; Steve Denning, "The Origin of 'the World's Dumbest Idea': Milton Friedman," *Forbes*, June 25, 2013, www.forbes.com/sites/stevedenning/2013/06/26/the-origin-of-the-worlds-dumbest -idea-milton-friedman/#1754dd8870e8; Stephen Gandel, "All-Time 100 Nonfiction Books: *Capitalism and Freedom*," *Time*, August 17, 2011, http://entertainment.time.com /2011/08/30/all-time-100-best-nonfiction-books/slide/capitalism-and-freedom-by-milton -friedman; "A Heavy-Weight Champ at Five Foot Two," *Economist*, November 23, 2006, www.economist.com/special-report/2006/11/23/a-heavyweight-champ-at-five-foot-two; Holcomb B. Noble, "Milton Friedman, Free Markets Theorist, Dies at 94," *NYT*, November 16, 2006, www.nytimes.com/2006/11/16/business/17friedmancnd.html; Burgin, *Great Persuasion*, 152–85.

35. Milton Friedman, *Capitalism and Freedom*, 1–5.

36. Jack, "Producing," 514–30.

37. Milton Friedman, *Capitalism and Freedom*, 5, 108–9; Friedman and Friedman, *Free to Choose*, x–xi.

38. Jack, "Producing," 514–30.

39. Friedman and Friedman, *Free to Choose*, xii, 309.

40. Jack, "Producing," 514–30.

41. Jack, 514–30; Burgin, "Age of Certainty"; Burgin, *Great Persuasion*; Taylor, "Modern Social Imaginaries," 91–124; O'Connor, "Financing the Counterrevolution," 160–66.

42. During the 1970s, the number of colleges and universities offering entrepreneurship and small-business courses increased from eight to almost 200. Moreton, "Make Payroll, Not War," 54–55, 66–70.

43. Phillips-Fein, *Invisible Hands*, 11.

44. Rodgers, *Age of Fracture*; Meeropol, *Surrender*.

45. Margaret Thatcher, interview by Douglas Keay for *Woman's Own*, September 23, 1987, transcript, Margaret Thatcher Foundation, www.margaretthatcher.org /document/106689.

46. Speakes, *Speaking Out*; Troy, *Morning in America*, 8–12 62; Marcus, *Happy Days*, esp. 60–90; Schoenwald, *Time for Choosing*, 190–220, esp. 191–97; Ehrman, *Eighties*, 1–48.

47. Phillips-Fein, *Invisible Hands*, esp. chaps. 4–8, quote on 100–101.

48. Ronald Reagan, "Second Inaugural Address," in Boyer, *Reagan as President*, 97–98; Ronald Reagan, "Strategic Defense Initiative," Boyer, *Reagan as President*, 207–8; Ronald Reagan, "Evil Empire," in Schweizer and Hall, *Landmark Speeches*, 89–93; Ashford, "Conservative Agenda," 206.

49. Reagan, "First Inaugural Address," in Schweizer and Hall, *Landmark Speeches*, 75; Reagan, "Time for Choosing," 53–54; Ronald Reagan radio addresses, September 21, 1976, April 16, 1979, January 19, 1977, transcripts in Skinner, Anderson, and Anderson, *Reagan*, 227–30, 271.

50. Troy, *Morning in America*, 63.

51. Reagan, "First Inaugural Address," 77; Reagan, "Second Inaugural Address," 96; Ronald Reagan, "Acceptance Speech," in Boyer, *Reagan as President*, 23.

52. Phillips-Fein, *Invisible Hands*, 180–81, 202–3. She notes the term "supply-side" was originally a scornful term used by Herbert Stein, chairman of the Council of Economic Advisors under Nixon and Ford, but Jude Wanniski started to promote it in his columns for the *Wall Street Journal*. Ronald Reagan radio address, January 9, 1978, transcript in Skinner, Anderson, and Anderson, *Reagan*, 395; Ashford, "Conservative Agenda," 196–97.

53. Troy, *Morning in America*, 74; Self, *All in the Family*, 339–425.

54. Reagan, "Time for Choosing," 51.

55. Reagan, 46.

56. Reagan, "Second Inaugural Address," 96.

57. Ronald Reagan radio address, November 30, 1976, transcript in Skinner, Anderson, and Anderson, *Reagan*, 134–35; Jacobs, "Conservative Struggle," 193–209; Ashford, "Conservative Agenda," 196.

58. Reagan, "First Inaugural Address," 76; Reagan radio addresses, September 21, 1976, April 16, 1979, January 19, 1977, 227–30, 271.

59. Phillips-Fein, *Invisible Hands*, 244.

60. T. Boone Pickens Jr., "My Case for Reagan," *Fortune*, October 29, 1984, reprinted in Boyer, *Reagan as President*, 88.

61. Troy, *Morning in America*, 67.

62. Reagan, "Evil Empire," 86, 90; Flippen, *Jimmy Carter*, 293–96.

63. For my purposes, "activist evangelical" denotes people of religious and political conservatism who advocate for evangelical Protestants and ministries to become more involved in politics, policy, and government. Precise scholarly and theological questions about the distinctions between modernist, fundamentalist, evangelical, born-again, Pentecostal, and charismatic Christians are too intricate and not related to my emphasis on dominant discourses and mainstream cultural formations, which engage broad narrative and affect. For a review of conservative Protestants, see Woodbury and Smith, "Fundamentalism et al."; and Worthen, *Apostles of Reason*.

64. Marsden, *Fundamentalism and American Culture*; Boyer, "Evangelical Resurgence," 29; Hart, *That Old-Time Religion*, esp. 25–53, 201–21; Flippen, *Jimmy Carter*, 73, 77–80.

65. Fones-Wolf and Fones-Wolf, "Managers and Ministers," 113, 120, 124.

66. Dochuk, *From Bible Belt*; Fones-Wolf and Fones-Wolf, *Struggle*; Fones-Wolf and Fones-Wolf, "Managers and Ministers."

67. Moreton, *To Serve God*, 145–72; Kruse, *One Nation under God*, 76–82.

68. "About Liberty," Liberty University, www.liberty.edu/aboutliberty.

69. Shires, *Hippies*, 105–7, 159, 188–89.

70. Hart, *That Old-Time Religion*, 78–96.

71. Kruse, *One Nation under God*, 49–64.

72. Billy Graham, *Hope*; Billy Graham, *Facing Death*; Billy Graham, *How to Be*; Billy Graham, *Angels*; "I Believe in God!," *Reader's Digest*, July 1978, 110–13; "Soul Saving," *Time*, January 23, 1978, 78; M. G. Stoddard, "Billy Graham: The World Is His Pulpit," *Saturday Evening Post*, March 1986, 42–45; K. L. Woodward, "All the Presidents' Man," *Newsweek*, April 21, 1980, 117.

73. Billy Graham, *How to Be*, ix–x, 86–87, 141.

74. Billy Graham, *Angels*, xi–xiii, xix.

75. "Excerpts from President's Speech," *NYT*, March 9, 1983, A18.

76. McAlister, *Epic Encounters*, 6–8.

77. Bourdieu, *Field of Cultural Production*, part 1; McAlister, *Epic Encounters*, 7–8.

78. Williams, *Marxism and Literature*, 128–35. He describes a structure of feeling as "a distinction from more formal concepts of 'world-view' or 'ideology' . . . meanings and values as they are actively lived and felt . . . elements of impulse, restraint, and tone; specifically affective elements of consciousness and relationships: not feelings against thought, but thought as felt and feeling as thought." It is a structure, but still in process, in a living interrelating continuity, but with connecting characteristics and hierarchies (Williams, 132).

79. Coppola, *Godfather*.

80. Bourdieu, *Field of Cultural Production*.

81. Kimberly Potts, "The 25 Most Essential Roseanne Episodes," *Vulture*, March 20, 2018, www.vulture.com/article/roseanne-most-essential-episodes.html.

82. *Roseanne*, season 1, episode 7, "The Memory Game," produced by Carsey-Werner, aired December 13, 1988, on ABC; *Roseanne*, season 1, episode 23, "Let's Call It Quits," produced by Carsey-Werner, aired May 2, 1989, on ABC.

83. *Who's the Boss?*, season 4, episode 19, "Housekeepers Unite," produced by Hunter-Cohan, aired March 15, 1988, on ABC.

84. *Gilmore Girls*, season 6, episode 6, "Welcome to the Dollhouse," produced by Warner Bros., aired October 18, 2005, on the WB.

85. Tanzina Vega, "In Ads, the Workers Rise Up and Go to Lunch," *NYT*, July 7, 2012; Stuart Elliott, "In New Ad Campaign, Orbitz Comes Out as Pro-vacation," *Media Decoder* (blog), *NYT*, May 4, 2012, http://mediadecoder.blogs.nytimes.com/2012/05/04/in-new-ad-campaign-orbitz-comes-out-as-pro-vacation.

86. Dolo Amber, "I just had a 'Norma Rae' moment at the Mall-wart . . .," Democratic Underground forum, June 24, 2004, www.democraticunderground.com/discuss/duboard.php?az=view_all&address=105x1317808; Dougall Fraser, "I'm the Norma Rae of Spin Class," *Dougall Fraser* (blog), August 27, 2014, www.dougallfraser.com/im-the-norma-rae-of-spin-class; Lee Ann Huntley, "Trump is having a Norma Rae moment it will take the National guard to get him out of there," Facebook, November 5, 2020, https://www.facebook.com/lee.a.huntley/posts/3800452179965041 .

87. Stephen Metcalf, "Calling Norma Rae," review of *Nickel and Dimed: On (Not) Getting By in America* by Barbara Ehrenreich, *Los Angeles Times*, May 27, 2001, www.latimes.com/archives/la-xpm-2001-may-27-bk-2976-story.html.

88. Michael Powell, "At Cablevision, Norma Rae's Been Escorted Outside," *NYT*, February 12, 2013.

89. Jack Mirkinson, "The Media vs. the American Worker," *Salon*, September 7, 2015, www.salon.com/2015/09/07/the_media_vs_the_american_worker_how_the_1_percent_hijacked_the_business_of_news.

90. Norma Rae (band website), www.normaraeband.com/bio (site discontinued, new band site https://normaraeband.com).

91. Leonie Haimson, "Last Night's PEP Meeting on Verizon Contract and Its 'Norma Rae' Moment," *NYC Public School Parents* (blog), August 18, 2011, https://nycpublicschoolparents.blogspot.com/2011/08/last-nights-pep-meeting-on-verizon.html.

92. Kara Smith, "Ithaca Community Calls on Cuomo to 'Respect' Public Education," NYSUT, March 20, 2015, www.nysut.org/news/2015/march/ithaca-community-calls-on-cuomo-to-respect-public-education.

93. Orleck, *We Are All,* 21–28. See original article at Peter Amsel, "NagaWorld Staff Go Norma Rae," Calvin Ayre (website), June 29, 2013, https://calvinayre.com/2013/06/29/casino/nagaworld-casino-staff-go-norma-rae-on-nagacorp.

94. Orleck, *We Are All,* 21–24; Amsel, "NagaWorld Staff."

95. Norma Rae flyer, Janus protest, AFL-CIO, May 2018, from Massachusetts AFL-CIO training the author attended.

Epilogue

1. Constance Grady, "Staging 'West Side Story' in 2020," *Vox*, March 11, 2020, www.vox.com/culture/2020/3/11/21166360/west-side-story-review-broadway-ivo-van-hove; Tim Teeman, "Ivo van Hove's 'West Side Story' Broadway Revival Aims to Shock," *Daily Beast*, February 21, 2020, www.thedailybeast.com/ivo-van-hoves-west-side-story-broadway-revival-aims-to-shock-but-ends-up-lost-in-time; Marilyn Stasio, review of *West Side Story*, directed by Ivo van Hove, Broadway Theater, New York, *Variety*, February 20, 2020, https://variety.com/2020/legit/reviews/west-side-story-review-broadway-ivo-van-hove-1203507979; Jerry Portwood, "'West Side Story' Revival Breaks All the Rules," *Rolling Stone*, February 20, 2020, www.rollingstone.com/music/music-live-reviews/west-side-story-broad

way-review-ivo-van-hove-955669; Charles McNulty, "'West Side Story' Blasts Back to Broadway," *Los Angeles Times*, February 20, 2020, https://www.latimes.com/entertainment -arts/story/2020-02-20/ivo-van-hove-west-side-story-broadway-review.

2. Spielberg, *West Side Story*.

3. Winant, *Next Shift*.

4. Television schedule, Turner Classic Movies, 8:00 p.m., *NYT*, May 21, 2012, C7; television schedule, Fox Mov, 7:00 p.m., *NYT*, February 25, 2010, C7.

5. Troy Turner, "The Life and Death of Norma Rae," *Opelika-Auburn News*, November 24, 2016; Associated Press, "Opelika Textile Mill Burns at Site Used in 'Norma Rae,'" *Tuscaloosa News*, November 16, 2016.

6. This valorization of the physical toll and bodily strain of labor is part of white working-class conservatism that also serves the neoliberal turn. Roll, *Poor Man's Fortune*.

7. Turner, "Life and Death"; Fred Woods, "'Old Mill' Features Fondly in Opelika Memories," *Opelika Observer*, April 3, 2015, http://opelikaobserver.com/old-mill-features -fondly-in-opelika-memories; Stanton, "Performing the Postindustrial," 89–93.

8. Cowie and Heathcott, *Beyond the Ruins*. This collection contains studies of sites of deindustrialization. As noted, workers and neighbors have immediate and disruptive experiences of deindustrialization in their city or county when a major manufacturer closes. Their perspective is significant to understanding the working class, but it is not descriptive of the overall array of industrial capitalism.

9. Thomas and Santiago, *Rethinking*, 107.

10. Orleck, *Storming Caesars Palace*; Chappell, *War on Welfare*; Ross and Solinger, *Reproductive Justice*; Walker-McWilliams, *Reverend Addie Wyatt*; Thomas and Santiago, *Rethinking*, 10–11, 53, 88.

11. Orleck, *Storming Caesars Palace*; "Building Southern Synergy," SisterSong, www .sistersong.net/building-southern-synergy-programs; "Centering Black Women's Issues and Leadership," SisterSong, www.sistersong.net/centering-black-womens-issues -leadership; Ross et al., *Radical Reproductive Justice*.

12. Alessa Dominguez, "Ryan Murphy's New Show Is the Queer Fairy Tale We Needed," *BuzzFeed News*, June 2, 2018, www.buzzfeednews.com/article/pdominguez /ryan-murphy-pose-fx-queer-trans-stories; Debra Birnbaum and Cynthia Littleton, "Ryan Murphy Inks Mammoth Overall Deal," *Variety*, February 13, 2018, https:// variety.com/2018/tv/news/ryan-murphy-netflix-overall-deal-fox-1202698305; John Koblin, "Ryan Murphy Heads to Netflix in Deal Said to Be Worth Up to $300 Million," *NYT*, February 13, 2018, www.nytimes.com/2018/02/13/business/media/netflix-ryan-murphy .html.

13. Tim Stack, "Why Ryan Murphy Is Donating All His Profits from *Pose*," *Entertainment Weekly*, June 7, 2018, https://ew.com/tv/2018/06/07/ryan-murphy-pose-profits; Hank Stuever, "Ryan Murphy's Pose Is a Fabulous—if Preachy—Restoration Effort," *Washington Post*, June 1, 2018, https://www.washingtonpost.com/entertainment/tv /ryan-murphys-pose-is-a-fabulous--if-preachy--restoration-effort/2018/06/01/2ce794e2 -6548-11e8-a69c-b944de66d9e7_story.html; Willa Paskin, "*Pose*," *Slate*, May 31, 2018, https://slate.com/culture/2018/05/ryan-murphys-pose-reviewed.html; Philip Galanes, "Ryan Murphy and Janet Mock on 'Pose,' Diversity, and Netflix," *NYT*, May 23, 2018,

www.nytimes.com/2018/05/23/arts/television/pose-ryan-murphy-janet-mock.html; Emily Nussbaum, "Mr. Big: How Ryan Murphy Became the Most Powerful Man in TV," *New Yorker*, May 14, 2018, 52–67.

14. *Pose*, season 1, episode 2, "Access," produced by Color Force, Brad Falchuk Teley-Vision, and Ryan Murphy Television, aired June 10, 2018, on FX.

15. *Pose*, season 2, episode 1, "Acting Up," produced by Color Force, Brad Falchuk Teley-Vision, and Ryan Murphy Television, aired June 11, 2019, on FX; Colin Clews, "1989. ACT UP Disrupt Mass," *Gay in the 80s* (blog), December 10, 2019, www.gayin the80s.com/?s=st+patrick.

16. The title comes from a term reportedly invented in Boyle Heights that combines *gente*, meaning "people," with "gentrified" and denotes gentrification by Latinos. Noemí Pedraza, "'Gentefied': A Love Letter to Boyle Heights," *Boyle Heights Beat* (blog), February 24, 2020, https://boyleheightsbeat.com/gentefied-a-love-letter-to-boyle-heights.

17. *Gentefied*, season 1, episode 7, "Brown Love," produced by MACRO and Sector 7, aired February 21, 2020, on Netflix.

18. *Gentefied*, season 1, episode 9, "Protest Tacos," produced by MACRO and Sector 7, aired February 21, 2020, on Netflix.

19. Sally Field, typed note on monogrammed stationery, September 3, 2009, drawer 2, CLS; Sally Field, "'I Started to Cry': Sally Field on Bringing *Norma Rae* to Cannes," *Literary Hub*, September 24, 2018, https://lithub.com/i-started-to-cry-sally-field-on -bringing-norma-rae-to-cannes; Field, *In Pieces*, 344.

20. Kathie O'Donnell, "WestPoint Stevens Junk Offering Increased to $950 Million," *Bond Buyer*, December 1, 1993, 2; "WestPoint Stevens' $600 Million Offering Seen Winning Strong Demand from Investors," *Bond Buyer*, November 30, 1993, 2; Kenneth N. Gilpin, "West Point-Pepperell Buyer Steps Down as Chairman," *NYT*, October 24, 1992; Rudolph A. Pyatt Jr., "For J.P. Stevens, 175th Anniversary Now a Requiem," *Washington Post*, July 3, 1988; "WestPoint Gets 85% of J.P. Stevens Stock," *Wall Street Journal*, May 10, 1988, 51; Robert J. Cole, "3-Month Battle for J.P. Stevens Ends," *NYT*, April 26, 1988, D1.

21. "WestPoint Stevens Reaches Agreement in Principle with Noteholders," PR Newswire, June 2, 2003, 1.

22. Times Wire Reports, "Mill That Inspired 'Norma Rae' Will Close," *Los Angeles Times*, April 27, 2003; Associated Press, "WestPoint Stevens Closing Norma Rae Textile Facility," *GoUpstate*, April 27, 2003, https://www.goupstate.com/story/news/2003/04/27 /westpoint-stevens-closing-norma-rae-textile-facility/29667507007/; *Times-News* and *Daily Herald* clippings, folder 9, CLS; UNC-TV, envelope with letter about Christine Rogers story, June 17, 2003, folder 16, drawer 2, CLS; Minchin, *Empty Mills*, 11.

23. "Crystal Lee 'Norma Rae' Sutton Is Battling Cancer," NC State AFL-CIO, July 11, 2008, http://aflcionc.org/crystal-lee-norma-rae-sutton-is-battling-cancer; Sue Sturgis, "Real 'Norma Rae' Dies of Cancer after Insurer Delayed Treatment," *Facing South* (blog), September 14, 2009, https://www.facingsouth.org/2009/09/real-norma-rae-dies -of-cancer-after-insurer-delayed-treatment; Susie Madrak, "'Norma Rae' Dead at 68 after Struggle with Insurance Company to Get Chemo," *Crooks and Liars*, September 14, 2009, http://crooksandliars.com/susie-madrak/norma-rae-dead-68-after-two-year-stru#.

24. Clippings, binder 25, CLS; Sturgis, "Real 'Norma Rae' Dies."

25. Crystal Lee Sutton, "The Rest of the Story: Norma Rae," interview, *Reelz Time*, March 6, 2008, video cassette, drawer 1, CLS; "Killer Coke Update," Killer Coke, November 2, 2009, http://killercoke.org/nl091102.php; "4. In Memory of a True Labor Leader and Hero," Killer Coke, http://killercoke.org/nl091102.php; "IUF/UITA: Coca-Cola Workers Worldwide," IUF, www.iuf.org/ccww (site discontinued, updated site https://www.iuf.org/campaigns/coca-cola-campaign/).

26. Sturgis, "Real 'Norma Rae' Dies."

27. Polanyi-Levitt, "Origins and Implications," 274–75; Gautier-Mayoral, "Puerto Rican Model," 1–26; Dypski, "Caribbean Basin Initiative," 110.

28. International Trade Association, *Guide*, 1–4, 8–10.

29. Larry Rohter, "Puerto Rico Fighting to Keep Its Tax Breaks for Business," *NYT*, May 10, 1993, A1; James Surowiecki, "The Puerto Rican Problem," *New Yorker*, April 6, 2015, 22; Cabán, "Puerto Rico."

30. Prashad, *Poorer Nations*; "CPEC Special Economic Zones (SEZs)," CPEC Authority, http://cpec.gov.pk/special-economic-zones-projects; Frank Holmes, "China's New Special Economic Zone Evokes Memories of Shenzhen," *Forbes*, April 21, 2017, www.forbes.com/sites/greatspeculations/2017/04/21/chinas-new-special-economic-zone-evokes-memories-of-shenzhen/#a83334576f23; "China's Special Economic Zones: Experience Gained," World Bank, 2015, www.worldbank.org/content/dam/Worldbank/Event/Africa/Investing%20in%20Africa%20Forum/2015/investing-in-africa-forum-chinas-special-economic-zone.pdf.

31. D. T. Max, "Made in Italy: The Chinese Immigrants Who Assemble Designer Bags in Tuscany," *New Yorker*, April 16, 2018, 50–57.

32. Dennis Hevesi, "Crystal Lee Sutton, the Real-Life 'Norma Rae,' Is Dead at 68," *NYT*, September 15, 2009, B17.

33. Cat Warren, "From the Editor: Waiting for Norma Rae," AAUP, July–August 2011, www.aaup.org/article/editor-waiting-norma-rae; Martha Grevatt, "Crystal Lee Sutton Fought for Union Rights," *Workers World*, October 10, 2009, www.workers.org/2009/us/crystal_lee_sutton_1015; Linda Meric, "VOICES: Employee Free Choice, Let's Do It for 'Norma Rae,'" *Facing South* (blog), October 1, 2009, www.facingsouth.org/2009/10/voices-employee-free-choice-lets-do-it-for-norma-rae.html; Sturgis, "Real 'Norma Rae' Dies"; "LHF Salutes Crystal Lee Sutton, the Real Norma Rae," Labor Heritage Foundation, September 22, 2009, https://www.laborheritage.org/lhf-salutes-crystal-lee-sutton-the-real-norma-rae/; Connie Schultz, "The 'Real Norma Rae' Dies, but Her Fight Lives On," *Cleveland*, September 16, 2020, www.cleveland.com/schultz/2009/09/the_real_norma_rae_dies_but_he.html; James Ridgeway, "Real-Life 'Norma Rae' Dies after Battle with Insurance Company," *Mother Jones*, September 16, 2009, www.motherjones.com/politics/2009/09/real-life-norma-rae-dies-after-battle-insurance-company.

34. Maggie Jones, "Crystal Lee Sutton: The Organizer," *NYT Magazine*, December 27, 2009, M35; Patricia Sullivan, "Labor Organizer Was Inspiration for 'Norma Rae,'" *Washington Post*, September 16, 2009, B5; David Macaray, "Goodbye Norma Rae," *CounterPunch*, September 24, 2009, www.counterpunch.org/2009/09/24/goodbye-quot-norma-rae-quot; "Goodbye Norma Rae: Eulogy for Crystal Lee Sutton," *Salt Spring News*, September 24, 2009, http://saltspringnews.com/modules.php?op=modload&name=News&file=article&sid=19723 (site discontinued); Jill, "American

Icon 'Norma Rae' Dies after Struggling with Her Insurance Company," *Feministe*, September 16, 2009, www.feministe.us/blog/archives/2009/09/16/american-icon-norma -rae-dies-after-struggling-with-her-insurance-company-to-cover-her-chemo (site discontinued); Bruce Raynor, "Crystal Lee Sutton, the Real 'Norma Rae,' Was a Fighter to the End," *Huffington Post*, September 14, 2009, www.huffingtonpost.com/bruce-raynor /crystal-lee-sutton-the-re_b_286077.html; "Crystal Lee Sutton Dies at 68," *Daily Herald*, September 14, 2009, www.rrdailyherald.com/news/crystal-lee-sutton-dies-at/article _8fc25d9d-3717-5439-8796-dcc44bf90511.html (site discontinued); Emery P. Delesio, "Crystal Lee Sutton: Inspiration for Movie 'Norma Rae' Dies at 68," Tributes (website), September 12, 2009, www.tributes.com/obituary/read/Crystal-Lee-Sutton-86758725.

35. Joe Maniscalco, "On Broadway, Casting Directors Keep Up the Fight," *LaborPress*, December 12, 2017, http://laborpress.org/on-broadway-casting-directors-keep-up-the -fight; "Rosanne Cash Is Writing a *Norma Rae* Musical," *Broadway Buzz*, December 11, 2017, www.broadway.com/buzz/190654/rosanne-cash-is-writing-a-norma-rae-musical; Ginger Adams Otis, "Stage Slight on B'Way: Casting Agent Axed from 'Rae' amid Union Try," *New York Daily News*, December 10, 2017.

Preview

1. Annie Palmer, "Amazon Workers Plan Strike at Staten Island Warehouse to Demand Coronavirus Protections," CNBC, March 29, 2020, www.cnbc.com/2020/03/29 /amazon-workers-in-staten-island-plan-strike-over-coronavirus-safety.html; Brittany Kriegstein and Larry McShane, "No Regrets for Amazon Workers Fired after Staten Island Protest," *New York Daily News*, March 31, 2020, www.nydailynews.com/new-york /ny-staten-island-amazon-firing-20200331-edshv23qlnfq3mavj4gde4gqgm-story. html; Brian Fung, "Fired Amazon Worker Sues over Pandemic Working Conditions," *CNN Business*, November 12, 2020, www.cnn.com/2020/11/12/tech/amazon-worker -lawsuit/index.html; Angelika Maldonado, "Here's How We Beat Amazon," interview by Eric Blanc, *Jacobin*, April 2, 2022, https://jacobin.com/2022/04/amazon-labor-union -alu-staten-island-organizing.

2. Véronique Hyland, "Can Labor Activists Be Style Icons?," *Elle*, May 18, 2022, www .elle.com/fashion/a40021642/union-drip-twitter.

3. Charlotte Alter, "He Came Out of Nowhere and Humbled Amazon," *Time*, April 25, 2022, https://time.com/6169185/chris-smalls-amazon-labor-union; Ari Levy and Annie Palmer, "Amazon Workers Just Voted to Join a Union," CNBC, April 2, 2022, www .cnbc.com/2022/04/02/amazon-workers-just-voted-to-join-a-union-heres-what-happens -next-.html; Christian Smalls (@Shut_downAmazon), "You're focused on me I'm focused on We," Twitter, April 15, 2022, https://twitter.com/Shut_downAmazon/status /1515026465288560652.

4. Sarah Jaffe (@sarahijaffe), Twitter, April 1, 2022, https://twitter.com/sarahljaffe /status/1509984045949763591; Nicki Washington (@dr_nickiw), Twitter, April 3, 2022, https://twitter.com/dr_nickiw/status/1510629314219364354.

5. *Meteor* (@themeteor), "How did @Shut_downAmazon and @amazonlabor win despite a massive effort by Amazon to oppose him?," Twitter, June 6, 2022, https://twitter .com/themeteor/status/1533917353569931264; Julie (@JuliaCintheCLE), "Great event tonight with @Shut_downAmazon! Thank you for reigniting the labor movement in

Cleveland!!," Twitter, June 9, 2022, https://twitter.com/JuliaCintheCLE/status/1535071514361745409; Laila Dalton (@lailaddaltonn), Twitter, June 14, 2022, https://twitter.com/lailaddaltonn/status/1536789208194437120; Christian Smalls (@Shut_down Amazon), "Yes! it is official I will be sharing my life's story with the world to continue to inspire. I'm so grateful to be able to say I will be writing a book . . . ," June 14, 2022, https://twitter.com/Shut_downAmazon/status/1536707229117829124; Diane (@Intrepid Reportr), "Solidarity with @Shut_downAmazon," Twitter, June 22, 2022, https://twitter.com/IntrepidReportr/status/1539645122320945152; Joseph Sikora (@josephsikora4), "Mr. Christian smalls is the real deal. Putting his heart and soul time energy and money where his mouth is," Twitter, June 22, 2022, https://twitter.com/JosephSikora4/status/1539608218128859137; @allthingslabor, "Look who I ran into last night. @Shut_downAmazon one of my working class heroes," Twitter, June 26, 2022, https://twitter.com/allthingslabor_/status/1541046292075450376; Jesse Jackson Sr. (@RevJJackson), ".@Shut_downAmazon Happy Birthday! Keep Hope Alive, my friend," July 5, 2022; Vail Kohnert-Yount (@vailkoyo), "so much to say about how amazing this weekend's @PeoplesParity convening was, but first—here is my & @jaredodessky's contribution to the @UnionDrip discourse," Twitter, July 10, 2022, https://twitter.com/vailkoyo/status/1546179527960920065.

6. Byerly, "Crystal Lee Sutton," in *Hard Times*, 215.

7. Wes Enzinna, "What Will Chris Smalls Do Next?," *New York*, July 18, 2022, and cover photo with "The Organizer," https://nymag.com/intelligencer/article/chris-smalls-amazon-profile.html.

8. Lisa Lucas (@likaluca), "Truly truly truly truly couldn't be prouder that @Pantheon Books will publish @Shut_downAmazon's forthcoming memoir," Twitter, June 13, 2022, https://twitter.com/likaluca/status/1536338139601588225.

BIBLIOGRAPHY

Archival Collections

Alabama Department of Archives and History, Montgomery, AL (Digital Collections)
Alamance Community College, Graham, NC
    Crystal Lee Sutton Collection
Archives and Special Collections at the Dodd Center, University of Connecticut,
    Storrs, CT
    American Thread Company Records, 1953–1978
    Center for Oral History Interviews Collection
        Peoples of Connecticut, 1973–1976
        Millworkers of Willimantic, 1979–1980
    Waterbury (CT) Area Immigrant Oral History Collection
Carnegie Mellon University, Pittsburgh, PA H. John Heinz III Collection (Digital
    Collections)
Centro Library and Archives, Hunter College–CUNY, New York, NY
    Bureau of Insular Affairs, Records of the PRRA 1918–1949 Microfilm Collection
    El Centro de Estudios Puertorriqueños Collection
    ILGWU/ UNITE Collection
    Kathy Andrade Papers
    Library of Congress Relating to Puerto Rico, Materials from the
    Offices of the Government of Puerto Rico in the United States Collection, 1930–93
        Bureau of Employment and Identification, and Migration Division Records
Connecticut Historical Society, Hartford, CT
    City Directories
    Hispanic Collection
Kheel Center for Labor-Management Documentation and Archives, Catherwood
    Library, Cornell University, Ithaca, NY
    Amalgamated Clothing and Textile Workers Union (ACTWU): Textile Division,
        Organizing Department, National Textile Recruitment and Training Pro-
        gram, Political and Legislative Department, International Affairs Depart-
        ment, and Legal Department
    International Ladies' Garment Workers' Union (ILGWU): Research Department,
        Operations Department, Zimmerman Papers, Justice Photographs, and
        Communications Department Photographs
    Justice, official publication of the International Ladies' Garment Workers' Union,
        1919–1995
    Union of Needletrades, Industrial, and Textile Employees (UNITE): Research
        Department Historic Files
Margaret Herrick Library, Academy of Motion Picture Arts and Sciences, Los
    Angeles, CA

Communikon Audience Test Reports
James Wong Howe Papers
Martin Ritt Papers
SMU Collection of Ronald I. Davies Oral Histories on the Performing Arts
Sydney Pollack Papers
National Archives in New York City
    Puerto Rican Records: National Recovery Administration Territorial Office for
        Puerto Rico
    Records of the Puerto Rico Reconstruction Administration
    Records of the Wage and Hour and Public Contracts Divisions
North Carolina Digital Heritage Center at the Wilson Special Collections Library,
        University of North Carolina (Digital NC)
Osborne Library at the American Textile History Museum, Lowell, MA
        (closed 2014)
Research Archives at Wistariahurst Museum, Holyoke, MA
Schlesinger Library at the Radcliffe Institute, Harvard University, Cambridge, MA
    Woman Alive! Collection, 1974–1977
Special Collections, Clemson University, Clemson, SC (Digital Finding Aids)
    "Corporate History," J.P. Stevens and Company, 1813–1989
Special Collections, Georgia State University Library, Atlanta, GA (Digital
        Collections)
    M. H. Ross Papers
Special Collections, Smith College, Northampton, MA
    Sophia Smith Collection of Women's History
        Ms. Foundation for Women Records, 1973–2008
        National Congress of Neighborhood Women Records, 1974–1999
        Gloria Steinem Papers, 1940–2000
Springfield History Library and Archives, Lyman and Merrie Wood Museum of
        Springfield History, Springfield, MA
Windham Textile and History Museum, Willimantic, CT

Periodicals

Bond Buyer	*Ladies' Home Journal*
Boston Globe	*Los Angeles Times*
Business Week	*MacLean's*
Central New Jersey Home News	*Mademoiselle*
(New Brunswick)	*McCall's*
Chicago Daily Tribune	*Ms.*
Chicago Tribune	*New Leader*
Cineaste	*Newsweek*
Forbes	*New York*
Fortune	*New York Daily News*
Hartford (CT) Courant	*New Yorker*
Harvard Crimson (Cambridge, MA)	*New York Times*
InSTYLE	*New York Times Magazine*
In These Times	*North Augusta (SC) Star*

Off Our Backs
On Location
Opelika-Auburn (AL) News
Palm Beach (FL) Post
People
Philadelphia Inquirer
Playboy
Progressive
Reader's Digest
Redbook

Saturday Evening Post
Senior Scholastic
Teen
Time
Tuscaloosa (AL) News
US News and World Report
Wall Street Journal
Washington Post
Washington Post and Times Herald

Guides, Commentaries, Treatises, Reports

Airov, Joseph. *The Location of the Synthetic Fiber Industry: A Case Study in Regional Analysis.* Cambridge, MA: MIT Press, 1959.

Arthur D. Little, Inc. *Report on New Industries for Puerto Rico, to Puerto Rico Development Corporation.* C-57289. Cambridge, MA: Arthur D. Little, Inc., 1942.

———. *Report on Ten-Year Industrial Plan for Puerto Rico, to Puerto Rico Economic Development Administration.* Written 1951. Washington, DC: International Cooperation Administration, Technical Aids Branch, Office of Industrial Resources, 1961.

Bolin, Richard L. "What Puerto Rico Faced in Being the First to Create EPZs in 1947." Speech given to Latin American Free Trade Zones Committee Conference on behalf of the Flagstaff Institute's and World Export Processing Zone Association's Award for Creativity, presented to Puerto Rico/Puerto Rico Industrial Development Company. San Juan, Puerto Rico, September 9, 2004. Transcript at https://explorersfoundation.org/archive/409t1-english.pdf.

———. *Why Export Processing Zones Are Necessary*, no. 1, ver. 1.02. Flagstaff, AZ: WEPZA and the Flagstaff Institute, 2004.

Caudill, Harry M. *Night Comes to the Cumberlands: A Biography of a Depressed Area.* Boston: Little, Brown, 1962.

Council for Pan American Democracy. *Starvation in Puerto Rico: Recommendations for the Immediate Relief of Our Caribbean Gibraltar.* New York: Publication of the Council for Pan American Democracy, 1943.

Edmunds, George Franklin. *The Insular Cases: The Supreme Court and the Dependencies.* Boston: New England Anti-imperialist League, 1901.

Farman, Melvin. *A Brief History.* Pamphlet for Arthur D. Little, Inc. Cambridge, MA: Arthur D. Little, Inc., [1965?].

Friedman, Milton. *Capitalism and Freedom.* With the assistance of Rose D. Friedman. Chicago: University of Chicago Press, 1962.

Friedman, Milton, and Rose Friedman. *Free to Choose: A Personal Statement.* New York: Harcourt Brace Jovanovich, 1980.

Graham, Billy. *Angels: God's Secret Agents.* Nashville, TN: W Publishing Group, 1975.

———. *Facing Death and the Life After.* New York: Grason, 1987.

———. *Hope for the Troubled Heart.* Irving, TX: Word, 1991.

———. *How to Be Born Again.* Nashville, TN: W Publishing Group, 1978.

Handlin, Oscar. *The Newcomers: Negroes and Puerto Ricans in a Changing Metropolis.* Cambridge, MA: MIT Press, 1959.

———. *Race and Nationality in American Life*. New York: Little, Brown, 1957.

International Trade Administration. *Guide to the Caribbean Basin Initiative*. Washington, DC: US Department of Commerce, November 2000.

Magee, John F. *Arthur D. Little, Inc.: At the Moving Frontier*. New York: Newcomen Society of the United States, 1985.

McConnell, Donald W. *Economic Trends and the New Deal in the Caribbean*. New York: Publication of the Council for Pan American Democracy, 1940.

McWilliams, Carey. *Factories in the Field: The Story of Migratory Farm Labor in California*. Boston: Little, Brown, 1939.

Mills, C. Wright, Clarence Senior, and Rose Kohn Goldsen. *The Puerto Rican Journey: New York's Newest Migrants*. New York: Harper and Row, 1950.

Mitchell, Broadus. *The Rise of Cotton Mills in the South*. Johns Hopkins University Studies in Historical and Political Science 39, no. 2. Baltimore: Johns Hopkins University Press, 1921. Reprint, Middletown, DE: Leopold Classic Library, 2016.

Nuñez, Elsa. "Poultry, Thread, and Whitewater." Paper presented at the Rethinking the Latin@ Intellectual Ecology Conference, University of Connecticut, Storrs, CT, October 12, 2007.

Osburn, Donald D. *Negro Employment in the Textile Industries of North and South Carolina*. Research Report 1966–10. Washington, DC: Office of Research and Reports, Equal Employment Opportunity Commission, 1966.

Padfield, Harland, and William E. Martin. *Farmers, Workers, and Machines: Technological and Social Change in Farm Industries of Arizona*. Tucson: University of Arizona Press, 1965.

Pesotta, Rose. *Bread upon the Waters*. New York: Dodd, Mead, 1944. Reprint, Ithaca, NY: ILR Press, 1987.

Rowan, Richard L. *The Negro in the Textile Industry*. Vol. 4 of *Studies of Negro Employment*, edited by Herbert R. Northrup, Richard L. Rowan, Darold T. Barnum, and John C. Howard. Philadelphia: Industrial Research Unit, Wharton School of the University of Pennsylvania, 1970.

Senior, Clarence O. *The Puerto Ricans of New York City*. Under the direction of C. Wright Mills. New York: Bureau of Applied Social Research, Columbia University, 1948.

Tugwell, Rexford Guy. *The Stricken Land: The Story of Puerto Rico*. New York: Doubleday, 1947.

Wagenheim, Kal. *A Survey of Puerto Ricans on the US Mainland in the 1970s*. New York: Praeger, 1975.

Zimmerman, Klaus F. "Circular Migration: Why Restricting Labor Mobility Can Be Counterproductive." *IZA World of Labor*, May 2014. https://wol.iza.org/articles/circular-migration.

Oral History and Primary Source Collections, Autobiographies, Memoirs

Boyer, Paul, ed. *Reagan as President: Contemporary Views of the Man, His Politics, and His Policies*. Chicago: Ivan R. Dee, 1990.

Byerly, Victoria. *Hard Times, Cotton Mill Girls: Personal Histories of Womanhood and Poverty in the South*. Ithaca, NY: ILR Press, 1986.

Conway, Mimi. *Rise Gonna Rise: A Portrait of Southern Textile Workers*. New York: Anchor/Doubleday, 1979.

Field, Sally. *In Pieces: A Memoir*. New York: Grand Central Publishing, 2018.

Honey, Michael K. *Black Workers Remember: An Oral History of Segregation, Unionism, and the Freedom Struggle*. Berkeley: University of California Press, 1999.

McGilligan, Pat. *Interviews with Screenwriters of the 1960s*. Backstory 3. Berkeley: University of California Press, 1997.

Moreno, Rita. *Rita Moreno: A Memoir*. New York: Celebra, 2013.

Ramírez, Norma E. Boujouen. "The Puerto Rican Experience in Willimantic: A Reflective Account Thirty Years Later." Keynote speech at the Latino Migration Exhibit at the Windham Textile and History Museum, Willimantic, CT, April 19, 2013. Transcript in author's possession.

Reagan, Ronald. *Speaking My Mind: Selected Speeches*. New York: Simon and Schuster, 1989.

Santiago, Esmeralda. *When I Was Puerto Rican: A Memoir*. New York: Addison-Wesley, 1993.

Schmidt, Samuel. *In Search of Decision: The Maquiladora Industry in México*. Ciudad Juárez, Mexico: Universidad Autónoma de Ciudad Juárez and the Flagstaff Institute, 2000.

Schweizer, Peter, and Wynton C. Hall, eds. *Landmark Speeches of the American Conservative Movement*. College Station: Texas A&M University Press, 2007.

Skinner, Kiron K., Annelise Anderson, and Martin Anderson, eds. *Reagan in His Own Hand: The Writings of Ronald Reagan That Reveal His Revolutionary Vision for America*. New York: Simon and Schuster, 2001.

Speakes, Larry. *Speaking Out: The Reagan Presidency from Inside the White House*. With Robert Pack. New York: Charles Scribner's Sons, 1988.

Steedman, Carolyn Kay. *Landscape for a Good Woman: A Story of Two Lives*. New Brunswick, NJ: Rutgers University Press, 1986.

Suggs, George G., Jr. *"My World Is Gone": Memories of Life in a Southern Cotton Mill Town*. Detroit, MI: Wayne State University Press, 2002.

Wagenheim, Kal, and Olga Jiménez de Wagenheim, eds. *The Puerto Ricans: A Documentary History*. Princeton, NJ: Markus Wiener, 2013.

Interviews and Conversations

Alexander, Sydenham. Telephone conversations with author. June 22, 2021, and July 26, 2022.

Jordan, Cathy, and Jay Jordan. Conversation with author. Graham, NC. June 18, 2013.

Koritz, Richard. Telephone interview with author. February 10, 2016.

Martínez, Aracelis. Written interview questions from author, translated by Irma Medina. Springfield, MA. February 10, 2018.

Medina, Irma. Interview with author. Springfield, MA. February 17, 2018.

Rumelt, Richard (former International Ladies' Garment Workers' Union district manager for western Massachusetts). Telephone conversation with author. March 28, 2019.

Russo, Gisele Desautels. Conversation with author. Storrs, CT. November 28, 2017.

Salgado-Cartagena, Maria. Conversation with author. Springfield, MA. December 3, 2017.

Stevenson, Ted (retired import/export manager for Ludlow Textiles). Conversation with author. Springfield, MA. August 26, 2022.

Winslow, Paul (former International Ladies' Garment Workers' Union district manager for western Massachusetts). Telephone conversation with author. March 14, 2019.

Filmography

Barret, Elizabeth, dir. *Stranger with a Camera*. Produced by Elizabeth Barret and Judi Jennings. Whitesburg, KY: Appalshop, 2000.

Biberman, Herbert, dir. *Salt of the Earth*. Produced by Paul Jarrico. Independent Productions Corporation/International Union of Mine, Mill, and Smelter Workers, 1954.

Coppola, Francis Ford, dir. *The Godfather*. Produced by Gray Frederickson and Albert S. Ruddy. Los Angeles: Paramount Pictures, 1972.

Kopple, Barbara, dir. and prod. *Harlan County, USA*. New York: Cabin Creek Films, 1976.

Mann, Anthony, dir. *God's Little Acre*. Produced by Sidney Harmon. Los Angeles: Security Pictures, 1958.

Perez, Rosie, dir. *¡Yo soy boricua, pa'que tu lo sepas!* Produced by Roger Sherman. Malibu, CA, and New York: Moxie Firecracker Films and IFC, 2006.

Ritt, Martin, dir. *Norma Rae*. Produced by Alexandra Rose and Tamara Assayev. Los Angeles: Twentieth Century-Fox, 1979; DVD, 2001.

Robbins, Jerome, and Robert Wise, dirs. *West Side Story*. Produced by Robert Wise and Saul Chaplin. Los Angeles: Mirisch Corporation and Seven Arts Productions, 1961.

Spielberg, Steven, dir. *West Side Story*. Produced by Steven Spielberg, Kristie Macosko Krieger, and Kevin McCollum. Los Angeles: Amblin Entertainment and 20th Century Studios, 2021.

Doctoral Dissertations and Theses

Alterman, Jon B. "Egypt and American Foreign Assistance, 1952–1956." PhD diss., Harvard University, 1997.

Boujouen, Norma Esther. "'Menea Esas Manos': Factory Work, Domestic Life and Job Loss among Puerto Rican Women in a Connecticut Town." PhD diss., University of Connecticut, 1990.

Loiselle, Aimee. "Corpse, Lover, Mother: Feminism in American Commercial Films of the 1970s and 1980s." Master's thesis, University of Vermont, 1998.

Matías-Ortiz, Andrés. "Ambivalent Solidarities: Homeworkers, Needlework Unions, and the ILGUW in Puerto Rico, 1930–1940." Master's thesis, University of Wisconsin–Madison, 2001.

Silva, Liana M. "'I Like to Live in América': *West Side Story* and *A Raisin in the Sun* as Urban Stories about Home and Citizenship." In "Acts of Home-Making: Home and

Urban Space in Twentieth Century African American and Puerto Rican Cultural Productions," 109–48. PhD diss., State University of New York, Binghamton, 2012.

Tellew, Fuad. "Private Foreign Investment as a Possible Aid for the Economic Growth of Iraq." PhD diss., University of Southern California, 1959.

Books

Acevedo-Muñoz, Ernesto R. *West Side Story as Cinema: The Making and Impact of an American Masterpiece*. Lawrence: University of Kansas Press, 2013.

Adler, William M. *Mollie's Job: A Story of Life and Work on the Global Assembly Line*. New York: Touchstone Books of Simon and Schuster, 2001.

Ahmed, Sara. *The Cultural Politics of Emotion*. Edinburgh, UK: Edinburgh University Press, 2014.

Amador, José. *Medicine and Nation Building in the Americas, 1890–1940*. Nashville, TN: Vanderbilt University Press, 2015.

Appelbaum, Eileen, and Rose Batt. *Private Equity at Work: When Wall Street Manages Main Street*. New York: Russell Sage Foundation, 2014.

Appleby, Joyce. *The Relentless Revolution: A History of Capitalism*. New York: W. W. Norton, 2010.

Ayala, César J., and Rafael Bernabe. *Puerto Rico in the American Century: A History since 1898*. Chapel Hill: University of North Carolina Press, 2007.

Baerga, María del Carmen, ed. *Género y trabajo: La industria de la aguja en Puerto Rico y el Caribe hispánico*. San Juan: Editorial de la Universidad de Puerto Rico, 1993.

Banner, Stuart. *How the Indians Lost Their Land: Law and Power on the Frontier*. Cambridge, MA: Belknap Press of Harvard University Press, 2005.

Barber, Llana. *Latino City: Immigration and Urban Crisis in Lawrence, Massachusetts, 1945–2000*. Chapel Hill: University of North Carolina Press, 2017.

Barker, Deborah. *American Cinema and the Southern Imaginary*. Athens: University of Georgia Press, 2011.

Barrett, James R. *History from the Bottom Up and the Inside Out: Ethnicity, Race, and Identity in Working-Class History*. Durham, NC: Duke University Press, 2017.

Beckert, Sven. *Empire of Cotton: A Global History*. New York: Vintage Books, 2014.

Beller, Jonathan. *The Cinematic Mode of Production: Attention Economy and the Society of the Spectacle*. Lebanon, NH: Dartmouth College Press/University Press of New England, 2006.

Bender, Daniel E. *Sweated Work, Weak Bodies: Anti-sweatshop Campaigns and Languages of Labor*. New Brunswick, NJ: Rutgers University Press, 2004.

Benmayor, Rina, Ana Juarbe, Celia Alvarez, and Blanca Vázquez. *Stories to Live By: Continuity and Change in Three Generations of Puerto Rican Women*. New York: Centro de Estudios Puertorriqueños, 1987.

Benton, James C. *Fraying Fabric: How Trade Policy and Industrial Decline Transformed America*. Champaign: University of Illinois Press, 2022.

Beruff, Jorge Rodríguez. *Strategy as Politics: Puerto Rico on the Eve of the Second World War*. San Juan: Editorial Universidad de Puerto Rico, 2007.

Biles, Roger. *The South and the New Deal*. Lexington: University of Kentucky Press, 1994. Reprint, 2015.

Bockman, Johanna. *Markets in the Name of Socialism: The Left-Wing Origins of Neoliberalism*. Palo Alto, CA: Stanford University Press, 2011.

Bodnar, John. *Blue-Collar Hollywood: Liberalism, Democracy, and Working People in American Film*. Baltimore: Johns Hopkins University Press, 2003.

Bonacich, Edna, and Richard P. Appelbaum. *Behind the Label: Inequality in the Los Angeles Apparel Industry*. With Ku-Sup Chin, Melanie Myers, Gregory Scott, and Goetz Wolff. Berkeley: University of California Press, 2000.

Bonacich, Edna, Lucie Cheng, Norma Chinchilla, Nora Hamilton, and Paul Ong, eds. *Global Production: The Apparel Industry in the Pacific Rim*. Philadelphia: Temple University Press, 1994.

Borda, Jennifer. *Women Labor Activists in the Movies: Nine Depictions of Workplace Organizers, 1954–2005*. New York: McFarland, 2010.

Boris, Eileen, Dorothea Hoehtker, and Susan Zimmermann, eds. *Women's ILO: Transnational Networks, Global Standards, and Gender Equity*. Leiden, Netherlands: Brill and ILO, 2018.

Bourdieu, Pierre. *Distinction: A Social Critique of the Judgement of Taste*. London: Routledge, 1984.

———. *The Field of Cultural Production: Essays on Art and Literature*. Edited by Randal Johnson. New York: Columbia University Press, 1993.

Briggs, Laura. *Reproducing Empire: Race, Sex, Science and US Imperialism in Puerto Rico*. Berkeley: University of California Press, 2002.

Brown, Leslie. *Upbuilding Black Durham: Gender, Class, and Black Community Development*. Chapel Hill: University of North Carolina Press, 2008.

Burgin, Angus. *The Great Persuasion: Reinventing Free Markets since the Great Depression*. Cambridge, MA: Harvard University Press, 2012.

Burnett, Christina Duffy, and Burke Marshall, eds. *Foreign in a Domestic Sense: Puerto Rico, American Expansion, and the Constitution*. Durham, NC: Duke University Press, 2001.

Cahn, Susan. *Sexual Reckonings: Southern Girls in a Troubling Age*. Cambridge, MA: Harvard University Press, 2007.

Caldwell, Erskine. *God's Little Acre*. New York: Penguin Books, 1933.

Campbell, Edward D. C., Jr. *The Celluloid South: Hollywood and the Southern Myth*. Knoxville: University of Tennessee Press, 1981.

Canaday, Margot. *The Straight State: Sexuality and Citizenship in Twentieth-Century America*. Princeton, NJ: Princeton University Press, 2009.

Cardona, Luis Antonio. *A History of the Puerto Ricans in the United States of America: The Coming of the Puerto Ricans*. Rockville, MD: Carreta, 1990.

Casey, Michael. *Che's Afterlife: The Legacy of an Image*. New York: Vintage Books, 2009.

Cerny, Philip. *Rethinking World Politics: A Theory of Transnational Neopluralism*. London: Oxford University Press, 2010.

Chappell, Marisa. *The War on Welfare: Family, Poverty, and Politics in Modern America*. Philadelphia: University of Pennsylvania Press, 2010.

Chibbaro, Anthony. *The Charleston Exposition*. Images of America Series. Mount Pleasant, SC: Arcadia, 2001.

Chomsky, Aviva. *Linked Labor Histories: New England, Colombia, and the Making of the Global Working Class*. Durham, NC: Duke University Press, 2008.

Choy, Catherine Ceniza. *Empire of Care: Nursing and Migration in Filipino American History*. Durham, NC: Duke University Press, 2003.

Clark, Daniel J. *Like Night and Day: Unionization in a Southern Mill Town*. Chapel Hill: University of North Carolina Press, 1997.

Cline, Elizabeth L. *Overdressed: The Shockingly High Cost of Cheap Fashion*. New York: Portfolio/Penguin, 2012.

Cobb, James C. *Away Down South: A History of Southern Identity*. New York: Oxford University Press, 2005.

———. *The Selling of the South: The Southern Crusade for Industrial Development, 1936–1990*. Urbana: University of Illinois Press, 1993.

Cobble, Dorothy Sue. *Dishing It Out: Waitresses and Their Unions in the Twentieth Century*. Urbana: University of Illinois Press, 1991.

———. *The Other Women's Movement: Workplace Justice and Social Rights in Modern America*. Princeton, NJ: Princeton University Press, 2005.

Cohen, Lizabeth. *A Consumer's Republic: The Politics of Mass Consumption in Post-war America*. New York: Random House, 2003.

Collins, Jane L. *Threads: Gender, Labor, and Power in the Global Apparel Industry*. Chicago: University of Chicago Press, 2003.

Colón, Alice. *Género y mujeres Puertorriqueñas: Tercer encuentro de investigadoras*. Río Piedras: Universidad de Puerto Rico, 1994.

Cook, Blanche Wiesen. *Eleanor Roosevelt*. Vol. 2, *The Defining Years, 1933–1938*. New York: Penguin Books, 2000.

Cooper, Frederick. *Colonialism in Question: Theory, Knowledge, History*. Berkeley: University of California Press, 2005.

Couldry, Nick. *Media Rituals: A Critical Approach*. London: Routledge, 2003.

Cowie, Jefferson. *Capital Moves: RCA's Seventy-Year Quest for Cheap Labor*. New York: New Press, 2001.

———. *Stayin' Alive: The 1970s and the Last Days of the Working Class*. New York: New Press, 2012.

Cowie, Jefferson, and Joseph Heathcott, eds. *Beyond the Ruins: The Meanings of De-industrialization*. Ithaca, NY: ILR Press, 2003.

Cox, Karen L. *Dreaming of Dixie: How the South Was Created in American Popular Culture*. Chapel Hill: University of North Carolina Press, 2011.

Dean, Mitchell. *Governmentality: Power and Rule in Modern Society*. London: SAGE, 1999. Reprint, 2010.

de Lauretis, Teresa. *Technologies of Gender: Essays on Theory, Film, and Fiction*. Bloomington: Indiana University Press, 1987.

Denning, Michael. *The Cultural Front: The Laboring of American Culture in the Twentieth Century*. London: Verso, 1996.

———. *Culture in the Age of Three Worlds*. New York: Verso, 2004.

Dietz, James L. *Economic History of Puerto Rico: Institutional Change and Capitalist Development*. Princeton, NJ: Princeton University Press, 1986.

———. *Puerto Rico: Negotiating Development and Change*. Boulder, CO: Lynne Rienner, 2003.

Dochuk, Darren. *From Bible Belt to Sunbelt: Plain-Folk Religion, Grassroots Politics and the Rise of Evangelical Conservatism*. New York: W. W. Norton, 2011.

Duany, Jorge. *The Puerto Rican Nation on the Move: Identities on the Island and in the United States*. Chapel Hill: University of North Carolina Press, 2002.

Duggan, Lisa. *The Twilight of Equality? Neoliberalism, Cultural Politics, and the Attack on Democracy*. Boston: Beacon, 2004.

Ehrman, John. *The Eighties: America in the Age of Reagan*. New Haven, CT: Yale University Press, 2005.

Ekbladh, David. *The Great American Mission: Modernization and the Construction of an American World Order*. Princeton, NJ: Princeton University Press, 2010.

English, Beth. *A Common Thread: Labor, Politics, and Capital Mobility in the Textile Industry*. Athens: University of Georgia Press, 2006.

Enstad, Nan. *Ladies of Labor, Girls of Adventure: Working Women, Popular Culture, and Labor Politics at the Turn of the Twentieth Century*. New York: Columbia University Press, 1999.

Farrell, Amy Erdman. *Yours in Sisterhood: Ms. Magazine and the Promise of Popular Feminism*. Chapel Hill: University of North Carolina Press, 1998.

Feldstein, Ruth. *Motherhood in Black and White: Race and Sex in American Liberalism, 1930–1965*. Ithaca, NY: Cornell University Press, 2000.

Findlay, Eileen Suárez. *Imposing Decency: The Politics of Sexuality and Race in Puerto Rico, 1870–1920*. Durham, NC: Duke University Press, 1999.

———. *We Are Left without a Father Here: Masculinity, Domesticity, and Migration in Postwar Puerto Rico*. Durham, NC: Duke University Press, 2014.

Flippen, J. Brooks. *Jimmy Carter, the Politics of Family, and the Rise of the Religious Right*. Athens: University of Georgia Press, 2011.

Fones-Wolf, Elizabeth. *Selling Free Enterprise: The Business Assault on Labor and Liberalism, 1945–1960*. Urbana: University of Illinois Press, 1994.

Fones-Wolf, Elizabeth, and Ken Fones-Wolf. *Struggle for the Soul of the Postwar South: White Evangelical Protestants and Operation Dixie*. Urbana: University of Illinois Press, 2015.

Foster, Gwendolyn Audrey. *Performing Whiteness: Postmodern Re/Constructions in the Cinema*. Albany: State University of New York Press, 2003.

Gabin, Nancy. *Feminism in the Labor Movement: Women and the United Auto Workers, 1935–1975*. Ithaca, NY: Cornell University Press, 1990.

Galvin, Miles. *The Organized Labor Movement in Puerto Rico*. Cranbury, NJ: Associated University Presses, 1979.

Garebian, Keith. *The Making of West Side Story*. Toronto, ON: ECW, 1995.

Glasser, Ruth. *Aquí Me Quedo: Puerto Ricans in Connecticut; Los Puertorriqueños en Connecticut*. Middletown: Connecticut Humanities Council, 1997.

Glenn, Evelyn Nakano. *Forced to Care: Coercion and Caregiving in America*. Cambridge, MA: Harvard University Press, 2010.

———. *Unequal Freedom: How Race and Gender Shaped American Citizenship and Labor*. Cambridge, MA: Harvard University Press, 2004.

Go, Julian. *American Empire and the Politics of Meaning: Elite Political Cultures in the Philippines and Puerto Rico during US Colonialism*. Durham, NC: Duke University Press, 2008.

Goldberg, Greg. *Antisocial Media: Anxious Labor in the Digital Economy*. New York: New York University Press, 2018.

Graham, Allison. *Framing the South: Hollywood, Television, and Race during the Civil Rights Struggle*. Baltimore: Johns Hopkins University Press, 2001.

Gramsci, Antonio. *Prison Notebooks*. Vols. 1–3. Translated by Joseph A. Buttigieg and Antonio Callari. New York: Columbia University Press, 2011.

Green, Hardy. *On Strike at Hormel: The Struggle for a Democratic Labor Movement*. Philadelphia: Temple University Press, 1991.

Greene, Julie. *The Canal Builders: Making America's Empire at the Panama Canal*. New York: Penguin, 2009.

Gregory, Mollie. *Women Who Run the Show: How a Brilliant and Creative New Generation of Women Stormed Hollywood*. New York: St. Martin's, 2002.

Grewal, Inderpal. *Transnational America: Feminisms, Diasporas, Neoliberalisms*. Durham, NC: Duke University Press, 2005.

Guglielmo, Jennifer. *Living the Revolution: Italian Women's Resistance and Radicalism in New York City, 1880–1945*. Chapel Hill: University of North Carolina Press, 2012.

Haberland, Michelle. *Striking Beauties: Women Apparel Workers in the United States South, 1930–2000*. Athens: University of Georgia Press, 2015.

Hahamovitch, Cindy. *No Man's Land: Jamaican Guestworkers in America and the Global History of Deportable Labor*. Princeton, NJ: Princeton University Press, 2011.

Hahn, Steven. *A Nation under Our Feet: Black Political Struggles in the Rural South from Slavery to the Great Migration*. Cambridge, MA: Harvard University Press, 2003.

Hale, Grace Elizabeth. *Making Whiteness: The Culture of Segregation in the South, 1890–1940*. New York: Random House, 1999.

———. *A Nation of Outsiders: How the White Middle Class Fell in Love with Rebellion in Postwar America*. New York: Oxford University Press, 2011.

Hall, Jacquelyn Dowd, Mary Murphy, James Leloudis, Robert Korstad, LuAnn Jones, and Christopher B. Daly. *Like a Family: The Making of a Southern Cotton Mill World*. Chapel Hill: University of North Carolina Press, 1987.

Hall, Stuart, ed. *Representation: Cultural Representations and Signifying Practices*. London: SAGE Publications with Open University, 1997.

Hardy-Fanta, Carol, and Jeffrey N. Gerson, eds. *Latino Politics in Massachusetts: Struggles, Strategies, and Prospects*. New York: Routledge, 2002.

Harkins, Anthony. *Hillbilly: A Cultural History of an American Icon*. New York: Oxford University Press, 2005.

Hart, D. G. *That Old-Time Religion in Modern America: Evangelical Protestantism in the Twentieth Century*. Chicago: Ivan R. Dee, 2002.

Hartford, William. *Where Is Our Responsibility? Unions and Economic Change in the New England Textile Industry, 1870–1960*. Amherst: University of Massachusetts Press, 1996.

———. *Working People of Holyoke: Class and Ethnicity in a Massachusetts Mill Town, 1850–1960*. New Brunswick, NJ: Rutgers University Press, 1990.

Harvey, Bruce G. *World's Fairs in a Southern Accent: Atlanta, Nashville, and Charleston, 1895–1902*. Knoxville: University of Tennessee Press, 2014.

Harvey, David. *A Brief History of Neoliberalism*. New York: Oxford University Press, 2005.

High, Steven, and David W. Lewis. *Corporate Wasteland: The Landscape and Memory of Deindustrialization*. Ithaca, NY: ILR Press, 2007.

Hill, Erin. *Never Done: A History of Women's Work in Media Production*. New Brunswick, NJ: Rutgers University Press, 2016.

Hodges, James. *New Deal Labor Policy and the Southern Cotton Textile Industry, 1933–1941*. Knoxville: University of Tennessee Press, 1986.

Honey, Michael K. *Southern Labor and Black Civil Rights: Organizing Memphis Workers*. Urbana: University of Illinois Press, 1993.

Hong, Grace Kyungwon. *The Ruptures of American Capital: Women of Color Feminism and the Culture of Immigrant Labor*. Minneapolis: University of Minnesota Press, 2006.

Hunter, Tera. *To 'Joy My Freedom: Southern Black Women's Lives and Labors after the Civil War*. Cambridge, MA: Harvard University Press, 1998.

Hyde, Anne F. *Empires, Nations, and Families: A History of the North American West, 1800–1860*. Lincoln: University of Nebraska Press, 2012.

Imada, Adria L. *Aloha America: Hula Circuits through US Empire*. Durham, NC: Duke University Press, 2012.

Jackson, Carlton. *Picking Up the Tab: The Life and Movies of Martin Ritt*. Bowling Green, OH: Bowling Green State University Popular Press, 1994.

Jacobson, Matthew Frye. *Roots Too: White Ethnic Revival in Post–Civil Rights America*. Cambridge, MA: Harvard University Press, 2006.

———. *Whiteness of a Different Color: European Immigrants and the Alchemy of Race*. Cambridge, MA: Harvard University Press, 1998.

Jameson, Fredric. *Postmodernism, or The Cultural Logic of Late Capitalism*. New York: Verso, 1991.

Janiewski, Dolores. *Sisterhood Denied: Race, Gender, and Class in a New South Community*. Philadelphia: Temple University Press, 1985.

Jewell, Katherine Rye. *Dollars for Dixie: Business and the Transformation of Conservatism in the Twentieth Century*. Cambridge: Cambridge University Press, 2017.

Jones, Jacqueline. *Labor of Love, Labor of Sorrow: Black Women, Work and the Family, from Slavery to the Present*. New York: Vintage Books, 1985.

Kahn, E. J., Jr. *The Problem Solvers: A History of Arthur D. Little, Inc*. Boston: Little, Brown, 1986.

Kaplan, E. Ann. *Women and Film: Both Sides of the Camera*. New York: Methuen, 1983.

Kiernan, Ben. *Blood and Soil: A World History of Genocide and Extermination from Sparta to Darfur*. New Haven, CT: Yale University Press, 2007.

Kirby, Jack Temple. *Media-Made Dixie: The South in the American Imagination*. Baton Rouge: Louisiana State University Press, 1978.

Klein, Christina. *Cold War Orientalism: Asia in the Middlebrow Imagination, 1945–1961*. Berkeley: University of California Press, 2003.

Koistinen, David. *Confronting Decline: The Political Economy of Deindustrialization in Twentieth-Century New England*. Gainesville: University Press of Florida, 2013.

Korrol, Virginia E. Sánchez. *From Colonia to Community: The History of Puerto Ricans in New York City*. Berkeley: University of California Press, 1994.

———. *Pioneros II: Puerto Ricans in New York City, 1948–1998*. Images of America Series. Mount Pleasant, SC: Arcadia, 2010.

Korstad, Robert, and James LeLoudis. *To Right These Wrongs: The North Carolina Fund and the Battle to End Poverty and Inequality in America in the 1960s.* Chapel Hill: University of North Carolina Press, 2010.

Krippner, Greta R. *Capitalizing on Crisis: The Political Origins of the Rise of Finance.* Cambridge, MA: Harvard University Press, 2012.

Kruse, Kevin M. *One Nation under God: How Corporate America Invented Christian America.* New York: Basic Books, 2015.

———. *White Flight: Atlanta and the Making of Modern Conservatism.* Princeton, NJ: Princeton University Press, 2005.

Kuhn, Clifford M. *Contesting the New South Order: The 1914–1915 Strike at Atlanta's Fulton Mills.* Chapel Hill: University of North Carolina Press, 2001.

Latham, Michael E. *The Right Kind of Revolution: Modernization, Development, and US Foreign Policy from the Cold War to the Present.* Ithaca, NY: Cornell University Press, 2011.

Leifermann, Henry P. *Crystal Lee: A Woman of Inheritance.* New York: Macmillan, 1975.

Lemann, Nicholas. *The Promised Land: The Great Black Migration and How It Changed America.* New York: Knopf, 1991.

Lichtenstein, Nelson. *The Retail Revolution: How Wal-Mart Created a Brave New World of Business.* 2nd ed. New York: Picador, 2010.

———, ed. *Wal-Mart: The Face of Twenty-First-Century Capitalism.* New York: New Press, 2006.

Lichtenstein, Nelson, and Elizabeth Tandy Shermer, eds. *The Right and Labor in America: Politics, Ideology and Imagination.* Philadelphia: University of Pennsylvania Press, 2012.

Lloréns, Hilda. *Imaging the Great Puerto Rican Family: Framing Nation, Race, and Gender during the American Century.* Lanham, MD: Lexington Books, 2014.

Lopez, Iris. *Matters of Choice: Puerto Rican Women's Struggle for Reproductive Freedom.* New Brunswick, NJ: Rutgers University Press, 2008.

MacLean, Nancy. *Democracy in Chains: The Deep History of the Radical Right's Stealth Plan for America.* New York: Viking, 2017.

———. *Freedom Is Not Enough: The Opening of the American Workplace.* New York: Russell Sage Foundation, 2006.

Maldonado, A. W. *Teodoro Moscoso and Puerto Rico's Operation Bootstrap.* Gainesville: University Press of Florida, 1997.

Marcus, Daniel. *Happy Days and Wonder Years: The Fifties and the Sixties in Contemporary Cultural Politics.* New Brunswick, NJ: Rutgers University Press, 2004.

Marsden, George M. *Fundamentalism and American Culture: The Shaping of Twentieth-Century Evangelicalism, 1870–1925.* Oxford: Oxford University Press, 1980.

Matos Rodríguez, Félix V., and Linda C. Delgado, eds. *Puerto Rican Women's History: New Perspectives.* Armonk, NY: M. E. Sharpe, 1998.

Matthews, Scott L. *Capturing the South: Imagining America's Most Documented Region.* Chapel Hill: University of North Carolina Press, 2018.

McAlister, Melani. *Epic Encounters: Culture, Media, and US Interests in the Middle East since 1945.* Berkeley: University of California Press, 2001. Reprint, 2005.

McCoy, Alfred W., and Francisco A. Scarano, eds. *Colonial Crucible: Empire in the Making of the Modern American State*. Madison: University of Wisconsin Press, 2009.

McElya, Micki. *Clinging to Mammy: The Faithful Slave in Twentieth-Century America*. Cambridge, MA: Harvard University Press, 2007.

———. *The Politics of Mourning: Death and Honor in Arlington National Cemetery*. Cambridge, MA: Harvard University Press, 2016.

McGirr, Lisa. *Suburban Warriors: The Origins of the New American Right*. Princeton, NJ: Princeton University Press, 2002.

McGreevey, Robert. *Borderline Citizens: The United States, Puerto Rico, and the Politics of Colonial Migration*. Ithaca, NY: Cornell University Press, 2018.

McGuigan, Jim. *Neoliberal Culture*. New York: Palgrave Macmillan, 2016.

McPherson, Tara. *Reconstructing Dixie: Race, Gender, and Nostalgia in the Imagined South*. Durham, NC: Duke University Press, 2003.

Meeropol, Michael. *Surrender: How the Clinton Administration Completed the Reagan Revolution*. Ann Arbor: University of Michigan Press, 1998.

Meléndez, Edgardo. *Sponsored Migration: The State and Puerto Rican Postwar Migration to the United States*. Columbus: Ohio State University Press, 2017.

Meléndez-Badillo, Jorell A. *The Lettered Barriada: Workers, Archival Power, and the Politics of Power in Puerto Rico*. Durham, NC: Duke University Press, 2021.

Miller, Edward H. *A Conspiratorial Life: Robert Welch, the John Birch Society, and the Revolution of American Conservatism*. Chicago: University of Chicago Press, 2022.

Miller, Gabriel. *The Films of Martin Ritt: Fanfare for the Common Man*. Jackson: University Press of Mississippi, 2000.

Minchin, Timothy. *"Don't Sleep with Stevens!": The J.P. Stevens Campaign and the Struggle to Organize the South, 1963–1980*. Gainesville: University Press of Florida, 2005.

———. *Empty Mills: The Fight against Imports and the Decline of the US Textile Industry*. Oxford, UK: Rowman and Littlefield, 2012.

———. *Hiring the Black Worker: The Racial Integration of the Southern Textile Industry, 1960–1980*. Chapel Hill: University of North Carolina Press, 1999.

Mirowski, Philip, and Dieter Plehwe, eds. *The Road from Mont Pèlerin: The Making of the Neoliberal Thought Collective*. Cambridge, MA: Harvard University Press, 2009.

Moreton, Bethany. *To Serve God and Wal-Mart: The Making of Christian Free Enterprise*. Cambridge, MA: Harvard University Press, 2009.

Ong, Aihwa. *Neoliberalism as Exception: Mutations in Citizenship and Sovereignty*. Durham, NC: Duke University Press, 2006.

Orleck, Annelise. *Common Sense and a Little Fire: Women and Working-Class Politics in the United States, 1900–1965*. 2nd ed. Chapel Hill: University of North Carolina Press, 2017.

———. *Storming Caesars Palace: How Black Mothers Fought Their Own War on Poverty*. Boston: Beacon, 2005.

———. *"We Are All Fast-Food Workers Now": The Global Uprising against Poverty Wages*. Boston: Beacon, 2018.

Ortiz, Altagracia, ed. *Puerto Rican Women and Work: Bridges in Transnational Labor*. Philadelphia: Temple University Press, 1996.

Ownby, Ted. *American Dreams in Mississippi: Consumers, Poverty, and Culture, 1830–1998*. Chapel Hill: University of North Carolina Press, 1999.

Panitch, Leo, and Sam Gindin. *The Making of Global Capitalism: The Political Economy of American Empire*. London: Verso, 2012.

Payne, Charles M., and Adam Green, eds. *Time Longer Than Rope: A Century of African American Activism, 1850–1950*. New York: New York University Press, 2003.

Perdue, Theda. *Race and the Atlanta Cotton States Exposition of 1895*. Athens: University of Georgia Press, 2010.

Phillips-Fein, Kim. *Fear City: New York's Fiscal Crisis and the Rise of Austerity Politics*. New York: Picador, 2017.

———. *Invisible Hands: The Making of the Conservative Movement from the New Deal to Reagan*. New York: W. W. Norton, 2010.

Phillips-Fein, Kim, and Julian E. Zelizer, eds. *What's Good for Business: Business and American Politics since World War II*. London: Oxford University Press, 2012.

Prashad, Vijay. *The Poorer Nations: A Possible History of the Global South*. New York: Verso, 2012.

Ray, Robert B. *A Certain Tendency of the Hollywood Cinema, 1930–1980*. Princeton, NJ: Princeton University Press, 1985.

Republican Newspaper Group. *Nuestra Historia: A History of Latinos in Western Massachusetts*. With Mass Mutual. Springfield, MA: Republican Heritage Book and Travel Series, 2013.

Richards, Lawrence. *Union-Free America: Workers and Antiunion Culture*. Urbana: University of Illinois Press, 2008.

Ring, Natalie. *The Problem South: Region, Empire, and the New Liberal State, 1880–1930*. Athens: University of Georgia Press, 2012.

Rivera, A. G. Quintero. *Patricios y plebeyos: Burgueses, hacendados, artesanos y obreros; Las relaciones de clase en el Puerto Rico de cambio de siglo*. Río Piedras, PR: Ediciones Huracán, 1988.

Roberts, Glenda S. *Staying on the Line: Blue-Collar Women in Contemporary Japan*. Honolulu: University of Hawaii Press, 1994.

Rockman, Seth. *Scraping By: Wage Labor, Slavery, and Survival in Early Baltimore*. Baltimore: Johns Hopkins University Press, 2009.

Rodgers, Daniel T. *Age of Fracture*. Cambridge, MA: Harvard University Press, 2011.

Rodríguez, Manuel R. *A New Deal for the Tropics: Puerto Rico during the Depression Era, 1932–1935*. Princeton, NJ: Markus Wiener, 2010.

Rodríguez-Silva, Ileana. *Silencing Race: Disentangling Blackness, Colonialism, and National Identities in Puerto Rico*. New York: Palgrave Macmillan, 2012.

Roediger, David R. *The Wages of Whiteness: Race and the Making of the American Working Class*. New York: Verso, 1991. Reprint, 1999.

———. *Working toward Whiteness: How America's Immigrants Became White*. New York: Basic Books, 2005.

Roll, Jarod. *Poor Man's Fortune: White Working-Class Conservatism in American Metal Mining, 1850–1950*. Chapel Hill: University of North Carolina Press, 2020.

Rosen, Ellen Israel. *Making Sweatshops: The Globalization of the US Apparel Industry*. Berkeley: University of California Press, 2002.

Ross, Loretta J., Lynn Roberts, Erika Derkas, Whitney Peoples, and Pamela

Bridgewater Toure, eds., *Radical Reproductive Justice*. New York: Feminist Press, 2017.

Ross, Loretta J., and Rickie Solinger. *Reproductive Justice: An Introduction*. Oakland: University of California Press, 2017.

Roth, Benita. *Separate Roads to Feminism: Black, Chicana, and White Feminist Movements in America's Second Wave*. Cambridge: Cambridge University Press, 2004.

Salmond, John A. *Gastonia, 1929: The Story of the Loray Mill Strike*. Chapel Hill: University of North Carolina Press, 1995.

———. *The General Textile Strike of 1934: From Maine to Alabama*. Columbia: University of Missouri Press, 2002.

Sassen, Saskia. *A Sociology of Globalization*. New York: W. W. Norton, 2007.

Schoenwald, Jonathan. *A Time for Choosing: The Rise of Modern American Conservatism*. Oxford: Oxford University Press, 2001.

Schoultz, Lars. *Beneath the United States: A History of US Policy toward Latin America*. Cambridge, MA: Harvard University Press, 1998.

Schulman, Bruce. *From Cotton Belt to Sun Belt: Federal Policy, Economic Development, and the Transformation of the South, 1938–1980*. London: Oxford University Press, 1991.

———. *The Seventies: The Great Shift in American Culture, Society, and Politics*. Boston: Da Capo, 2001.

Schulman, Bruce, and Julian Zelizer, eds. *Rightward Bound: Making America Conservative in the 1970s*. Cambridge, MA: Harvard University Press, 2008.

Schulman, Peter A. *Coal and Empire: The Birth of Energy Security in Industrial America*. Baltimore: Johns Hopkins University Press, 2015.

Self, Robert O. *All in the Family: The Realignment of American Democracy since the 1960s*. New York: Hill and Wang, 2012.

Sennett, Richard. *The Culture of the New Capitalism*. New Haven, CT: Yale University Press, 2006.

Sernett, Milton C. *Harriet Tubman: Myth, Memory, and History*. Durham, NC: Duke University Press, 2007.

Shenin, Sergei Y. *The United States and the Third World: The Origins of Postwar Relations and the Point Four Program*. Huntington, NY: Nova Science, 2000.

Shires, Preston. *Hippies of the Religious Right*. Waco, TX: Baylor University Press, 2007.

Slobodian, Quinn. *Globalists: The End of Empire and the Birth of Neoliberalism*. Cambridge, MA: Harvard University Press, 2018.

Smyth, J. E. *Nobody's Girl Friday: The Women Who Ran Hollywood*. Oxford: Oxford University Press, 2018.

Sparrow, Bartholomew H. *The Insular Cases and the Emergence of American Empire*. Lawrence: University Press of Kansas, 2006.

Steger, Manfred B., and Ravi K. Roy. *Neoliberalism: A Very Short Introduction*. London: Oxford University Press, 2010.

Stein, Judith. *Pivotal Decade: How the US Traded Factories for Finance in the Seventies*. New Haven, CT: Yale University Press, 2011.

Stoler, Ann Laura. *Along the Archival Grain: Epistemic Anxieties and Colonial Common Sense*. Princeton, NJ: Princeton University Press, 2010.

Sugrue, Thomas J. *Sweet Land of Liberty: The Forgotten Struggle for Civil Rights in the North*. New York: Random House, 2008.

Sullivan-González, Douglass, and Charles Reagan Wilson, eds. *The South and the Caribbean*. Jackson: University Press of Mississippi, 2001.

Thomas, Lorrin, and Aldo A. Lauria Santiago. *Rethinking the Struggle for Puerto Rican Rights*. New York: Routledge, 2019.

Thompson, Lanny. *Imperial Archipelago: Representation and Rule in the Insular Territories under US Dominion after 1898*. Honolulu: University of Hawaii Press, 2010.

Torres, Andrés, ed. *Latinos in New England*. Philadelphia: Temple University Press, 2006.

Torres, Andrés, and José E. Velázquez, eds. *The Puerto Rican Movement: Voices from the Diaspora*. Philadelphia: Temple University Press, 1998.

Trías Monge, José. *Puerto Rico: The Trials of the Oldest Colony in the World*. New Haven, CT: Yale University Press, 1997.

Troy, Gil. *Morning in America: How Ronald Reagan Invented the 1980s*. Princeton, NJ: Princeton University Press 2005.

Vance, Sandra S., and Roy V. Scott. *Wal-Mart: A History of Sam Walton's Retail Phenomenon*. New York: Twayne, 1994.

Venator Santiago, Charles R. *Puerto Rico and the Origins of US Global Empire: The Disembodied Shade*. New York: Routledge, 2015.

Vera, Hernán, and Andrew Gordon. *Screen Saviors: Hollywood Fictions of Whiteness*. Lanham, MD: Rowman and Littlefield, 2003.

Walker-McWilliams, Marcia. *Reverend Addie Wyatt: Faith and the Fight for Labor, Gender, and Racial Equality*. Champaign: University of Illinois Press, 2016.

Waterhouse, Benjamin. *Lobbying America: The Politics of Business from Nixon to NAFTA*. Princeton, NJ: Princeton University Press, 2013.

Weible, Robert, ed. *The Continuing Revolution: A History of Lowell, Massachusetts*. Lowell, MA: Lowell Historical Society, 1991.

Whalen, Carmen. *From Puerto Rico to Philadelphia: Puerto Rican Workers and Postwar Economies*. Philadelphia: Temple University Press, 2001.

Whalen, Carmen, and Víctor Vázquez-Hernández, eds. *The Puerto Rican Diaspora: Historical Perspectives*. Philadelphia: Temple University Press, 2005.

Wilkerson, Jessica. *To Live Here, You Have to Fight: How Women Led Appalachian Movements for Social Justice*. Champaign: University of Illinois Press, 2019.

Williams, Raymond. *Marxism and Literature*. Oxford: Oxford University Press, 1977.
———. *Politics and Letters: Interviews with the New Left Review*. New York: New Left Books, 1979.

Winant, Gabriel. *The Next Shift: The Fall of Industry and the Rise of Health Care in Rust Belt America*. Cambridge, MA: Harvard University Press, 2022.

Windham, Lane. *Knocking on Labor's Door: Union Organizing in the 1970s and the Roots of a New Economic Divide*. Chapel Hill: University of North Carolina Press, 2017.

Worthen, Molly. *Apostles of Reason: The Crisis of Authority in American Evangelicalism*. Oxford: Oxford University Press, 2014.

Zaretsky, Natasha. *No Direction Home: The American Family and the Fear of National Decline, 1968–1980*. Chapel Hill: University of North Carolina Press, 2007.

Zieger, Robert, ed. *For Jobs and Freedom: Race and Labor in America Since 1865.* Louisville: University Press of Kentucky, 2007.

———. *Southern Labor in Transition, 1940–1995.* Memphis: University of Tennessee Press, 1997.

Ziff, Trisha, ed. *Che Guevara: Revolutionary and Icon.* New York: Harry N. Abrams, 2006.

Articles and Chapters

Akram-Lodhi, A. Haroon. "What's in a Name: Neo-conservative Ideology, Neo-liberalism, and Globalization." In *The Neoliberal Revolution: Forging the Market State*, edited by Richard Robison, 156–72. New York: Palgrave Macmillan, 2006.

Alvarez, Celia. "El Hilo Que Nos Une/The Thread That Binds Us: Becoming a Puerto Rican Woman." *Oral History Review* 16, no. 2 (Fall 1988): 29–40.

Amador, Emma. "'Women Ask Relief for Puerto Ricans': Territorial Citizenship, the Social Security Act, and Puerto Rican Communities, 1933–1939." *Labor* 13, no. 3–4 (December 2016): 105–30.

Ashford, Nigel. "The Conservative Agenda and the Reagan Presidency." In *The Reagan Years: The Record in Presidential Leadership*, edited by Joseph Hogan, 189–213. Manchester, UK: Manchester University Press, 1990.

Baerga, María del Carmen. "El género y la construcción social de la maginalidad del trabajo femenino en la industria de la confección de ropa." In Baerga, *Género y trabajo*, 3–55.

Baerga-Santini, María del Carmen. "La defensa el trabajo industrial a domicilio: Mujeres en comtra de la sindicalización en Puerto Rico, 1920–1940." *Historia y sociedad*, no. 1 (1994): 33–58.

———. "Trabajo diestro sin trabajadores diestras: La (des)califación en la industria de la aguja en Puerto Rico, 1914–1940," *La Ventana*, no. 9 (1999): 158–89.

Barreto, Amílcar Antonio. "The Evolving State of Latino Politics in New England." In Torres, *Latinos in New England*, 291–310.

Beckert, Sven, Angus Burgin, Peter James Hudson, Louis Hyman, Naomi Lamoreaux, Scott Marler, Stephen Mihm, Julia Ott, Philip Scranton, and Elizabeth Tandy Shermer. "Interchange: The History of Capitalism." *Journal of American History* 101, no. 2 (2014): 503–36.

Benmayor, Rina. "For Every Story There Is Another Story Which Stands Before It." In Benmayor et al., *Stories to Live By*, 1–12.

Bonacich, Edna, and Khaleelah Hardie. "Wal-Mart and the Logistics Revolution." In Lichtenstein, *Wal-Mart*, 163–88.

Bonacich, Edna, and David V. Waller. "Mapping a Global Industry." In Bonacich et al., *Global Production*, 21–41.

Boris, Eileen. "Needlewomen under the New Deal in Puerto Rico, 1920–1945." In Ortiz, *Puerto Rican Women*, 33–54.

———. "Organization or Prohibition? A Historical Perspective on Trade Unions and Homework." In *Women and Unions: Forging a Partnership*, edited by Dorothy Sue Cobble, 207–25. Ithaca, NY: ILR Press, 1993.

Bourdieu, Pierre. "The Forms of Capital." In *Handbook of Theory and Research for the Sociology of Education*, edited by J. G. Richardson, 241–58. New York: Greenwood Press, 1986.

Boyer, Paul S. "The Evangelical Resurgence in 1970s American Protestantism." In Schulman and Zelizer, *Rightward Bound*, 29–51.

Brown, Wendy. "Neoliberalism, Neoconservatism, and De-democratization." *Political Theory* 34, no. 6 (December 2006): 690–714.

Burgin, Angus. "Age of Certainty: Galbraith, Friedman and the Public Life of Economic Ideas." *History of Political Economy* 45, no. S1 (December 2013): 191–219.

Burnett, Christina Duffy, and Burke Marshall. "Between the Foreign and the Domestic: The Doctrine of Territorial Incorporation, Invented and Reinvented." In Burnett and Marshall, *Foreign*, 1–37.

Cabán, Pedro. "Puerto Rico in Crisis and the Shifting Dictates of Empire." *Centro Journal* 33, no. 1 (Spring 2021): 7–40.

Carbado, Devon W., Kimberlé Williams Crenshaw, Vicki M. Mays, and Barbara Tomlinson. "Intersectionality: Mapping the Movements of a Theory." *DuBois Review* 10, no. 2 (2013): 303–12.

Carter, Eric D. "Where's Che? Politics, Pop Culture, and Public Memory in Rosario, Argentina." *FOCUS on Geography* 55, no. 1 (2012): 1–10.

Charlton, Hannah. Introduction to Ziff, *Che Guevara*, 7–14.

Cho, Sumi, Kimberlé Crenshaw, and Leslie McCall. "Toward a Field of Intersectionality Studies: Theory, Applications, and Praxis." *Signs* 38, no. 4 (Summer 2013): 785–810.

Connell, Raewyn. "Understanding Neoliberalism." In *Neoliberalism and Everyday Life*, edited by Susan Braedley and Meg Luxton, 22–36. Montreal, QC: McGill–Queen's University Press, 2010.

Cripps, Thomas. "Frederick Douglass: The Absent Presence in 'Glory.'" *Massachusetts Review* 36, no. 1 (Spring 1995): 154–63.

Crespino, Joseph. "Civil Rights and the Religious Right." In Schulman and Zelizer, *Rightward Bound*, 90–105.

Cruz, José E. "Pushing Left to Get to the Center: Puerto Rican Radicalism in Hartford, Connecticut." In Torres and Velázquez, *Puerto Rican Movement*, 69–87.

Davine, Lauren. "Could We Not Dye It Red at Least? Color and Race in *West Side Story*." *Journal of Popular Film and Television* 44, no. 3 (2016): 139–49.

de Jong, Greta. "'With the Aid of God and the F.S.A.': The Louisiana Farmers' Union and the African American Freedom Struggle in the New Deal Era." In Payne and Green, *Time Longer Than Rope*, 230–75.

del Moral, Solsiree. "Colonial Citizens of a Modern Empire: War, Illiteracy, and Physical Education in Puerto Rico, 1917–1930." *New West Indian Guide* 87, no. 1–2 (2013): 30–61.

Dobbin, Frank, Isaac Martin, and William H. Sewell Jr. "Book Symposium: Greta R. Krippner, Capitalizing on Crisis." *Trajectories* 23, no. 2 (Spring 2012): 1–15.

Duany, Jorge. "Portraying the Other: Puerto Rican Images in Two American Photographic Collections." *Discourse* 23, no. 1 (Winter 2001): 119–53.

Dypski, Michael Cornell. "The Caribbean Basin Initiative: An Examination of Structural Dependency, Good Neighbor Relations, and American Investment." *Journal of Transnational Law and Policy* 12, no. 1 (Fall 2002): 95–136.

Ferrero, Ignacio, W. Michael Hoffman, and Robert E. McNulty. "Must Milton Friedman Embrace Stakeholder Theory." *Business and Society Review* 119, no. 1 (2014): 37–59.

Findlay, Eileen. "Artful Narration: Puerto Rican Women Return Migrants' Life Stories." *Journal of Women's History* 22, no. 4 (Winter 2010): 162–84.

———. "Slipping and Sliding: The Many Meanings of Race in Life Histories of New York Puerto Rican Return Migrants in San Juan." *Centro Journal* 24, no. 1 (Spring 2012): 20–43.

Fink, Joey. "In Good Faith: Working-Class Women, Feminism, and Religious Support in the Struggle to Organize J.P. Stevens Textile Workers in the Southern Piedmont, 1974–1980." *Southern Spaces*, July 2014. https://doi.org/10.18737/M7J60K.

Fones-Wolf, Elizabeth, and Ken Fones-Wolf. "Managers and Ministers: Instilling Christian Free Enterprise in the Postwar Workplace." *Business History Review* 89, no. 1 (Spring 2015): 99–124.

Foulkes, Julia L. "Seeing the City: The Filming of *West Side Story*." *Journal of Urban History* 41, no. 6 (2015): 1032–51.

Frederickson, Mary. "'I Know Which Side I'm On': Southern Women in the Labor Movement in the Twentieth Century." In *Women, Work and Protest: A Century of US Women's Labor History*, edited by Ruth Milkman, 156–80. Boston: Routledge and Kegan Paul, 1985.

Friedman, Tami J. "Exploiting the North-South Differential: Corporate Power, Southern Politics, and the Decline of Organized Labor after World War II." *Journal of American History* 95, no. 2 (September 2008): 323–48.

Garcia, Gervasio Luis. "I Am the Other: Puerto Rico in the Eyes of North Americans, 1898." *Journal of American History* 87, no. 1 (June 2000): 39–64.

Gautier-Mayoral, Carmen. "The Puerto Rican Model and the Caribbean Basin Initiative: A New Form of South-South Cooperation?" *Caribbean Studies* 23, no. 1/2 (1990): 1–26.

Gayle, Janette. "'Invaders': Black Ladies of the ILGWU and the Emergence of the Early Civil Rights Movement in New York City." The Gotham Center for New York City History (October 2016). https://www.gothamcenter.org/blog/invaders-black-ladies-of-the-ilgwu-and-the-emergence-of-the-early-civil-rights-movement-in-new-york-city.

Glaessel-Brown, Eleanor E. "A Time of Transition: Colombian Textile Workers in Lowell in the 1970s." In Weible, *Continuing Revolution*, 341–75.

Glasser, Ruth. "Mofongo Meets Mangú: Dominicans Reconfigure Latino Waterbury." In Torres, *Latinos in New England*, 103–24.

Go, Julian. "Chains of Empire: Projects of State: Political Education and U.S. Colonial Rule in Puerto Rico and the Philippines." *Comparative Studies in Society and History* 42, no. 2 (April 2000): 333–62.

Gónzalez, Lydia Milagros. "La industria de la aguja de Puerto Rico y sus orígenes en los Estados Unidos." In Baerga, *Género y trabajo*, 59–81.

Greene, Julie. "Movable Empire: Labor, Migration, and US Global Power during the Gilded Age and Progressive Era." *Journal of the Gilded Age and Progressive Era* 15, no. 1 (January 2016): 4–20.

Grosfoguel, Ramón. "Puerto Rican Labor Migration to the US: Modes of Incorporation, Coloniality, and Identities." *Review* (Fernand Braudel Center) 22, no. 4 (1999): 503–21.

Hahamovitch, Cindy, and Rick Halpern. "Not a 'Sack of Potatoes': Why Labor Historians Need to Take Agriculture Seriously." *International Labor and Working-Class History* 65 (Spring 2004): 3–10.

Hall, Stuart. "Encoding and Decoding in the Television Discourse." Paper for the Council of Europe Colloquy, University of Leicester September 1973. https://core.ac.uk/download/pdf/81670115.pdf.

Hallam, Julia. "*Working Girl*: A Woman's Film for the Eighties, Female Spectators and Popular Film." In *Gendering the Reader*, edited by Sara Mills, 173–98. New York: Harvester/Wheatsheaf, 1994.

Hanagan, Michael, and Marcel van der Linden. "New Approaches to Global Labor History." *International Labor and Working-Class History* 66 (Fall 2004): 1–11.

Hernandez, Deborah Pacini. "Quiet Crisis: A Community History of Latinos in Cambridge, Massachussetts." In Torres, *Latinos in New England*, 149–70.

Hodges, James. "J.P. Stevens and the Union Struggle in the South." In *Class and Community in Southern Labor History*, edited by Gary M. Fink and Merl E. Reed, 53–64. Tuscaloosa: University of Alabama Press, 1994.

———. "The Real Norma Rae." In Zieger, *Southern Labor in Transition*, 251–72.

Jack, Caroline. "Producing Milton Friedman's *Free to Choose*: How Libertarian Ideology Became Broadcasting Balance." *Journal of Broadcasting and Electronic Media* 62, no. 3 (2018): 514–30.

Jackson, Ben. "At the Origins of Neo-liberalism: The Free Economy and the Strong State, 1930–47." *Historical Journal* 53, no. 1 (January 2010): 125–51.

Jacobs, Meg. "The Conservative Struggle and the Energy Crisis." In Schulman and Zelizer, *Rightward Bound*, 193–209.

Johnson, Robert David. "Anti-imperialism and the Good Neighbor Policy: Ernest Gruening and Puerto Rican Affairs, 1934–1939." *Journal of Latin American Studies* 29, no. 1 (February 1997): 89–110.

Johnson, Val Marie. "Introduction, Special Section: Chronologies and Complexities of Western Neoliberalism." *Social Science History* 35, no. 3 (Fall 2011): 323–36.

Jones, G. L. "Sweatshops on the Spanish Main." In Wagenheim and Jiménez de Wagenheim, *Puerto Ricans*, 163–65.

Jones, William P. "'Simple Truths of Democracy': African Americans and Organized Labor in the Post–World War II South." In *The Black Worker: A Reader*, edited by Eric Arnesen, 250–70. Urbana: University of Illinois Press, 2007.

Juarbe, Ana. "Anastasia's Story." In Benmayor et al., *Stories to Live By*, 13–24.

Kaplan, Amy, and Donald Pease. Introduction to *Cultures of United States Imperialism*, edited by Amy Kaplan and Donald Pease, 1–40. Durham, NC: Duke University Press, 1994.

Kimble, James J., and Lester C. Olson. "Visual Rhetoric Representing Rosie the Riveter: Myth and Misconception in J. Howard Miller's 'We Can Do It!' Poster." *Rhetoric and Public Affairs* 9, no. 4 (Winter 2006): 533–69.

Larner, Wendy. "Neo-liberalism: Policy, Ideology, Governmentality." *Studies in Political Economy* 63, no. 1 (Autumn 2000): 5–25.

Lewis, Gordon K. "Puerto Rico: A Case Study of Change in an Underdeveloped Area." *Journal of Politics* 17, no. 4 (November 1955): 614–50.

Luxton, Meg. "Doing Neoliberalism: Perverse Individualism." In *Neoliberalism and Everyday Life*, edited by Susan Braedley and Meg Luxton, 163–83. Montreal, QC: McGill-Queen's University Press, 2010.

Macpherson, Anne S. "Birth of the US Colonial Minimum Wage: The Struggle over the Fair Labor Standards Act in Puerto Rico, 1938–1941." *Journal of American History* 104, no. 3 (December 2017): 656–80.

———. "Citizens v. Clients: Working Women and Colonial Reform in Puerto Rico and Belize, 1932–45." *Journal of Latin American Studies* 35, no. 2 (May 2003): 279–310.

Maza, Sarah. "Stories in History: Cultural Narratives in Recent Works of European History." *American Historical Review* 101, no. 5 (December 1996): 1498–1500.

McGirr, Lisa. "A History of the Conservative Movement from the Bottom-Up." *Journal of Policy History* 14, no. 3 (2002): 331–39.

———. "Now That Historians Know So Much about the Right, How Should We Best Approach the Study of Conservatism?" *Journal of American History* 98, no. 3 (December 2011): 765–70.

McGuinness, Aims. "Searching for 'Latin America': Race and Sovereignty in the Americas in the 1850s." In *Race and Nation in Modern Latin America*, edited by Nancy Appelbaum, Anne S. Macpherson, and Karin Alejandra Rosemblatt, 87–107. Chapel Hill: University of North Carolina Press, 2003.

Memou, Antigoni. "Re-appropriating Che's Image: From the Revolution to the Market and Back Again." *Ephemera* 13, no. 2 (2013): 449–51.

Moreton, Bethany E. "Make Payroll, Not War." In Schulman and Zelizer, *Rightward Bound*, 52–70.

Muñiz-Mas, Félix O. "Gender, Work, and Institutional Change in the Early Stage of Industrialization: The Case of the Women's Bureau and the Home Needlework Industry in Puerto Rico, 1940–1952." In Matos Rodríguez and Delgado, *Puerto Rican Women's History*, 181–205.

Muñoz Marín, Luis. "'The Sad Case of Port Rico.'" In Wagenheim and Jiménez de Wagenheim, *Puerto Ricans*, 170–78.

New York State Curriculum. "Old Voices, New Voices: Mainland Puerto Rican Perspectives and Experiences." *Organization of American Historians Magazine of History* 10, no. 2 (Winter 1996): 36–42.

O'Connor, Alice. "Financing the Counterrevolution." In Schulman and Zelizer, *Rightward Bound*, 148–69.

Ortiz, Altagracia. "'En la aguja y el pedal eché la hiel.'" In Ortiz, *Puerto Rican Women*, 55–81.

———. "Puerto Rican Women Workers in the Twentieth Century: A Historical Appraisal of the Literature." In Matos Rodríguez and Delgado, *Puerto Rican Women's History*, 38–61.

———. "Puerto Rican Workers in the Garment Industry of New York City, 1920–1960." In *Labor Divided: Race and Ethnicity in United States Labor Struggles, 1835–1960*, edited by Robert Asher and Charles Stephenson, 105–30. Albany: State University of New York Press, 1990.

Palley, Thomas I. "Financialization: What It Is and Why It Matters." In "Finance-Led

Capitalism? Macroeconomic Effects of Changes in the Financial Sector Conference," 1–31. Working paper no. 525, Levy Economics Institute of Bard College, Annandale-on-Hudson, NY, December 2007.

Panitch, Leo, and Martin Konings. "Myths of Neoliberal Deregulation." *New Left Review*, no. 57 (May-June 2009): 67–83.

Paredez, Deborah. "'Queer for Uncle Sam': Anita's Latina Diva Citizenship in *West Side Story*." *Latino Studies* 12, no. 3 (2014): 332–52.

Pastor, Robert. "Sinking in the Caribbean Basin." *Foreign Affairs* 60, no. 5 (Summer 1982): 1038–58.

Petrovic, Misha, and Gary G. Hamilton. "Making Global Markets: Wal-Mart and Its Suppliers." In Lichtenstein, *Wal-Mart*, 107–42.

Polanyi-Levitt, Kari. "The Origins and Implications of the Caribbean Basin Initiative: Mortgaging Sovereignty?" *International Journal* 40, no. 2 (Spring 1985): 229–81.

Ríos, Palmira N. "Export-Oriented Industrialization and the Demand for Female Labor: Puerto Rican Women in the Manufacturing Sector, 1952–1980." *Gender and Society* 4, no. 3 (September 1990): 321–37.

Rivera, Ralph. "Latinos in Massachusetts: Growth and Geographical Distribution." *New England Journal of Public Policy* 8, no. 2 (1992): 51–65.

Rooks, Daisy. "The Cowboy Mentality: Organizers and Occupational Commitment in the New Labor Movement." *Labor Studies Journal* 28, no. 3 (Fall 2003): 33–62.

Sedgewick, Augustine. "What Is Imperial about Coffee? Rethinking 'Informal Empire.'" In *Making the Empire Work: Labor and United States Imperialism*, edited by Daniel E. Bender and Jana K. Lipman, 312–33. New York: New York University Press, 2015.

Silvestrini, Blanca. "Women as Workers: The Experience of the Puerto Rican Woman in the 1930s." In *The Puerto Rican Woman: Perspectives on Culture, History, and Society*, edited by Edna Acosta-Belén, 59–74. Westport, CT: Greenwood, 1986.

Simon, Bryant. "The Appeal of Cole Blease in South Carolina: Race, Class, and Sex in the New South." *Journal of Southern History* 62, no. 1 (February 1996): 57–86.

———. "Race Reactions: African American Organizing, Liberalism, and White Working-Class Politics in Postwar South Carolina." In *Jumpin' Jim Crow: Southern Politics from Civil War to Civil Rights*, edited by Jane Dailey, Glenda Elizabeth Gilmore, and Bryant Simon, 239–58. Princeton, NJ: Princeton University Press, 2000.

———. "Rethinking Why There Are So Few Unions in the South." Special issue, "Labor in Georgia." *Georgia Historical Quarterly* 81, no. 2 (Summer 1997): 465–84.

Sosar, David P. "A Tale of Two Cities: Holyoke, Massachusetts and Hazleton, Pennsylvania." *International Journal of Education and Social Sciences* 2, no. 1 (January 2015): 71–81.

Stanton, Cathy. "Performing the Postindustrial: The Limits of Radical History in Lowell, Massachusetts." *Radical History Review*, no. 98 (Spring 2007): 81–96.

Sugrue, Thomas J., and John D. Skrentny. "The White Ethnic Strategy." In Schulman and Zelizer, *Rightward Bound*, 171–92.

Suri, Jeremi. "Détente and Its Discontents." In Schulman and Zelizer, *Rightward Bound*, 227–45.

Taylor, Charles. "Modern Social Imaginaries." *Public Culture* 14, no. 1 (Winter 2002): 91–124.

Thomas, Lorrin. "'How They Ignore Our Rights as American Citizens': Puerto Rican Migrants and the Politics of Citizenship in the New Deal Era." *Latino Studies* 2, no. 2 (2004): 140–59.

Thompson, Lanny. "Aesthetics and Empire: The Sense of Feminine Beauty in the Making of the US Imperial Archipelago." *Culture and History Digital Journal* 2, no. 2 (December 2013): 1–24.

———. "Representation and Rule in the Imperial Archipelago: Cuba, Puerto Rico, Hawai'i, and the Philippines under US Dominion after 1898." *American Studies Asia* 1 (2002): 3–39.

Toplin, Robert Brent. "Norma Rae: Unionism in an Age of Feminism." *Labor History* 36, no. 2 (Spring 1995): 282–98.

"Two Rewettable Fabrics." *Marine Engineering*, no. 76 (August 1, 1971): 71.

Vázquez Erazo, Blanca. "The Stories Our Mothers Tell: Projections-of-Self in the Stories of Puerto Rican Garment Workers." *Oral History Review* 16, no. 2 (Fall 1988): 23–28.

———. "Postscript." *Oral History Review* 16, no. 2 (Fall 1988): 41–46.

Vera, Hernán, and Andrew Gordon. "Sincere Fictions of the White Self in the American Cinema: The Divided White Self in Civil War Films." In *Classic Hollywood, Classic Whiteness*, edited by Daniel Bernardi, 263–80. Minneapolis: University of Minnesota Press, 2001.

Wakefield, Dan. "Long Night's Journey." In Wagenheim and Jiménez de Wagenheim, *Puerto Ricans*, 271–77.

Wallis, Brian. "Che Lives!" In Ziff, *Che Guevara*, 23–31.

Whalen, Carmen. "Colonialism, Citizenship, and the Making of the Puerto Rican Diaspora: An Introduction." In Whalen and Vázquez-Hernández, *Puerto Rican Diaspora*, 1–42.

———. "'The Day the Dresses Stopped': Puerto Rican Women, the International Ladies Garment Workers' Union, and the 1958 Dressmaker's Strike." In *Memories and Migrations: Locating Boricua and Chicana Histories*, edited by Vicki Ruiz and John Chávez, 121–50. Urbana: University of Illinois Press, 2008.

———. "Radical Contexts: Puerto Rican Politics in the 1960s and 1970s and the Center for Puerto Rican Studies." *Centro Journal* 21, no. 2 (Fall 2009): 221–55.

———. "Sweatshops Here and There: The Garment Industry, Latinas, and Labor Migrations." Special issue, "Sweated Labor: The Politics of Representation and Reform." *International Labor and Working Class History* 61, no. 1 (Spring 2002): 45–68.

Wilson, Mark R. "The Advantages of Obscurity: World War II Tax Carryback Provisions and the Normalization of Corporate Welfare." In Phillips-Fein and Zelizer, *What's Good for Business*, 16–44.

Woodbury, Robert D., and Christian S. Smith. "Fundamentalism et al.: Conservative Protestants in America." *Annual Review of Sociology* 24 (1998): 25–56.

Woods, Colleen. "Building Empire's Archipelago: The Imperial Politics of Filipino Labor in the Pacific." Special issue, "Labor and Empire." *Labor* 13, no. 3-4 (December 2016): 131–52.

Ziff, Trisha. "Guerrillero Heroico." In Ziff, *Che Guevara*, 15–22.

INDEX